The Treatment of Sex Offenders with Developmental Disabilities

A *Practice Workbook*

William R. Lindsay

WILEY-BLACKWELL

A John Wiley & Sons, Ltd, Publication

This edition first published 2009
© 2009 John Wiley & Sons Ltd.

Wiley-Blackwell is an imprint of John Wiley & Sons, formed by the merger of Wiley's global Scientific, Technical, and Medical business with Blackwell Publishing.

Registered Office
John Wiley & Sons Ltd, The Atrium, Southern Gate, Chichester, West Sussex, PO19 8SQ, UK

Editorial Offices
The Atrium, Southern Gate, Chichester, West Sussex, PO19 8SQ, UK
9600 Garsington Road, Oxford, OX4 2DQ, UK

350 Main Street, Malden, MA 02148-5020, USA

For details of our global editorial offices, for customer services, and for information about how to apply for permission to reuse the copyright material in this book please see our website at www.wiley.com/wiley-blackwell.

The right of William Lindsay to be identified as the author of this work has been asserted in accordance with the Copyright, Designs and Patents Act 1988.

Library of Congress Cataloging-in-Publication Data

Lindsay, William R.
  The treatment of sex offenders with developmental disabilities : a practice workbook / William Lindsay.
      p. cm.
  Includes bibliographical references and index.
  ISBN 978-0-470-74160-3 – ISBN 978-0-470-06202-9
  1. Offenders with mental disabilities.   2. Offenders with mental disabilities–Rehabilitation.
  3. Sex offenders–Mental health serives.   4. People with mental disabilities and crime.
  5. Criminal psychology.   I. Title.
    HV6133.L56 2009
    365'.6672–dc22   2008052404

A catalogue record for this book is available from the British Library

Typeset in 10/13pt Galliard by Aptara Inc., New Delhi, India

1 2009

Contents

List of Figures

Participants gave their written consent for use of any material. All figures have been altered where required in order to change or remove any information that might enable identification of any participant.

Foreword

The area of intellectually disabled sexual offenders is a particularly challenging one and up until relatively recently has been ignored by frontline researchers and program developers. Alongside innovators such as James Haaven in the United States, over the years Bill Lindsay has consistently argued for the need to develop specialized programs and assessment measures for intellectually disabled sex offenders. In this excellent book Professor Lindsay presents a comprehensive approach to the assessment and treatment of intellectually disabled sex offenders that is exhaustive in its approach and meticulous in its attention to research and theory. Professor Lindsay is an extremely able and incisive researcher whose suggestions for the treatment of sex offenders are thoroughly grounded in empirical data. Moreover, his rich experience as a clinical psychologist and therapist is evident in the book and he always makes sure he attends to the nuances and complexities of practical work with sex offenders. In fact, what sets this book apart from a number of recent texts on intellectually disabled sex offenders is that is written by a practicing scientist *and* therapist.

This is a large book containing twenty chapters and two appendices. Structurally the book is divided into three major sections, background theory and research, treatment considerations, and a treatment section where twelve chapters are devoted to a thorough description of how to treat clinical problems ranging from cognitive distortions to sexual fantasies. There are excellent chapters on the assessment section on risk assessment and the relevance of self-regulation offence pathways for intellectually disabled sex offenders. A valuable feature of the first section is that it provides a theoretical and research context for the subsequent more practical chapters and helps readers to understand the rationale and nature of the interventions outlined. For me the highlight of the theoretical section is the presentation of Professor Lindsay's own treatment model which is compromised of the skilful integration of several etiological and practice theories that emphasizes the importace of addressing sex offenders specific offence related problems and also facilitating their attachments and reentry to the community. It represents a supple framework for the assessment and treatment of intellectually disabled sex offenders and displays a fine sense of what is useful in current theory and relevant for this group of offenders. In the following two sections the application of the treatment model to specific problems areas is well detailed and each chapter is full of useful practical suggestions and ideas. Therapists should come away from a close reading of the applied section with a clear idea of how to systematically assess and comprehensively treat intellectually disabled offenders. Researchers are also likely to have their appetites wetted by the numerous astute observations Professor Lindsay makes about offense related attitudes and factors.

I thoroughly recommend this book to specialists working with intellectually disabled sex offenders and those working with sex offenders of normal intellectual functioning. One of the great achievements of Professor Lindsay's book resides in its demonstration that it is possible to attend to and build strengths in offenders while also reducing risk for further sexual reoffending. In addition, an important thread running throughout the book is the thesis that if sex offenders are to successfully desist from further offending they need to re enter our community, regain their status as fellow citizens and have the opportunity to turn their lives around with the help of family, community members, and practitioners. A critical component of this process of redemption and reentry is the acquisition of the necessary personal and social resources to live better and less harmful lives. This book will be of immense help to those who are committed to such goals.

Professor Tony Ward
Victoria University of Wellington
New Zealand.

Preface

This book is the product of many years of working with men with intellectual disabilities who have perpetrated inappropriate sexual behaviour and sex offences. I began working with sex offender groups in 1987 and have continued with both intellectual disability and mainstream offenders. One of the exciting aspects of any clinical field is the possibility of combining research developments with clinical work and I hope that the reader will recognise the synthesis of both throughout the book. I have ha d the privilege to work closely with many talented colleagues; our clinical observations have informed our research and research has driven our clinical work.

In developing my work I have drawn on many influences including mainstream writing on sex offenders, the voluminous research on intellectual disabilities, extensive treatment reports and clinical trials in behavioural and cognitive therapy, psychometric assessment research and risk assessment research. The chapters reflect these various research and treatment strands with practical methods for proceeding with work in these various tasks. Like all practising clinicians, I have also assessed and treated hundreds of patients who have influenced all my approaches and methods.

One purpose in writing this book is to help professionals working with offenders with intellectual disabilities to feel they can develop competence in important areas of working with these clients. I have been very aware over the years that colleagues are keen to engage with clients but are unsure of how and where to start. There is always the frustration of reading about important clinical innovations and at the same time being unsure of their application in one's own clinical setting. I have tried to outline the theoretical and research developments with an emphasis on how they can be applied to sex offenders with intellectual disabilities.

In 2004 John Taylor, Peter Sturmey and myself edited a book for Wiley entitled "Offenders with Developmental Disabilities" and we observed that research and practice developments had been growing considerably. Since that time, the pace has quickened with many authorities and services now recognising the nature of the clinical and social problems to be addressed and turning to the increasing volume of research work for some guidance on assessment, treatment and organisation of services. The requirements are such that, now, developments will occur to address the service need with or without sound writing and research to underpin their validity. It is my hope that publications such as this and those of others will indeed provide parameters for new practices.

I do not think that this book is a finished article on the topic of treatment for sex offenders with intellectual disability. I have no doubt that the next ten years will bring important, clinically effective innovations to the field. It is essential to conduct treatment with an understanding of its derivation and an open mind to validated, reliable changes emerging from the work of others. In this way treatment will not atrophy in a set of tired familiar techniques. I have witnessed treatment groups where the facilitator goes through the motions of presentation with no real understanding of the reasons for application or the specific requirements of the individuals in treatment. That is not to say that we should be swayed by every fad and fashion to arrive – there are and will be plenty of them. It is just to make a plea for continued awareness of clinical progress in the field.

One issue of terminology requires to be addressed in any book on intellectual disabilities. I have preferred "intellectual disability" and "developmental disability" as internationally recognised terms to refer to this client group. However until very recently the American Association of Intellectual and Developmental Disabilities has endorsed the term "mental retardation" and this is still widely recognised in North America. In Canada these is widespread use of "developmental disabilities " to refer to the client group. One has to be careful in interpreting this latter term since developmental disabilities can include disorders which, although highly prevalent in populations of individuals with intellectual disability, also include a number of people who function, intellectually, at a higher level. Here I am thinking of disorders on the Autistic spectrum. Closer to home, in the U.K. we have for some time used the term "learning difficulty" to describe the population. The reader should realise that all these references to the population are synonymous (apart from the exceptions mentioned in relation to developmental disability) and all relate to people who fulfil three diagnostic criteria. The person should have an intelligence quotient below 70 IQ points as measured by a reputable and well standardised assessment such as the Wechsler Adult intelligence scale – third edition. The IQ should take into account the standard errors of the test. The second criterion is that the individual should have significant deficits in adaptive behaviour, again as measured by a recognised standardised assessment. Different classification systems recommend slightly different criteria in adaptive behaviour but they all use it as a requirement of classification. The third criterion is that any such deficits should have a childhood onset, generally prior to age 18.

Over the years, i have noticed that professionals are apprehensive about working with sex offenders and even about accepting sex offenders into their services. This is understandable given the valence afforded to this group in the public consciousness. That is one reason why this type of treatment and service intervention should always be conducted within the auspices of a clinical team. To have one's colleagues to balance judgement and support intervention is immensely valuable. I would like to acknowledge the help of several people in the development of my work which has culminated in this book. So many colleagues have fashioned my thinking over the years. I have also been fortunate to have strong work partners to help in what is clearly a contentious clinical area. Anne Smith, the consultant psychiatrist with whom I worked for two decades has been a constant support and latterly Fabian Haut, Steve Young and Fergus Douds have been influential. More recently Peter Oakes and Farooq Ahmad have challenged my thinking on service delivery. Many nursing staff have spent years of their professional lives helping to keep groups running constantly including Ronnie Allan, Steve Scott, Evelyn Kelly, Paul Winters, Lesley Murphy, Danny Murphy, Lorna Cox, John Whitelaw, Tom Morgan and others. I am in huge debt to Charlotte Quinn and Pamela Reid for their administrative support. I am also indebted to various staff at Wiley for their patience and perseverance, especially at a time when so many staff and editorial changes were afoot.

Bill Lindsay
November 2008.

About the Author

Bill Lindsay, PhD, is Consultant Clinical Psychologist, Lead Clinician in Scotland and Head of Research for Castlebeck Care, Darlington, U.K. He is also Chair of Learning Disabilities and Forensic Psychology at the University of Abertay, Dundee. He holds a visiting chair at Northumbria University, Newcastle. An author of over 200 scientific articles and book chapters his research interests include the fields of cognitive behavioural therapy for people with intellectual disabilities and forensic psychology. He is a fellow of both the British Psychological Society and the International Association for the Scientific Study of Intellectual Disabilities. Previously he was a consultant psychologist in the State Hospital, Scotland with responsibilities for intellectual disabilities and mainstream sex offender treatment. He was also head of Clinical Psychology Learning Disability services in Tayside, UK. He has been a member of various advisory groups to both the Scottish and U.K. governments and chaired the Scottish Forensic Network working group on forensic intellectual disability services. He is currently associate editor for the Journal of Applied Research in Intellectual Disabilities and the Journal of Intellectual and Developmental Disabilities while also on the editorial board for the British Journal of Clinical Psychology and Psychiatry, Psychology and Law.

Part One
Background Research and Theory

Chapter 1

Introduction to Offenders, Sex Offenders and Abusers with Intellectual Disability

The relationship between intellectual disability and crime seems to have fascinated writers and researchers in the field for well over a century. Both Scheerenberger (1983) and Trent (1994) have described in detail the historical association between low intelligence and crime in the late nineteenth and early twentieth centuries. Up until that time, people with intellectual disability (ID) were generally considered a burden on, rather than a menace to, society. Scheerenberger (1983) writes that during the eighteenth and nineteenth centuries, living conditions were harsh for people with ID especially in urban areas with growing industrialisation. In rural areas, they tended to work long hours in poverty but in industrial settings they were unable to be in employment or be accepted into apprentice programmes. The impetus for change was undoubtedly Darwin's theory of evolution, which Galton (1883) employed to argue for the role of genetics in individual greatness in his book *Hereditary Genius*. Others, notably Goddard (1912), employed the same methods for ID to devastating effects.

In fact, these authors were part of a general movement which increasingly regarded ID as a menace. Scheerenberger (1983) notes, 'By the 1880s, mentally retarded persons were no longer viewed as unfortunates or innocents who, with proper training, could fill a positive role in the home and/or community. As a class they had become undesirable, frequently viewed as a great evil of humanity, the social parasite, criminal, prostitute, and pauper' (p. 116). In 1889, Kerlin (reviewed by Trent, 1994) argued that crime, rather than being the work of the devil, was the result of an individual's inability to understand moral sense and also their physical infirmity, both of which were non-remediable and inherited. Kerlin and others certainly linked ID with a range of social vices including drunkenness, delinquency, prostitution and crime, but Goddard (1910) moved these concepts on basing his arguments on Mendelian laws of hereditary. His first contribution was to reclassify ID using the term feeblemindedness to include all forms of ID. Those with the mental age of 2 years or less were termed 'idiots', with a mental age of 3–7 years 'imbeciles' and with a mental age of 8–12

The Treatment of Sex Offenders with Developmental Disabilities William Lindsay
© 2009 John Wiley & Sons, Ltd

years 'morons'. Crucially, the addition of the latter category more than doubled the number of feeble-minded people. His interest in genetics then led him to conclude that there was a causal relationship between feeblemindedness and social vice. The conceptualisation of people with ID, and their significantly growing numbers, moved from a social burden to a social menace. Goddard (1911) and others proposed two solutions for this increasing problem – segregation and sterilisation – which continued to have a significant impact for decades to come.

In the spirit of Galton and his work on genius, several authors, including Goddard (1911), published pedigree studies apparently confirming the inherited nature of feeblemindedness and its causal link to crime. Trent (1994) summarises these studies writing that they 'reinforced the belief in the linkage of rapidly multiplying mental defectives and a host of social problems: crime, prostitution, abusive charity, juvenile delinquency, venereal diseases, illegitimate births, and drunkenness' (p. 178).

At the same time, considerable advances were being made in mental testing with similarly devastating effects on the population of people with ID. Terman (1911), one of the pioneers of psychometric testing, wrote, 'There is no investigator who denies the fearful role of mental deficiency in the production of vice, crime and delinquency … not all criminals are feeble minded but all feeble minded are at least potential criminals' (p. 11). In his book, *The Criminal Imbecile*, Goddard (1921) concluded, 'Probably from 25% to 50% of the people in our prisons are mentally defective and incapable of managing their affairs with ordinary prudence' (p. 7). As the century progressed, with the influence of Mendelian theories of inheritance, advances in mental testing and concerns about increasing numbers, the causal link between ID and crime tightened. In a contemporary review of the available scientific studies, MacMurphy (1916) concluded, 'Mental defectives with little sense of decency, no control of their passions, with no appreciation of the sacredness of the person and the higher reference of life, become a centre of evil in the community, and inevitably, lower the moral tone … perverts and venereal diseased are overwhelmingly mental defective, as in public drunkenness and shoplifting and the picking of pockets are acts of the feeble minded and one of the large proportions shown by statistics' (quoted in Scheerenberger, 1983, p. 153).

As part of this movement, Fernald (1909, 1912) had written and spoken enthusiastically of the link between ID, its widespread prevalence, and a range of social problems including prostitution, crime, sexual perversion, poverty and their menace to the community. However, despite his huge influence as a persuasive orator, unlike others, he also seems to have paid some attention to reliable, behavioural observations. He reviewed the discharges from the institution with which he was involved from 1890 to 1914 and the results are reported to have surprised him. Of the 1537 individuals who had been discharged, less than half could be followed up, but he found that around 60% of the men and 36% of the women were doing well in the community. This positive result, although not remarkable by modern standards, was a surprise to him and others working with the certainty of the causative link between ID and crime (Fernald, 1919). He considerably altered his position and began advocating innovative programmes and even community placement: 'We know that a lot of the feeble minded are generous, faithful and pure minded. I never lose an opportunity to repeat what I am saying now, that we have really slandered the feeble minded. Some of the sweetest and most beautiful characters I have ever known have been feeble minded people' (Fernald, 1918, reported in Trent, 1994, p. 158). However, his views were not shared by many of his colleagues (e.g. Goddard, 1921) and, in any case, the damage had essentially already been done. In the opening address to the American Association on Mental Deficiency in 1921, hugely pejorative references were made about people with ID filling the courts and paralysing schools. Over a decade later, Glueck (1935) studied 500 delinquent juveniles with ID and concluded that ID was a complicating factor in crime, that a far higher proportion of boys with ID fell into delinquent groups and that they were less able to participate in rehabilitation programmes. Sutherland (1937) concluded that between 20% and 50% of delinquents residing in prisons had ID.

There is no doubt, then, that ID and crime were inextricably related in a manner which fostered a cultural prejudice. This cultural prejudice is perhaps typified by Terman's resonating phrase 'the fearful role of mental deficiency' which, coming from such an authoritative and presumably for the time, enlightened source, gives us today a flavour of the extent of these views. These views were pervasive over five decades and can still be detected occasionally when local services for people with ID wish to establish a group home in a particular residential area. Managers and workers in these services are well aware of the outcry that can ensue when local residents fear that the presence of individuals with ID will have a deleterious effect on the neighbourhood. I myself have been to several such meetings and the usual fears are that people with ID will behave in an extremely disinhibited fashion, that it will become widely known that a home for people with ID is placed in the community, and that this will have a depressing effect on house prices. At one meeting, one woman summed up the fears by stating, 'Who in their right mind would want a house like this in their street? Why do you have to have it here?' These fears are, of course, nonsense and it is the case that people with ID are generally quiet, conservative, sociable and extremely good neighbours. It is a salutary lesson that the parameters of scientific respectability can stoke public perceptions of prejudice and threat. Thankfully, we have probably re-entered an era where, once again, ID and crime are no longer inextricably linked. For decades, no one has seen ID as a causative factor in crime and it is foolish to emphasise ID in any discussion or treatise on criminology.

Prevalence of People with ID in Criminal Populations

Despite the debunking of any close relationship, researchers continue to review the role of ID in criminal populations. Farrington and colleagues (Farrington, 1995, 2005), in their meticulous longitudinal studies of delinquency and crime, have found low IQ to be one of a number of risk factors associated with crime. However, their definition of low IQ is above the range of ID (an IQ of 85 or below) and, as such, cannot be considered in any way definitive in relation to this population. Despite a wealth of investigations, there is no clarity on the proportion of people with ID in criminal populations. Neither can we be clear about whether or not the type of offences committed by individuals with ID differs in frequency from those committed by mainstream offenders. Holland (2004) and Lindsay and Taylor (2008) have noted a number of methodological differences between studies which give rise to significant differences in both overall prevalence and the rates of specific offences. Firstly, the study setting seems to have a considerable impact on the recorded prevalence rates of individuals with ID. In a classic study on mentally disordered offenders, Walker and McCabe (1973) found that 35% of inmates were diagnosed as having ID and reported that there were very high conviction rates for arson (15%) and sexual offences (28%) when compared to other groups in their sample. This major study, among others, has led to the belief that sexual offences and arson are overly represented in this group of offenders.

However, a recent study (Hogue *et al.*, 2006) reviewed the same group but did so across different settings of maximum security, medium/low security and community forensic services, all for individuals with ID. These authors found a considerable disparity in rates of index offence depending on the setting. With respect to arson, 2.9% of offenders in the community were referred for fire-raising while 21.4% in the medium/low secure setting were referred for an arson offence. Similarly, there was a significant difference between percentage of participants who had committed a violent offence with 42.5% in the high secure setting and 11.6% in the community. Studies conducted in either setting independently would have come to different conclusions regarding the rates of arson and violence in this client group. Therefore, the effect of the setting is extremely important when considering prevalence rates of specific offences.

A second major variable is the method used to identify ID. Some studies have used recognised IQ assessments while others have relied on self-report. Holland (1991) noted widely varying prevalence rates of ID (2.6–39.6%) reported in studies on prison populations in the United States. It was clear that various studies used different methods to assess ID. A study by MacEachron (1979) of 436 adult male offenders in state penal institutions in Maine and Massachusetts employed recognised intelligence tests and found prevalence rates of ID between 0.6% and 2.3%. Studies which use a screening method for assessing IQ, such as the Hayes Ability Screening Index (Hayes, 2002) or the Aamons Quick Test (Ammons and Ammons, 1958), will automatically overestimate the prevalence of ID since it is the function of screening tests to be over-inclusive with a view to further assessment.

The methodological differences between studies continue with two recent pieces of research finding markedly different rates of offenders with ID in prison settings. Crocker *et al.* (2007) attempted to assess 749 offenders in a pre-trial holding centre in Montreal. In fact, for a number of reasons including refusal to participate, administrative difficulties and technical problems, they were only able to assess 281 participants with three subscales of the Individual Mental Ability Scale (Chevrier, 1993). They reported that 18.9% were in the 'probable ID range' with a further 29.9% in the borderline ID range (full scale IQ of 71–85). However, in a study of 102 prisoners in Victoria, Australia, Holland and Persson (2007) found a prevalence rate of less than 2% using the Wechsler Adult Intelligence Scale. In the latter study, all prisoners were assessed routinely by trained forensic psychologists while in the former study only around one-third of potential participants were included in the study. In addition, three subscales of an intelligence test were used in the former study while in the latter a full WAIS (the most comprehensively validated IQ test) was used for all participants. It is difficult to reconcile these two recent studies, but it is likely that the difference in assessment methods and comprehensiveness of the sample were significant contributors to the disparity in results.

A third major variable is whether or not individuals with borderline intelligence are included in the sample. As can be seen from the study by Crocker *et al.* (2007), the prevalence rate would increase from 18.9% of individuals with 'probable ID' to 48.8% if the definition were to include individuals with borderline ID. In the study by Hayes (1991a, b) of prisoners in New South Wales, Australia, she found that 2% fell within the formal classification of ID and a further 10% were identified in the range of borderline intelligence. Any review of a normal curve indicates that the percentage of the population increases dramatically as one moves from two standard deviations below the mean (IQ of 70, the cut-off for a classification of ID) through the ranges of borderline intelligence (IQ cut-off 80 or 85 depending on the definition) towards the mean. These differences in percentage of the population will also be reflected in the criminal population and prevalence will increase accordingly. Therefore, inclusion criteria are extremely important when considering overall prevalence of criminals with ID and the incidence of specific types of crime.

In addition to the variables discussed above, social policy decisions are likely to have a massive impact across every aspect of service delivery, service use and research. It is not a coincidence that the relatively recent increase in research on offenders with ID has coincided with policies of deinstitutionalisation. As a result of these policies, large institutions in the developed world have closed and the courts no longer have an automatic diversion option of transfer to hospital prior to legal proceedings. As one older offender said to me in a sex offender group, 'they didn't used to have probation, you just got locked up in hospital.' Therefore, more offenders with ID are living in the community and accessing criminal justice services across the range from contact with police to periods of imprisonment. In a follow-up study of 91 offenders with ID on statutory care orders in Denmark, Lund (1990) found a doubling of the incidence of sex offending when comparing sentencing figures for 1973 and 1983. He suggested that this rise may have been a result of policies of deinstitutionalisation, whereby people with ID are no longer detained in hospitals for indeterminate lengths of time. He concluded that those with a propensity towards offending would be more likely to be living in the community and, as a result, would be more likely to be subject to the normal legal processes should they engage in offending behaviour.

For many years, it has been considered that sexual offences feature prominently in offences committed by men with ID. Walker and McCabe (1973), in their study conducted in highly secure hospitals, found that 28% of their sample with ID had committed sexual offences, which was a higher conviction rate than other groups in their sample. In a series of studies on the relationship between IQ and offences against children, Blanchard and colleagues (Blanchard *et al.*, 1999, 2008; Cantor *et al.*, 2005) have found that men who commit offences against children have a lower average IQ. However, although the IQ difference is significant, the group of men who commit

offences against children still have an average IQ of around 90, which is well in excess
of the ID range. Hogue *et al.* (2006) found no differences between their three cohorts
in the rate of sexual offending, which were high at between 34% and 50%. However,
Green, Gray and Willner (2002) reported a phenomenon of considerable importance
to this issue. They found that men with ID who had committed offences against
children were significantly more likely to be reported to the criminal justice service
than men who had committed sexual offences against adults. They felt that any group
of offenders with ID would be likely to have an over-representation of men who
had committed sexual offences against children as a result of this ascertainment bias.
Therefore, these methodological issues and social policy factors are likely to have a
considerable impact on results found in various studies.

Low IQ as a Risk Factor

Although the causal link between ID and crime has now been discredited, criminol-
ogists remain fascinated by the extent to which low IQ is a risk factor in crime. In a
comprehensive review of the role of intelligence and its relationship to delinquency,
Hirschi and Hildelang (1977) concluded that the relationship between intelligence
and delinquency was at least as strong as the relationship of either class or race and
delinquency. Several authors have found that boys with lower IQs have at least twice
the rate of referral to juvenile court than that found for boys with higher IQs (e.g.
Goodman, Simonoff and Stevenson, 1995; Kirkegaard-Sorensen and Mednick, 1977;
Reiss and Rhodes, 1961; Rutter, Tizard and Whitmore, 1970).

It is important to note that all of these studies investigate the relationship between
lower IQ and crime employing participants in the IQ range of 80–120. In the early
stages of their highly influential longitudinal studies, West and Farrington (1973)
reported the results of a longitudinal study of 411 boys conducted over a period of
10 years. By comparing the boys with an IQ of over 110 with those who had an IQ of
less than 90, they found that a quarter of the former group had a police record while
half of the latter group had such a record. Further analysis revealed that 1 in 50 of
those with an IQ over 110 recorded recidivism while 1 in 5 with an IQ of less than 90
re-offended. They noted that for some boys offending began at the age of 8, and in
their regression analysis they established the predictive value of inconsistent parenting,
poor housing at 8–10 years, troublesome behaviour at 8–10 years, an uncooperative
family and low IQ. Their studies of crime and deviance in later years (Farrington, 1995,
2005) found that the best predictors were invariably previous convictions from 10 to
13 years. For example, convictions at 14–16 years were predicted best by convictions
at 10–13 years. Having convicted parents and being rated as daring and dishonest
had additional predictive effects. Convictions at 17–20 years were best predicted by
convictions at 14–16 years and adult convictions were best predicted by convictions in
previous age ranges. An unstable job record, low family income and a hostile attitude
towards police also made additional predictive contributions to the probability of an
adult criminal career. This cycle begins with troublesome behaviour, uncooperative
families, poor housing, poor parental behaviour and low IQ at the age of 8. The higher

the number of risk domains (families, childhood behaviour, schooling, low IQ, etc.), the higher the probability of later delinquency and criminality (Stouthamer-Loeber *et al.*, 2002).

Although this research invokes the concept of low IQ as a risk factor for crime, there are factors which complicate and confuse the issue significantly. The first is straightforward in that Farrington and colleagues do not generally review individuals with IQ less than 70. Their studies focus on low average IQ and borderline intelligence. The second that poor housing and low family income are significantly associated as risk factors for a criminal career. Emerson (2007) cites a wealth of information on the association between poverty and ID to the extent that those in the most disadvantaged sections of society had four or five times the risk of mild and moderate ID when compared to those in the least disadvantaged sections. He goes on to cite evidence relating poverty to increased mortality, poorer health and mental health, poorer educational attainment, social exclusion and poorer outcomes across a wide range of indicators of quality of life. Emerson and Turnbull (2005) also found higher rates of antisocial behaviour in adolescents with ID living in conditions of poverty when compared to those who did not. In the series of studies of individuals with ID, it was found that household poverty and neighbourhood deprivation were associated with increased rates of emotional and behavioural difficulties among children and adults (Emerson, Robertson and Wood, 2005), having higher rates of psychological distress (Emerson, 2003) and higher rates of being a victim of crime (Emerson, Robertson and Wood, 2005). Household poverty and lower socio-economic positions were associated with increased risk in a range of lifetime hazards with a corresponding threat to health and well-being. The important point about this research is that poverty is likely to have a significant mediating role when considering the relationship between IQ and crime.

Several studies have investigated the relationship between ID and crime rather than low IQ. McCord and McCord (1959) evaluated an early intervention study with 650 underprivileged boys in Massachusetts. The boys were divided into 325 matched pairs and assigned to treatment and control conditions. There was a relationship between IQ and the rates of conviction in that for the treatment group 44% of those in the IQ band 81–90 had a conviction while 26% of those with an IQ above 110 had a conviction. However, the 10% of individuals in the lowest IQ group (less than 80) had an intermediate rate of conviction at 35%. This was lower than that recorded in the IQ band 81–90. Furthermore, of those in the higher IQ band who were convicted of crime, none went to a penal institution while the highest percentage going to a penal institution, 19%, were in the lowest IQ band. The results were similar in the control group, with 50% in the IQ band 81–90 convicted of crime and 25% in the IQ band less than 80 convicted, although the numbers in the latter cohort were small.

Two further studies support this finding. Maughann *et al.* (1996) and Rutter *et al.* (1997) followed up children who had demonstrated severe reading difficulties in school. It might be considered that a significant proportion of the children with severe reading difficulties had developmental and IDs. The authors were somewhat surprised, given the background of the relationship between IQ and crime, when they found that the rate of adult crime among boys who had significant reading difficulties was slightly lower than the rate of adult crime in the general population comparison group. Similarly, antisocial behaviour in childhood was less likely to persist into adult life when it was accompanied by reading difficulties. The finding still held true when psychopathology and social functioning were controlled. Therefore, while there may be a relationship between low average IQ and crime, when individuals with an intellectual level of over 1.5 standard deviations below the mean are studied, the relationship seems to break down with those in the lowest intellectual bands showing lower rates of crime.

One recent piece of evidence on the assessment of risk in offenders with ID provides interesting data with regard to rate of offending. Gray *et al.* (2007) compared 145 offenders with ID against 996 mentally disordered offenders. They reported that the ID group had a significantly lower number of previous convictions (average = 8.3) than the non-ID group (average = 11.8). Following these individuals up for between 2 and 12 years, they reported that the ID group had a reconviction rate of around half that of the non-ID group. At the 2-year follow-up point, 4.8% of the ID group and 11.2% of the non-ID group had committed violent offences, while at the same follow-up point, 9.7% of the ID group and 18.7% of the non-ID group had committed general offences. Again, these differences were significant suggesting that offenders with ID had a lower rate of previous offending and a lower rate of re-offending. These data certainly do not support any hypothesis that offenders with ID commit more offences or have a higher rate of recidivism than other types of offenders.

Conclusions

The historical link between ID and crime had a drastic effect on people with ID at the beginning of the twentieth century. What came to be considered as 'the menace of the feeble minded' (Trent, 1994) was a significant motivation for extensive programmes of segregation and, to a lesser extent, sterilisation. The impact lasted for decades and its effect probably still lingers in the form of lesser prejudices. There still remains a fascination for the issue of the proportion of people with ID in the criminal justice services. For the reasons outlined in this chapter, even recent studies have found widely varying percentages. Studies have used different measures of ID, have employed different inclusion criteria, have been conducted in different settings, and have been implemented in different cultures. All of these factors will remain in future studies and suggest that the question is ultimately unanswerable. It is unlikely that we will nail down a specific proportion of individuals with ID who commit crime or a specific proportion of criminals who have ID. Neither will we be able to specify the specific proportion of individuals who commit sexual crimes. The most important outcome is that, whatever the proportion, it is sufficient to warrant research and clinical activity into assessment and treatment of offenders and sex offenders with ID. Given the effects on victims, the perpetrator himself and his wider social network, there is ample incentive to embark on this work.

The relationship between intelligence and crime is robust but the most comprehensive studies have been conducted using the variables of low average and borderline intelligence. They have not generally partialled out those individuals with ID. When this group is partialled out for comparison with groups of individuals with low average and average IQ, studies have found that the group with ID perpetrates lower rates of crime and reconvictions. Again, the conclusion can only be that whether or not rates are slightly higher or slightly lower, there is a significant problem with offenders with ID which warrants our clinical attention.

Chapter 2

Assessment of Offence-Related Issues

Assessment is a crucial starting point not only for defining the idiomatic formulation of the issues surrounding the individual events but also, even more basically, in defining the population. The type of cognitive assessment used, whether it is a review of educational history or a detailed analysis of cognitive assessment, is likely to make a difference to the individuals included within a service. It is important to gain as much detailed information about a person's educational history and cognitive functioning prior to developing formulation for an individual's offending behaviour. It will be noted later in this chapter that several offence-related variables vary with intellectual ability and the level of intellectual disability will be a factor in any consideration of the aetiology of the sexual offence.

There are a number of theoretical and empirical reasons why a developmental history is a good starting point for the assessment of an individual sex offender. The Violence Risk Appraisal Guide (VRAG) and Sex Offender Risk Appraisal Guide (SORAG), both developed by Quinsey *et al.* (1998, 2006), are well-established risk assessments predicated on early research when the variables related to risk assessment were first outlined (Harris, Rice and Quinsey, 1993). Both these assessments are widely researched actuarial instruments and of several studies comparing the predictive accuracy of risk assessment instruments on a range of databases, most employ either the VRAG or the SORAG as a comparator (see later), presumably because of their extensive psychometric derivation and long history. Both these instruments include a number of childhood and developmental variables which contribute significantly to predictive accuracy. Both include an item on whether or not the individual has lived with both biological parents throughout their childhood. If they have not lived with both biological parents, then this increases the risk for future offences. Although ticking one or other box seems a peremptory way of reviewing a person's developmental history, the item is a summary of research on attachment issues throughout an individual's childhood.

Marshall (1989a) argued that sex offenders may fail to develop secure attachments in childhood and that these disruptions to attachment may result in a subsequent failure to learn interpersonal skills and failure to develop the positive self-concept required to enter into intimate relationships with other adults. Subsequently, this lack of intimacy skills and poor self-concept result in a sex offender experiencing emotional loneliness through lack of interpersonal contact. However, the individual is likely to continue to experience a drive for sexual contact and emotional closeness which results in them seeking these basic human needs through forced sex or sexual deviancy. This model was further developed by Ward, Hudson and Marshall (1996) when they hypothesised three styles of insecure attachment each of which may lead to a failure to achieve intimacy with adult relationships. These will be reviewed in greater detail in Chapter 5 but the issue from the point of view of assessment is that combined with other factors these intimacy deficits may lead to offenders seeking intimacy through sexually inappropriate means or sexual offending. In a subsequent study of 147 offenders, they found that insecure attachment was associated with all types of offending including sexual and non-sexual, violent offending. In addition, rapists tended to have more dismissive attachment styles while child molesters were more likely to have either fearful or preoccupied attachment styles. More recently, Stirpe *et al*. (2006) assessed the attachment style of 101 sexual and non-sexual offenders using the Adult Attachment Interview. Similar to previous researchers, they found that sexual offenders reported a greater level of insecure attachment styles although all offenders tended towards insecure attachments.

In a study of violent men with intellectual disability (ID), Novaco and Taylor (2008) investigated 105 male forensic patients to determine whether their exposure to parental anger and aggression was related to assault and violence in a hospital setting. Historical records, staff ratings, self-reports and clinical interviews were employed to assess participants' propensity towards anger and aggression and childhood exposure to parental anger and aggression. They found that witnessing parental violence in childhood was significantly related to anger and aggression in adulthood. This is another piece of research evidence, conducted specifically on offenders with ID, which underlines the importance of the nature and quality of childhood attachment experiences and childhood family experiences in the development of adult offending behaviour.

The upshot of these various theoretical models and research outcomes is that a review of developmental attachments in childhood is important in the assessment of sex offenders with ID. Unfortunately, a recent study on one particular assessment for attachment style (Keeling, Rose and Beech, 2007a) found that the Relationship Scales Questionnaire (RSQ: Griffin and Bartholomew, 1994) had poor psychometric properties when tested on special needs offenders (mean IQ 71.3). The RSQ is based on the attachment model of Bartholomew and Horowitz (1991) on which the Ward, Hudson and Marshall (1996) work was based. It assesses the four categories of attachment – secure, preoccupied, avoidant-fearful and avoidant-dismissive. However Keeling, Rose and Beech (2007a) found that the scales generally had poor internal consistency and low convergent validity with another attachment questionnaire. Therefore, at present, the assessors should gather interview information in order to gain a perspective on the individual sex offender's relationship and attachment history. In this regard, Novaco and Taylor (2008) employed a set of 10 interview questions which were scored dichotomously and which generated a simple four point rating of the individual's experience of parental anger and aggression in childhood. Therefore, a simple, robust rating of parental violence proved to have good reliability and predictive validity in relation to adult aggression.

The VRAG and SORAG also review childhood history of behavioural problems at school. Indeed, this item is so important and valid that in the 2006 revision of the assessments they propose that the Child and Adolescent Taxon, which is a more detailed review of behavioural and attachment problems in childhood, may be a suitable substitute for the Psychopathy Checklist – Revised (Hare, 1991) in the categorisation of risk. Behavioural problems in childhood can generally be assessed through detailed information (using interview and historical documents) on behavioural problems at school. These are graded from no problems, through some difficulties (e.g. some oppositional behaviour at school or minor truancy), to severe behavioural problems and truancy. Therefore during interview the assessor would wish to ascertain the extent to which behavioural difficulties in childhood resulted in exclusion from school or being expelled from school. The differences between these two categories may be important in that a child can be excluded for one or two days for a single occurrence that does not recur over the course of the person's whole education, whereas being expelled usually arises after repeated, persistent and severe behavioural difficulties. The assessor will have to make a judgement when there are a series of repeated exclusions from school which do not result in the child being expelled over the course of education. However, once again, this summary item on the VRAG/SORAG is an indication of a complex range of developmental issues and interpersonal experiences.

The reason why these two issues, attachment and behavioural problems in childhood, have been dealt with in such detail is to emphasise that interviewing the sex offender with ID and, if possible, relatives and carers is an important first step to assessment. The interview and gathering of historical information should be guided by our knowledge of research showing important factors in the aetiology of sexual offending. The research on sexual offending and offenders with ID will be reviewed in this and following chapters. However, it is unlikely that all of this information will emerge at an early stage in assessment. In our own services, assessment will continue for months after the onset of treatment. A clear example of this is the assessment of sexual abuse in childhood. It is undoubtedly an important factor in the aetiology of sexual offending (Beail and Warden, 1995; Lindsay *et al.*, 2001) but offenders may be extremely reluctant to disclose such intimate personal information during a formal assessment period. In a further study, Lindsay *et al.* (2001) found that it might take up to a year for an individual to feel secure enough with professionals involved in services and confident enough in confidentiality for them to reveal details of personal sexual abuse. Clearly if the offender has corresponding difficulties with attachments and relationships, this could be an additional obstacle in their willingness to reveal highly personal, intimate information. In this way, assessment is likely to continue throughout the treatment period.

As mentioned earlier, cognitive assessment is extremely important as part of the initial evaluation of sex offenders with ID. Others (Lezak, Howieson and Loring, 2004; Kaufman and Lichtenberger, 1999) have explained the uses and functions of various intellectual assessments with much greater detail and knowledge than I would be able to. However, there are two fundamental aspects of cognitive assessment which should guide assessment and treatment procedures with all clients with ID including offenders. Firstly, it is important to establish the basic level of intellectual ability possessed by the individual in order to have a greater understanding on how to structure assessment and treatment procedures. At a very simple level, an individual who falls in the range of moderate or severe ID (an IQ less than 50) is likely to have greater difficulty in understanding the laws and mores of society. If such an individual has engaged in inappropriate sexual behaviour, they may lack the intellectual ability to gain a full understanding that such behaviour is against the conventions of society. While this is an extreme example, it is certainly true that as an offender's intellectual ability decreases below the cut-off for a formal classification of ID (an IQ of 70), then it may become increasingly difficult for them to engage with assessment and treatment procedures. An assessor will have to be acutely aware of the need to adapt all aspects of engagement with the client from interviewing, through the use of psychometric assessment, to the adaptation of treatment procedures. This is true for both the client's perception and understanding of the information presented and the way in which professionals decide to communicate such information. The use of adapted methods of communicating, recording information, presenting information and conducting treatment will be presented extensively throughout this book. In addition, it will be seen later in this chapter that the level of intellectual ability may have implications for the pathway sex offenders choose in the perpetration of incidents and may also have implications for the long-term treatment and management of individuals.

A second fundamental application of cognitive assessment is to review the relative strengths and weaknesses on an individual's intellectual profile. The *Wechsler Adult Intelligence Scale – Third Edition* (Wechsler, 1999) allows the assessor to investigate four basic intellectual functions through an analysis of the subtests. These four basic functions are verbal comprehension, perceptual organisation, working memory and processing speed and, as I have indicated, others have explained these basic functions with greater authority and knowledge than I will in this text. Relative deficits in any of these functions will have implications for the way in which the client is able to understand information, retain information and assimilate information. If, for example, the individual has a relative deficit in working memory even when compared to other individuals with ID, then appropriate adjustments in repetition of information and memory aids may have to be made during treatment procedures. This is especially true for those individuals working in mainstream settings with offender who they consider to have lower intellectual functioning. I am regularly asked to assess certain sexual offenders who are not responding as expected to even procedures which have been adapted for lower functioning offenders. Invariably, cognitive assessment reveals a specific deficit in some basic intellectual function be it working memory, processing speed or verbal comprehension which explains the difficulty which the individual is having with material. When appropriate adjustments are made for this individual, then they are more able to engage with material being dealt with in sex offender group treatment.

Research on Assessment

In the remainder of this chapter, I will review relevant research on the assessment of sex offenders with ID. Research on offence-related issues can be subdivided into research which is conducted on general offenders with ID but which is also relevant to sex offenders, and research which is specific to sexual offenders. The former would include work on the assessment of social problem solving, the assessment of emotional instability and emotional regulation and the considerable amount of research on a disposition towards anger and hostility. The latter includes assessment of sexual knowledge, cognitive distortions related to sexual offending, self-regulation pathways adopted by sexual offenders and assessment of sexual preference or sexual deviancy.

Risk assessment is the second broad group of studies. Again these are split into two areas related to static/actuarial risk and dynamic/proximal risk. Static variables are those which do not change in a person's history. Therefore, parental stability, behavioural problems at school, teenage alcohol and drug problems and offending history will all be included as static variables. One static variable, age, does change, with risk decreasing as the individual gets older (Quinsey *et al.*, 2006). Dynamic risk variables are those factors which are considered changeable in the offender. Hanson and Harris (2000) split dynamic risk factors into stable and acute variables. The former are factors which are relatively stable in the person's life such as a propensity towards hostility or a propensity towards substance abuse. While these factors are indications of disposition, they may be amenable to change through protracted periods of treatment. Acute factors are immediate to the situation in that the person may be actively angry or hostile or may be currently intoxicated or abusing substances. Acute dynamic factors can be more long lasting, for example the individual may currently have access to victims.

There is clearly considerable overlap between offence-related factors and dynamic risk factors. Anger and hostility are considered important offence-related assessments and are also considered to be important dynamic/proximal risk factors. Therefore, in the following review of assessment studies, there will be overlap between these two areas of assessment.

Assessment of Offence-Related Issues

Thornton (2002) has developed a framework for the consideration of dynamic risk factors in sex offenders which includes issues that would be considered for offence-related interventions. He set out four domains, the first of which was socio-affective functioning. This refers to the way in which the individual being assessed relates to other people and includes aspects of negative affect such as anger, anxiety, depression and low self-esteem. In relation to sexual incidents, low self-esteem and loneliness have been found to feature prior to incidents of inappropriate or violent sexual behaviour (Beech *et al.*, 2002) and, in earlier parts of this chapter, I have reviewed some of the research on emotional loneliness and attachment and the way it relates to sexual offending. The second domain is related to distorted attitudes and beliefs and there has been considerable interest in relation to cognitive distortions for sex offenders (Ward, Hudson and Keenan 1998; Ward and Hudson, 2000). The third domain, self-management, refers to the individual's current ability to engage in appropriate problem solving, impulse control and a general ability to regulate their own behaviour. Clearly these are offence-related issues and deficits in such self-regulation would be relevant to the assessment of increased immediate risk. Self-regulation has also been employed as the fundamental principle guiding recent developments in the assessment and treatment for sex offenders (Ward and Hudson, 2000; Ward, Hudson and Keenan, 1998). The fourth domain mentioned in the framework was offence-related sexual preference which was split into sexual drive and deviant sexual preference. Although this categorisation is proposed for dynamic risk factors, I will consider offence-related issues under each of these separate headings, since there is such a degree of conceptual overlap.

Socio-affective functioning

Most of the information on assessment of socio-affective functioning is gained through self-report questionnaires. This is true for the whole field of psychological assessment of affective functioning. The normal process is that the researcher will give out a series of self-report questionnaires to participants who will then fill them out and return them. At the outset, it is important to understand that none of this is true for any groups of participants, including offenders, with ID. Because of the literacy deficits involved in the population, all assessments will be read out to participants in a structured setting. However, the very nature of this process means that all assessments are conducted under conditions of structured interview rather than self-report. The assessor has not only the participant's verbal response to the question but will also be able to observe their behavioural and emotional response to the questions. This is a considerable strength in such assessments with individuals with ID but it also means that assessment will take much longer. I always think that administration of even a short self-report questionnaire of 20 items is likely to take up to an hour to administer. This lengthy process is a considerable strength in that the assessor has an increased amount of time in direct contact with the participant and as has been mentioned, the assessor has behavioural observations or reactions to assessment questions. Therefore one can observe the enthusiasm and conviction a person may have for certain items and topics. We can gain impressions of indifference to questions, reluctance to engage with items and, crucially, any lack of understanding a client may be having with questions or issues. However, it also means that all processes including assessment and treatment in relation to offenders with ID take much longer. This is an aspect which anyone working in this field should take into account.

Antisocial and hostile attitude emerge most frequently from studies reviewing dynamic risk factors in offenders. Indeed, in the field of ID, hostility and anger have attracted a large amount of research when compared with other dynamic risk factors. Research on aggressive behaviour has suggested that it presents a serious risk for staff in ID services (Taylor, 2002). Kiely and Pankhurst (1998) investigated the incidence of violence experienced by staff working in an ID service in a UK National Health Service Trust. They discovered that there were almost five times as many recorded incidents of service user violence as in the Trust's sister Psychiatric Service, with 81% of respondents in the Intellectual Disability Service reporting physical assaults at the hands of clients over the previous 12 months. They also reported that staff felt more cautious and wary in dealing with their assailant after the assault and lost confidence in their ability to work. Other studies have reported similar negative reactions by staff to aggressive individuals including feelings of fear, anger and annoyance (Rose and Cleary, 2007), and high states of staff turnover and burnout (Hastings, Horne and Mitchell, 2004). Anger and aggression have a negative impact on the lives of people with ID in a number of ways. Taylor (2002) suggested that aggressive behaviour is the primary reason why people with ID are admitted or readmitted to institutions. Therefore, for a number of reasons, there has been a large amount of research in this field.

Novaco and Taylor (2004) sought to evaluate the reliability and validity of anger assessment procedures with 129 male in-patients with ID, most of whom had forensic histories. In this study, specially modified self-report measures of anger disposition (Novaco Anger Scale (NAS), Novaco, 2003; Spielberger State-Trait Anger Expression Inventory (STAXI), Spielberger, 1996), anger reactivity (NAS Provocation Inventory (NAS-PI), Novaco, 2003) and informant rated anger attributes (Ward Anger Rating Scale (WARS), Novaco, 1994) were investigated with regard to their internal consistency, stability and concurrent predictive validity. The STAXI and NAS showed substantial intercorrelations, providing evidence for concurrent validity for these instruments. WARS staff ratings for patient anger, based on Ward observations, were found to have high internal consistency and to correlate significantly with patient anger self-reports. Anger, self-reported by the participants, was significantly related to their record of assaultive behaviour in hospital. Predictive validity was assessed retrospectively, examining patient assault behaviour in the hospital as predicted by patient rated anger in a hierarchical regression analysis. Controlling for age, length of stay, IQ, violent offence and personality measures, the NAS total score was found to be significantly predictive of whether the patient physically assaulted others in the hospital and the total number of physical assaults. This is a particularly important finding since it demonstrates that a dispositional assessment (NAS total score) has predictive validity in terms of assaultative behaviour of offenders.

Alder and Lindsay (2007) reported on a provocation inventory which was shorter than the NAS and easily accessible. The Dundee Provocation Inventory (DPI) was developed within the context of Novaco (1975) analysis of the functions of anger. The DPI is a self-report measure specifically developed for use with individuals with ID. It covers a range of social situations which could produce an anger reaction depending on the individual's appraisal of events and construction of threat. The DPI samples a range of situations which might engender emotions such as disappointment, jealousy and embarrassment to assess the extent to which an individual reports that they could produce anger. It is rated on a Likert-type scale, with a pictorial representation of the scale to aid understanding, in view of the fact that self-reports are more reliable for people with ID if visual information is included (Finlay and Lyons, 2001). Alder and Lindsay (2007) assessed a group of 114 individuals on the DPI. Sixty-two of these individuals were also administered the NAS and the NAS-PI. The first set of findings was that there were high correlations between the DPI and the NAS ($r = 0.57$) and the DPI and the NAS-PI ($r = 0.75$). All of the items, an item to total correlation greater than $r = 0.48$ and there was high internal consistency in the instrument ($\alpha = 0.91$). In a further factor analysis, they found that the most easily interpreted structure was a five factor solution of threat to self-esteem, locus of control, resentment, frustration and rejection. These factors can be considered as basic self-schemata. In other words, they are likely to represent assumptions about the world which offenders may hold. They may feel that the community is an environment which threatens self-esteem or they may feel a drive to control social surroundings in uncertain situations. Actions arising from such schemata may give rise to aggressive responses. Threat to self-esteem has a clear relationship to the findings that have emerged from recent studies by Jahoda *et al.* (2001) and Payne and Jahoda (2004) who found that efforts to defend self-image were primary in the development of both anger and feelings of depression in people with ID. This further emphasises the importance of self-image and self-esteem in the development of offending in this client group (Beech *et al.*, 2002).

Although hostile attitude and anger emerge persistently from studies assessing risk for future violent and sexual incidents, it has to be acknowledged that sex offenders with ID tend to show lower levels of anger than other offenders with ID. Lindsay *et al.* (2006c) in a study of 247 offenders with ID, found that sex offenders showed significantly lower levels of anger and aggression than other male offenders or female offenders. For the present chapter, we have recently reanalysed the Alder and Lindsay (2007) data, with some additional data from new participants with a view to establishing means and standard deviations for different groups. These can be seen in Table 2.1. Sex offenders reported lower levels of anger and aggression on each factor when compared to other client groups including violent offenders with ID. The table provides data which can be used to compare individual assessments with various client groups. Where anger is present in the perpetration and development of a sexual offence, it may be a particularly potent dynamic risk factor.

In a further development, Taylor *et al.* (2004) developed the Imaginal Provocation Test (IPT) as an additional idiographic anger assessment procedure with people with ID that taps key elements of the experience and expression of anger, is sensitive to change associated with anger treatment and is easily modifiable for idiographic uses. The IPT produces four indices relevant to the individual client's experience of anger: anger reaction, behavioural reaction, a composite of anger and behavioural reaction and anger regulation. They administered the IPT to 48 participants prior to beginning an anger treatment and showed that the indices had good internal consistency. The assessment had reasonable concurrent validity when correlated with the STAXI and NAS. Therefore it would appear that there are rapid, flexible and sensitive idiographic

Table 2.1 Mean scores and standard deviations for each group for each factor and for the overall DPI score (Alder and Lindsay)

	Factor A Threat to self-esteem		Factor B Locus of control		Factor C Resentment		Factor D Frustration		Factor E Rejection		Total DPI	
	Mean	SD	Mean	SD	Mean	SD	Mean	SD	Mean	SD	Mean	SD
Anger referrals ($N = 39$)	10.1	4.7	4.9	2.9	2.9	2.7	3.4	2.5	7.1	3.6	28.3	14.2
Sex offenders ($N = 8$)	8.4	5.3	5.8	3.5	3.0	2.8	2.4	2.0	5.8	2.3	25.3	13.7
All participants ($N = 116$)	9.7	4.9	4.3	3.1	2.1	2.4	3.4	2.4	6.9	3.3	26.4	12.9

assessments of anger among people with ID and that these assessments have reasonable psychometric properties.

Moving on to other socio-affective variables, Lindsay (2005) has stressed the importance of promoting social contact, interpersonal relationships and community identification in sex offenders with ID, both from a practical and theoretical standpoint. Such increased social inclusion allows others to monitor the individual offender and ensures that their views and attitudes are constantly being adjusted, reviewed and even challenged by ordinary social contact. As we have seen earlier, social isolation and loneliness have been shown to be important aspects in the development of the cycle leading up to a sexual offence in mainstream offenders. In the recent study, Steptoe *et al.* (2006) compared a cohort of 28 sex offenders with ID and 28 control participants with ID. They were reviewing quality of life as measured by the Life Experience Checklist (LEC: Ager, 1990) and relationships as measured by the Significant Others Scale (SOS: Power, Champion and Aris, 1988). They found that the two groups did not differ on the home, opportunities and freedom domains of the LEC but that although they had similar opportunities to establish relationships, the sex offender cohort showed significantly lower scores on the relationships domain. This was replicated on the SOS in that the sex offenders showed poorer relationships than the control participants but, interestingly, there was no difference in their satisfaction regarding relationships. Therefore, although the sex offender cohort had more impoverished relationships than control participants, they reported being quite happy with this more restricted range. This led to the conclusion that the promotion of appropriate relationships, contact with the community and pro-social influences are an important area for assessment and treatment.

Lindsay *et al.* (2006c) also found that sex offenders were recorded as showing lower levels of anxiety than other male or female offenders. A similar finding was also reported by Lindsay and Skene (2007) in a study of a mixed group of 108 participants with ID. They administered adapted versions of the Beck Anxiety Inventory (BAI) and the Beck Depression Inventory (BDI). In a joint factor analysis of all items, two main factors emerged representing anxiety and depression separately. They then analysed each assessment separately and found that the emerging structures were similar to that of studies on mainstream participants. For the BAI, three main factors emerged representing somatic complaints relating to balance, subjective anxiety and somatic aspects of feeling hot. For the BDI, three factors emerged once again comprising of emotional cognitions relating to the perception of self such as sadness, pessimism, self-criticism and irritability; secondly loss of function such as loss of interest, indecisiveness and loss of energy; and thirdly somatic changes in sleep and appetite. The study also found that sex offenders ($n = 33$) reported the lowest level of anxiety and depression when compared to other groups such as other offending males, anxiety referrals and depression referrals. Therefore in these results, similar to those of Steptoe *et al.* (2006), the picture emerges of a group of individuals who, taken as a whole may be somewhat quieter, less sociable and less emotionally labile than other offenders with ID.

Two recent studies have evaluated the psychometric properties of several assessments with sex offenders with ID. Four assessment instruments were adapted and tested on a small cohort of sexual offenders with special needs by Keeling, Rose and Beech (2007a). They recruited 16 sexual offenders with special needs and 53 mainstream sexual offenders to investigate the psychometric properties of the Social Intimacy Scale (SIS; Miller and Lefcourt, 1982), the RSQ (Griffin and Bartholomew, 1994), the Criminal Sentiments Scale (CSS: Gendreau *et al.*, 1979) and the Victim Empathy Distortion Scale (VEDS: Beckett and Fisher, 1994). One of the difficulties with their study was that 'special needs' was not synonymous with ID and included participants with organic deficits but who were in the range of average IQ. They based their choice of assessments on good theoretical and empirical evidence that sex offenders have been identified as having intimacy deficits (reflected in the SIS), attachment difficulties (reflected in the RSQ), have often been identified as possessing criminal attitudes and negative social influences (reflected in the CSS) and have specific difficulties in relation to victim empathy (reflected in the VEDS). They found that the adapted version of the SIS was psychometrically consistent with the original version and the adapted version correlated highly with the original. As has been mentioned earlier, the RSQ showed poorer psychometric properties with inadequate internal consistency and the CSS similarly showed poor psychometric properties and poor convergence with other similar scales. The original and adapted version of the VEDS were highly correlated, it had good test re-test reliability and also showed high convergence with another assessment of victim empathy, replicating studies with mainstream offenders by Beckett and Fisher (1994). Therefore, both the SIS and VEDS appeared to retain good psychometric properties when adapted for sex offenders with special needs.

In a study conducted in the context of the English prison service sex offender programme, Williams, Wakeling and Webster (2007) investigated the psychometric properties of six adapted measures with 211 men who had undertaken the treatment programme and had low intellectual functioning. The mean IQ for the sample was 71.9 with a range from 56 to 80 IQ points, which is somewhat higher than other samples in the field but not markedly so. Six instruments were employed in the study. The Sex Offender Self Appraisal Scale (SOSAS) was a measure of cognitive distortions related to sex offences (see later for discussion and Chapter 12); the Sex Offender Opinion Test (SOOT) and Victim Empathy Consequences Task (VECT) evaluated attitudes to victims; the Self Esteem Questionnaire (SEQ) and Emotional Loneliness Scale (ELS) assessed personal variables while the Relapse Prevention Interview (RPI) reviewed risk factors. They found that three tests had good internal consistency with alphas over 0.8 (the SOOT, the RPI and the ELS) and three had adequate internal consistency with alphas over 0.75 (the SOSAS, the VECT and the SEQ). Factor analyses of the tests found logical underlying structures but each of the analyses accounted for less than 40% of the total variance. These authors also found that all the assessments except the ELS reflected improvements after completion of the programme.

There are now a range of assessments which have been developed and adapted on offenders with ID and which allow an assessor to gather reliable and valid information from this client group. These assessments include the NAS, the BAI, the BDI, the SOS, the LEC, the DPI and the IPT and the range of assessments employed by Keeling, Rose and Beech (2007a) and Williams, Wakeling and Webster (2007). These tests allow us to augment interview material and historical background information with valid psychometric data. In this way, we can begin to make a very structured assessment of socio-affective functioning.

Assessment of attitudes, cognitions and beliefs

A considerable amount of work has been completed on knowledge and beliefs on sexual interaction with sex offenders with ID and control participants. With this client group, it is important not only to review cognitive distortions but also to consider the level of sexual knowledge an individual may have. Indeed, one of the first hypotheses put forward to account for inappropriate sexual behaviour in this group was that lack of sexual knowledge may lead the individual to attempt inappropriate sexual contact precisely because they are unaware of the means to establish appropriate interpersonal and sexual relationships. This hypothesis was entitled 'counterfeit deviance' and was first mentioned by Hingsburger, Griffiths and Quinsey (1991) and was noted by Luiselli (2000) to be the most influential basis for the development of treatment services for sex offenders with ID. The term refers to behaviour which is undoubtedly deviant but may be precipitated by factors such as lack of knowledge, limited opportunities to establish sexual relationships, sexual naivety and poor social and heterosexual skills rather than a preference or sexual drive towards inappropriate objects. Therefore remediation should focus on educational issues and developmental maturation rather than inappropriate sexuality. Griffiths, Quinsey and Hingsburger (1989) gave a number of examples illustrating the concept of counterfeit deviance and developed a treatment programme, part of which was based significantly on sexual and social education.

In a review of variables associated with the perpetration of sexual offences in men with ID, Lindsay (2004) noted that, surprisingly, there were no controlled tests of this hypothesis. This was despite the fact that the notion is relatively easy to test under controlled conditions. Counterfeit deviance would suggest that some men with ID commit sexual offences because they have poorer social-sexual knowledge, do not understand the rules and mores of society and are unaware of taboos relating to sexuality. Therefore, men with ID who have committed sexual offences should have poorer sexual knowledge than those who do not.

Since then, a number of studies have appeared testing this hypothesis. Talbot and Langdon (2006) employed the Bender Sexual Knowledge Questionnaire (Bender *et al.*, 1983) to assess the sexual knowledge of 11 sex offenders with ID who had been in treatment, 13 who had not been in treatment and 26 control participants (non-offenders) with ID. There were no significant differences between the untreated sex offenders and the non-offenders and the author's conclusion was 'limited sexual knowledge may not be a factor that sufficiently places men with ID at risk of committing sexual offences' (p. 529). Lambrick and Glaser (2004) in a review of sex offenders with ID reported from their service that a number of offenders had excellent social skills and a good understanding of the issues related to sexuality. They also concluded that poor sexual knowledge was unlikely to be a primary reason for the perpetration of sexual offences in these individuals.

Two sets of authors have tested this hypothesis directly. Michie *et al.* (2006) hypothesised that a consequence of counterfeit deviance would be that men who have committed inappropriate sexual behaviour or sexual offences should have poorer sexual knowledge than those who had not. They conducted two studies using the Socio-Sexual Knowledge and Attitudes Test (SSKAT: Wish, McCombs and Edmondson, 1979) comparing groups of sex offenders with ID and control participants. In the first study, comparing 17 male sex offenders with 20 controls, they found that of 13 subscales in the SSKAT, three comparisons, birth control, masturbation and sexually transmitted diseases, showed significant differences between the groups and in each case the sex offenders had higher levels of sexual knowledge. There were no differences between the groups on age or IQ. In a second comparison, 16 sex offenders were compared with 15 controls. There were significant differences between the groups on seven scales and in each case the sex offenders showed higher levels of sexual knowledge. The authors then pooled the data for all 33 sex offenders and 35 control participants. They found a significant positive correlation between IQ and SSKAT total score for the control group ($r = 0.71$) but no significant relationship between IQ and SSKAT total score for the sex offender cohort ($r = 0.17$). They presented two possible reasons for this finding. The first was that, by definition, all the sex offender cohort have some experience of sexual interaction. It is unlikely that these experiences of sexual interaction are random and one might therefore conclude that these sex offenders have given some thought and attention to sexuality at least in the period prior to the perpetration of the inappropriate sexual behaviour or sexual abuse. Therefore, we can be sure that they have at least one experience of sexual activity which is not the case for the control participants. The second possible explanation was that these individuals have a developmental history of increased sexual arousal. This in turn may have led to selective attention and interest in sexual information gained from informal sources. Such persistence of attention would lead to a greater retention of information through rehearsal and perhaps to a greater level of associated appropriate sexual activity such as masturbation. These behavioural and informal educational experiences would lead to a higher level of sexual knowledge. In this latter hypothesis, sexual arousal and sexual preference are hypothesised to have an interactive effect with knowledge acquisition and, perhaps, attitudes and beliefs. However, once again, these authors showed that sex offenders did not have a poorer level of sexual knowledge than non-sexual offenders. Therefore poor knowledge of appropriate sexual behaviour could not be invoked as a reason for the sex offence.

Lunsky *et al.* (2007) conducted a more sensitive analysis of this issue in a comparison of 48 men with ID who had committed sexual offences and 48 men with ID who had no known sexual offence history. They administered the Socio-Sexual Knowledge and Attitudes Assessment Tool – Revised (SSKAAT-R: Griffiths and Lunsky, 2003) which is an updated and revised version of the SSKAT. They split the sexual offenders into a group of 27 participants who had committed repeated or forced offences and 16 participants who had committed inappropriate sexual behaviour such as public masturbation or inappropriate touching. When comparing the two main groups of sex offenders and controls, they found that the former had higher levels of sexual knowledge than the matched group of non-offenders. However in their more subtle analysis, they found that the persistent, forceful offenders had a greater level of knowledge and more liberal attitudes than the inappropriate offenders who had similarly conservative attitudes to the control group. This was a significant finding with a large effect size and they concluded that the counterfeit deviance hypothesis may continue to pertain to inappropriate offenders rather than persistent deviant offenders.

It is generally recognised that cognitive distortions which justify, minimise or mitigate sexual offences are crucial in the offending cycle of perpetrators. A number of assessments have been developed to assess these cognitive distortions and these developments have spread to the field of ID. Kolton, Boer and Boer (2001) employed the Abel and Becker Cognitions Scale (Abel *et al.*, 1998) with 89 sex offenders with ID. They found that the response options of the test needed to be changed to a dichotomous assessment to reduce extremity bias and the revised assessment preserved the psychometric integrity of the original test. Keeling, Rose and Beech (2007a) revised the VEDS (Beckett and Fisher, 1994) for use with special needs sexual offenders. They found that the adapted scale correlated significantly with the original ($r = 0.78$), had good internal consistency ($\alpha = 0.77$) and good test/re-test reliability ($r = 0.88$). It also had good convergent validity with a further test of empathy. The VEDS was also used in an evaluation of sex offender pathways by Langdon, Maxted and Murphy (2007) where they found that it did not differentiate between different types of sexual offenders with ID.

The most widely reported assessment of attitudes and beliefs associated with sexual offending is the Questionnaire on Attitudes Consistent with Sexual Offending (QACSO: Lindsay *et al.*, 2004c). The QACSO consists of seven scales assessing attitudes which could be considered permissive of or consistent with seven different types of sexual offences. The types of attitudes assessed are those which minimise the harm to the victim, which mitigate the offender's responsibility, which move some of the responsibility for the offence onto the victim and other attitudes which might excuse the actions of the offender for various reasons. The first section covers attitudes related to rape and woman with questions such as 'If a man rapes a woman, is it just a bit of fun?' There is a scale related to dating abuse which the authors had thought might be related to some types of sexual assault on women with questions such as 'If a girl invites you back to her place for coffee, is she really asking you back for sex?' There are three scales on non-contact offences. The voyeurism scale contains questions such as 'Is staring at a woman's body a good way of showing her that you find her attractive?' The exhibitionism scale contains items such as 'When a man shows his penis to a woman, does it really turn her on?' And the stalking and sexual harassment scale contains items such as 'Is it okay to follow woman as long as you don't touch them?' Two further scales complete the instrument: the offences against children scale contains items such as 'Do you think sex with children does harm if the adult is gentle?' and the scale on homosexual assault contains items such as 'If a man rapes another man would it do him any harm?' Finally, the QACSO contains a social desirability scale which is empirically derived from the original pool of items and will be explained later.

Broxholme and Lindsay (2003) completed a pilot project on the QACSO which assessed six of these seven scales (the stalking and sexual harassment scale had not yet been included). They found that the scales discriminated significantly between groups of sexual offenders with ID and a group of non-sexual offenders with ID. A further, more extensive study was completed by Lindsay, Whitefield and Carson (2007). They compared 41 sex offenders with ID, 34 other types of male offenders with ID (generally violent or alcohol-related offences), 30 non-offenders with ID and 31 mainstream, non-offending males. Using three methods to compute reliability, they excluded certain items as unreliable. Items which did not discriminate significantly between groups were also excluded. They then reviewed the remaining items within each scale and computed internal consistency. Items which reduced internal consistency were also dropped from the main assessment. This then left these authors with three types of items within each scale which they classified as A items (those which discriminated between groups, had good internal consistency and good reliability), B items (those which discriminated between groups, had good reliability but reduced the internal consistency within each scale) and C items (those which lacked adequate psychometric properties or did not discriminate between groups). Five items which did not discriminate between groups but which had good reliability were retained to make up a social desirability scale. These items failed to discriminate because all groups had high (unsocialised) average scores on them. The logic behind the social desirability scale was that those men who scored low on this scale were likely to be masking their true attitudes since all groups in the study had equally high scores on all five items.

The QACSO has been used by two research groups in addition to the original authors. Rose *et al.* (2002) used the instrument to assess outcome in a sex offender treatment group for five men with ID. Although they reported large effect sizes (not calculated by the original authors), numbers were too few for the treatment effects to achieve statistical significance. Rose *et al.* (2007) reported a further treatment intervention on a group of six sex offenders with ID. On this occasion, treatment effects reported on the QACSO achieved statistical significance. Langdon and Talbot (2006) also used the QACSO to assess levels of cognitive distortions in sex offenders and found that this cohort had significantly higher scores on the QACSO than non-offenders. In a study on pathways into sex offending (see later; Ward, Hudson and Keenan, 1998), Langdon, Maxted and Murphy (2007) used the QACSO to assess differences in attitudes between different types of offenders, finding no significant differences between the groups.

In addition to demonstrating differences between sexual offenders, non-sexual offenders and non-offenders, Lindsay *et al.* (2006b) tested attitudinal differences between offenders against women, offenders against children and exhibitionists. They conducted two separate studies on two separate sites and in both, offenders against women had higher scores than the other cohorts on the rape and attitudes to women scale while the offenders against children had higher scores on the child scale than the other cohorts. Therefore there were some indications of specificity in cognitive distortions between offenders against women and offenders against children. The exhibitionists showed no specific elevation in relation to other sex offending cohorts and there were no significant differences between groups on the scales related to non-contact offences. In a series of case studies, Lindsay *et al.* (1998a,b,c) and Lindsay *et al.* (1999) showed improvements following treatment on the QACSO and Lindsay and Smith (1998) found that sex offenders treated for 2 years showed significantly greater improvements on the QACSO than men treated for 1 year. Therefore, these authors have found that the QACSO has utility in demonstrating the effects of treatment and may also have some utility in discriminating between offenders against adults and offenders against children.

Self-management and self-regulation

Self-regulation has become a fundamental concept in the assessment and treatment of sex offenders since the publication of the Ward and Hudson (2000) and Ward, Hudson and Keenan (1998) model of self-regulation pathways in the perpetration of sexual offences and recidivism. Ward and Hudson (1998) proposed four basic pathways for offending into which sex offenders can be categorised. These four pathways were split into two pathways with approach goals and two pathways with avoidant goals. The nature of the pathway within each goal (approach or avoidant) is determined by whether the self-regulation style is active or passive. The first is the approach/explicit pathway in which the individual has a clear wish to offend sexually and uses explicit plans and procedures to carry out the act. The approach/automatic pathway involves the individual engaging in over learned behavioural scripts which are consistent with sexual offending. Their behaviour may be poorly planned and somewhat impulsive within the context of these behavioural scripts. The third pathway is avoidant/active where the individual attempts to control their thoughts and behaviour which might lead towards sexual offending. However, their strategies are ineffective and counterproductive leading to an increased risk of sexual offending. Clear examples of this are increasing alcohol intake to try and control sexual impulses or masturbating to inappropriate sexual fantasies in an effort to satiate and eliminate these impulses. The fourth pathway is avoidant/passive where the individual may wish to avoid sexual offending or abusive incidents but lacks coping skills to prevent it from happening.

Several authors have reported empirical support for this model. Bickley and Beech (2002) conducted a validation of the model with 87 men who had committed sexual offences against children. They found that all but a handful of these individuals could be reliably categorised according to the four pathways. In addition, men with active or explicit pathways had significantly lower rates of previous conviction. Forty one point four per cent of the sample were allocated to the approach/explicit pathway, 34.5% to the approach/automatic pathway, 16.1% to the avoidant/active pathway and 8.1% to the avoidant/passive pathway. Webster (2005) investigated the model with reference to 25 men who had re-offended following sex offender treatment. He found that all but four could be allocated reliably to a pathway and that the majority were approach/explicit offenders. The results supported the view of Hudson and Ward (2000) that approach/explicit men were likely to be the most difficult to change in treatment.

In a further test of the model, Yates and Kingston (2006) assessed 80 men convicted of rape offences against adults, incest offences and offences against extra-familial children. They found that incest offenders tended to follow an avoidant pathway while rapists towards an approach pathway. Interestingly, static and dynamic risk factors varied across pathways with those following approach pathways having higher static risk than those following the avoidant/passive pathway. Those following an approach/automatic pathway had a higher level of dynamic risk factors than other participants. They concluded that their study suggested that different types of sexual offenders may have different treatment needs leading to variations in treatment planning.

In their application of the sex offending pathways model to offenders with ID, Keeling and Rose (2005) referred to research which found that offenders with ID were characterised as having low self-esteem, low self-worth and unassertiveness. They also drew on research which suggested that insight was required to understand the consequences of one's actions and without insight, it seemed unlikely that sex offenders with ID would engage in conscious explicit planning. Therefore they would be more likely to be aligned with passive or automatic styles of self-regulation strategies. As a result, they felt that the avoidant/passive or approach/automatic pathways might be most likely classifications for sex offenders with ID. They concluded that 'What does seem clear from the literature is that intellectually disabled sex offenders seemed to have very little in common with the offender who relapses via the approach/explicit pathway' (p. 81).

In a pilot evaluation of these hypotheses, Keeling, Rose and Beech (2006) conducted a study of 16 sex offenders with special needs and found that these individuals could be assigned reliably to one of the four sex offender pathways. However, against the predictions of Keeling and Rose (2005), all but one participant was assigned to the active pathways. Two problems with this study were the small sample and the fact that the experimental group included a number of individuals who had an IQ in the average range but had special needs for reasons of poor literacy or brain damage, making comparisons with ID offenders difficult. In another study, Langdon, Maxted and Murphy (2007) classified 34 sex offenders with ID and borderline intelligence, using the four pathways model. They reported that six (18%) fell into the avoidant pathways while 28 (82%) fell into the active pathways with almost half (16: 47%) in the approach/explicit pathway. This latter finding is more similar to that in mainstream offenders found by Bickley and Beech (2002) when they classified their sample as 75.9% approach offenders and 24.1% avoidant. However, it was still the case that the considerable majority fell into the active pathways. In addition, Langdon, Maxted and Murphy (2007) found that offenders with a passive strategy had lower levels of general intellectual functioning than offenders with an active strategy. There were no differences between offenders falling into different pathways on number of known offences, victim empathy, socio/sexual knowledge or victim type.

A final study evaluating the Ward and Hudson Pathways Model of the sexual offence process arrived at similar conclusions regarding pathway allocation. Similar to the other two studies, Lindsay, Steptoe and Beech (2008) used the Offence Pathway Checklist developed by Bickley and Beech (2002) to allocate 62 sexual offenders with

ID to one of the four self-regulation pathways. They also found that participants could be reliably allocated to one of the pathways with disagreement on only two participants. They found that the overwhelming majority (95.1%) of participants were allocated to approach pathways. This reinforced the previous findings of Keeling, Rose and Beech (2006) and Langdon, Maxted and Murphy (2007). Given that so few participants were assigned to the avoidant pathways, all subsequent analyses were confined to categories of self-regulation style rather than approach or avoidant goals. Of the 62 participants, 35 were allocated to explicit/active self-regulation while 27 were allocated to automatic/passive self-regulation. Explicit/active offenders had a higher rate of contact offences, a lower rate of non-contact offences and a lower re-offending rate at 3 years follow-up. They also found, similar to Langdon, Maxted and Murphy (2007) that the automatic/passive offenders had a significantly lower mean IQ.

It is interesting that these three studies have consistently allocated the majority of sexual offenders with ID to categories of approach goals. This is against the prediction from Keeling and Rose (2005) that because of the issues of low self-esteem, lack of ability to develop clear sexual offending strategies, problem solving deficits and poor coping skills, sex offenders with ID would be more likely to be allocated to avoidant and passive pathways. The available literature does suggest some preliminary explanations for these findings. It has already been noted that some studies have found that sex offenders with ID show lower levels of emotional disregulation than other client groups. For example, Lindsay and Skene (2007) found that of the various groups studied on the BAI and BDI, sex offenders reported the lowest levels of emotional instability.

Impulsivity is a personal characteristic which is often cited in relation to sex offenders in general and also sex offenders with ID. Ward and Hudson (1998) in their elucidation of the offence pathways of mainstream sex offenders mention impulsivity in relation to a number of subtypes. Not all pathways rely on impulsive reactions from the sex offender. Indeed, the approach/explicit pathway does not invoke impulsivity at all and the extent to which it is incorporated into other pathways is variable. For example, although Ward and Hudson (1998) invoke impulsivity in relation to the approach/automatic pathway, if an offender employs an approach/automatic pathway in which they engage in routine high risk behaviours without the explicit intention to offend, one could argue that they are arranging their routines in order to maximise the probability of offending opportunities. In this way, impulsivity would not appear to play a central role in the offence cycle.

Several authors (Nussbaum *et al.*, 2002; Cohen *et al.*, 2002) have conducted studies in which it appeared that sex offenders were less impulsive than other types of offenders when these personality traits were measured systematically. Parry and Lindsay (2003) compared 22 sex offenders with 6 non-offenders and 13 other types of offenders using the Barratt Impulsiveness Scale (Barratt 1994) adapted to suit the client group. They found that sex offenders reported lower levels of impulsiveness than other types of offenders. However, they felt that there may be subgroups of clients with ID who do indeed have higher levels of disinhibition and impulsivity and that this should be incorporated into assessment and treatment considerations.

Although this finding may appear counterintuitive, some colleagues who work in the field of offenders with ID have been unsurprised by this result. When they work with sex offenders and other types of offenders they have noticed that the sex offender group are quieter, less demonstrative and more self-contained. It may be that we are overly influenced by the very high risk individuals who are extremely disinhibited and take up a great deal of staff time, attention and concern. These individuals are always at the forefront of clinical team discussions, staff observation and escorting duties and incident reports. In such instances we might advise staff to look behind this individual when they are being observed in the common room and they are likely to see four or five sex offenders with ID quietly reading the paper and keeping themselves to themselves. In this way, impulsivity may appear to be a highly significant feature in the client group but, in fact, we may place too much of our opinion on a small number of individuals who are extremely difficult to manage and cause a great deal of concern.

Opportunism is a clearer concept than impulsivity. Carers may remark to me, 'He is so impulsive, as soon as you turn your back he will do something.' The important point is that he employed some self-restraint until staff reduce their level of vigilance. Here, they seem to be referring to a lack of long-term self-restraint and the willingness, to produce something that is viewed as impulsive behaviour, to take advantage of any opportunity even if the short-term consequences are likely. Therefore the high level of opportunism combined with a low perceived level of threat (see Chapters 5 and 6).

These ideas merge the available research evidence with clinical observations to offer some explanation of unusual findings. As such, the tentative hypotheses about self-regulation, impulsivity and emotional stability require a great deal of further testing before we can incorporate them into the reliable body of knowledge on this client group. What is clear is that there is a great deal of work to be done in this field in order to help clinicians make reliable judgements and assessments with a view to conducting more effective treatment which is appropriate to each sex offender with ID.

Sexual preference and sexual drive

In mainstream sex offender work, inappropriate sexual preference and sexual drive have been considered as primary motivation by several authors (Blanchard *et al.*, 1999; Harris *et al.*, 2003). Although some of this work is beginning to extend to men with lower intellectual functioning, there are no studies which specifically assess sexual drive and sexual preference in sex offenders with ID. One can draw inferences from other studies which review the persistence of offending and investigate the relationship between sexual preference and IQ. Some of the main inferences have been drawn from studies which have noted previous sexual offending and patterns of offending and cohorts of referred clients. Day (1994) reported in a study of 31 sexual offenders referred to his clinic, that all of them had previous recorded incidents of inappropriate sexual behaviour or sexual offences. This would suggest that there is considerable persistence in the sexual behaviour of these men rather than the incident being isolated. Lindsay *et al.* (2004b) found that for 62% of referrals, there was either a previous conviction for a sexual offence or clear documented evidence of sexual abuse having been perpetrated by the individual. If one considers the social context of an individual with ID, any incident of sexual abuse is typically met with a great deal of criticism towards the offending individual on the part of his victim's family or his care givers. This would be a considerable disincentive to the further commission of additional sexual offences and one must conclude that sexual drive and sexual preference may be significant factors in the persistence of this behaviour in the face of such criticism. Therefore, there is some oblique evidence which would suggest that sex offenders with ID show some persistence in their sexual behaviour.

However, other pieces of evidence, although not directly testing sexual drive, do suggest a somewhat more complicated picture. Lindsay, Steptoe and Beech (2008) in their study of sex offence pathways, found that approach/explicit offenders had a significantly lower rate of re-offending 3 years after they had been incorporated in treatment. This ran counter to the hypothesis, suggested by Hudson and Ward (2000) that approach/explicit offenders would have a higher rate of re-offending. In order to account for this finding, Lindsay, Steptoe and Beech (2008) revisited the hypothesis of 'counterfeit deviance'. They felt that although sex offenders with ID had a greater level of sexual knowledge and, by implication, they have had a greater developmental interest in sexual matters (Michie *et al.*, 2006; Lunsky *et al.*, 2007), they may still have retained a poor understanding of the extent to which society condemns inappropriate sexual behaviour and may not have developed appropriate self-regulation mechanisms with regard to sex (this thesis is developed in Chapter 6). In addition, some individuals with ID may have a general difficulty in developing self-restraint strategies and this generalised difficulty is likely to be reflected also in sexual self-restraint. All of the individuals in their study received extended treatment which focused predominantly on challenging cognitive distortions related to sexuality and promoting self-regulation and self-restraint. Given that this cohort of approach/explicit offenders has a lower rate of re-offending, rather than the higher rate hypothesised, one explanation is that these individuals may have indeed lacked appropriate strategies to regulate and control their sexuality.

Therefore there was some support for the hypothesis of counterfeit deviance, especially in the light of the fact that these individuals may have had a higher level of sexual knowledge and sexual interest. Treatment may have served to reinforce strongly the understanding that such sexual activity is socially taboo and also help to promote the effective self-restraint strategies which a normally able individual might develop through maturation experiences. These individuals were better able to develop self-regulation and restraint strategies which countermand the notion of a pervasive persistence in sexual behaviour with these individuals. In fact, it suggests that treatment may be particularly effective in promoting self-regulation strategies for sexual drive in this classification of sexual offenders with ID. Treatment certainly appears to have been far more successful than the undifferentiated criticism, without the promotion of coping strategies, which these individuals may have previously experienced.

Two important studies, although again not directly relevant, can further inform on the issue of sexual preference. Blanchard *et al.* (1999) investigated patterns of sexual offending in 950 participants. They found that lower functioning sex offenders were significantly more likely to commit offences against younger children and male children. Although the proportion of variance is not high, this information, coming as it does from a well conducted series of studies, constitutes evidence that inappropriate sexual preference plays at least some role in this client group. They also reported that their results suggest that choices of male or female victims by offenders with ID were not primarily determined by accessibility (or other circumstantial factors) but, rather, by their relative sexual interest in male and female children. Cantor *et al.* (2005) published a detailed meta-analytic study of previous reports which have included reliable data on IQ and sexual offending. In a reanalysis of data on 25 146 sex offenders and controls, they found a robust relationship between lower IQ and sexual offending but specifically, lower IQ and paedophilia. They hypothesised that 'a third variable – a perturbation of prenatal or childhood brain development – produces both paedophilia and low IQ' (p. 565). They go on to accept that psychosocial influences are likely to be important but incomplete in explaining paedophilia, emphasising the value of investigating the range of hypotheses presented for the genesis of sexual offending. However, this information on the relationship between intellectual ability and sexual preference, coming as it does from a highly reliable research group, prevents more persuasive evidence than the essentially anecdotal accounts of previous authors (e.g. Day, 1994; Lindsay *et al.*, 2004b). Therefore, sexual drive and sexual preference are likely to be important considerations within any treatment programme and Lindsay, Steptoe and Beech (2008) suggest that treatments which promote coping skills, self-regulation and self-restraint may be effective in this regard. Lindsay (2005) certainly argues that self-regulation and self-control of any inappropriate sexual drive or preference is an essential aspect of any treatment programme.

Conclusions to Offence-Related Assessment

I have used Thornton's (2002) framework to consider assessment of socio-affective functioning, attitudes, cognitions and beliefs related to sexual offending, self-regulation and sexual drive and sexual preference. There are a number of assessments which have been adapted and researched recently to assess various aspects of socio-affective functioning. Some studies have shown that sex offenders have lower levels of emotional instability than control groups while others have indicated that, consistent with mainstream sexual offenders, social isolation may be a very important aspect to consider during both assessment phases and treatment phases. There have now been a number of studies reviewing sexual knowledge, attitudes and beliefs which suggest that sexual offenders generally have a level of sexual knowledge consistent with non-offenders or a level of knowledge greater than non-offenders. Lunsky *et al.* (2007) found that persistent sexual offenders had the greatest knowledge of sexual matters when compared to naïve offenders and control participants. Lindsay, Whitefield and Carson (2007) found that sexual offenders have a significantly higher number of attitudes which excused or justified sexual assault when compared to control participants. In addition, there was some evidence that these cognitive distortions show some specificity between offenders against adult women and offenders against children.

It is gratifying that there are an increasing number of appropriate instruments for this highly salient field of assessment. Sex offenders with ID could be reliably allocated to self-regulation pathways and some studies have shown that such allocation may be important from the point of view of treatment and management. Individuals allocated to passive/automatic pathways had lower recorded IQ and higher rates of re-offending. This suggests that alternative, perhaps additional, treatment and management arrangements should be included in their programmes. It was also noted that impulsiveness may be generally lower in sex offenders when compared to other types of offenders with ID but that when impulsiveness is noted in individuals, it may be extremely important. There were also some suggestions regarding persistence and sexual preference in this client group and these issues should certainly be incorporated into treatment programmes.

Chapter 3

Risk Assessment

Over the past 5 years, risk assessment has become increasingly important for intellectual disability services. Acknowledging this development, Lindsay and Beail (2004) reviewed a number of important issues in relation to the adoption and development of risk assessment for people with ID. In the absence of a body of knowledge relevant to the field, they noted that individual services for people with ID tended to develop their own risk assessments or adapted versions of existing risk assessments. Such idiosyncratic and piecemeal initiatives can lead to a number of difficulties. Firstly, there may be diversions of opinion, without any empirical support, on the important factors related to risk for this client group. Secondly, there is less opportunity for the field to develop a consistent body of knowledge in relation to the value of risk assessment or even factors involved. For example, Camilleri and Quinsey (2008) note a number of risk assessments which have been used with offenders with ID. They reviewed some elaborate clinical risk assessments which had received strong recommendations despite lack of evidence for their predictive validity or, indeed, reliability. A final concern regarding lack of consistency across agencies is that the results of the risk assessments are likely to produce different figures. One area may feel they have a large number of individuals who fall in the high-risk categories while another agency, with a similar population, may consider that they have very few individuals in the high-risk categories and a large number of individuals in the categories of medium risk for the perpetration of future incidents. In fact, these differences may reflect the different methods of assessment or the different factors emphasised in the assessments rather than differences in the population. In this way, national or even regional planning for services can be thrown into some degree of confusion. Of course, the main reason for the development of reliable and valid risk assessment is in order that we can predict which individuals in our services are most likely to commit further incidents of offending behaviour and sexual abuse while, on the other hand, predict those individuals who are least at risk

The Treatment of Sex Offenders with Developmental Disabilities   William Lindsay
© 2009 John Wiley & Sons, Ltd

of perpetrating further incidents. It is on the basis of such information that major decisions about treatment and management are made.

Risk assessment falls into two main categories – assessment which is based on static/historical variables such as history of violent incidents, childhood behaviour problems and mental health diagnostic information; and those assessments which are based on dynamic/proximal variables, such as current access to victims, hostile and antisocial attitude and cognitions which might justify sexual assault. As has been reviewed in the previous chapter, dynamic variables are essentially similar to offence-related variables and have been dealt with extensively. However, in this chapter, I will look at these dynamic variables to review their predictive utility in relation to future occurrence (or non-occurrence) of violent or sexual incidents.

Actuarial Risk Assessments

One of the first evaluations of an actuarial risk assessment with any offenders with ID was by Tough (2001). She employed two risk assessments with 81 sex offenders with ID referred to an assessment and treatment service. The Rapid Risk Assessment for Sex Offender Recidivism (RRASOR: Hanson, 1997) is a simple four item checklist including previous sexual offences, age of the perpetrator, relationship to the victim and sex of the victim. The original developers found that the RRASOR significantly predicted those who did commit a further sexual offence and those who did not, with a medium effect size (Receiver Operator Characteristics (ROCs), auc = 0.68) (Hanson and Thornton, 2000). Tough (2001) also used the Static-99 (Hanson and Thornton, 1999), which included all the RRASOR items plus other items related to general criminality. She found that the RRASOR was significantly correlated with future sexual incidents ($r = 0.31$) and predicted future sexual incidents with a medium effect size. The Static-99, on the other hand, was not significantly related to future incidents and did not predict future incidents any better than chance. Harris and Tough (2004) employed the RRASOR as a means of allocating individuals with ID into their services. By accepting referrals of only low or medium risk, as judged by the RRASOR, they argued that they could target limited resources at an appropriate group. In this way, actuarial risk assessments were used for a very practical purpose, targeting treatment and management in order to maintain sex offenders of medium risk in community services.

There have been a number of studies in the last 5 years which investigate the utility of known risk factors for future offending when applied to groups of offenders with ID. This has built on work developing risk assessment on mainstream offenders. Lindsay, Elliot and Astell (2004) conducted a study to review the predictive potential of a range of previously identified variables and their relationship with recidivism. They employed 52 male sex offenders with an average IQ of 64.3 (range 56–75 IQ points); and at least 1 year had elapsed since conviction for the index offence (mean period of discharge was 3.3 years). They included 15 static/historical variables and 35 proximal/dynamic variables, all of which had either been identified in previous research or added on the basis of clinical experience. The significant variables to emerge from the regression models included antisocial attitude, poor relationship with mother, low self-esteem, lack of assertiveness, poor response to treatment, offences involving physical violence, staff complacency, an attitude tolerant of sexual crimes, low treatment motivation, erratic attendance, unexplained breaks from routine, deterioration of family attitudes, unplanned discharge and poor response to treatment. Interestingly, certain variables, some of which emerge strongly in mainstream studies, were not associated with recidivism. These included a previous criminal lifestyle, employment history, criminal companions and antisocial influences, diverse sexual crimes and deviant victim choice.

This information may indicate the way in which those of us working in this field should adjust our evaluations in relation to this client group. For example, very few individuals with ID have an employment history reflected in the fact that this does not emerge as a significant variable. In other words, neither the recidivists nor the non-recidivists would have any employment history and so it did not differentiate between categories. On the other hand, individuals often have alternative regimes of special educational placement, occupational placements and the like which serve to make up the weekly regime. Non-compliance with this regime did emerge as a significant variable suggesting that individuals with ID might be judged in relation to their peers. Non-compliance with the regime does emerge significantly from mainstream research on risk assessment and perhaps reflects similar underlying psychological processes in individuals. This in turn suggests that the individual working with that offender should have a basic grasp of the general cultural context of people with ID. For example, a probation officer, familiar with mainstream offenders and their employment histories, may excuse the non-attendance of an ID offender at their occupational placement in the belief that it sounded tedious and boring and the officer him/herself would not enjoy it either. Alternatively, they may make allowances for the ID offender on the basis of their disability, lowering their expectations regarding punctuality and persistence on the basis of the individual's handicap. From the point of view of our own research, this would be precisely the wrong thing to do in that engagement with the placement regime and its corresponding pro-social influences is likely to be a protective factor regarding risk. Lindsay (2005) has written of the theoretical and practical importance of engaging offenders with ID in society in the form of interpersonal contacts, occupational placements and so on. These theoretical aspects will be dealt with in Chapter 5. In the meantime, this emerges as a clear risk factor which has important ramifications for management of the offender.

A specific test of the predictive value of one actuarial variable was conducted by MacMillan, Hastings and Caldwell (2004) when they compared actuarial assessment and clinical judgement for the prediction of physical violence in a forensic ID sample. They studied 124 individuals over a 1-year follow-up period and found that the actuarial process (previous assaults) resulted in medium to large effect sizes for prediction (ROC, auc = 0.77). (The Receiver Operator Characteristic provides a value between 0 and 1. The higher the value of the area under the curve, auc, the better the prediction of those individuals who go on to and those individuals who do not perpetrate an incident. For a more detailed description, see MacMillan, Hastings and Caldwell (2004).) Therefore, these authors found that it was possible to make reasonable predictions of who was at risk for violence in forensic populations with ID. Although this study was on violence rather than sexual offences, it serves as a specific illustration of the predictive value of one actuarial variable, that is, whether or not the person has perpetrated a previous assault.

Effectiveness of Actuarial Assessment Instruments

The first systematic evaluation of a standard risk assessment when applied to individuals with ID was conducted by Quinsey, Book and Skilling (2004) with the Violence Risk Appraisal Guide (VRAG) (Quinsey *et al.*, 1998, 2006. The VRAG and its sexual counterpart, the Sexual Offence Risk Appraisal Guide (SORAG), are the most widely researched and evaluated risk assessments in the mainstream criminal population. Most studies comparing the relative accuracy of risk assessments use the VRAG as a comparator. For example, Barbaree *et al.* (2001) compared the VRAG, SORAG, RRASOR, Static-99 (Hanson and Thornton, 1999) and the Multifactorial Assessment of Sex Offender Risk for Recidivism. They compared these various instruments on 215 mainstream sex offenders in Canada who had been released from prison for an average of 4.5 years. This study found that the VRAG, SORAG, RRASOR and Static-99 successfully predicted general recidivism and sexual recidivism.

Other authors have compared the predictive accuracy of various instruments across a range of clients and cultures. Kroner and Mills (2001) compared the predictive accuracy of the Psychopathy Checklist – Revised (PCL-R: Hare, 1991), the VRAG and the HCR-20 (comprising the historical scale, the clinical scale and the risk management scale; Webster *et al.*, 1995) with 97 normally able male offenders in Canada. They found no statistically significant differences between the instruments, although the VRAG had the highest prediction correlations for minor and major misconducts. Sjostedt and Langstrom (2002) compared the accuracy of several instruments, including the VRAG, on the prediction of recidivism among 51 mainstream offenders convicted of rape and followed up for 92 months in Sweden. They found that only the RRASOR showed predictive accuracy for sexual recidivism whereas the other instruments showed some predictive accuracy with violent non-sexual recidivism. Bartosh *et al.* (2003) compared several instruments including the SORAG to predict recidivism in 251 sexual offenders in the United States. They categorised their participants in terms of index offence type and found that none of the four tests had consistent predictive accuracy across categories. However, the Static-99 and SORAG emerged as the most consistent instruments in terms of predictive accuracy. Harris *et al.* (2003) compared the VRAG, the SORAG, the RRASOR and Static-99 and the prediction of recidivism for 396 sex offenders in Canada. All four instruments predicted recidivism with significantly greater accuracy than chance. The prediction of violent recidivism was considerably higher for the VRAG and SORAG with effect sizes large for violent recidivism and moderate for sexual recidivism.

Langton *et al.* (2007) conducted a considerable extension of the Barbaree *et al.* (2001) study with 468 mainstream sex offenders followed up for an average of 5.9 years. They compared a number of risk assessments including the VRAG, SORAG, RRASOR, Static-99 and its more recent development, the Static-2002 (Hanson and

Thornton, 2003). They compared the various risk assessments on their ability to pre-dict non-violent offending, any offending, serious offending and sexual offending. All the instruments apart from the RRASOR significantly predicted non-violent offending with the VRAG and SORAG showing the largest (medium) effect sizes. All instru-ments significantly predicted any offending and serious offending with the VRAG and SORAG showing the largest effect sizes for any offending and those two assessments plus the Static-2002 showing the largest effect sizes for serious offending. For sexual offending, the Static-2002 showed the largest predictive effect and the VRAG the smallest (it should be remembered that the VRAG is designed to predict violent of-fending). My main point in reviewing these studies is firstly to show that although different assessments are used in different comparative studies, it seems that the VRAG and SORAG are often included as a comparison. Secondly, results suggest that they compare favourably with these other assessments. It is therefore gratifying that the first formal evaluation of a standardised risk assessment has been completed with the VRAG.

Quinsey, Book and Skilling (2004) carried out a 16-month follow-up of 58 clients with ID of whom 67% exhibited antisocial behaviour and 47% exhibited a violent or sexual misbehaviour. They found that the VRAG showed significant predictive value with a medium effect size (auc = 0.69). They also found that monthly staff ratings of client behaviour were significantly related to antisocial incidents. One of the interesting developments in this study was that they substituted the PCL-R (Hare, 1991), a somewhat technical item on the VRAG, with a Child and Adolescent Taxon (CAT) which is a much simpler measure of antisociality. As has been mentioned in the previous chapter, the CAT is based on interview and file material regarding childhood behavioural difficulties. Quinsey *et al.* (2006) in their revision of the VRAG have found that the CAT can substitute the PCL-R with no significant reduction in accuracy. This is likely to be a very important advance in the field of ID offenders since the CAT, being a less technical evaluation, is more easily derived than the PCL-R. They concluded that the VRAG was a reasonably accurate estimate of long-term risk in this client group.

Two more recent studies have employed larger samples of offenders with ID to investigate the value of risk assessment in this population. Gray *et al.* (2007) compared 145 individuals with ID (118 males and 27 females) against 996 mentally disordered without ID (843 males and 153 females). They compared the VRAG, the Psychopathy Checklist – Screening Version (PCL-SV: Hart, Cox and Hare, 1995) and the HCR-20 for predictive validity with both groups from 2- to 12-year follow-up. Using ROC aucs, all three instruments significantly predicted those who would and those who would not perpetrate a future incident. The predictive values for the ID group were generally similar or greater than those for the non-ID group on both violent and general offending. For the HCR-20, predictions for the ID group were considerably higher than controls for violent offending (auc = 0.79 for the ID group against auc = 0.68 for the non-ID group) and significantly higher for general offending (auc = 0.81 for the ID group against auc = 0.68 for the non-ID group). For all three instruments, on the ID group, they found large effect sizes for the prediction of both violent and general offences.

In the second study, Lindsay *et al.* (2008) conducted a comparison of actuarial risk assessments on offenders with ID. They employed 212 violent and sexual offenders with ID as participants, 73 drawn from high secure services, 70 from medium/low secure services and 69 from a community forensic service. These individuals were followed up for 1 year for incident recording. They employed the VRAG, the Static-99 and the Risk Matrix-2000 (Thornton *et al.*, 2003), which has sections for assessing risk of violence (RM-2000/V) and risk for sexual incidence (RM-2000/S) with a combined score (RM-2000/C). Lindsay *et al.* (2007a) found that the VRAG was a reasonable predictor for future violent incidents with a medium effect (auc = 0.72), the Static-99 predicted future sexual incidence with a medium effect size (auc = 0.71) and the RM-2000/V (auc = 0.61) and the RM-2000/S (auc = 0.62) predicted somewhat less well with small effect sizes. The authors wrote that the findings on the RM-2000 should not discourage future research as, because it is relatively simple to use, it has the potential for considerable utility if it can be found to have similar predictive ability to other risk assessments. However, this study does give further validation to both the VRAG and Static-99, which have had endorsement from the results of several studies and researchers across cultures and countries. Following the overall risk prediction effects, Lindsay *et al.* (2008) compared the three separate cohorts using these risk assessments and found that the VRAG and RM-2000/C demonstrated an orderly pattern among the groups with the high secure participants having higher scores than the medium secure participants who in turn had higher scores than the low secure participants. This trend was most notable on the VRAG.

In the study conducted by Lindsay *et al.* (2008), the differences between groups on the VRAG reflected the differences between groups on the recorded number of violent offenders with 69% of participants in the high secure setting having perpetrated a violent offence; 35% in the medium/low secure setting and 24% in the community setting. Therefore, it might be considered that a finding that risk assessment values discriminate between participants assigned to different levels of security is unremarkable. However, there is a considerable debate in the field of ID on whether pathways to offender services reflect inherent characteristics of individuals or the ability of local services to deal with such persons. Although we might make the hypothesis that level of risk of violence will increase according to increased level of security, we cannot be confident that this hypothesis will be supported because the community forensic service employed in this study is relatively comfortable catering to more difficult forensic cases. Therefore, it is notable that the risk assessment comparison between participants in different levels of security does indeed indicate increasing violence according to security. In this regard, the authors also reported no difference in the level of sexual offences recorded across the three samples. Fifty-six per cent of participants in high secure, 58% in medium secure and 55% in the community sample had perpetrated sexual offences. This latter finding was reflected in the fact that assessments for risk of future sexual offending did not show differences between the groups. It does suggest that low secure and community services are more able to deal with sexual offenders, irrespective of their risk for future sexual offences. It also seems to suggest that where physical violence accompanies a sexual offence, the individual is more likely to be transferred to levels of higher security.

Although there are not many studies on which to base a conclusion about static/actuarial risk assessment, these studies do provide some encouragement on the applicability of risk assessment to offenders with ID. There are now three evaluations of the VRAG, and the one which was conducted by the authors of the assessment found a marginally lower predictive value. One study has found a medium effect size for the predictive value of the Static-99 while another report has used its predecessor, the RRASOR, to determine which referrals are appropriate for treatment. On the RM-2000/C, although the effect sizes on prediction were smaller, it did discriminate between groups of high secure, medium/low secure and community offenders. Therefore, there is some research which has produced promising initial evaluations for the use of established risk assessments with this client group.

It is interesting that one of the basic findings of this small body of research is that assessments which have been established on mainstream populations have broadly equivalent predictive values when applied to forensic ID populations. It might be considered that individuals with lower intellectual functioning commit crime and antisocial behaviour for a range of reasons specific to the population and related to lower functioning. This is the principle behind the hypothesis of 'counterfeit deviance', which was discussed in the previous chapter. This hypothesis presents the argument that sexual offences in this population are due to ID specific variables such as lack of sexual knowledge, poor understanding of social conventions, an inadequate grasp of the law and so on. However, risk assessment research to date would suggest that the standard variables uncovered originally by Harris, Rice and Quinsey (1993) are as relevant to offenders with ID as they have been found to be in mainstream offenders. Therefore, previous violence, poor attachments in childhood, childhood maladjustment and antisociality have been found to be as relevant to this client group as to other client groups. Although research is at an early stage and further studies are required in order to establish these principles in offenders with ID, even at this stage, it is an important finding.

Structured Clinical Judgement

The reason why actuarial prediction of risk has been studied with such intensity is because clinical judgement has previously been shown to be extremely poor in relation to risk prediction with violent offenders. There are many examples in the literature with reports of poor predictive validity in relation to clinical judgement (Borum, 1996; Elbogen, 2002; Litwack, 2001; Quinsey *et al.*, 1998). In the field of ID, one recent study (Smith and Willner, 2004) investigated the process of clinical judgement using staff analyses of case vignettes. No consistent judgements emerged from staff ratings, underlining the variability of clinical judgement. However, in a study predicting violence in 124 in-patients with intellectual disability, MacMillan, Hastings and Caldwell (2004) demonstrated that when clinical judgement was structured and made by the clinical team, risk prediction improved considerably to the extent that it was consistent with actuarial prediction. Several researchers and clinicians have been unhappy with the restrictions placed on the assessor by actuarial instruments and have developed a number of assessments which provide a compromise between clinical judgement and actuarial prediction. These are Structured Clinical Judgement instruments, of which the most frequently reported is the Historical Clinical Risk – 20 Items (HCR-20; Webster *et al.*, 1995).

There is now a considerable quantity of research work on the HCR-20 in a range of settings for individuals without intellectual disability. Most of this research has been carried out in forensic psychiatric settings or with mentally disordered offenders. Grann, Belfrage and Tengstrom (2000) conducted a 2-year follow-up of 404 forensic patients who had committed violent offences. They found that the H Scale (10 historical items) predicted significantly for both offenders with a diagnosis of schizophrenia (auc = 0.71) and offenders with personality disorder (auc = 0.71). In a 2-year follow-up of 70 psychiatric patients who had committed violent acts, Dolan and Khawaja (2004) reported that the HCR-20 total score significantly predicted self or collateral reports of violence (auc = 0.76) and documented incidents of re-offending (auc = 0.71). There is now a considerable body of research attesting to the clinical utility of the HCR-20 in terms of its ability to predict future violent incidents (Lindsay and Beail, 2004).

In an investigation of the use of the HCR-20 with 212 adult males with ID from forensic settings, Taylor *et al.* (2008) found that the HCR-20 scales and total score had a high inter-rater agreement, that the H Scale and total score had good internal consistency ($\alpha = 0.75$ in both cases), that it correlated significantly with the VRAG and violent incidents recorded over a period of 1 year and that it was unrelated to IQ. Participants who perpetrated at least one further violent incident over a follow-up period of 1 year had significantly higher scores on the H Scale, C Scale (5 clinical items) and the R Scale (5 risk management items). The total score was a significant predictor for future violence over the follow-up period of 1 year (auc = 0.72) with further significant but somewhat lower predictive values for the H Scale (auc = 0.68), the C Scale (auc = 0.67) and the R Scale (auc = 0.62). In a study of 60 offenders from a high secure setting, Morrissey *et al.* (2007a) found that scores on the HCR-20 had a significant predictive relationship with institutional violence (auc = 0.68–0.77). In a further analysis, Morrissey *et al.* (2007b) reported that with 73 participants with ID in a maximum secure setting the HCR-20 total score was significantly negatively correlated with treatment progress ($r = -0.32$) and had a significant predictive relationship with positive progress (auc = 0.69). Therefore, the HCR-20 would appear to have as much utility in services for offenders with ID as it has been shown to have in mainstream mentally disordered offender populations.

Personality Disorder and Offenders with ID

In the previous section, it has been demonstrated that the variables which have been found to predict violent and sexual incidents in mainstream offenders are also relevant to the prediction of incidents in offenders with ID. One of the variables which emerges consistently from studies and has been employed with many of the major risk assessments is that of personality disorder. Indeed, one assessment of a specific personality disorder – the PCL-R (Hare, 1991), although not designed as a risk as- sessment – has been found consistently and significantly to predict future violence. Personality disorder (PD) has been associated strongly with offending and recidivism in mainstream populations. The crucial finding is that certain PDs, especially antisocial PD, are reasonable predictors of future aggression and are significantly more preva- lent among inmates of correctional settings (Fazel and Danesh, 2002). In addition, psychopathy as measured by the PCL-R is related to certain PDs, including antisocial PD, and has been found to be a good predictor of violent recidivism (e.g. Hemphill, Hare and Wong, 1998; Grettan *et al.*, 2001; Walters, 2003). A final important finding is that antisocial PD and the PCL-R make significant contributions to the prediction of recidivism in a range of offences (Harris *et al.*, 2003). Therefore, from a number of points of view, research on PD has been shown to produce extremely important findings in relation to the planning and development of forensic mental health and offender services and treatment, and the prediction of future violent incidents.

DSM-IV and ICD-10 are two standard classification systems for psychiatric disor- ders which have classifications for a range of PDs. Both have a categorical structure to classification and have the same strengths and weaknesses. Both have undergone review and revision for individuals with ID. The review of ICD-10 classifications takes into account an ID perspective (the DC-LD, Royal College of Psychiatrists, 2001). From the point of view of PD, there are interesting basic alterations in DC-LD. Firstly, it recommends that, because of developmental delay in these individuals, diagnosis should not be made until at least 21 years of age. In addition, DC-LD requires the initial confirmation of PD unspecified before progressing to a more specific diagnosis of PD. PD unspecified requires that the characteristics must not be a direct conse- quence of the person's ID and also states specifically that there must be associated significant problems in occupational and/or social functioning. Therefore, the impact of personality on the person's general, social and occupational functioning is explicitly considered as a requirement for diagnosis. The DSM-IV classificatory system has also undergone a review for considerations specific to ID (DM-ID, National Association for Dual Diagnosis, 2007). DSM-IV has extensive trait descriptions for 10 specific PDs in three clusters. Cluster A includes paranoid PD, schizoid PD and schizotypal PD; Cluster B includes antisocial PD, borderline PD, histrionic PD and narcissis- tic PD; and Cluster C includes avoidant PD, dependent PD and obsessive compulsive PD. DM-ID also emphasises a number of cautions in relation to the diagnosis of PD (Lindsay *et al.*, 2007a). This endorses the age limit of 21 years and also specifies that a diagnosis of PD should not include deficits related to the intellectual disability itself such as a higher level of dependency through an innate lack of ability to manage one's own affairs. A further caution of DM-ID is that any initial diagnosis of PD should be provisional and revisited after 1 year in order to assess any impact of remedial or rehabilitation procedures which are widely in existence in ID services.

A further important caveat, in relation to people with ID, has been recommended strongly by researchers in this field. Lindsay *et al.* (2006a) and Morrissey *et al.* (2007a) have written that a diagnosis of PD or psychopathy has a considerable pejorative connotation in the general population. Such pejorative labels should be used for this population with extreme caution. People with ID are devalued in the first place. The label to describe the population of individuals with ID has been changed repeatedly throughout the twentieth century partly because each term takes on the devaluing connotations that are associated with the population. If, as clinicians, we were to be incautious with the use of PD classifications, it would add another devaluing label to this population. Therefore, diagnosis of PD in this client group should be made with the utmost caution.

There has been a steady, slow development of research on ID and PD. These began with early idiosyncratic writings which focused on personality characteristics such as weakness, simplicity, immaturity and instability (Earl, 1961). Two more recent analyses have reviewed scientific work based on recognised diagnostic classifications (Alexander and Cooray, 2003; Reid *et al.*, 2004). The first systematic investigation into PD in adults with ID was conducted by Corbett (1979) when he reported a prevalence rate of PD of 25% in a large community sample of 402 participants. Over the following 10 years, others found similar, relatively high rates of PD in this population. For example, Reid and Ballinger (1987) found a rate of severe PD of 22% in a general, institutionalised population of people with ID. They found a predominance of explosive PD in males, cyclothymic PD in females and an approximately equal distribution of hysterical PD between males and females. More recent work has produced more fluctuating figures with regard to prevalence of PD.

Reviewing the literature, Alexander and Cooray (2003) comment on the lack of reliable diagnostic instruments, difference between ICD-10 and DSM-IV diagnostic systems, confusion of definition and personality theory and the difficulties of distinguishing PD from other problems integral to ID, for example communication problems, sensory disorders and developmental delay. In reviewing the fluctuating prevalence rates from different studies, they sensibly conclude, 'The variation in the co-occurrence of personality disorder in (*Intellectual Disability*) with prevalence rates ranging from 1% to 91% ... is too large to be explained by real differences' (p. 528). They recommend tighter diagnostic criteria, greater use of behavioural observation and increased use of informed information. Naik, Gangadharan and Alexander (2002) held these cautions in mind when they conducted a study of 230 out-patients with ID in which they found a prevalence rate of PD of 7%. Of these individuals diagnosed with PD, 59% were classified with dissocial/antisocial PD, 28% emotional unstable PD and 10% with both diagnoses. They found a high percentage of co-morbidity with Axis I disorders and 59% had one or more admission to hospital.

In a study on the same population reported previously (70 offenders with ID from a high secure setting, 73 from a medium/low secure setting and 69 from a community forensic setting), Lindsay *et al.* (2006a) took considerable care to address previous criticisms of PD research. Extensive training of research assistants and clinical informants was conducted, care was taken to ensure inter-rater reliability, and multiple information sources were employed including file reviews, clinical informants, carers and nursing staff. They reported an overall rate of 39% of participants diagnosed as having PD, and given that the three cohorts were administratively selected for having been referred to offender services for people with ID, they argued that the relatively high rate of diagnosis seemed reasonable. By far, the most common diagnosis in these samples was antisocial PD with participants in the high secure setting having a significantly greater rate of diagnosis. Those diagnosed with PD were found to have a significantly higher level of risk for violence as measured by actuarial measures of risk, when compared to those with no diagnosis of PD. However, those with a PD diagnosis did not differ significantly from those without on actuarial measures of risk of sexual recidivism. The authors went on to combine PD classifications with PCL-R data to construct a simple dimensional system of increasing indications of PD. They found strong relationships between increasing indications of PD and actuarial measures of risk for future violence (VRAG and RM-2000/V). Relationships with actuarial measures of sexual risk were less strong, less consistent and less significant. The Static-99 showed a significant, orderly relationship with increasing PD, while the RM-2000/S was not significant. Therefore, the data suggested that PD had a strong relationship with risk for violence but a less strong relationship with risk for sexual incidents.

In a further analysis of their data, Lindsay *et al.* (2007c) found that similar factor structures emerged from PD data in this client group as those found in mainstream studies. In an analysis of PD data from 168 participants from high secure hospitals, Blackburn *et al.* (2005) found that two super-ordinate factors emerged representing 'acting out' and 'anxious-introverted' underlying personality difficulties. These reflected similar super-ordinate factors to emerge from a previous study (of 379 university students) by Morey (1988). In a similar confirmatory factor analysis, Lindsay *et al.* (2007c) found that two super-ordinate factors emerged representing 'acting out' and 'anxious/avoidant/inhibited'. These two factors accounted for a similar amount of variance as in the Blackburn *et al.* (2005) study (38%) and were essentially orthogonal. The findings add weight to the emerging picture that a classification of PD, if used with caution and based on appropriate information, may have similar utility in offenders with ID as it does with mainstream offenders. However, it should be remembered, particularly with reference to sex offenders with ID, that the relationship between PD and risk for sexual offending was not as strong as the relationship between PD and risk for violent offending.

In a similar vein, Morrissey and her colleagues (2007a) have investigated the value of the concept of psychopathy as a predictor for violence in offenders with ID. Morrissey (2003) developed clinical guidelines for the use of the PCL-R with offenders with ID in order to facilitate research in the field. She felt that a number of conceptual and practical difficulties should be considered including differences in the presentation of the core characteristics of the disorder, confusion between symptoms arising from intellectual limitations and those arising from PD, restricted opportunities to manifest all the characteristics for psychopathy and problems with patient interview as a methodology for this population. On the basis of these guidelines, Morrissey *et al.* (2005) reported findings on the applicability, reliability and validity of the PCL-R in 203 offenders with ID. They reported acceptable internal consistency for the measure with good reliability for affective and interpersonal facets ($\alpha = 0.74$–0.79) and somewhat poorer reliability for lifestyle and antisocial facets of psychopathy ($\alpha = 0.62$–0.64). Attempts to overcome coding difficulties were based on the guidelines published by Morrissey (2003), and inter-rater reliability for the total scale, convergent and discriminant validity were all found to be similar to those observed in other populations. Full scale IQ was not found to be correlated with the PCL-R total or either Factor I (affective and interpersonal style) or Factor II (antisocial lifestyle) subscales, indicating that the measure was not reflecting aspects of global cognitive dysfunction. The PCL-R was significantly associated with level of security, with concurrent independent measures of externalising behaviour problems and with various measures of risk. It was also related to interpersonal behaviour in that high scorers were rated as more dominant, coercive and hostile than low scorers on the interpersonal CIRCLE personality measure (Blackburn and Renwick, 1996).

In a further analysis, Morrissey *et al.* (2007a) investigated the predictive validity of the PCL-R in a sample of 60 offenders with ID in a high secure forensic psychiatric setting. In contrast to research on mainstream offenders, they found that PCL-R scores did not significantly predict any type of aggressive behaviour. Neither did they find a relationship between PCL-R factor scores and institutional violence over the 12-month period. Morrissey *et al.* (2007b) further reviewed the PCL-R in 73 participants in a high secure ID service by investigating its relationship with treatment progress over a 2-year period. They found that PCL-R total score and Factor I scores (interpersonal and affective aspects) were significantly and inversely associated with positive moves from high to medium secure conditions within the follow-up period. The PCL-R scores were also significantly associated with negative treatment progress (moves to more restricted treatment conditions). Interestingly, they found that the personality-based aspects of psychopathy, specifically deficient affective experience, were stronger predictors of progress than the behavioural or antisocial aspects. They suggested a number of reasons for this finding including the fact that participants with such personality characteristics may be disruptive and unmotivated during treatment, may be less likely to engage with treatment, may produce less positive and trusting attitudes from staff, and may have a negative effect in their dealings with prospective receiving services. Therefore, while there was no relationship between the PCL-R and institutional violence, there was certainly a significant relationship with treatment progress.

These findings are all the more significant when we consider sex offenders with ID. It has been noted that studies have reported equivalent numbers of sex offenders across levels of security. Therefore, a relatively significant number of individuals are likely to be appropriate for sex offender treatment in community as well as other secure settings. If it is the case that personality features are related to treatment engagement and treatment progress, then it is important for therapists to consider these features and make appropriate adjustments to ensure engagement with treatment in all settings. Where individuals are showing poorer participation with treatment, it may be necessary to invoke other management and motivational procedures in order to ensure progress.

Assessment of Dynamic Risk

As mentioned in the previous chapter, there is considerable overlap between dynamic risk and offence-related issues and the research on these assessments has been reviewed extensively in the previous chapter. In this section, I will consider only those studies which have looked at the predictive value of dynamic variables in relation to future incidents. Lindsay, Elliot and Astell (2004) investigated a number of dynamic variables in relation to sex offence recidivism and found that antisocial attitude, low self-esteem, attitudes tolerant of sexual crimes, low treatment motivation, deteriorating treatment compliance and staff complacency all contributed to the predictive model. The most significant dynamic predictors were antisocial attitude, denial of crime, allowances made by staff and deteriorating compliance. Boer, Tough and Haaven (2004) proposed an assessment for risk manageability in sex offenders with ID. They included a number of stable and acute dynamic variables related to staff, environment and offenders themselves. These included staff attitudes and knowledge of clients, communication and consistency among supervisory staff, environmental changes such as new staff, complacency in staff, offender's attitudes and compliance, offender coping ability, relationships, antisociality and various changes in these factors. Although they did not provide evidence for the effectiveness of this measure, Lindsay, Elliot and Astell (2004) did find that many of these variables contributed towards the predictive model for sexual recidivism in their study.

Quinsey, Book and Skilling (2004) conducted a field trial of dynamic indicators with 58 participants. They found that ratings of inappropriate and antisocial behaviour were the best predictor of subsequent inappropriate violent or sexual behaviour. In addition, there were differences between clients who precipitated and those who did not precipitate incidents on the dynamic variables of compliance, dynamic antisociability and inappropriate/antisocial behaviour. There were increases in inappropriate antisocial behaviour, mood problems, social withdrawal and denial of problems in the month prior to the month in which a new incident occurred.

Quinsey, Book and Skilling (2004) employed a design whereby they compared assessments taken 6 months prior to an incident, assessments taken in the month prior to the incident and assessments taken during the month of the incident. They recorded significant increases in the assessments taken in the month prior to the incident and argued, logically, that in those assessments taken prior to the occurrence of an incident, the assessor could not know that an incident was going to take place in the following month. Therefore, if these assessments could be shown to predict incidents, then the variables under investigation would be highly important and clinically significant.

Employing a similar design, Lindsay *et al.* (2004a) tested the Dynamic Risk Assessment and Management System (DRAMS) on which staff made daily ratings of client's mood, antisocial behaviour, aberrant thoughts, psychotic symptoms, self-regulation, therapeutic alliance, compliance with routine and renewal of emotional relationships. Ratings were compared between those taken on the day of the incident, the day prior to the incident and a further control day at least 7 days distant from an incident. Although there were only five participants with full data sets on appropriate days, there were significant increases in ratings for the day prior to the incident for mood, antisocial behaviour, aberrant thoughts and DRAMS total score. Steptoe *et al.* (2008) conducted a larger study on the predictive validity of the DRAMS with 23 forensic patients in a high secure setting. Predictions were made against independently collected incident data and concurrent validity was assessed against the Ward Anger Rating Scale (WARS: Novaco and Taylor, 2004). The sections of mood, antisocial behaviour and intolerance/agreeableness had significant predictive values with incidents (auc > 0.70) and there were highly significant differences, with large effect sizes, between assessments taken 1 or 2 days prior to an incident and control assessments conducted at least 7 days from an incident. Therefore, dynamic risk assessment appears to perform well in both concurrent and predictive validity in relation to offenders with ID including sex offenders. In a critique of these studies, Camilleri and Quinsey (2008) noted that several of the items in the DRAMS did not have a significant predictive relationship with subsequent incidents. They made the important point that assessing and targeting variables which are not related to recidivism may be at best of little value and, at worst, a waste of valuable staff time and therapeutic input. They write, 'This poses a significant problem for targeting criminogenic needs – there is little reason to believe that targeting items that do not predict recidivism would reduce risk' (p. 17). This is an extremely important consideration which is very relevant to forensic ID services.

One further series of studies has investigated the value of dynamic risk variables in the prediction of violent and sexual incidents. Lindsay *et al.* (2008b) used two instruments in order to calculate their value in predicting incidents over the subsequent year. The Short Dynamic Risk Scale (SDRS: Quinsey, 2004) is an eight-item rating scale that records a range of dynamic factors including hostile attitude, coping skills, self-care skills and consideration of others. The Emotional Problem Scale (EPS: Prout and Strohmer, 1991) is a rating instrument developed for individuals with mild ID. It includes scales on thought disorder, physical aggression, non-compliance, anxiety, distractibility, depression, hyperactivity, withdrawal, self-esteem, verbal aggression, somatic concerns and sexual maladjustment. The EPS factor analyses into two main factors: externalising behaviour problems (physical aggression, non-compliance, hyperactivity and verbal aggression) and internalising behaviour problems (anxiety, depression and self-esteem). The SDRS was completed on 145 offenders with ID and the EPS completed on 169, both at the beginning of the study. Over the follow-up period of 1 year, the SDRS had a significant predictive relationship with incidents (auc = 0.72) as did the EPS, externalising scale (auc = 0.75), and the EPS, internalising scale (auc = 0.73). A further development was completed by Hogue *et al.* (2006) when they made a more detailed study of the EPS with 172 offenders with ID from a range of security settings. Participants in maximum security were rated on the EPS as having significantly higher levels of internalising behaviour problems including depression, anxiety and low self-esteem. There were no differences between participants from different levels of security on externalising behaviour problems apart from physical aggression where, once again, the participants from high security had higher levels. Therefore, these two assessments of dynamic risk, the SDRS and the EPS, have promise in relation to the prediction of future sexual and violent incidents.

Conclusions

I have reviewed the various studies on risk assessment with offenders with ID and have attempted to make conclusions about the relative value of various assessments that have been investigated. There is no doubt that there has been a significant increase in the amount of research being conducted in this field. However, it is my impression, having visited a number of services in the United Kingdom, North America and Australia and having discussed the issues with clinicians involved, that the clinical use of risk assessment is moving ahead quicker than the research which might substantiate its value.

There have been a number of studies on both static and dynamic risk on violent and sexual offenders with ID and these studies have suggested a number of important hypotheses. There is no doubt that the variables originally established by Harris, Rice and Quinsey (1993) have applicability in offenders with ID. This can be seen with the significant predictive results derived from studies using the VRAG and Static-99. However, these instruments are composite assessments and it may be that some of the variables contained in them are more highly predictive than others. The point noted by Camilleri and Quinsey (2008) is extremely important. From a criminogenic position, there is little point assessing and directing treatment interventions upon variables which have no relevance in reducing risk. They have pointed this out in relation to the DRAMS but the argument is equally relevant for the various items on the VRAG, SORAG, Static-99 and RM-2000, all of which have been used with offenders with ID. Interestingly, there may be value, from a psychological position, in that improving contentment, personal abilities, and so on, may be personally important to the individual. It is likely, however, that improved psychosocial adjustment and reduction of risk are closely related in that good psychological adjustment may promote reductions in hostility, greater compliance and better personal engagement.

Lindsay, Elliot and Astell (2004) noted that there were several variables in their analysis which were not related to future sexual incidents even though all of these variables had been found to be significant predictors with mainstream sex offenders and violent offenders. Indeed, it is notable from their study that there were more dynamic variables retained in the regression model than static variables in the prediction of future sexual incidents. If one then considers that a single assessment using the SDRS and EPS resulted in predictions for the following year which were as significant or more significant than established static risk assessments, then one might surmise that dynamic variables may be at least as important and perhaps more important with sex offenders with ID.

Chapter 4

Treatment of Inappropriate Sexual Behaviour

Probably because of the contentious nature of the topic, sex offender treatment has come under a great deal of scrutiny over the past 20 years. Researchers have reported the effects of treatment on a range of personal characteristics including sexual arousal to deviant stimuli, attitudes consistent with sexual offending, interpersonal problem solving skills, social skills, anger, depression, anxiety and sexual behaviour. However, as Quinsey (1998) points out, the issue of specific interest in relation to social policy makers is whether or not individuals re-offend. In this regard, it seems to me that sex offender treatment is judged by a different yardstick than therapies for other psychological difficulties. A single relapse (re-offence) is considered unequivocally as a treatment failure. However, in other therapies such as those dealing with anxiety, depression, phobias and even violence, a single relapse would be at worst considered a setback. For other therapies, a single relapse might even be considered a success when compared to the individual's rate of pre-treatment episodes. If an individual had experienced five or six bouts of chronic depression prior to treatment and following treatment had a period of 15 years in which he or she was symptom free prior to having a relapse, most therapists would view this as a considerable treatment success. However, if an individual has committed five or six sexual offences and similarly following treatment did not re-offend until 15 years later, it is considered a treatment failure and is viewed with a different interpretation. Cann, Falshaw and Friendship (2004) conducted a 21-year follow-up of sexual offenders discharged from prison in England and Wales. Their interpretation of individuals who had spent 15 years in the community prior to re-offending was that he had been 'at risk in the community' for 15 years. Although these results are essentially similar, it is clear that sex offender treatment is, rightly, considered with much greater caution. This has proved a huge strength for the field of sex offender treatment and healthy robust arguments continue to the present time on the validity of the large number of treatment outcome and follow-up studies in the area. As a clinician and researcher, I consider this a benefit which is not always afforded to colleagues working in other areas.

A Short Review of Outcome and Follow-up Research in Mainstream Sex Offender Treatment

It is difficult to partial out behavioural and cognitive behavioural treatments, but there is some evidence from review studies that it may be important to do so. In a meta-analysis of sex offender treatments, Hanson *et al.* (2002) reported that 'Current treatments (any treatment currently offered and cognitive behavioural treatments offered since 1980) were associated with significant reductions in both sexual and general recidivism whereas the older treatments were not' (p. 187). 'Older treatments' were predominantly behavioural, employing techniques such as aversion therapy, reorientation of sexual preferences through masturbatory reconditioning and promotion of social competence. Furby, Weinrott and Blackshaw (1989) reviewed this (mostly pre-1980) literature and concluded that the existing evaluations were undermined by methodological weaknesses and that there was no evidence of a positive treatment effect. Therefore, it seemed that psychological treatment employing only behavioural techniques was unlikely to produce positive and lasting change.

Hall (1995a) conducted a meta-analysis of cognitive behavioural treatments, only including studies which employed a comparison group. He found 12 studies that appeared after the Furby, Weinrott and Blackshaw (1989) review and found a small but significant treatment effect and concluded that cognitive behavioural treatments were superior to purely behavioural treatments. However, critics noted that the strongest treatment effect came from comparisons between treatment completers and those who dropped out of treatment. Treatment drop-outs may be a poor comparison since they are likely to have characteristics related to recidivism risk such as confrontational behaviour, antisocial personality, impulsivity, lack of reliability, poorer lifestyle habits and relative youth (Wierzbicki and Pekerik, 1993). In a further analysis, Hall (1995b) found that when the drop-out cohorts were removed from the meta-analysis, the treatment effect was no longer significant. In a third meta-analysis, Gallacher *et al.* (1999) reviewed 25 comparison group studies examining psychological or hormonal treatments. They concluded that there was a significant treatment effect for cognitive behavioural treatments but, unlike Hall (1995a), found insufficient evidence to support medical/hormonal treatments.

Two more recent reviews have ended with conflicting conclusions. Hanson *et al.* (2002) conducted a meta-analysis of 43 studies with a combined *n* of 9454. They found that the sexual offence recidivism rate for the treatment groups combined was 12.3% compared to 16.8% for the comparison groups combined. A similar pattern was recorded for non-sexual recidivism with overall rates lower for the treatment groups (29%) than for the comparison groups (39.2%). As mentioned earlier, cognitive behavioural treatments were associated with higher reductions in both sexual recidivism (9.9% for the treatment groups, 17.4% for the comparison groups) and general recidivism (32% for the treatment groups, 51% for the comparison groups). Behavioural treatments (older forms of treatment) seem to have little effect on recidivism. Therefore, in this carefully controlled meta-analysis, cognitive behavioural sex offender treatment reduced recidivism by almost a half.

The robust nature of the debate surrounding the effectiveness of sex offender treatment is illustrated by the fact that, reviewing the same studies, a contemporaneous paper by Rice, Harris and Quinsey (2001) came to different conclusions. They meticulously reviewed the methodology of all the studies they gathered. This is a common practice for sex offender treatment reviews but less prevalent for other psychological problems. Following their analysis, they concluded that all but three studies were suspect. The first robust study was that of Romero and Williams (1983) in which they randomly assigned sex offenders to an intensive probation and psychodynamic group psychotherapy plus probation. For those who completed the optimum 40 weeks of psychotherapy, the re-arrest rate for sex offenders was significantly higher than those assigned to intensive probation alone. While the methodological limitations in this study should caution the conclusion that treatment had a negative effect, there was no evidence for a reduction in re-offending. The second study was conducted by Borduin *et al.* (1990) with adolescent sex offenders, in which they employed a multi-systemic community-based therapy including intervention for school problems, social deficits, peer difficulties and family conflict. Although the number of participants was small (8 in each group), officially recorded re-arrest data showed a large positive effect for treatment. The third study was an interim report (Marques, 1999) on the evaluation of a cognitive behavioural programme for incarcerated child molesters and rapists at Atascadero State Hospital. The study has been conducted to the highest standards of randomised control design with random assignment to treatment and no treatment conditions and a second comparison group matching treatment refusers to treated individuals. Treatment also had a high degree of programme integrity. When offenders who completed treatment were compared with untreated volunteers, there were no significant positive effects of treatment.

These three studies, which employed the highest standards of experimental design, had equivocal outcomes with the best studies showing no effects of treatment. Rice, Harris and Quinsey (2001) were, therefore, less optimistic in their conclusions than Hanson *et al.* (2002). While they gave a number of recommendations to promote investigation into treatment effectiveness, they did note programme characteristics which are more likely to be ineffective or associated with increased recidivism including 'confrontation without skill building, a non-directive approach, a punitive orientation, a focus on irrelevant or non-criminogenic factors..., the use of highly sophisticated verbal therapies, ... and a low risk clientele' (p. 306). Reviewing the whole correctional treatment literature, they also identified characteristics of programmes that would have some chance of success in reducing sex offender recidivism. These characteristics included 'a skill based training approach emphasising problem solving and self-management skills, the modelling of pro-social, anti-criminal behaviours and attitudes, a directive but non-punitive orientation, a focus on modifying antecedents to criminal behaviour, a supervised community component..., and a moderately high risk clientele' (p. 306).

While these reviews have been compiled, follow-up studies continue to be published with the same contradictory outcomes. Individuals treated in the Regional Treatment Centre (RTC) sex offender treatment programme in Ontario have been studied by a number of research groups. Quinsey, Khanna and Malcolm (1998) followed up 483 participants, 213 of whom had received sex offender treatment, 183 who were judged as not requiring treatment, 52 who had refused to be assessed, 27 who were assessed by judged to be unsuitable for treatment and 9 who were considered to require treatment but did not receive it for a variety of reasons. A further 45 participants met all of the criteria for inclusion but were not released. Participants were followed up for an average of 44 months and it was found that those participants who had been treated had a higher rate of sexual recidivism than men who were not treated. Individuals who were not considered appropriate for treatment generally fell into lower risk categories and so the authors re-analysed the data controlling for risk and found that treated participants remained significantly more likely to commit a further sexual offence.

This pessimistic outcome can be compared to the results of Looman, Abracen and Nicholaichuk (2000) in a study which drew participants from the same pool of individuals in RTC. They reviewed archives of treated and untreated offenders making rigorous attempts to match individuals on age of index offence, date of index offence and prior criminal history. They found 89 treated and 89 untreated individuals who were so matched, all of whom could be followed up for a period of around 5 years (average follow-up 9.9 years). These authors found that 23.6% of the treated group were convicted for a new sexual offence whereas 51.7% of the untreated group committed another sexual offence. The same effect was seen for non-sexual offences with 61.8% of the treated group committing a non-sexual offence and 74.2% of the untreated group committing such an offence. They also analysed their data comparing men who had only one sexual conviction and men who had more than one sexual conviction finding similar results throughout, that is, the treated group had significantly lower re-offending rates than the untreated group. In a further study on a different population in Canada, Nicholaichuk *et al.* (2000) compared 296 treated and 283 untreated sexual offenders for an average of 6 years after their release from prison. Similar to the Looman, Abracen and Niecholaichuk (2000) study, controls were matched on age at index offence, date of index offence and prior criminal history. They found a significant treatment effect for both the number and severity of new sexual and non-sexual offences. Therefore, these authors made more optimistic conclusions regarding the effect of sex offender treatment.

Additional outcome studies have appeared in the last few years. McGrath *et al.* (2003) compared 56 participants who had completed sex offender treatment with 49 who entered but did not complete treatment and 90 who refused treatment services. They employed valid measures of risk and found that although participants were not randomly assigned to treatment conditions, there were no between-group differences on participants' pre-treatment risk for sexual recidivism. Treatment was based on cognitive behavioural and relapse prevention principles, participants were sentenced to 4 or more years of incarceration, and the average follow-up period was almost 6 years. Treatment completers had a sexual re-offence rate of 5.4% compared to 30.6% for the treatment drop-outs and 30% for the no treatment groups. As the authors acknowledged, the methodological weaknesses may arise from the fact that the comparison groups (treatment drop-out and treatment refusers) may have been subject to the same biases as have been found in previous studies, that is, they may be more confrontational, less willing to accept a regulated lifestyle, more impulsive and so on. However, they did find retrospectively that the groups were matched on level of risk on the Static-99. Seabloom *et al.* (2003) reported similar successful outcomes for a treatment programme with adolescent sex offenders. Treatment components were multi-systemic including individual therapy, group therapy, family therapy and extended group sessions which took place in a retreat. Fifty individuals completed the programme, 51 withdrew or dropped out and all were followed up for a minimum of 14.68 years (average 18.34). Throughout this extremely lengthy follow-up, none of the completers committed a sexual re-offence while 8% of those who withdrew were convicted for a further sexual offence. The same effect was seen when comparing arrests and convictions for all types of offences with the completers showing lower rates (8%) than the non-completers (21.6%). While this study was not as well controlled as other studies and is undermined by the flaw mentioned previously in relation to using drop-outs as a comparison, the length of follow-up allows one to have some optimism concerning those who complete treatment.

Consistent with the pattern of rigorous and contradictory findings in the field, two studies provide a significant caution to these optimistic outcomes. Hanson, Broom and Stephenson (2004) conducted a 12-year follow-up of 724 sexual offenders who had been treated in a range of community programmes with 403 in the treated group and 321 in the untreated comparison cohort. After controlling for year of release, follow-up time and static risk factors, they found that the differences between the treated and untreated groups were virtually zero. The sexual recidivism rate in the treated group was 21.4% after 12.5 years and that compared to 22.2% after 10 years in the untreated group. Although some treatment programmes were judged to approximate to contemporary standards of relapse prevention and cognitive behavioural treatment, participants receiving these treatments fared little better than the rest. They noted that their findings contrasted with the positive effects of cognitive treatment reported in previous reviews (Hanson *et al.*, 2002).

The treatment programme which has received the greatest amount of attention is the California Sex Offender Treatment Project mentioned previously (Marques, 1999). This was designed as a randomised control trial and treatment was conducted according to relapse prevention and cognitive behavioural principles. The final report was published by Marques *et al.* (2005) with 704 offenders randomly assigned to the treatment condition, volunteer control condition and non-volunteer control condition. Nearly three quarters (72.4%) had offended against children with the remainder (27.6%) against adults, 167 of the treatment condition completed and 37 dropped out. None of the control participants dropped out of the study. Overall, no significant differences were found among the three groups in their rates of sexual or violent re-offending during an 8-year follow-up period. However, examination of subsets of the treated group revealed that those individuals who achieved treatment targets had significantly lower re-offence rates than those who did not. In addition, the assessments for achievement of targets were significant predictors of sexual offence recidivism, emphasising the importance of continuing with assessment during and after treatment (Beech *et al.*, 2002). In general, they felt that their findings supported the measurement of dynamic factors during treatment which might predict re-offending or indicate treatment benefit. Because of its meticulous randomised control design, this study has on the one hand been hailed as a definitive finding on the lack of treatment outcome effect, and on the other has been severely criticised for its methodological limitations.

William Marshall and colleagues have developed and implemented sex offender programmes for many years. Marshall *et al.* (2006) described this integrated programme for the treatment of sex offenders which has been operating in a Canadian Federal Prison for 15 years and they followed up 614 sexual offenders who had entered into treatment. Ninety-six per cent of the participants completed treatment and they followed up 534 participants who had been discharged for an average of 5.42 years. There were 352 offenders against children and 182 rapists in their sample. Fourteen of the offenders against children and three rapists had committed a further sexual offence which represented an overall sexual re-offence rate of 3.2%. Based on the actuarial risk levels of the sample, they estimated that the expected recidivism rates of an untreated group similar to their own would be 16.8% for sexual offences and 40% for non-sexual offences. The figures which they found of 3.2% sexual recidivism and 13.6% general recidivism were significantly lower than the expected rates derived from actuarial risk measures. Based on published government costings, they went on to estimate that in addition to the fact that the programme had saved many potential victims from suffering at the hands of sexual re-offenders, it also produced a financial saving to society of approximately 1 395 000 Canadian dollars per year.

Marshall and Marshall (2007) reviewed not only the Marques *et al.* (2005) study but also the appropriateness of the randomised control design for the evaluation of sex offender treatment. They forwarded a number of arguments on why these rigorous designs are inappropriate for such evaluation. They pointed out the difficulties involved in recruiting a no treatment control group. Firstly, psychological treatment is so obvious when it is being delivered and when it is not being delivered that it is highly unlikely that participants would remain blind to the fact that they were not receiving treatment; a fact which is not likely in a drug trial. Secondly, if offenders were to sign up for such a design and as a result did not receive treatment, it may affect their parole board evaluation and judgement of risk for future sexual offending, subsequently jeopardising their release. In fact, these authors suggested that those assigned to a no treatment control may actually resent the fact and harbour some opposition and hostility to the regime as a result. They also argued that the requirements of treatment integrity determined that studies adopt a manualised programme which would be followed by the facilitators. Such manualisation reduces the effects of therapist variables which have been shown to account for a significant proportion of the potency of treatment (Beech and Hamilton-Giachristis, 2005). One specific criticism of the Marques *et al.* (2005) study was that 'Intoxication while offending' turned out to be an important variable and many of the control group may have had treatment for substance abuse. This paper in turn produced a considerable debate on the web site of the Association for the Treatment of Sexual Abusers with one contributor suggesting that had Marques *et al.* (2005) study produced positive results for sexual abuse treatment, treatment supporters would have been 'shouting it from the rooftops'. On the other hand, those who doubt the effect of treatment may well have been scrutinising the design for weaknesses.

This debate will go on and on and on. There are good studies supporting both treatment effectiveness and a lack of effect. There are excellent scientists reviewing treatment design, outcome results and treatment processes. As I have said, it is a considerable luxury in this field that there is such a learned and trenchant debate, although my guess is that it may be less comfortable for the leading protagonists.

Treatment for Sex Offenders with Intellectual Disability

In mainstream work on the treatment of sex offenders, programmes tended to focus on changing deviant sexual preference, especially those interventions for offenders against children (Kelly, 1982), with 78% of studies at that time employing aversion therapy. Some programmes added components aimed at enhancing social functioning, the most comprehensive of which was that of Marshall and Barbaree (1988). However, generally, interventions were focused on specific issues related to sexuality rather than the general social functioning and adaptation in sex offenders. To some extent, the same is true in the field of ID. A number of authors presented case studies on the treatment of public masturbation. Using behavioural methods, they showed a reduction in public masturbation through reinforcement and over-correction (Luiselli *et al.*, 1977), a mild punishment in the form of contingent lemon juice (Cook *et al.*, 1978), and techniques of extinction or differential reinforcement (Polvinale and Lutzker, 1980).

In contrast, the first significant and influential development in the field was a comprehensive treatment programme aimed at improving social functioning, improving sexual awareness and sexual knowledge, extending relationships, improving coping skills and reducing inappropriate sexuality (Griffiths, Quinsey and Hingsburger, 1989). These authors took as a starting point the fact that these individuals may have restricted social and sexual opportunities which caused them to develop inappropriate choices. They wrote 'Clearly, the (*previous*) treatment objectives for developmentally delayed individuals who display sexually inappropriate behaviour have been restrictive rather than rehabilitative. Considering that many of the individuals who display inappropriate sexual behaviour may not know how to express sexuality in an appropriate manner, the punishment for inappropriate sexual expression places the individual in a sexual void' (p. 11). They go on to argue that a rehabilitative programme with a wide ranging social and sexual focus would be far more appropriate and they then describe a comprehensive treatment programme focusing on interpersonal relationships and interpersonal skills to maintain such relationships while acknowledging the importance of focusing on inappropriate or deviant sexual preferences.

With each client, these authors first employed a range of assessments including assessment of sexual knowledge, an analysis of the client's living situation, social skills assessment including role-play and videotape and assessment of sexual preference. They then developed a multifactorial treatment plan which was designed to review risky aspects of the environment, increase personal and social skills and address the issues of sexuality. Specific aspects of training included sex education, social competency training, training in relationships, training in coping skills and personal responsibility and, where appropriate, intervention for inappropriate sexual preference which included aversion in imagination and measures to promote appropriate masturbation. Even at this early stage in the development of treatment for offenders with ID, they included protective relapse prevention procedures in their methods. These varied from Level 1, simple ongoing case management, through Level 2 which represented proactive interventions such as booster sessions and ongoing discussions to continue support and prevent relapse. Level 3 was implemented when clients began to show signs of negative emotional states, indications of loss of control and any tendency towards isolation or cognitive distortions. This level of relapse prevention included interventions with care givers to support the person in addressing any setbacks and difficulties. The highest level of relapse prevention, Level 4, included the complete re-evaluation of the client's needs, an increase in supervision and possible resumption of intervention to decrease inappropriate sexual behaviour, modify inappropriate sexual interest and general re-institute a number of treatment aspects. These authors also reported on a series of 30 case studies in which they recorded no re-offending and described a number of successful cases to illustrate their methods.

The authors also emphasised the importance of communication between the treatment and support teams which is a theme that I have emphasised continually when I have been doing workshops and teaching on work with offenders with ID. Since Griffiths, Quinsey and Hingsburger (1989) mentioned communication specifically in this early programme outline, it is worth reviewing several particular points. It is seldom mentioned in the literature but, during workshops and teaching exercises, I always emphasise the importance of communication at three levels. The first is at the level of case conferences, which has always been germane to the management of anyone with intellectual disability who is incorporated into services. More recently, this macro-level of communication has been incorporated into the legal system with regard to offenders in general in the form of MAPPA Meetings in the United Kingdom. The second level of communication is to ensure that everyone who is involved in the day-to-day treatment and management of the individual has a clear idea of their responsibilities. This form of communication is at a closer level and probably requires fairly regular updates on how treatment is progressing. Although this form of communication is more usual when the individual is an in-patient or resident in services, for sex offenders it is important that these aspects are reviewed regularly for all cases, even those individuals who are living independently.

The third level of communication is a micro-level of information exchange between the relevant individuals in a person's life. It may be that services are concerned about breaks in routine for an individual or periods where they have unexplained absences. In these cases, an arrangement can be made that the person's routine is made known to all individuals who are involved. The communication would be such that when the person leaves the house to go to their placement in the morning, then a family member or carer might phone the treatment centre or the occupational centre to inform them that they had now left and they would be expected to arrive in (say) 20 minutes. When the individual arrives, the treatment or occupational centre would then phone back to inform the carer of his arrival. In this way, everyone is fairly sure that the agreed routine has been followed. If there is a deviation from this routine, then a number of things might happen. If it is sufficiently concerning, the police might be informed although this would generally be unusual. However, the discrepancy in time can be discussed during treatment sessions and counselling sessions so that the importance of self-regulation and appropriate routines are made completely clear to the individual involved. It is not uncommon for men who are on probation or attending for treatment to have such arrangements in place.

Griffiths, Quinsey and Hingsburger (1989) developed, perhaps, the most comprehensive example of behavioural management approaches and Plaud *et al.* (2000) wrote that they had been the most common psychological treatments for the management of sexual offending in this client group. Haaven, Little and Petre-Miller (1990) described a wide ranging series of treatments including social skills training, sex education and promotion of self-control in a comprehensive programme which addressed sexual offending under a behavioural management regime. Essentially, they described a secure in-patient treatment unit and associated treatment programme. At the time of writing, they reported on 27 convicted sexual offenders who had committed a range of offences, predominantly against children. They detailed a very comprehensive treatment programme which employed 'individualised treatment planning... creating a total change in how each client relates to himself and the world' (p. 21). This treatment programme included the development of a modified therapeutic community, individualised treatment, the employment of group processes and extensive transition arrangements and community follow-up. Therefore, although the programme was based on a number of behavioural methods developed by Griffiths, Quinsey and Hingsburger (1989), there were comprehensive interventions directed at the individual's lifestyle, relationships and social networks. It is another indication that from its early beginnings, treatment for sex offenders with ID has focused not only on the criminogenic aspects of the individual's difficulties but also on their general lifestyle.

Other, somewhat less comprehensive behavioural management approaches have also been employed. Grubb-Blubaugh, Shire and Balser (1994) employed a behavioural management and peer review approach in a closed unit to promote appropriate socialised skills in a group of sex offenders and abusers. They developed a 'jury system' which consisted of peer review with recommended positive or negative consequences for individuals' behaviour. There were 12 adult male participants in the study and they recommended consequences such as group socialisation for the day, elimination of shopping and telephone privileges, community service hours, removal of a personal television and a simple warning. This peer review system and the consequences for behaviour that were derived from it resulted in significant reductions in a range of non-compliant, aggressive and sexually inappropriate behaviours. This system was implemented in a closed unit, and while the authors noted improvements in a range of behavioural skills, there was little opportunity for individuals to demonstrate these skills or indeed any self-control outside the closed unit.

This observation that many sex offenders with ID continue to be supported and supervised years after the cessation of treatment is a methodological issue which makes it difficult to review and evaluate the effectiveness of therapy in this field. Practically, it is a considerable strength that it is possible to continue to offer services to these very difficult clients. However, when reviewing the effectiveness of therapy, it is impossible to partial out the effectiveness of a treatment intervention from the effectiveness of simple, continued monitoring. This difficulty has continued to the present day and is illustrated by a treatment study of six sex offenders with ID by Craig, Stringer and Moss (2006). Following a 7-month treatment programme incorporating sex education, addressing cognitive distortions, reviewing the offence cycle and promoting relapse prevention, they found no significant improvements on any measure including assessment of sexual knowledge. However, despite this lack of treatment progress, they also reported no further incidents of sexual offending during a 12-month follow-up. In their description of individual participants, they wrote that all six received 24-hour supervision and so presumably had little or no opportunity to re-offend. Therefore, despite the lack of treatment progress, continued supervision may have ensured successful medium-term outcomes. Where individuals are continually supervised, the value of follow-up data is obviously compromised.

Plaud *et al.* (2000) reviewed aversion therapy techniques and masturbatory reconditioning techniques in some detail. With reference to deviant sexual arousal, aversion therapy links thoughts and behaviour associated with deviant sexual arousal with an aversive image or event. This then results in a negative reaction to the deviant sexual stimulus. The aversive stimulus or event may be tactile, olfactory, behavioural or imagined. The aim is to link the aversive consequence with the offence cycle in order to promote self-regulation and self-restraint skills in the real setting, through the employment of the aversive connotation. Lindsay (2004) has described a case example of the successful use of such techniques in treatment. This was the case of a man who had offended against a girl of 8 and had previously downloaded a number of child images from the Internet, and who disclosed during treatment that he was beginning to masturbate to an image of watching a prepubescent girl in a park. The technique involved encouraging him to imagine the scene as it would normally come to him and then inserting aversive stimuli into the sequence. The first aversive stimulus was being tapped on the shoulder by a policeman while he was watching the girl, having to report his name and since he was a known sex offender being taken to the police station. The second aversive event in the sequence was the presence of two large young men who noticed that he was a single man watching a girl in a park and came over to him in an accusing and aggressive manner. Both of these sequences were rehearsed frequently over several consecutive treatment sessions and the client reported that they were successful in reducing his sexual arousal to this particular deviant sexual stimulus. While there have been a number of studies on these procedures in the general sex offending literature (Marquis, 1970; Marshall, 1969), there are no systematic studies of this technique with individuals who have ID. However, they remain promising techniques which can be employed fairly easily either in individual or group settings. Further examples are given in the section later, dealing with sexual fantasy.

As has been mentioned earlier with reference to the mainstream sex offender literature, the most significant treatment developments over the last 20 years have been the
use of cognitive and problem solving techniques. These methods have been developed
to a sophisticated degree in mainstream offenders and a central assumption in cognitive
therapy is that sex offenders hold a number of cognitive distortions regarding sexuality which support the perpetration of sexual offences. Cognitive distortions fall into a
number of categories including mitigation or even denial of responsibility, denial of
harm to the victim, denial or mitigation of intent to offend, thoughts of entitlement,
mitigation through the claim of an altered state such as depression or intoxication and
complete denial that an offence has occurred. There have been several reports which
have considered these cognitive processes during treatment of sex offenders with ID.
In an early study, O'Conner (1996) developed a problem solving intervention for
13 adult male sex offenders. This involved consideration of a range of risky situations
in which offenders had to develop safe solutions for both themselves and the potential
victims. She reported positive results from the intervention with most subjects having
achieved increased community access. However, as noted above, the extent to which
this increased community access was supervised is not mentioned in the report.

In a series of case studies (Lindsay *et al.*, 1998a,b,c; Lindsay *et al.*, 1999), we
reported on the treatment of men with ID who had offended against children, exhibitionists and stalkers. Treatment was developed on the basis of cognitive intervention
in which various forms of denial and mitigation of the offence were challenged over
treatment periods of up to 3 years. There were three fairly distinctive aspects of these
reports. Firstly, after each session, we assessed client attitudes in relation to their specific offence. It was during this period that we were developing the QACSO (described
extensively in Chapters 2 and 20). Therefore, it was possible to link the content of each
session to the impact on specific cognitive distortions. The second fairly distinctive
aspect was that all participants lived in the community and had unsupervised access to
their usual community routines such as leisure facilities, occupation, transport, shops,
entertainment and so on. The reports did not, therefore, have the drawback noted
earlier of continued close supervision which is a problem with so many studies in this
field. The third distinctive feature was the extent of the follow-up. We did not publish
any of the outcomes until we had data for at least 4 years following referral. Several
participants had follow-ups of up to 7 years.

Across the case studies, it became clear that some aspects of cognition were easier
to change than others. Those based on factual information such as the age of consent
changed much more readily than those based on more entrenched opinions such as
the view that victims share some of the responsibility. Interestingly, we found that
certain attitudes, which were derived from the sex offender literature, did not change.
Those were related to the view that sexual offences are associated with power to a
greater degree than they are with sex. Most of the participants retained the view
that the purpose of sexual assault was to gain sexual gratification rather than achieve
power over the individual. While they accepted that there were power imbalances in
the relationship, their view was that the goal was essentially sexual. At the time of
writing, despite participants having free access to the community, there was only one

case of recidivism among the offenders against children and none in the exhibitionist offenders. The incident of recidivism in the child case was relatively minor and the individual was incorporated once again into treatment. There was, however, a series of more severe recidivism incidents in one of the stalking cases. These case studies provided some basis for optimism in treatment given that they did not suffer from some of the drawbacks in previous cases such as continued supervision and short follow-ups. However, they did not possess the requirements of adequate evaluation in that there were no control conditions where individuals received other types of treatment or no treatment at all.

Courtney, Rose and Mason (2006) found support for the centrality of cognitive distortions in the offence process, in a qualitative study of nine male sex offenders with ID. Following interviews and detailed analysis using grounded theory techniques, they concluded that all aspects of the offence process were linked to the offender attitudes and beliefs such as blaming others, denial of the offence, seeing themselves as the victim and claiming ignorance of skills necessary to initiate an appropriate social encounter. They reported that 'it seemed to be an attempt to distance themselves, as if to deny taking part' (p. 185). These cognitive distortions of blaming others (mitigation of responsibility), seeing themselves as the victim (mitigation of responsibility through claiming an altered state or claiming mitigating circumstances) and denial of the offence are issues which have been reported extensively in the mainstream literature. Complete denial of any memory of taking part in the incident is a similar conclusion to that drawn by Lindsay and Smith (1998) when they wrote that some men with ID deny the offence to such an extent that they strive to believe that it never happened. It has always seemed to me that some of my clients strive to attain a 'magical' circumstance whereby if they do not mention the incident and if staff and family around them never mention the incident, then it never happened. It is not simply a belief that it never happened, it is a new fact. Therefore, a crucial aspect of treatment is to explore these aspects of denial, develop a disclosure and offence account section in treatment and review other aspects of cognitive distortions.

Other therapists and researchers have begun to develop and report more systematic evaluations of sex offender treatment with this client group. Rose *et al.* (2002) reported on a 16-week group treatment for five men with ID who had perpetrated sexual abuse. The group treatment employed self-control procedures, consideration of the effect on victims and identifying emotions within oneself in addition to sex education, appropriate assertiveness and avoiding situations involving risk. Participants were assessed using the QACSO attitudes scale, a measure of locus of control, a sexual behaviour and law scale and victim empathy scale. The only significant differences from baseline to post-treatment were found on the locus of control scale. This indicated a more external locus of control after the intervention. The authors acknowledged that treatment was short in comparison to the normal programme of sex offender treatment, which usually lasts from 1 year to 18 months, but they reported no re-offending at 1-year follow-up.

Rose and his colleagues in a further study (Rose *et al.*, 2007) again found changes in locus of control following a community-based sex offender treatment programme. This programme had two interesting features. Firstly, there was no formal compulsion for individuals to attend. In other programmes, participants are often subject to court ordered treatment, probationary disposals or deferred sentences. Secondly, most studies employed participants who have a measured intellectual ability in the range of around 60–75 IQ points. The participants in the Rose *et al.* (2007) study were somewhat less able with an IQ range of 49–70 IQ points and a mean IQ of 57. As with the Lindsay *et al.* (1998a,b,c,d) case studies, participants had free access to the community, travelled independently or lived with their family. The programme employed methods to increase motivation, develop victim empathy, address cognitive distortions and develop relapse prevention programmes. This is a more comprehensive cognitive-based intervention than some of the earlier programmes described previously. They assessed participants using the QACSO and the Nowickie-Strickland Locus of Control Scale (Nowicki, 1976). Six participants completed the programme and there were significant improvements on both measures. One of the interesting issues for this research group was the question why locus of control should become more external. They felt that, following treatment, sex offenders with ID might begin to understand that they are under more scrutiny and observation than they had previously realised. They also hypothesised that there may be more generalised changes as a result of extensive treatment in that participants may realise they have less control over their lives than they had previously thought. They reported no recidivism over a 16-month period despite that participants maintained their community access. They also felt that the relapse prevention plan (Keeping Safe Plan) was important for both participants themselves and carers in maintaining the lack of recidivism.

The importance of cognitive behaviour therapy was incorporated into a treatment framework by Lindsay (2005). He hypothesised that two basic treatment components were required to promote change in this client group. The first was intervention directed at offence-related issues such as sexual preference and cognitive distortions. The second was intervention aimed at promoting engagement with society and development of pro-social relationships. This theoretical framework will be described further in the next chapter but Rose *et al.* (2007) specifically related their study to this analysis. They concluded that it was possible to provide successful sex offender treatment in the community. They noted that they encouraged group members to remain engaged in all other aspects of their daily lives including occupation, leisure and social activities to maintain their quality of life. They then concluded that they supported the Lindsay (2005) model which promoted these two strands of treatment: intervention on sexual offending issues while encouraging engagement and commitment to society.

Three structured treatment comparison studies have been conducted based on cognitive behavioural treatment methods. Unfortunately, all three fall well short of the standards required by randomised control comparisons. It is, therefore, important that while we consider them, we bear in mind that they have significant methodological shortcomings. Lindsay and Smith (1998) compared seven individuals who had been in treatment for 2 or more years with another group of seven who had been in treatment for less than 1 year. The comparisons were serendipitous in that time and treatment reflected the probation sentences delivered by the court. Therefore, participants were not randomly allocated and the sample sizes were small. However, there were no significant differences between the two cohorts in terms of severity or type of offence.

Those who had been in treatment for less than 1 year showed significantly poorer progress and were more likely to re-offend than those treated for at least 2 years. There were significant differences between the groups in improvement recorded on scales of the QACSO in favour of the 2-year treatment and two-thirds of those treated for only 1 year re-offended while none of those treated for 2 or more years re-offended. They concluded that shorter periods of treatment may be of limited value for this client group.

A second comparison was conducted by Keeling, Rose and Beech (2007b) when they compared 11 'special needs' offenders and 11 mainstream offenders matched on level of risk, victim, sex, offence type and age. This was another comparison of convenience in that the 11 'special needs' offenders were the target group and the 11 mainstream offenders were chosen from a large pool. The authors noted a number of limitations in their study including the fact that 'special needs' was not synonymous with ID and, as a result, they were unable to verify the intellectual differences between the mainstream and 'special needs' populations. In fact, the average IQ was 71 with one participant in the low-average intellectual range and deemed suitable because of illiteracy. Two individuals in the range of borderline intellectual functioning had 'special needs' as a result of acquired brain injury. Further limitations were that the treatments and assessments were not directly comparable because both required modification and adaptation to be suitable for the 'special needs' population. The outcome was that there were few differences between the groups after treatment but, more significantly, follow-up data were collected for an average of 16 months. For the 'special needs' group, there were no further recorded incidents of sexual offending during this time despite the fact that all had been released from prison. Murphy and Sinclair (2006) reported on the cognitive behavioural treatment of 52 men who had sexually abusive behaviour and mild ID. Treatment groups ran over a period of 1 year and there were significant improvements in sexual knowledge, victim empathy and cognitive distortions at post-treatment assessment. In addition, there were reductions in sexually abusive behaviour at 6-month follow-up. However, although their study was designed to include control participants, it was not possible to recruit participants for a range of unforeseen administrative reasons. They did note, however, that those who re-offended had a significantly higher rate of Autistic Spectrum Disorder. Therefore, in these studies, the control comparisons have not been randomised, have been controls of convenience or researchers have not been able to gather sufficient control participants due to a range of administrative obstacles.

Over the years, I have conducted a number of evaluations on the clinical effectiveness of the offender service run by myself and colleagues. Lindsay *et al.* (2004b) compared 106 men who had committed sexual crimes or sexually abusive incidents with 78 men who had committed other types of offences or serious incidents. There was a significantly higher rate of re-offending in the non-sex offender cohort (51%) than in the sex offender cohort (19%). In a subsequent, more comprehensive evaluation, Lindsay *et al.* (2006c) compared 121 sex offenders with 105 other types of male offenders and 21 female offenders. Re-offending rates were reported for up to 12 years after the index offence. There were no significant differences between the groups on IQ and the sex offender cohort tended to be older than the other two cohorts.

Female offenders had higher rates of mental illness although rates for male cohorts were generally high at around 32%. The differences in re-offending rates between the three groups were highly significant with rates of 23.9% for male sexual offenders, 19% for female offenders and 59% for other types of male offenders. The significant differences were evident for every year of follow-up except year one.

There are a number of observations to be made about these outcome results. Firstly, 23.9% re-offending for male sex offenders is higher than the base rate for recidivism reported in mainstream offenders (Hanson *et al.*, 2002). Therefore, it is not a particularly good outcome in terms of the number of men who have offended at least once over follow-up periods of up to 12 years. Indeed, the re-offending rate of 59% for other types of male offenders would not encourage much optimism for the development of services for this client group. However, we also followed up the number of offences committed by recidivists and compared this number with the number of offences committed 2 years prior to treatment. In making this comparison, we noted that some men had committed so many offences prior to being referred that this would be likely to skew the data in favour of finding a post-treatment reduction. Therefore, we limited the ceiling for offences to 15 and anything over 15 was discounted. This was important since we noted cases such as an individual who had committed up to 400 incidents of sexual abuse offences against female relatives and these kinds of numbers may have skewed considerably the findings in favour of a treatment effect. In fact, the highest number of offences committed after treatment was 13 and this was not a sexual case. Comparing pre- and post-referral rates for only those individuals who had re-offended, the number of sexual offences fell from 235, 2 years prior to referral, to 68, up to 12 years after referral. This represented around a 70% reduction in the number of incidents which we concluded was a significant amount of harm reduction in those individuals who did commit further offences. In addition, although we did not report it, when we include the non-recidivists, the number of incidents 2 years prior to referral rises to 879. If we then compare the 68 incidents following referral, this represents a reduction of around 92% in recorded incidents indicating a considerable amount of harm reduction as a result of interventions. Therefore, there is some evidence that treatment interventions may significantly reduce recidivism rates in sex offenders with ID. Where recidivism does occur, treatment may result in fewer abusive incidents. A further service outcome evaluation was published by McGrath, Livingston and Falk (2007) on 103 sex offenders with ID. They followed participants up for an average of 5.8 years and found a recidivism rate of 10.7% with only 20 new offences. However, it was not clear how many participants received 24-hour supervision. These outcomes are reasonably positive and suggest that we can have some optimism regarding the establishment of treatment services for sex offenders with ID and the efficacy of targeted treatment for this client group.

Conclusions

This chapter has reviewed significant developments both in the treatment of mainstream sexual offenders and in treatment for sex offenders with ID. The main advances have been in cognitive behavioural approaches for sex offenders. However, it is clear that since its inception, sex offender treatment for individuals with ID has incorporated far wider, general elements than a simple focus on offending issues. Griffiths, Quinsey and Hingsburger (1989) incorporated a comprehensive treatment involving social skills, problem solving, building relationships and addressing occupational issues in addition to interventions for sexual behaviour. Rose *et al.* (2007) noted the importance of addressing lifestyle issues as well as sexual issues and in our own treatment services, interventions had been broad based with a focus on community integration as well as inappropriate sexual behaviour. The outcomes have been reasonable with a number of conclusions being drawn. Longer treatments seem more effective than shorter treatments. One of the reasons for this is likely to be a result of the intellectual disability itself. Several authors have noted the repetitive nature of treatment (e.g. Rose *et al.*, 2007) and constant rehearsal and repetition requires greater amounts of time. The repetition is required because of the intellectual limitations of the individuals and their difficulty in coming to terms with fairly complex material and treatment approaches. The second conclusion is that there is some evidence for the effectiveness of more comprehensive treatments. The results from studies which have employed broad-based approaches which promote engagement with the community, maintenance of a range of community placements and promote quality of life have reported positive outcomes. A third conclusion from this review is that one has to be careful when reviewing studies in the field. Several studies have mentioned the continued supervision of participants over lengthy periods of up to 2 years. This clearly affects the opportunities that are available to participants for re-offending since constant monitoring is certainly put in place in order to prevent potential incidents. Therefore, outcome evaluations and follow-up are completely compromised in that one is unable to conclude whether or not treatment has had any effect on recidivism rates. This is most clearly illustrated by the study of Craig, Stringer and Moss (2006) when they reported no significant improvements on any measure following treatment but no recidivism during 12 months follow-up when all participants continue to be supervised. We can only conclude that simple supervision prevented incidents rather than any impact of treatment. Similarly, we should be wary of the available treatment comparisons since they all suffer from significant methodological shortcomings. Having said that, the recidivism data reported by Rose *et al.* (2007) and Lindsay *et al.* (2006a) are persuasive, considering the fact that participants continued to have free access to the community.

Chapter 5

Theories of Sexual Offending and Intellectual Disability

In the study of criminal behaviour, theoretical models have moved the field forward substantially. These models have been both explanatory and predictive and have generated considerable amounts of research. For example, there have been a number of theories based on genetics which have promoted research to determine the extent to which biological mechanisms of inheritance affect the likelihood of criminal behaviour. Many of these studies have looked at familial patterns with antisocial behaviour in children or criminal behaviour in adulthood associated with a relatively high frequency of similar problems in parents. The risk of antisocial and criminal behaviour in boys whose fathers have received at least one prison sentence has been found to be around five times greater than those boys whose fathers were not registered with the police (Kandel *et al.*, 1988). Twin studies have also contributed to these models. Christiansen (1977) analysed data on 3586 twin pairs and found 52% concordance for criminal behaviour for identical male pairs and 22% concordance for fraternal male pairs. This, and other studies, certainly suggests a role for genetic inheritance.

Several sociological theories have been extremely influential in directing the nature of research and services for criminal groups. The adoption of mainstream or subcultural values in teenage years has been highlighted by several theorists. Cohen (1955) suggested that boys entered into delinquency because they were conforming to the expectations and encouragement of their delinquent subculture. This model proposed that the material and vocational aspirations of all boys tended towards those of the middle classes. Boys from lower socio-economic groups were disadvantaged in competition towards these aspirations because they were less likely to be schooled in the skills of the middle classes. Faced with lower ability to achieve these goals using legitimate, middle class means, these individuals were more likely to use subcultural delinquent methods to fulfil these aspirations. One of the main criticisms of this theory was the view that delinquency and crime were a result of lack of commitment to the conventions of society, rather than a disparity between middle class aspirations

The Treatment of Sex Offenders with Developmental Disabilities   William Lindsay
© 2009 John Wiley & Sons, Ltd

and perceived personal potential. Delinquent individuals would no longer have these aspirations, leading to a general disillusionment with society and low personal aspirations among those who have become delinquent (Gibbons and Krohn, 1986). Hirschi (1969) developed these theories based on the established relationship between lower socio-economic status and higher rates of crime. His control theory paid attention to both positive learning of criminal behaviours through association with criminal subcultures, and also the development of self-control through appropriate social learning in being law abiding. Hirschi felt that the success of social training was dependent on four factors: attachment, commitment, involvement and belief, all in relation to society. This will be outlined in more detail later in this chapter.

The point about this short introduction is to illustrate that theoretical developments have been very important in furthering criminological research and services. This is also true in sexual offending and I will now go on to review some of the main theories of sexual offending and their relevance and relationship to intellectual disabilities. For this chapter, I have drawn heavily on the excellent volume, *Theories of Sexual Offending* by Ward, Polaschek and Beech (2005).

The Counterfeit Deviance Hypothesis

Although there is no theory to account for criminality in offenders with intellectual disability, there is a basic theory which makes a number of hypotheses concerning the genesis of inappropriate sexual behaviour or sexual offending in sex offenders with intellectual disability (ID). The counterfeit deviance hypothesis was developed by Hingsburger, Griffiths and Quinsey (1991) and is specifically aimed to give a theoretical explanation for some inappropriate sexual behaviour in this client group. They noted that people with ID often live in circumstances in which appropriate heterosexual relationships, sexual development and the acquisition of sexual knowledge are not supported. Indeed, those of us who have worked in these settings will understand that for many individuals with ID, the development of sexual relationships has either been ignored or discouraged. Therefore, many individuals will have had little experience of learning about a range of issues related to sexuality and a number of factors will contribute to inappropriate sexual behaviour which are related to developmental and environmental issues for people with ID rather than sexual deviance. These authors are not so naïve as to discount real sexual deviance in this client group. While acknowledging that a small number of individuals will have deviant sexual preferences, they point out that this makes it all the more important to differentiate counterfeit deviance. They also acknowledge that the effects of inappropriate sexual behaviour, no matter the reason, will have a significant impact on the victims. From the perspective of the victim, the important aspect is the assault or incident itself, irrespective of the cause. However, from the point of view of management and treatment, theoretical causes and pathways are of utmost importance.

The counterfeit deviance hypothesis is perceptive in integrating issues pertinent to IDs and issues pertinent to sex offending. In addition to acknowledging real deviance and impact on victims, they also note that some paraphilias can also be relatively benign. They acknowledge that such deviant sexual attraction occurs in the non-ID population and is only of concern when men express this attraction publicly. They note that some men are likely to express their deviant sexuality in private through masturbation. This paper was published in 1991 prior to the development of Internet-based pornography. With easier access through the Internet to deviant sexual material, there would appear to have been a sharp increase in paedophilia. This is highly unlikely in that these men previously expressed this aspect of their sexuality in private. The availability of Internet pornography now makes these acts public. However, even without the development of the Internet, such expression was never as private for men with ID as it was in the mainstream population. Men with ID often live in supported circumstances where carers can enter their bedroom or otherwise interrupt private periods with the possibility of discovering even reasonably well-concealed inappropriate sexual behaviour.

For what is essentially a $3^1/_2$ page article in a professional newsletter, Hingsburger, Griffiths and Quinsey have written a surprisingly comprehensive theory based on the proposal that much of the inappropriate sexual behaviour displayed by men with ID is based on the lack of sexual knowledge, poor understanding of social conventions and lack of opportunity for appropriate sexual expression. This produces behaviour which is undoubtedly deviant but arises from systemic developmental and environmental experiences rather than inappropriate or deviant sexual attraction to violence or children. Because it is a comprehensive account related specifically to ID, I will begin with the counterfeit deviance hypothesis. Aspects which arise from it are also relevant to other theories of sexual offending and the way in which they can be adapted for sex offenders with ID.

Hingsburger, Griffiths and Quinsey stressed the importance of differentiating counterfeit deviance from true sexual deviance. Individuals should not be classified as deviant when in fact the problem lies in a system which has failed to provide appropriate opportunities and learning for sexual expression. Additionally, individuals should not receive medication for a problem which has a systemic rather than biological source. This latter point continues to be increasingly relevant in an era where antilibidinal medication is increasingly viewed as a viable option for treatment. Finally, accurate classification will help therapists to devise more effective and tailored treatment programmes.

The 11 sub-hypotheses can be considered as pathways into sexual offending, all of which can be viewed as counterfeit and unrelated to sexual deviance. These hypotheses can be grouped into those which deal with the environment, those which deal with heterosexual relationships, those considering developmental issues and those pertaining to medical factors. The first group of hypotheses relate to environmental issues. The first is the *structural hypothesis* which considers environments where appropriate sexual expression is prohibited. Men and women with ID frequently live in supported circumstances and if these environments, staff groups and so on do not respect privacy and appropriate sexual expression, then these individuals are likely to seek privacy elsewhere. Those of us who have worked in this field are all too familiar with establishments where sexuality has occurred in a public but secluded area, for example behind the shed, behind the garage, in an area of the toilets. While this may be viewed with some permissiveness in teenagers as an indication of developmental experience, in adults, even with ID, it can often be considered with greater censure. However, these individuals may simply be looking for a place where staff are less likely to find them. Linked to this hypothesis is the *behavioural hypothesis* which suggests that staff may pay more attention to sexual expression in clients by telling them to stop it or redirecting them. This increased attention in itself can increase the importance and probability of any behaviour including sexual behaviour. Therefore when assessing inappropriate sexual behaviour, we should consider the contingencies which have been employed over the past few weeks and months. A third environmental hypothesis is the *perpetual arousal hypothesis* which considers that people with ID who masturbate frequently or in public have a high sexual arousal. However, the authors propose that a lack of opportunity for appropriate sexual expression and a possible lack of privacy result in more frequent public masturbation. Since these individuals are seen to masturbate more frequently, staff wrongly assume that their frequency is higher than others who are able to take advantage of a high degree of privacy. Another aspect of this hypothesis is that certain people with ID may find it physically difficult to masturbate to orgasm resulting in a higher frequency of masturbatory activity. Finally, in relation to environmental variables, the *modelling hypothesis* notes that when carers or families support people with ID, they are likely to behave in what with others would be an inappropriate manner. They may invade modesty and privacy to help with dressing and bathing, see clients naked more frequently and touch them in ways which would be inappropriate with others. While this is a necessary part of caring, it can be seen that such modelling by staff could be misinterpreted as normal interaction by clients. If clients were to begin to copy these patterns of interaction, they would undoubtedly be considered deviant.

Hingsburger, Griffiths and Quinsey also note the restrictions on relationships which are placed on individuals with ID and constitute a second group of hypotheses. Because of ways in which some clients are protected or viewed as 'eternal children' they may not be afforded the opportunities to meet appropriate partners and develop appropriate relationship and social skills. This is the *partner selection hypothesis* and suggests that the lack of opportunity to meet age appropriate consenting partners may lead to clients taking advantage of inappropriate opportunities with staff or children. Those of us who work in this field are often aware that some clients can be inappropriately familiar even when a stranger enters a supported establishment. The second, related hypothesis is the *inappropriate courtship hypothesis* which notes the lack of experience people with ID may have in developing complex interpersonal relationship skills. This might result in men attempting to form relationships through inappropriate and highly intrusive means because the complex skills of forming relationships, developing relationships and sustaining relationships over a longer term have never been learned. This lack of knowledge may also result in difficulties in differentiating between sexual and non-sexual relationships and appropriate or inappropriate behaviour. A third factor which is also specifically related to developmental issues is the *sexual knowledge hypothesis*. Here, the authors acknowledge two aspects: Firstly, that individuals may have lacked the experiences necessary for developing sexual knowledge and secondly that when lifelong, developmental experiences are presented, the ID itself may restrict the learning of subtle cues and experiences. Through the 1980s and 1990s, there was a considerable effort to redress these deficits (Bender *et al.*, 1983; Lindsay *et al.*, 1992) but it is likely that even extensive sex education courses cannot substitute for years of developmental learning about sexuality and relationships. As a result, men with ID may have inadequate sexual knowledge on how to deal with situations involving heterosexual relationships.

Two further developmental hypotheses are included in this theory. The *learning history hypothesis* considers the importance of men growing up in protected or institutional environments. Firstly, this may result in the well-documented phenomenon that where male teenagers grow up in all male institutions, there is a higher rate of same sex activity. Therefore, in these situations men may only have access to learning in the context of same sex activity. As a result, they may develop with an expectation that men generally have sex with other men. In combination with some of the other hypotheses, this expectation may result in inappropriate or unskilled approaches to other potential partners. The cultural context of same sex partners has, thankfully, moved on considerably in the years since Hingsburger, Griffiths and Quinsey outlined their hypotheses. However, the point is still valid in that an expectation of same sex activity in combination with the other hypotheses may produce an incident based on erroneous assumptions. The same, of course, is true for heterosexual encounters in that this hypothesis also postulates that men with ID may not learn ways in which to make responsible, appropriate overtures to both men and women. Inappropriate advances may indeed be viewed as sexual offending. The final developmental hypothesis is the *moral vacuum hypothesis* which cites the importance of experiences and learning related to perspective taking. Through developmental experiences, most of us learn that our interpersonal behaviour has an impact on others. Where experiences have been restricted or, through an ID, a male has been unable to gain a full understanding concerning all aspects of interpersonal situations, they may not have developed perspective taking skills. Therefore, they may be seen as deficient in 'victim awareness' when this is actually related to ID and development.

Two final factors in their treatise relate to particular medical variables. The *medical hypothesis* suggests that communication difficulties may prevent an individual reporting a medical condition which results in apparently sexualised behaviour. They use the example of a urinary tract infection which may result in frequent genital touching which is nothing to do with sexuality. In addition, the *medication side effect hypothesis* suggests that some medications can cause loss of libido or sexual dysfunction. These changes in an individual, if poorly explained and poorly supported, may cause frustration or aggression which in turn may be related to attempts to gain sexual satisfaction to compensate for the side effects of medication.

Taken together, these hypotheses which make up the *counterfeit deviance hypothesis* constitute a number of pathways which can act either alone or in combination to cause inappropriate sexual behaviour which will undoubtedly be viewed as deviant. However, since these incidents may be driven by variables related to environmental factors, lack of experience of relationships, maladaptive or inadequate developmental learning or issues related to medical complaints, they are not sexually driven or sexually deviant. Therefore, the deviance is counterfeit.

Evaluation

The *counterfeit deviance hypothesis* is an excellent piece of work in that it takes account of factors related specifically to ID. Across all 11 sub-hypotheses it invokes the restrictions placed on the individual through their ID itself. This causes difficulties in communicating needs, difficulty in appreciating complex and subtle cues and restrictions in gaining knowledge through even repeated developmental experiences. It also takes account of the cultural restrictions imposed on people with ID which result in a reduced level of opportunity to gain social skills, interpersonal skills and knowledge about heterosexual interaction. Furthermore, it recognises that many individuals with ID may have maladaptive or distorted experiences through restricted living or institutional living. It would be comforting to be complacent about these factors nowadays. We could consider that developments in deinstitutionalisation have resulted in the distorted effects on development of institutional living becoming a thing of the past. However, Sturmey, Taylor and Lindsay (2004) have noted the recent development of markets for service provision especially in relation to offenders with ID. Some local service commissioners deal with forensic cases by referring them to out of area medium secure services which are expanding considerably. They suggest that there may be a phenomenon of reinstitutionalisation where cases are referred to specialist forensic facilities because local staff lack confidence in dealing with the risks associated with clients offending behaviour. Such a phenomenon may reinstate the likelihood of larger establishments dealing with difficult clients.

Perhaps because it was developed in the late 1980s, the *counterfeit deviance hypothesis* does not deal significantly with an understanding of the laws and conventions of society. As more and more clients live in the community and as a small percentage of them offend, it has been increasingly clear to me that it is extremely important to have a thorough understanding of the conventions and values of society. Where an individual has had a restricted or distorted upbringing, they may have failed to develop a full understanding of these conventions. While the developmental processes involved in such learning are fully covered in the *counterfeit deviance hypothesis*, it does not emphasise this aspect of social and cultural knowledge. Relatedly, it makes no mention of an understanding of society's laws. The *moral vacuum hypothesis* does invoke the concept of victim understanding and perspective taking but generally Hingsburger, Griffiths and Quinsey do not emphasise the development of moral understanding in relation to cultural conventions and laws. I will deal with this later in the final section of this chapter.

Although it took some years, there have now been a number of research evaluations which have tested the *sexual deviance hypothesis* directly. Lindsay (2005) wrote that it was surprising that the hypothesis had never been tested since it was relatively easy to evaluate certain aspects. The theory would suggest that lack of sexual knowledge, poor social and heterosocial skills, limited opportunities to establish sexual relationships and sexual naivety are instrumental in the perpetration of sexual offences. Therefore, men who commit inappropriate sexual behaviour should be poorer in relation to all of these skills than men who do not. As has been described in Chapter 2 on Assessment of Offence-Related Issues, several authors have now tested this hypothesis. To reiterate briefly, Talbot and Langdon (2006) compared groups of sex offenders with ID and non-offenders with ID finding no significant differences between untreated sex offenders and non-offenders. Clearly, the *counterfeit deviance hypothesis* would have predicted poorer sexual knowledge in the sex offenders. Michie *et al.* (2006) found higher levels of sexual knowledge in sex offenders with ID when compared to controls. They also found that the sexual knowledge of controls was related to IQ while sexual knowledge of sex offenders was unrelated. They felt that for sex offenders, sexual knowledge was more likely to be affected by sexual interest and sexual drive resulting in the lack of relationship with IQ. None of these findings support the *counterfeit deviance hypothesis.* Lunsky *et al.* (2007) conducted a more sensitive experiment splitting sexual offenders into deviant/persistent offenders and naïve/inappropriate offenders. They found that only the deviant/persistent offenders had greater levels of sexual knowledge than control participants and they concluded that the *counterfeit deviance hypothesis* may hold only with inappropriate offenders. Therefore, they suggested that the *counterfeit deviance hypothesis* may be more relevant to inappropriate offenders rather than deviant offenders. In fact, as has already been pointed out, Hingsburger, Griffiths and Quinsey took account of deviant persistent offenders in their original paper noting that a small percentage of men with ID may indeed be motivated by deviant sexual attraction. Therefore, the *counterfeit deviance hypothesis* may continue to be important in relation to a subsection of sexual offenders with ID.

I will return to adaptations and developments of the *counterfeit deviance hypothesis* towards the end of this chapter. I have dealt with it in such detail firstly because it is an account of inappropriate sexual behaviour which is specifically related to men with ID and secondly because it elucidates the processes relevant to people with ID, which may also be relevant to sexual offending. Therefore, in commenting on the following theories of sexual offending, I will employ all of these processes which have already been discussed.

Finkelhor's Precondition Model of Child Sexual Abuse

Perhaps because it was one of the first theories of sex offending, Finkelhor's (1984) Precondition Model of Child Sexual Abuse was extremely influential throughout the 1990s in the development of programmes for sexual offenders. It contains a number of factors which both explain why men might wish to offend sexually against children and describes the processes involved in committing such offences. Ward, Polatchik and Beech (2005) make the point that he was one of the first writers to acknowledge that sex offending was a complex multifactorial issue. Up to that point, treatment for sexual offenders had generally focused on the single factor of sexual arousal and had employed techniques such as masturbatory reconditioning, stimulus fading from child images to adult images and simple aversive techniques. The implication of such treatment is that the problem itself is univariate and can be treated by focusing on this single issue. Finkelhor (1984) postulated that the problem itself was multivariate and, by extension, treatment should focus on a number of interrelated factors. This was the first theory to employ such a comprehensive analysis and subsequent theories have generally followed this approach, focusing on a number of environmental, developmental and personal factors.

Four basic factors which have been implicated in the development of child sexual abuse were incorporated into the theory. The first is simply that some men are sexually aroused by children. The second is that for some men sex with children is more emotionally satisfying than sex with adults. This was referred to as emotional congruence with children. The third factor was that some men may be unable, for a range of reasons, to become sexually close to an adult and, therefore, fulfil their sexual needs in socially unacceptable ways with children. These three factors set out to account for deviant sexual interest. The final factor relates to the way in which this sexual interest can be transformed into the perpetration of a sexually abusive act. In the fourth factor, men become disinhibited and act in a manner outside of the normally accepted repertoire but in a way which is consistent with their sexual interest in children. Finkelhor considered that these factors work in combination to create conditions in which it is possible for men to perpetrate sexual abuse. If one of the factors is not activated or is working against the other three, then the sexual abuse will not occur. The factors may work consistently together or may function in a temporal sequence but they contribute to the sequential, temporal preconditions of child sexual abuse.

There are four preconditions relating to sexual abuse. These are motivation, overcoming internal inhibitors, overcoming external inhibitors and overcoming the resistance of a child.

Motivation to sexually offend

Motivation itself is separated by Finkelhor into three areas mentioned above. Firstly, the individual male must experience sexual arousal or sexual preference towards children. This can be caused by a number of factors. It is reasonably well documented that sex offenders as a group report higher rates of personal sexual abuse in childhood than other groups of men (Briggs and Hawkins, 1996; Dahawan and Marshall, 1996). It was postulated that such experiences of personal abuse may act as a disinhibition towards adult–child sexual contact and act as a learning incident which conditions sexual responses towards children. Early exposure to sexual behaviour as a child may also involve the use of pornography. Once again, this may prime responses concerning the sexualisation of children. These developmental causes result in basic sexual arousal towards children.

A second motivational factor is that for a variety of reasons, some men develop an emotional congruence with children. They may have a need to feel more powerful in relationships and children automatically fulfil this need or they may feel that interactions with children are safer in relation to self-esteem factors. Another possibility is that some men may have a distorted personal emotional development which results in them feeling more comfortable with children rather than adults. These needs are likely to be strongly reinforced by some children because it is simply the case that either through genetic priming or through persistent developmental learning children are culturally programmed to be comfortable with lower power relationships with adults. The third motivational factor is referred to as 'blockage'. In this, men are unable to meet their sexual needs with adults for a variety of reasons. These may include developmental reasons such as a fear of intimacy or poor heterosexual social skills. They may include current systemic reasons such as marital or relationship breakdown. This blockage results in motivation to engage children as replacements for adults in sexual situations. Taken together, these factors provide powerful motivation for avoiding or blocking sexual contact with adults and engaging children.

Overcoming internal inhibitors

While men may be motivated to have sex with a child, they will also be very aware of the social and cultural taboos placed on adult/child sexuality. Some of the motivational factors may have undermined their commitment and belief in these social taboos. If personal sexual abuse has occurred over a period in childhood then it may be that the prohibition of adult–child sex has been somewhat undermined within the individual's cognitive framework. However, there have to be a number of more immediate personal disinhibitors which allow the individual to overcome personal inhibitions. One of the most frequently cited variables which triggers the personal justification for sexual abuse is the range of cognitive distortions which have been outlined by several authors (e.g. Ward *et al.*, 1997) which provide personal permission for a man to continue the cycle of sexual offending. More immediate disinhibitors might be alcohol intoxication or a sense of entitlement resulting from a breakdown in normal sexual relationships. For example, where a man has had protracted arguments and confrontations with his partner or a breakdown in heterosexual relationships, he may use his lack of access to sexual opportunities as a justification for turning towards more vulnerable individuals such as children. This would be another, more immediate, cognitive distortion in that he may justify his sexual approaches by blaming his partner for denying him sex. These various factors allow the man to overcome his personal inhibitions and justify sexual approaches to children.

Overcoming external inhibitors

This precondition has been extremely influential in the development of sex offender treatment. The concept of preparing the situation, relationships and the victim in order to commit the sexual offence has been the focus of much of sex offender treatment over the years. Organising these opportunities has been called 'grooming' and has become a standard aspect of the lexicon of sex offender assessment and treatment. Planning may be quite explicit or implicit to the routines of the man involved. It can include reviewing situations and environments where vulnerable victims might be, it can involve gaining the trust of children through inducements and favours, it may incorporate getting to know certain families and developing trust with the children in the family or it may involve more comprehensive long-term planning with men becoming engaged with an organisation for children such as a sports team or youth club. However, overcoming external inhibitors does not always mean that the man will have an organised long-term or medium-term plan. He may also encounter a child unexpectedly in a certain situation which affords the possibility of unseen sexual abuse and he may take advantage of the situation. There are therefore a number of ways in which men can manipulate situations or take advantage of situations which reduce the chances of external control.

Overcoming the resistance of the child

At this point, the other preconditions are likely to have been met. The perpetrator is sufficiently motivated to offend, they have overcome their personal inhibitions to offend against children and they have organised or taken advantage of a situation whereby the external monitoring and control is reduced to such an extent that it is possible to commit a sexual offence. The final precondition is that the man must now overcome the resistance presented by the child. As with the previous preconditions, different sex offenders will employ a range of different methods to induce children into engaging sexually. They may pretend that they are playing with the children while moving the game increasingly towards sexual contact. They may use pornography to interest children in sexual behaviour and further interest them in exploring the stimuli in the pornography through sexual contact. This is not to say that children are aware of sexuality and its ramifications for the man in question, it is simply that the perpetrator is taking advantage of the natural curiosity of children but this time in a sexual context. He may use threats or violence towards the children in order to force them to engage in sexual activity. Alternatively, he may move the child increasingly towards sexual engagement and then use emotional blackmail to perpetuate the contact by threatening censure and punishment should parents, teachers or other adults find out about what has been occurring. One of the most common ways proposed is that men encourage children into sexual contact through inducements with sweets or inducements associated with adult behaviour such as cigarettes and alcohol. Giving alcohol to children acts as a further disinhibitor in that it is likely to interfere with cognitive capacities and resistance in children.

Evaluation

Finkelhor's theory was very influential in the development of treatment programmes because it recognised the complexity of sexual offending and also directed therapists to specific factors in this complex process. The factors would be invoked differently, depending on individuals although all individuals would essentially move through the temporal sequence. Therefore, treatment could focus on individual predisposing factors, individual motivational factors and idiomatic pathways which each man employed to perpetrate specific sexual offences. However, importantly, the theory provides a practical context in which these various factors can be addressed. Therefore, for example, therapists could focus on the specific way in which individuals dealt with their own internal inhibitors and could also focus on ways in which they planned situations in their life to circumvent and overcome various external obstacles and inhibitors. Each man would also employ their own ways of engaging children and overcoming any resistance which they presented. Therefore, although the theory is able to incorporate individual pathways into a sex offender treatment programme, it also allows the commonalities in various individual's approaches to be incorporated in a common framework. It further encourages therapists and offenders to review both distal and proximal factors in considering the cycle of offending.

From the point of view of ID, the model resonates with a number of areas of research in the field of sexual offending and in general research. The three factors which contribute towards the motivation precondition have all been considered at least to some degree in the field of ID. Finkelhor suggests that some men are sexually aroused by children and explains this in terms of developmental experiences in childhood. Increasingly, in mainstream sex offender work, inappropriate sexual preference and sexual drive have been suggested as primary motivation by several authors (Blanchard *et al.*, 1999; Harris *et al.*, 2003). As I have written in previous chapters, this work has certainly extended to the field of ID and it was noted that sex offenders show a degree of persistence in that a high percentage have a previous conviction or clear documented evidence of at least one previous, similar incident (Day, 1994; Lindsay *et al.*, 2002). Blanchard *et al.* (1999) reviewed 950 sex offenders and found that those with ID were more likely to commit offences against younger children and male children. In a meta-analysis and reanalysis of 25 146 sex offenders and controls, Cantor *et al.* (2005) found a robust relationship between lower IQ and sexual offending, specifically, lower IQ and paedophilia. In a further analysis on 832 adult male patients referred to a speciality clinic, Blanchard *et al.* (2008) again found a similar relationship between paedophilia and low IQ in a homogeneous population with fewer referral sources as they had found in a heterogeneous group of sexual offenders referred from multiple sources. This, they felt, cut down the possibility of a systematic bias in referral source which might have affected results from general sources. Therefore, although it accounts for a small percentage of the variance, there is some evidence that some men with ID may tend towards a sexual interest in children.

The other variables which are cited in the motivation precondition have also been researched in the field of ID. In relation to sexual abuse in childhood, similar results have been found with ID sex offenders as those in the mainstream offending population. Lindsay *et al.* (2001) found a higher rate of child sexual abuse reported in sex offenders with ID than in control participants. In the field of ID, there has been a considerable amount of work on developmental issues affecting self-esteem, negative social comparison and stigma (Jahoda *et al.*, 2006; Dagnan and Jahoda, 2006). This work has been done in relation to problems with anxiety, depression and hostility in individuals but it is clearly relevant to sex offenders in that those authors postulate a number of mechanisms whereby people with ID develop low self-esteem and cognitive schemata related to stigma through continual processes of negative social comparison. In mainstream settings, the social comparisons that people with ID make with non-disabled peers are likely to be unfavourable towards themselves (Szivos-Bach, 1993). In addition, they may have limited opportunities to develop varied roles and attributes related, for example, to employment or social intimate relationships. Having access to a range of roles is thought to buffer against negative social comparison and if sex offenders in particular with ID have less complex and poorly consolidated self-schemata, low self-esteem and stigma may be the result (Dagnan and Lindsay, 2008). Given the negative comparisons made in relation to mainstream groups, it certainly follows that sex offenders with ID may tend towards congruence with similarly vulnerable groups such as children. Therefore, the available evidence suggests that developmental experiences may make sex offenders with ID particularly vulnerable to these motivational preconditions.

Finkelhor's third set of motivational factors are related to blockage of sexual expression either through personal obstacles or systemic factors. The various sub-hypotheses outlined earlier on the *counterfeit deviance hypothesis* are clearly relevant to structural obstacles and personal obstacles which might prevent appropriate sexual expression. Living in supported circumstances where environments do not respect privacy, a lack of opportunity for appropriate sexual expression, lack of opportunity to meet age appropriate consenting partners, the lack of opportunities to develop complex interpersonal relationship skills and a developmental discouragement from learning about sexuality would all contribute towards personal and systemic obstacles in sexual expression. An inability to take advantage of interpersonal experiences and to learn the complex nature of social and sexual interaction may also contribute to blockage. Clearly the two medical hypotheses would be specific obstacles to sexual expression. It is fairly straightforward to see the way in which developmental experience in people with ID would present distal and proximal obstacles to sexual expression in adulthood. This, together with other relevant variables might produce specific vulnerability which is particularly relevant to this theoretical model.

In relation to the other three stages in the precondition model, research on sex offenders with ID has suggested similar processes to those found in mainstream offenders. One of the most important factors related to overcoming internal inhibition is that of personal attitudes and beliefs which permit sexual offending. Lindsay, Whitefield and Carson (2007) and Langdon and Talbot (2006) both found that sex offenders with ID held significantly higher levels of cognitive distortions than other types of offenders and non-offenders. Rose *et al.* (2007) also found high levels of cognitive distortions which were amenable to reduction through treatment in sex offenders with ID. Therefore, it may be that this population employ similar mechanisms to overcome internal inhibitors in relation to perpetrating incidents. In previous chapters we have noted that, contrary to expectations, sex offenders with ID employ predominantly approach pathways in relation to acts which they perpetrate. Of the predominant percentage who employ approach pathways, around half actively plan the circumstances of the offence. This suggests that at least some offenders with ID are able to explicitly, if only in a rudimentary fashion, plan circumstances whereby external inhibitors of the offence might be overcome. Even with approach/automatic offenders, the routines and behavioural scripts employed are likely to lead to situations in which external inhibitors are circumvented. These issues will be dealt with in more detail later in the following chapter but, for the time being, they provide some evidence that sex offenders with ID are able to overcome external inhibitors within the temporal pattern suggested by Finkelhor.

In my experience, when a sex offender with ID overcomes the resistance of the victim, it is done in much the same way as has been reported for mainstream sex offenders. Clients will occasionally use force to commit an offence, will use bribes of sweets, cigarettes and alcohol, will use threats of parental censure if the child tells of an incident or will use emotional blackmail saying that both the perpetrator and child will 'get into terrible trouble' if the child reveals the incident. Therefore, there is evidence that the Finkelhor Precondition Model may be as relevant to sex offenders with ID as it is to mainstream offenders. Indeed, aspects of the model are strengthened by both research on people with ID in general and by the counterfeit deviance hypothesis which illustrates several of the mechanisms employed in Finkelhor's Precondition Model and which are emphasised in the histories of sex offenders with ID.

The Marshall and Barbaree Integrated Theory

The Integrated Theory developed by Marshall and Barbaree (1990) has a focus on the importance of developmental experiences and as such has specific relevance for offenders with ID. It has an important emphasis on the development of attachment style and, although there is little specific research on the development of attachments in people with ID, there is some research which focuses on related, developmental issues. For Marshall and Barbaree, adolescence is a critical period in the development of personal understanding of aggressive and sexual impulses, the development of social and interpersonal skills, the development of problem solving and coping styles and the development of self-regulation skills in relation to both aggression and sexual impulses. Where individuals may have inadequate relationship skills, poor coping styles, low self-esteem and attachment difficulties, they are more likely to have significant problems in differentiating these various impulses and in developing appropriate self-regulation skills. During puberty and around this period of adolescents, biology provides the major developmental changes and the individual needs to acquire skills for coping with these changes. Men with a history of developmental adversity such as physical or sexual abuse or oppressive parenting may arrive at adolescence with poor skills to cope with these major biological and social changes. As a result, young men who may have already been vulnerable, do not develop adequate coping skills or the appropriate skills for developing social and sexual relationships in adulthood. This in turn primes certain men for a breakdown in future social and sexual relationships and predisposes them to inappropriate and even violent social and sexual relationships. Crucially, early developmental experiences produce vulnerabilities and these are compounded by inadequate coping with adolescent developmental experiences.

For Marshall and Barbaree, childhood is the period where males will develop basic relationship skills which they will then employ in the period of transition to adulthood. Poor parenting, insecure attachments and low self-esteem produce a range of skill deficits which preclude the individual from emotional coping and personal effectiveness. They then develop profound difficulties in personal and interpersonal problem solving which lead to a range of obstacles when it comes to establishing appropriate social relationships. Without appropriate social relationships, it logically follows that there cannot be appropriate, nurturing, close sexual relationships. Marshall and Barbaree also suggest that these individuals fail to develop the ability to differentiate adequately between aggressive and sexual impulses. In addition, exposure to antisocial attitudes and misogynistic attitudes at home or culturally, may reinforce further antisocial and misogynistic attitudes which produce greater vulnerability in these men for the perpetration of sexual offences. If they see women as inferior or have experience of being abused by an adult, these attitudes can carry through to adulthood and, indeed, be reinforced and strengthened during adolescence and adulthood. As a result, cognitive schemata and the corresponding cognitive distortions may develop in their attitudes towards women and children. These cognitive schemata are crucial in the perpetration and justification of sexual offences. They also promote behavioural routines which are consistent with firmly held attitudes and which will in turn provide further vulnerability factors for the perpetration of sexual offences.

The theory accounts for the development in adolescence of a world view which contains cognitive schemata that will remain relatively stable and which will be reinforced by chronic deficits in emotional regulation and relationship skills. With significant problems in emotional regulation and poor methods of discussing these difficulties with appropriate others, individuals can become increasingly isolated at a time when social identity is developing. Such isolation encourages the further development of idiosyncratic world views and cognitive schemata in the absence of pro-social influences. Therefore, the individual may develop deviant sexual fantasies which are reinforced through selective attention to media influences, pornography and so on and which will be reinforced through masturbation. This in turn further strengthens these various schemata through sexual coping. Sexual coping is a central concept in that Marshall and Barbaree suggest that men cope with emotional and interpersonal difficulties through appropriate sexual contact. However, if such appropriate contact is not available, they are likely to resort to inappropriate sexual strategies for coping with the various situations in their lives.

The probability of the sexual offence, or the actual occurrence of the offence is likely to be further promoted by disinhibitors such as alcohol or stress. The more vulnerable an individual is, as a result of their developmental experiences, then the less is required by way of disinhibitors. Stressors also come in the form of loss of relationships, emotional difficulties, loneliness or rejection and they are presented to an individual who is already lacking in ability to deal appropriately with difficult situations. It should also be remembered that Marshall and Barbaree perceive sexuality as a particular means of coping with such situations in men and this catastrophic fusion of variables may combine with a specific opportunity in the perpetration of a sexual offence. The authors also postulate a perturbation of neural mechanisms in the mid brain which is responsible for sexual and aggressive behaviours. They draw on evidence that sexual steroids are involved in activating both sexuality and aggression and then suggest that during adolescence, certain individuals fail to adequately discriminate these impulses, resulting in a tendency to fuse both sex and aggression. The massive release of male hormones during this age, if not appropriately dealt with through developmental coping, results in this confusion. All of these factors combine in generating a propensity towards offending against women and children.

Evaluation

Marshall and Barbaree's Integrated Theory focuses on developmental issues throughout childhood and adolescence. Crucial psychological and social processes which occur through pre-pubertal childhood equip boys to deal with the significant biological and social changes which will occur throughout adolescence. Disruptions in these various processes are likely to have important effects regarding sexual adjustment and subsequently, sexual offending. In many ways, it has similarities to Finkelhor's Precondition Model in that both stress the importance of developing skills which will enable adolescents and adults to form social and sexual relationships in an appropriate fashion. Major disruption to this process may result in distorted motivations to offend sexually. In this sense, both theories focus on developing vulnerabilities to commit sexual offences. Marshall and Barbaree place a greater emphasis on deficits in self-regulation skills which are caused by these processes. Crucially, they also postulate an interaction between these interpersonal, social and developmental processes and hormonal and biological challenges. If males become increasingly isolated through lack of appropriate skills for forming social and sexual relationships, this will allow them to develop idiosyncratic, distorted world views and cognitive schemata. The absence of pro-social influences means that these schemata are less likely to be challenged.

Another important aspect of the Integrated Theory is that men meet a number of personal needs through sexual activity. If they are unable to meet these needs in an adaptive fashion, they will choose a maladaptive fashion. This has resonance with the Precondition Theory in that one of Finkelhor's explicit motivational routes is that for men who choose to offend against children, adaptive sexuality with adults is 'blocked' for a variety of reasons. Perhaps the main strength of the Integrated Theory is that it accounts for motivation towards all types of sex offending including both adults and children. However, it is not clear on the nature of the differential pathways involved in different types of sexual offending.

From the point of view of sex offenders with ID, much of the research which is relevant to the Precondition Model also pertains to the Integrated Theory. There is an emerging research literature which links developmental problems in childhood to the experience of a range of mental health and other difficulties in adulthood for this client group. Individual factors for children with ID such as poorer problem-solving skills, difficulties with emotional control and communication difficulties are considered to make the person's interaction with their world more demanding and complex. For example, in a study of 107 adults with ID, Nezu *et al.* (1995) found a relationship between cognitive variables and depression. They reported levels of depressive symptoms correlated positively with increases in feelings of helplessness, increases in negative automatic thoughts and lower rates of self-reinforcement. Self-reinforcement and coping with feelings of helplessness are key developmental skills which act as protective buffers against the onset of problems through adolescence and adulthood. Several authors (e.g. Dagnan and Lindsay, 2008) have noted the importance of having access to a wide range of roles as a buffer against negative social comparison and associated problems with mental health in adulthood. If people with ID have a less complex range of social experiences, they are likely to have a correspondingly narrower range of roles with fewer opportunities to develop protective psychological buffers. For some men with ID, these processes are likely to have a significant impact when dealing with changes in adolescence in that they may have developed fewer skills or inadequate skills to deal with the challenges outlined by Marshall and Barbaree. Individual factors such as poorer problem solving, emotional control and communication difficulties are reasonably well established in people with ID. This body of research has linked these deficits to self-report ratings of depressive symptoms (Payne and Jahoda, 2004). There is also an emerging literature on attachment experiences of children with IDs and there is little doubt that disruptions in attachment have significant effects in later life (Chapter 2).

A second group of social factors relates to experiences of personal abuse, negative expectations, bullying and loss, all of which interfere with the development of adaptive skills for dealing with general life experiences and which are likely to promote a negative self-image and a negative world view. As has been mentioned, several authors have found a link between problems in self-esteem, social comparison, negative self-evaluation and the experience of stigma in this client group (Dagnan and Waring, 2004; Szivos-Bach, 1993).

The most frequently investigated attachment difficulty in adults with ID, including offenders, is childhood abuse. Many studies have reported increased rates of sexual and physical abuse in people with ID. In a review, Sequeira and Hollins (2003) noted that people with ID experience a range of symptoms, psychopathology and behavioural difficulties as a result of sexual abuse. Beail and Warden (1995) underlined the fact that severe disruptions of attachment, as evidenced by sexual abuse, are found significantly across the range of individuals with ID including sex offenders. Lindsay *et al.* (2006c) found high rates of sexual and physical abuse in all types of offenders. Therefore, there is ample evidence of severe disruption in psychological developmental processes all of which have been noted as important in the Integrated Theory. The counterfeit deviance hypothesis presents a number of ways in which men with ID may be blocked in the development and expression of sexuality.

Having noted the consistency between research on people with ID and the psychological and social mechanisms proposed in the Integrated Theory, we also have to acknowledge that the same research presents significant problems for the theory. Much of the research has been conducted on generic populations and it has been found that individuals with ID who develop mental health and relationship problems show a link between these disruptions and adult psychopathology. However, it is clear that they do not all go on to commit sexual offences. Indeed, a minority develop this kind of problem and it is not clear why some men with these developmental experiences go on to commit sexual offences while others do not. The research on self-regulation pathways suggests that up to half of the sex offenders with ID are approach offenders with active regulation strategies (Keeling, Rose and Beech, 2006; Langdon, Maxted and Murphy, 2007). Therefore, the hypothesised self-regulation deficits in the Integrated Theory may not be present.

Another issue which is difficult to explain on the basis of the Integrated Theory is that research studies have found that sex offenders tend to be older at the point of referral than other types of offenders (Hogue *et al.*, 2006; Lindsay *et al.*, 2006c).

One would expect that since these various processes are a result of difficulties in adolescence, the onset of inappropriate sexual behaviour might be correspondingly young. Certainly, there is no reason to predict that sex offenders might be older than other types of offenders when referred.

These logical difficulties are relevant to all theories which invoke developmental disruptions as causative variables for sexual offending, they are not confined to criticisms of the Integrated Theory. In this regard, a common difficulty for all such explanations of sexual offending is the information on sexual abuse. As has been mentioned, studies on sex offenders and other types of offenders with ID have shown that around 40% of sex offenders have themselves been physically abused in childhood. It follows that around 60%, a majority, do not report sexual abuse in childhood. This leaves us with considerable inconsistency in linking childhood sexual abuse to sexual offending in adulthood. A further difficulty from these studies is that around 5–10% of men who commit other types of offences do report sexual abuse in their own childhood. However, these men have not gone on to commit sexual offences in adulthood and this is a further inconsistency in linking these disruptions of attachment in childhood to sexual offending in adulthood. Some writers review this research sceptically with the conclusion that socio-psychological explanations for sexual offending do not hold much promise (Quinsey, 2004). However, the consistency with which studies from a variety of sex offender populations report an increase in childhood sexual abuse, suggests some consistent attachment factors are likely to be in play. Therefore, the Integrated Theory is likely to have significant relevance to at least a proportion of sex offenders with ID.

Hall and Hirschman's Quadripartite Model

Ward, Polaschek and Beech (2005) describe the Quadripartite Model as having much potential but being unjustly neglected. Hall and Hirschman (1991, 1992) formulated two versions of the model, one for rape and one for offences against children. They felt that a weakness of theories of sexual offending was that they tended to focus on one or two causative factors while sexual offending is a far more complex process with multiple causes. They proposed the theory which included four primary factors to account for a greater diversity of types of sexual offending.

The first factor is sexual arousal to an inappropriate stimulus. This is a clear physiological motivator, provides intrusive feelings in the individual and also provides persistent sexual urges towards the inappropriate stimulus such as violence or children. By placing physiological arousal as one of the four primary factors, Hall and Hirschman make a significantly different emphasis to that taken by Finkelhor or Marshall and Barbaree while at the same time taking account of the considerable amount of research on inappropriate sexual preference in men (e.g. Quinsey and Chaplin, 1988; Harris *et al.*, 1996). The second primary factor is that of cognitive distortions. These have been dealt with extensively in Chapter 2 and are essentially attitudes which permit a man to commit an incident of sexual abuse or justifications for the abuse. These cognitive distortions are equally relevant to violent offences against adults or offences against children. Hall (1996) wrote that such attitudes were germane to the degree of planning required in committing such acts. He also felt that a significant proportion of sexual offenders against children would evidence low levels of impulsivity which would allow the adoption of cognitive distortions in conjunction with planning. Importantly, this model suggests that the sex offenders are reasonably competent individuals who may plan certain acts based on their sexual motivation, their cognitive justifications for committing a sexual offence and in recognition of the costs and benefits of acting in such a manner.

The third primary factor is affective discontrol. This accounts for aspects which would lower normal inhibitors controlling sexuality. Hall and Hirschman (1991, 1992) recognise that sex offenders will experience a degree of anxiety or apprehension over the prospect of committing an illegal act, may experience guilt or the prospect of guilt when considering inappropriate sexual behaviour and may also experience a degree of victim empathy. These factors exert some behavioural and emotional regulation over the individual and their controlling influence must be weakened in order that the offence can take place. Therefore, emotional disregulation can occur through a number of means. It may be that the man himself is using ineffective strategies to control his sexuality. The two most usual examples of poor strategies are a reliance on masturbation in order to control deviant sexual fantasies or the use of alcohol to dampen inappropriate sexual impulses. However, other examples might be that an increase in emotional problems such as anxiety disorders or depression might cause the offender to act upon sexual impulses which have previously been under some emotional control. Emotional problems can disrupt the offenders self-regulation at any point before the offence, during treatment or during a relapse prevention follow-up. Another way in which emotional disregulation can trigger an offence is when offenders confuse emotional states such as loneliness and sexual desire. Isolation and lack of social contact allow the individual to focus on personal issues, emotional difficulties and sexual desire without their thoughts or cognitions being diverted to normal inhibitors such as anxiety over prosecution, or their understanding of harm to victims.

The fourth primary factor included in the Quadripartite Model is personality factors. These include a wide range of developmental issues most of which have already been covered in the previous section on the Integrated Theory such as attachment issues, physical or sexual abuse and other adverse developmental experiences. These various developmental disruptions contribute to personality difficulties which may lead the individual to develop an antisocial means of responding to others with a tendency to contravene social conventions and break social rules.

Hall and Hirschman felt that for any individual, one primary factor may predominate and be the major source of motivation for an offence. They also postulated that each individual has a 'Threat Threshold' which moderates and controls sexual behaviour. If the motivation generated by any of the primary factors exceeds the threshold then the likelihood of an offence becomes much greater. Alternatively, if the threat threshold is perceived as lowering in any particular situation, again an offence is more likely. Situational factors can influence a primary factor so that it rises above the normal threshold. Therefore, if a man's inappropriate sexual arousal increases for any reason above the threshold whereby his sexuality is controlled by perceived threat, then an offence may be more likely. If the threat threshold is lowered by the perception (cognitive distortion) that the victim is complicit in the sexual act, then the offence is more likely. Primary factors may combine to increase their potency over the threat threshold. Therefore, if the individual is experiencing increasing isolation and develops antagonistic views towards the world together with a sense of entitlement through dysfunctional personality traits, then the strength of the primary factors may rise over the threat threshold. In this way, the Quadripartite Model is a dynamic personalised analysis of the development of the sex offence process with attention between the various motivating factors and personal regulation of sexuality. Each of the four factors can be used to identify a particular type of offender with four subtypes corresponding to physiological, cognitive, poor emotional regulation and personality. In this way, one factor may predominate although there is a constant interaction between all these personal variables and the threat threshold.

Evaluation

The Quadripartite Model manages to account for a wider range of research than other models. This is especially true in relation to inappropriate sexual preference which, as mentioned above, has been shown consistently to be a factor in many larger scale studies of sexual offenders. In addition, it invokes the motivational influence of personality factors which, again, have been shown to feature prominently in risk prediction for sexual offences (e.g. Harris *et al.*, 2003). While invoking these two major personal factors in the development of sexual offences, the model does not ignore the importance of cognitive distortions and emotional regulation which are predominant features of other models. Indeed, it affords these factors equal weight in the general conceptual structure of how men commit sexual offences.

Two further important additions to the conceptual structure are added, explicitly, within the model. The first is that these factors interact and one may become predominant raising the individual's motivation over the inhibitory threshold. Therefore, inappropriate sexual preference for children may not, in itself, be sufficient to perpetrate a sexual offence. Research has certainly supported this hypothesis. In general studies, up to 20% of men have shown at least some sexual arousal towards child stimuli. However, it is clear that this percentage of men do not go on to commit sexual offences. In addition, Seto and colleagues (Seto, Cantor and Blanchard, 2006; Seto and Eke, 2005) have shown that only around 1% of men who have been convicted of child pornography offences actually go on to commit 'hands on' offences. One might conclude that these men considered child pornography offences to be private and, as a result, had considered that these situational factors lowered the threshold for the commission of this sexual offence. However, in order to commit a contact sexual offence, other primary factors would be required to come into play which was not the case with the majority of individuals in these studies. The second innovative feature in the model is the concept of an inhibitory threat threshold which promotes self-regulation in individuals. For various situational reasons perceived by the offender, this threshold may be lowered or, if personal motivational factors are invoked more strongly, motivation may rise above the self-regulation threshold. However, the concept of a threshold certainly invokes the concept of self-regulation and its importance in the perpetration of offences.

The concept of a self-regulation threshold is extremely useful in the field of ID. Individual's with ID may not adequately perceive the threat of prosecution. This might happen for a number of reasons, many of which have already been described in the section on the counterfeit deviance hypothesis. If certain men have not adequately understood the extent to which inappropriate sexual behaviour is socially condemned, they are likely to have an unrealistic appraisal of the threat which such behaviour presents. In addition, if, when they commit an act of inappropriate sexual behaviour, others react in an inconsistent fashion or in some other inappropriate manner such as understating or overstating its importance, then the perpetrator will continue to receive messages which are unrealistic regarding the extent of the threat threshold. Therefore, these offences may continue because of an inadequate perception of threat. The concept of a threat threshold can be used extensively in treatment through persistent discussion and demonstration of the extent to which such behaviour is inappropriate. These concepts have certainly been used in the current sex offender programme described later.

We have also seen the way in which issues related to developmental disruption are relevant to offenders with ID. This has been discussed in relation to both the Precondition Model and Integrated Theory. Research in sexual abuse, physical abuse, attachment difficulties and antisocial attitudes have all found that men with ID experience these difficulties with at least similar frequency to other groups. Research on personality factors and their importance in the field has also shown that these issues are as relevant to this client group as they are to other criminal groups (Lindsay *et al.*, 2006c, 2007d; Morrissey *et al.*, 2005). Similarly, earlier in this chapter, I have reviewed the importance of emotional control and emotional disregulation in this client group, especially in relation to negative social comparison and stigma. Therefore, at every level and on every major aspect, the Quadripartite Model seems particularly appropriate for consideration in relation to offenders with ID.

The Ward and Hudson Self-Regulation Pathways Model

Ward and Hudson (1998) developed a model which proposed four basic pathways of the sexual offence process. The model has been extremely influential in changing the way in which sex offender assessment and treatment has been conceptualised and delivered. It has also generated a considerable amount of research from a variety of research groups, some of whom work with offenders with ID. It is, therefore, likely to be particularly influential in the field of sex offenders with ID. Because the Self-Regulation Pathways Model is described at various points throughout this book, I will only briefly reiterate the main aspects here.

Ward and Hudson (1998) responded to a number of criticisms of the, then, prevalent model of sex offender treatment which was relapse prevention (RP; Pithers *et al.*,

1983, 1988). The RP Model was developed in the field of alcohol addiction and treat-ment for addictions. It highlights seemingly unimportant decisions or acts, in relation to personal stress, boredom, leisure, work and so on, which might seem individually trivial and defensible, but taken together construct a clear cycle and a pathway of re-lapse or, in sex offending, recidivism. Intervention on this cycle provides the offender with the knowledge and capacity to alter and avoid these decisions, cognitions and situations which might lead to lapses and relapses in the offence cycle. While RP has been invaluable in providing a coherent model for sex offender treatment, Ward and Hudson (1998) based their theoretical criticism on the fact that lapses and relapses in addiction are very different to those concepts in sex offending where one lapse constitutes a relapse and treatment failure. This led to several conceptual difficulties moving gratification effects close to violation effects. It also proposed a single overall conceptual model for sexual offending with a single process of relapse emphasising various negative events and skill deficits such as poor coping strategies and negative emotional states. Therefore, RP generally employed self-regulation failure while Ward and Hudson (1998) felt that some offenders explicitly planned the offence using good self-regulation skills. In this regard, their criticisms were similar to the concepts seen in the Quadripartite Model where Hall and Hirschman felt that several offenders are likely to have low impulsivity with explicit planning of their offence. Therefore, Ward and Hudson invoked the concept of self-regulation style rather than failure and different styles lead to different pathways in the offence process.

On the basis of personal accounts of sex offenders which were analysed using grounded theory, they identified clear patterns in the offending processes. These patterns were developed into four different pathways to offending. These pathways were defined by two distinct ways of establishing offence-related goals (approach or avoidance) and by two strategies of self-regulation (active or passive).

Ward and Hudson first acknowledge that men have a desire to commit inappropriate sexual behaviour. They will then have an understanding of the extent to which this behaviour is unacceptable and their appraisal of the acceptability of their wish for sexual behaviour determines whether they will adopt approach goals or avoidant goals. If the man adopts approach goals he is interested in the successful gratification of sexual desires and completion of the inappropriate sexual behaviour. The individual who adopts avoidant goals wishes to inhibit sexual desires and reduce the chances of perpetrating a sexual offence.

Self-regulation styles are then split into active and passive with the consequence of determining four basic offence pathways. These have been described earlier in Chapter 2 and it is only necessary to reiterate here that the first is an approach explicit pathway where the perpetrator actively plans a strategy which he wishes to carry out successfully. The second is the approach automatic pathway where the perpetrator engages in well-rehearsed cognitive and behavioural scripts which are likely to lead to successful gratification of sexual desires. In both of these approach pathways, the perpetrator is likely to evaluate the events positively. The offender who has a wish to avoid sexual offending may use an active self-regulation style which involves inappropriate or counterproductive strategies which eventually lead to sexual offending. Finally, the avoidant/passive pathway incorporates individuals who wish to prevent themselves from expressing inappropriate sexual behaviour but have such poor coping strategies that they can think of no effective ways to stop themselves offending.

Evaluation

The Self-Regulation Pathways Model has been productive, not least in the field of offenders with ID, in promoting research and promoting change in the assessment and treatment of offenders. Ward and colleagues have published two significant volumes in both assessment (Ward *et al.*, 2004) and treatment (Ward, Yates and Long, 2006). Keeling and Rose (2005) hypothesised that because of issues relating to the ID population itself such as poor self-esteem, negative social comparison, experience of stigma, poor coping skills and restricted experiences of social and sexual interaction, offenders with ID were more likely to adopt avoidant and passive offence pathways. However, as has been mentioned earlier, three studies have found that sex offenders with ID tend to adopt pathways which reflect approach goals with around equal proportions employing approach/explicit and approach/automatic pathways (Keeling, Rose and Beech, 2006; Langdon, Maxted and Murphy, 2007; Lindsay, Steptoe and Beech, 2008). Therefore, while the Self-Regulation Pathways Model is undoubtedly applicable to offenders with ID, greater consideration is required to accommodate these findings into a theory or model of the sex offence process in offenders with ID.

The Good Lives Model of Offender Rehabilitation

The Good Lives Model (GLM) was first proposed by Ward and Stewart (2003) and has been developed considerably by Ward and colleagues (Ward and Gannon, 2006; Ward and Marshall, 2004). GLM stresses the importance of constructing a balanced, pro-social personal identity in offenders. This is achieved through the utilisation and development of internal capabilities such as skills, attitudes and beliefs and the promotion of external conditions such as supports for the offender and opportunities for development. GLM proposes that it is a human function to pursue basic needs but that in sex offenders these needs become distorted for a variety of reasons. In the GLM, criminogenic needs and dynamic risk factors constitute the motivation for distorted outcomes, all of which make up a negative life model leading to sexual offending, therefore, the individual uses inappropriate means to achieve antisocial goals in an attempt to construct a fulfilling life. They may also lack the abilities and capacities to achieve a GLM. By promoting the internal and external conditions for achieving human needs in adaptive, pro-social ways, the assumption is that they will less likely to harm others or themselves. Therefore, treatment should focus on the promotion of ways in which offenders can achieve human goods and fulfil their needs in a socially acceptable fashion.

The GLM is, therefore, a far more generic theory incorporating issues relating to the motivation, aetiology, treatment and rehabilitation of sexual offenders and which takes account not only of risk factors but also offenders' human needs. Lindsay *et al.* (2007d) have written the GLM fits well with the Self-Regulation Pathways

Model in that the former constitutes a broad rehabilitation framework while the latter details specific aspects of assessment and therapy dealing with idiomatic features of an individual's offence process. Ward and Gannon (2006) developed this model considerably, elucidating both the assumptions underpinning GLM and the primary goods which individuals might seek. They state that the primary goals are life (healthy living and adaptive functioning), knowledge, excellence in work and play, excellence in agency (self-directedness), inner peace (an ability to control stress and emotional turmoil), friendship (intimate and family relationships), community, spirituality (some feeling of purpose in life), happiness and creativity. Assumptions underpinning GLM are that sexual offending represents a maladaptive attempt to pursue human goods and that these maladaptive strategies should be replaced by adaptive and coping skills, linked to the living situations of offenders and which lead to psychological well-being. A GLM plan should be constructed explicitly taking account of each offender's personal strengths, interests and living environments. Ward and colleagues propose that GLM has the theoretical resources to link a set of aetiological assumptions, explicit avenues for motivating offenders, a set of treatment principles and strategies, identification of internal and external conditions for achieving human goods and an underpinning set of rehabilitation values (primary goods) which function as a general framework to orientate therapists in case formulation and treatment planning.

GLM assumes that sex offenders, like the rest of us, are predisposed to seek a number of primary goods. The way in which they go about this is socially unacceptable but the process is no different from others who seek these human goods in a variety of socially acceptable ways. There is an emphasis on self-esteem and personal identity and the way in which we all pursue a good life as defined by the human values. Therefore, although it is not explicit in the way in which these values emerge, it clearly invokes the same developmental issues as have been invoked in other models of the sex offence process. Correspondingly, the GLM has explicit, practical suggestions for the way in which treatment goals are formulated and incorporated into a programme. Procedures which promote the acquisition of human goods and the fulfilment of primary needs should be incorporated into treatment. In addition, such treatment plans require to be individualised to take into account the specific needs of offenders and the likely situations he will have available to him. Therefore, skills taught to offenders should be done in the context of the situations they are likely to experience. Risk factors constitute problems or maladaptive ways in which offenders strive to achieve these basic human goods. Therefore, a treatment programme should take these into account by, on the one hand emphasising the problems which will result in pursuing human goods in this manner while, on the other, providing alternative, pro-social means for obtaining these human goods or an acceptable equivalent.

Evaluation

The GLM is a significant advance on existing models for the rehabilitation of sex offenders. Ward and Gannon (2006) criticised the RP Model which recommended the reduction of recidivism by reducing or eliminating each dynamic risk factor assessed in an individual. They described this as a 'pincushion model' (p. 79) where each risk factor was represented by a pin and treatment focused on the removal of each risk factor rather than promoting personal adaptive skills and pro-social opportunities. The GLM attempts to redress these shortcomings through the promotion of a Holistic Rehabilitation Model for sex offending. It has certainly had a significant impact on sex offender treatment programmes with most adopting procedures for the promotion of appropriate attachments, social relationships, adaptive routines and engaging work opportunities, all of which will fulfil human goods in a pro-social manner. While much of the GLM has proved novel and innovative in the field of sex offending, it comes as no surprise or innovation in the field of ID where Quality of Life (QOL) has been a central focus in the 30 years of research into deinstitutionalisation and community involvement.

Most of the features of the GLM have been germane to research on QOL. Healthy living, work, leisure, social relationships and friendship, spirituality and community integration are all mentioned as primary human goods in the GLM and have a long research history in the field QOL and ID. Most of this work has been linked to deinstitutionalisation with various writers (Ager, 1990; Bonham *et al.*, 2004; Cummins and Lau, 2003a; Emerson and Hatton, 1994) developing reliable and valid assessments for the evaluation of QOL in this client group and carrying out extensive research programmes in assessing the extent to which clients' QOL improves as a result of moving from institutions to community placement.

However, research in the field of ID has not predated GLM simply through work on QOL. Work on the assessment of personality and people with ID has focused to a large extent on an individual's source of motivation to engage with their surroundings. This has led to certain definitions of personality which rely on personal motivation. In essence, the GLM is also a motivational construction in that the various primary goods are needs for which we all seek fulfilment. In the field of ID, the starting point of most work in this area has been developmental, reviewing the way in which developmental experiences form personality characteristics in individuals with ID. In addition, personality factors are considered to be a framework for the way in which people with ID are motivated to interact with their environment. Therefore, in a series of studies with children, Switzky and colleagues (Switzky, 2001) reviewed the importance of intrinsic motivation in children who worked harder, required less praise for staying on task and maintained their performance longer when compared to externally motivated children when working under self-monitored conditions. By contrast, externally motivated individuals worked better when under closer supervision from teachers. These authors (e.g. Switzky and Haywood, 1991, 1992) concluded that self-regulation was an extremely important trait in people with ID when considering relatively independent living in less regulated settings. They felt that motivational orientation (intrinsic vs. extrinsic) was a central concept in personality development in individuals with ID.

In another model which has close similarities with GLM, Reiss and Havercamp (1997) outlined 16 basic values which provide motivation for all individuals including people with ID. They developed an assessment to tap these values (Reiss and Havercamp, 1998) and in a factor analytic study found a 15 factor solution which conformed to the basic values in their theoretical construction. They also found that people with and without ID showed the same motivational profiles in relation to achieving these basic values. In other words, people with ID and without ID pursue happiness through motivation for the same needs which they specified as social contact, curiosity, honour, family, independence, power, order, idealism, status, vengeance, romance, exercise, acceptance, tranquillity, eating and saving. Saving was the only item that did not emerge from the factor analysis. Aberrant environments which did not satisfy ordinary desires and psychological needs are likely to produce personality difficulties while aberrant motivation (e.g. desire for excessive amounts of positive reinforcement) are similarly likely to result in distortions of personality. This theory of development and motivation is fascinating and wide ranging in its view of personality and, while predating GLM, has clear parallels. The primary goods stated in GLM are listed below with their equivalents from the Reiss and Havercamp Personality Model.

The Good Lives Model	The Reiss Model
Excellence in work and play	Power/status
Inner peace	Tranquillity
Knowledge	Curiosity
Excellence in agency (self-directedness)	Honour/status
Friendship	Social contact/family/acceptance
Community	Social contact/acceptance
Spirituality	Idealism
Happiness	Order/tranquillity
Creativity	Curiosity
	Independence
	Vengeance
	Romance
	Exercise
	Saving

It is fairly clear that although the Reiss model of personality and motivation is not exactly consistent with the GLM, conceptually it is very similar. The basic tenet is that people are motivated for certain primary goods (GLM) or basic values (Reiss Model) and that these constitute the basic requirements for personal fulfilment. As has been mentioned, various researchers on motivation in people with ID (e.g. Switzky, 2001; Reiss and Havercamp, 1997) have considered it axiomatic that distorted environments will produce distortions in the way in which people fulfil these basic values and needs. It is also the case that individuals with aberrant personality traits (e.g. excessive extrinsic motivation) will seek to fulfil these basic human needs in distorted ways.

Two things flow from this research on QOL, personality and motivation in people with ID. Firstly, it is a short step to consider that sex offenders, with possible maladaptive desires and developmental experiences already outlined extensively in this chapter, might pursue basic human values in a distorted fashion. These distortions may in fact represent inappropriate sexual behaviour. Secondly, it is not surprising that when I first outlined a framework for the treatment of sex offenders with ID (Lindsay, 2005), QOL was a central feature in comprehensive treatment. In fact, this model had been developed independently of work on the GLM and had grown out of work on sex offending, QOL, personality and motivation in offenders with ID. However, the end result had considerable similarities with the GLM. This model for the treatment of sex offenders with ID will be outlined and developed in the next chapter. Developments will draw heavily on theoretical models for the treatment of mainstream sex offenders as well as research on QOL and personality in people with ID.

Chapter 6

A Theory for the Sex Offence Process and a Model for Treatment in Offenders with Intellectual Disabilities

Since I wrote the model underpinning a treatment approach for sex offenders with intellectual disability (ID; Lindsay, 2005), there has been a considerable amount of research in the field of offenders with ID and much of the work on general sex offending has been assimilated into the field. All of this research and assimilation has been included in previous chapters. In this chapter, I will integrate this information and attempt to interpret the significance of various empirical outcomes in respect of their impact on theoretical constructs for sex offenders with ID. I will also incorporate some of the main features of other theoretical constructions and assess the implication of research findings for their importance to ID. I will review issues of aetiology and motivation for offending, strategies for offending, theories of criminality and attempt to integrate these various pieces of information in order to construct a model to underpin the treatment approach and programme.

Motivation for Inappropriate Sexual Behaviour and Sexual Offences

Sexual offences are fairly easily defined since they are legally cast. Inappropriate sexual behaviour is harder to define but important in the context of offenders with ID. It has been clarified in earlier chapters that many incidents of inappropriate sexual behaviour in this client group go unreported. While this is commonly suspected in mainstream sexual offending, it is much clearer in offenders with ID since they are often observed and monitored much more closely. Therefore, there is objective evidence that inappropriate sexual behaviour has occurred which, had it been witnessed in a mainstream setting or, indeed a community setting outside the group home or care home, would have been prosecuted as a sexual offence. For a variety of reasons,

The Treatment of Sex Offenders with Developmental Disabilities William Lindsay
© 2009 John Wiley & Sons, Ltd

these incidents may not be reported. Police may feel that since the person is already in a supervised situation and since a successful prosecution is unlikely to make any difference or improvement to the supervision arrangements, there is little point in taking the matter forward. Carers may feel that because of the man's intellectual limitations, it would be unfair to involve the legal processes. In some cases (Holland, 2004), care homes may not wish to publicise the fact that an incident of inappropriate sexual behaviour has occurred in their establishment and may simply put in more stringent supervision arrangements to ensure that it does not happen again. Therefore, there are a variety of reasons why incidents may go unreported even when there is clear witnessed evidence that they have occurred. Because of this, it is important to define inappropriate sexual behaviour at the outset. Inappropriate sexual behaviour is sexual preference or sexual actions directed towards children, coercive or violent sex (rape or sexual assault), stalking, indecent exposure and bestiality. For a detailed discussion of sexual offences, paraphilias, inappropriate sexuality and the differences between these categories, the reader should review Griffiths *et al.* (2007).

Inappropriate Sexuality

In the 1970s, treatments for sexual offending and the principles on which they were based employed a model of anomalous sexual preference and sexual arousal to inappropriate objects and stimuli such as children or violence. Several phallometric studies demonstrated that a significant number of men showed a phallometric response to inappropriate stimuli. Typically, these studies present a variety of pictures to participants including adult women, adult men, boys, girls and situations involving sexual violence. Phallometric responses are then recorded to each set of stimuli (Quinsey and Chaplin, 1988). Similar studies have also been conducted on viewing time for these different stimuli, showing essentially similar results (Harris *et al.*, 1996).

   Using phallometric response as a classificatory condition, Blanchard and colleagues (Blanchard *et al.*, 1999, 2008; Cantor *et al.*, 2005) have investigated the relationship of a number of variables, including IQ, to sexual preference. In their first study (Blanchard *et al.*, 1999) they found that men who committed offences against younger children and male children had a significantly lower average IQ than those who committed offences against adults. While the average IQ of men who had offended against children was well in excess of the ID range, it was of interest that it was significantly lower. In a subsequent study of 454 men who had been accepted for clinical assessment for a variety of sexual offences, Cantor *et al.* (2005) assessed variables including number of victims, age of victims, number of consenting adult sexual partners and phallometric test results. Lower IQ scores were associated with a greater number of child victims while higher IQ scores were associated with a greater number of consenting, adult sexual relationships. A similar pattern was found for phallometric responses with lower IQ scores associated with greater responses to children and higher IQ associated with responses to adult stimuli. The mean IQ of the group showing responses to children was 89.5 which, again, is well in excess of the ID range. However, it was around 10 IQ points lower than the 'adult-oriented' group whose mean IQ was around average at 97.8. In a subsequent meta-analysis of 3187 offenders against children,

302 offenders against adults and 16 222 men convicted of non-sexual crimes, Cantor *et al.* (2005) found that offenders against children had significantly lower IQs than non-sexual offenders while sexual offenders against adults had an intermediate mean IQ. They also found a higher rate of non-right-handedness in paedophilic men which was nearly three times that of the other groups in the study.

One criticism of these studies is that they may be subject to referral bias. Green, Gray and Willner (2002) investigated the referral patterns of sex offenders with ID and found that those who committed more serious offences and offences against children were more likely to be referred to the judicial system. Those individuals who had committed less serious offences against adults were more likely to be diverted from the system. Therefore, they felt that there may be a systematic bias increasing the proportion of offenders with ID who had committed incidents against children when investigators review those going through the criminal justice system. In addition, agencies and carers working with individuals with ID are more likely to become concerned if the individual they are supervising shows a sexual preference towards children. Again, this might result in a disproportionate number of individuals being referred to treatment agencies who have not committed serious offences but have shown a sexual interest in children. In this way, the results found by Blanchard and colleagues on people referred either to treatment services or the criminal justice system may be biased. Their results may reflect this systemic referral difficulty.

Blanchard *et al.* (2008) investigated 832 adult male patients referred to their clinic for the evaluation of sexuality. They also investigated referral source in an attempt to address the issue of systemic bias. Specifically, their study was designed to review the relationships between IQ, handedness and erotic age preference. Overall, the study found that those men diagnosed as paedophilic had an average IQ of 90.75, the hebephilic (preference for pubescent males or females) group had an average IQ of 97.72 and the teleiophilic (preference for adult males or females) had an average IQ of 100.1. The 10-point difference in men with preferences for children is significant but considerably in excess of the ID range. However, the authors found similar results from homogeneous and heterogeneous referral sources and concluded that the difference was unlikely to be due to referral bias. As mentioned in Chapter 2, Cantor *et al.* (2005) hypothesised that 'a third variable – a perturbation of pre-natal or childhood brain development – produces both paedophilia and low IQ' (p. 565). It is reasonably well established that ID and non-right-handedness are significantly associated (Grouio *et al.*, 1999) but these various studies simply alert us to the fact that sexual preference is likely to be an important consideration in assessment and treatment for sex offenders with ID. The proportion of variance in the Blanchard studies is not large and they themselves acknowledge that psychosocial influences are likely to be important in any consideration of the aetiology of sex offences. However, these studies do provide the evidence that sexual preference is an important consideration for aetiology and treatment. It corresponds precisely with the sexual arousal factor in the Hall and Hirschman (1992) Quadripartite Model and it is likely to be a significant factor in the development of incidents in at least some sex offenders with ID.

Personality

With mainstream offenders, there is no doubt that clinical measures of antisociality are highly associated with offending and sexual offending. Hall and Hirschman (1992) hypothesised that personality problems were likely to be a primary factor in the development of sexual offences. They included traits emerging from adverse developmental experiences and an antisocial lifestyle. Harris *et al.* (2003) found that assessment of antisociality (the Psychopathy Checklist – Revised (PCL-R), Hare, 1991) in addition to phallometric measures was highly predictive of sexual recidivism. A number of risk assessments which incorporate personality disorder measures and evaluations of antisociality have found to be as predictive of future violent offences in offenders with ID as in mainstream offenders (Harris and Tough, 2004; Quinsey, Book and Skilling, 2004; Lindsay *et al.*, 2008b). In a higher order analysis of personality disorder diagnoses Lindsay *et al.* (2007c) found results consistent with studies on mainstream offender (Blackburn *et al.*, 2005) and non-offender (Morey, 1988). Morrissey *et al.* (2005, 2007a, b) found that the PCL-R scores were significantly associated with level of security and inversely associated with treatment progress in offenders with ID. Therefore, it is likely that personality correlates are an important factor in assessment and treatment of sex offenders in that significant antisociality may be associated with higher doses of treatment. In addition, although personality disorder is considered to be a relatively stable feature, Lindsay (2007) in a consideration of personality disorder classification has advised that any diagnosis in this client group should be provisional with reassessment conducted at least 1 year later in order to review stability.

Impulsiveness has often been considered to be an important personality variable which is significantly featured in sexual offenders (Hanson and Harris, 2000). Glaser and Deane (1999) in a study of sexual and non-sexual offenders with ID, concluded that impulsiveness was the most significant feature for both groups. Parry and Lindsay (2003) in a systematic comparison of sex offenders and non-sexual offenders found that sex offenders reported lower levels of impulsiveness. They suggested that impulsivity may be a significant factor when it is a feature of the individual and earlier (Chapter 2) these data were examined in more detail making the distinction between impulsivity and opportunism. Therefore, this personality feature remains an important consideration in assessment, treatment and supervision.

Psychological/Developmental Factors

This large group of aetiological factors has been implicated repeatedly in the aetiology of sex offences by a variety of researchers and theorists. All the theoretical models outlined in the previous chapter feature developmental factors prominently. Even the Blanchard group who have investigated the significant relationship between neurodevelopmental factors and sexual preference (Blanchard *et al.*, 1999, 2008; Cantor *et al.*, 2005) recognise that their neurodevelopmental explanations will not be sufficient to account for sexual offences. Disruptions to developmental attachments through childhood abuse, difficulties in relation to social comparison and stigma, developmental problems associated with negative social comparison and difficulties with peer relationships and systemic obstacles in the development of relationship skills all feature in developmental studies of populations with ID. As we have seen in the previous chapter, all of the developmental disruptions hypothesised as important in the aetiology of sexual offending have been found in people with ID. Clearly, the majority of this population does not develop problems with offending or sexual offending. However, if these factors are present to operate in conjunction with personality difficulties and problems with sexual preference then they may indeed exceed a certain threshold for committing inappropriate sexual behaviour in the manner hypothesised by Hall (1996). A further piece of evidence attesting to the importance of these variables is that, in the same way as they are predictive in mainstream offender studies, developmental variables have been found to predict recidivism in sex offenders with ID. Lindsay, Elliot and Astell (2004) found that attachment disruption, low self-esteem and lack of assertiveness contributed significantly to their Regression Model in the prediction of sex offence recidivism. Therefore, developmental variables are an important factor in the aetiology of sexual offences in this client group.

While major, prolonged developmental experiences do feature as important psychological predictors, studies of mental illness diagnosis and emotional disturbance have not reported higher levels in groups of sex offenders with ID. Lindsay *et al.* (2004b, 2006c) found that the levels of major mental illness recorded in groups of sex offenders were essentially similar to that found in other types of male offenders with ID at around 30%. This figure was exactly the same as the percentage reported by Day (1994) in his study of a group of sex offenders with ID. Lindsay and Lees (2003) and Lindsay and Skene (2007) found that sex offenders reported lower levels of anxiety and depression when compared to other groups. Therefore, while significant developmental factors do appear related to sex offenders with ID in general, a diagnosis of mental illness or emotional disregulation appears less explanatory in terms of aetiology.

Counterfeit Deviance

In my earlier consideration of this model (Lindsay, 2005) I was lukewarm about the explanatory power of counterfeit deviance in the aetiology of sexual offences. However, subsequent research has prompted a revision of this position. Firstly, Hingsburger, Griffiths and Quinsey (1991) themselves differentiated between different types of paraphilia. They acknowledged that a small percentage of individuals with ID become sexually aroused in ways that are offensive or dangerous. Therefore, while the Counterfeit Deviance Hypothesis accounts for a range of pathways into sexual offending which do not indicate aberrant sexual preferences, these authors clearly acknowledged the importance of sexual preference in some individuals. Lunsky *et al.* (2007) found that 'inappropriate' offenders had lower sexual knowledge than 'persistent, forceful' offenders and concluded that the Counterfeit Deviance Hypothesis was more likely to pertain to the former.

The Ward and Hudson (1998) Pathways Model has been particularly fruitful with regard to studies on offenders with ID. Keeling and Rose (2005) made specific hypotheses about the pathways likely to feature in this group. Since the population is characterised by low self-esteem, low self-worth, unassertiveness and poor problem-solving skills, they concluded that sex offenders with ID would be more likely to be aligned with passive, automatic styles of self-regulation and less likely to engage in conscious, explicit planning. They felt that avoidant/passive or approach/automatic pathways would feature most prominently. However, three studies based on these hypotheses (Keeling, Rose and Beech, 2006; Langdon, Maxted and Murphy, 2007; Lindsay, Steptoe and Beech, 2008) all found that sex offenders with ID tended to use approach pathways with equal numbers distributed between active and passive self-regulation strategies. This has a number of implications which endorse a revision of the Counterfeit Deviance Hypothesis.

Firstly, the fact that the majority of these men are assessed as employing approach goals suggests that there are very few who actively attempt to inhibit their sexual desires. This in turn suggests that few have a significant awareness of *the extent* to which these acts are socially unacceptable. If one considers that sexual preference and adverse developmental experiences may lead these men into a preference for coping in this way, then a reduced understanding of the extent to which it is inappropriate will reduce their wish to avoid offending. Secondly, Hudson and Ward (2000) hypothesised that approach/explicit offenders would have a higher rate of re-offending. In their study, Lindsay, Steptoe and Beech (2008) found the opposite with approach/explicit offenders having a significantly lower rate of re-offending following treatment. This reinforces the conclusion that these men may have an insufficient understanding of how inappropriate their behaviour is. One function of treatment is to reinforce the extent to which it is condemned by society. Once this realisation has been achieved, stronger self-regulation strategies can be reinforced. Therefore, while these individuals are not completely naive about the fact that their behaviour is inappropriate, they have not internalised the extent to which it is against the conventions of society. They have not previously appreciated the critical requirement for self-control in relation to sexual preference and the need to develop alternative relationship skills. In this way, the Counterfeit Deviance Hypothesis is revised to consider that these men realise that their behaviour is unacceptable but do not appreciate the extent to which it contravenes the conventions of society.

The Threat Threshold

Hall and Hirschman (1992) and Hall (1996) employed the concept of a threat threshold in their Quadripartite Model. If the external threat is seen as low, then the primary factors in their model may be sufficiently activated for the individual to make an appraisal that a sex offence is worth the risk. Alternatively, if the primary factors are activated strongly, they may exceed the perceived level of threat, again resulting in a sexual offence. Given the research cited above, the concept of a threat threshold seems particularly apposite in relation to offenders with ID. If a man has not fully appreciated the extent to which inappropriate sexual behaviour is condemned, then the threat threshold is likely to be lowered. In circumstances where developmental disturbances have been high and they are combined with a degree of sexual drive, then they may easily exceed lowered threat thresholds resulting in high rates of incidence. The severe criticism and sanctions meted out by carers and family may serve simply to mask an understanding of the wider views of society. It is also the case that the individuals themselves may be quite used to excessive criticism, and sanctions for a range of aberrant sexual behaviours are given the same status as other less important maladaptive interactions. One series of studies reinforces this interpretation. Rose *et al.* (2002, 2007) have demonstrated that following sex offender treatment there is a significant change in participants' perception of external locus of control which increased in both studies. Participants were more likely to understand that the agencies of society, for example police, courts and so on, were a significant factor in the control of the behaviour of citizens. Therefore, participants gain a greater understanding of the extent to which these agencies will condemn and control their behaviour. Therefore, the importance of self-regulation strategies is emphasised.

Accurate perception of the threat threshold will promote self-regulation strategies for behavioural scripts and cognitive self-schemata which may have developed through adverse developmental experiences or personality difficulties. These more effective self-regulation strategies will replace any poor problem-solving skills that may have featured previously in the individual and will certainly address any issues of inappropriate sexual preference. Therefore, these various factors combine in sex offenders with ID to account for the aetiology of sexual offending and the differential results on recidivism found in various studies and different offender groups.

Conclusions on Motivation for Inappropriate Sexual Behaviour

In terms of the aetiology of sexual offences, this model has found support for inappropriate sexual preference in the studies of Blanchard and colleagues. There is massive support for the disruption of developmental experiences in a range of studies. However, it is clear that while these developmental disruptions are relevant across the whole field of ID, only a small proportion commits inappropriate sexual behaviour. In studies of the developmental disruption which might seem most significant, that of childhood sexual abuse, it remains the case that most sex offenders with ID (around 60%) do not report sexual abuse in their childhood. Therefore, while developmental disruption is an important factor, it cannot be considered to be the major feature. Clearly it will operate in conjunction with the other factors. Current mental illness and emotional disregulation may be important in individual cases, but when one compares sex offenders to other client groups, they do not show a greater preponderance of these factors. Some studies have suggested that sex offenders as a group have better emotional regulation than other groups. Therefore, they cannot be considered primary factors in the development of sexual offences across cases. Personality factors appear to predict treatment progress and levels of security. Personality disorder characteristics also seem to feature in offenders with ID in ways similar to that of mainstream offenders. They may indeed be important when developing a treatment programme. If therapists can promote greater sociability and lower antisociality in offenders, then they are more likely to be compliant with their treatment regime and be accessible to treatment concepts. A revised formulation of the Counterfeit Deviance Hypothesis would suggest that offenders with ID do not appreciate fully the extent to which society condemns inappropriate sexual behaviour. By reinforcing this message and promoting a greater sense of external locus of control offenders are more likely to identify more accurately the level of threat which their behaviour will present. Finally, all of these factors contribute to the relationship between an individual's needs, their behavioural scripts, their cognitive schemata in relation to sexuality and, in particular, their cognitive schema regarding the level of threat which will be triggered by their behaviour and imposed by society.

Theories of Criminality, Quality of Life and Community Engagement in Sex Offenders with ID

Identification and engagement with the community and values of society have long been core concepts in sociological theories of criminality. Several authors have explored the mechanisms for the development of engagement in society showing that the disruption of developmental relationships or certain maladaptive patterns of family interaction are instrumental in promoting disengagement with society's values. Patterson and colleagues (Patterson, 1986; Patterson, Reid and Dischion, 1992) produced a major developmental model explaining the onset of delinquency and criminal behaviour. In an extensive series of studies based on learning and reinforcement theories, they found that from as early as 18 months, some families may promote a child's coercive behaviour such as tempter tantrums and hitting because those behaviours have functional value in terminating conflict. With repeated transactions and interactions, these behaviours are strengthened and firmly established. In other families, children learn interactions that are quite distinct from those learned in distressed families. In non-distressed families, in which pro-social behaviours are reinforced, the child learns that interaction such as talking and negotiating are followed by a termination of conflict. In distressed families, not only are coercive behaviours promoted, pro-social behaviours may not be particularly effective in terminating family conflict (Snyder and Patterson, 1995). Therefore, as these boys develop, they fail to learn pro-social behaviours, problem solving and language skills but become highly skilled in antisocial behaviours. Through major parenting processes such as discipline, positive parenting, monitoring and problem solving, coercive and pro-social skills emerge in children. In distressed family interactions, parental discipline reinforces coercive child behaviour, pro-social interpersonal academic and work skills are encouraged less and deviant problem solving is inadvertently taught which leads to the development of coercive, antisocial problem-solving styles in the termination of interpersonal conflict. In this way, world views, cognitive schemata and styles of engagement with society and the community are developed through repeated forms of family interaction.

In a separate series of studies, Farrington (1995, 2005) has found that delinquency in early adolescence is significantly associated with troublesome behaviour at 8–10 years, an uncooperative family at 8 years, poor housing at 8–10 years, poor parental behaviour at 8 years and low IQ at 8–10 years. Therefore, already at the age of 10 years, delinquent behaviour is associated with uncooperative families, poor housing and poor parental behaviour. These adverse developmental experiences continue to exert an influence on delinquent and criminal behaviour throughout teenage years and young adulthood. Farrington's studies of crime and deviancy in later years revealed that the best predictors were invariably previous convictions from 10 to 13 years. Adult criminal convictions at 21–24 years were best predicted by convictions in previous age ranges. An unstable job record, low family income, a hostile attitude towards police at the age of 14 also made additional predictive contributions to the probability of an adult criminal career. Importantly, the higher number of risk domains (e.g. uncooperative family, childhood behaviour, poor engagement with schooling) the higher probability of later delinquency and criminality (Stouthamer *et al.*, 2002). These are variables which have been implicated in the theoretical models outlined in the previous chapter and are clearly relevant to offenders with ID. The significant point is that, as with the studies by Patterson and colleagues, these studies establish a hypothesis concerning the relationship between developmental experiences, influence, societal and environmental factors and criminality.

As indicated at the beginning of the previous chapter, Cohen (1955) hypothesised that boys began committing crime because they were identifying with a delinquent subculture and conforming to its expectations. This hypothesis suggested that boys from lower socio-economic groups were disadvantaged in fulfilling their human needs and gaining human goods (using the terminology of Good Lives Model (GLM) and the Reiss Model) because they had not learned the skills of less disadvantaged boys. The model of family interactions forwarded by Patterson and colleagues illustrates the mechanisms in which these skills are developed or fail to develop. Therefore, these boys adopt illegal means to achieve their goals which are in turn consistent with the delinquent subculture. However, Cohen's (1955) hypothesis was criticised with the view that delinquency and crime were a result of lack of commitment to the conventions of society rather than a disparity between middle class aspirations and perceived personal potential. This lack of commitment would have the result that delinquent individuals would no longer have aspirations to fulfil human needs in ways valued by society.

These hypotheses concerning the general disillusionment with society and low personal aspirations among those who have become delinquent (Gibbons and Krohn, 1986) were combined with other emerging findings to create important theories of criminality. The established relationship between lower socio-economic status and higher rates of crime encouraged the development of sociological theories to explain this link. Control Theory (Hirschi, 1969) paid attention to both the positive learning of criminal behaviours through association with criminal subcultures, and also the development of self-control through appropriate social learning and the adoption of law abiding routines and cognitive schemata. Hirschi felt that the success of social learning was dependent on four factors: attachment, commitment, involvement and belief. Attachment referred to the extent to which the individual identified with the expectations and values of others within society such as teachers and parents. Commitment invokes a rational element in criminality. Individuals make subjective evaluations about the loss that they will experience following arrest and conviction. Involvement refers to the fact that many individuals are engaged in ordinary activities such as work, education and other occupational activities and have little opportunity to consider delinquency. The less involved individuals are with the day-to-day activities of society, the more likely they are to engage in criminal activity. Belief referred to the extent to which individuals accepted the laws of society as a reasonable framework for community cohesion.

There is a wealth of evidence consistent with this hypothesis. This evidence shows that negative attitudes to schoolwork and authority are indeed associated with delinquent and antisocial activity (Elliot, Huizinga and Ageton, 1985). This suggests that the disruption of attachments between children and authority figures such as parents and teachers, results in a failure to internalise parental values and promote social conformity. Schuerman and Kobran (1986) found that within any particular urban area, an increase in the long term unemployed population who are no longer seeking employment and a corresponding decrease in semi and unskilled job holders, was a major factor in the increase of crime in the area. Patterson and his colleagues (Patterson and Yoerger, 1997) provided a more subtle analysis of attachment in that they demonstrated that dysfunctional attachment rather than lack of attachment will promote criminal activity whereas functional attachment promotes engagement with social conventions and laws.

Community engagement and engagement with society is a core concept in the literature on IDs. As seen in the previous chapter, a number of researchers have found that there is a clear tendency to stigmatise and exclude such individuals. Negative social comparison in people with ID is a reasonably well-established concept for a proportion of the population. Therefore identification and engagement may, at the very least be disrupted in a proportion of individuals and at worst become completely undermined. There are a number of influential researchers in the field of ID who have developed models for community integration which have specific relevance to Control Theory and community identification for individuals with ID.

Control Theory and Offenders with ID

Control Theory provides a robust set of concepts into which we can place research on sex offenders with ID and which allows a consideration of the way in which community engagement, quality of life and identification with societal values may be disrupted.

Attachment. For Hirschi, attachment represents the extent to which individuals identify with the expectations and values of others within society, such as parents and teachers. The previous chapter has reviewed ways in which these attachments may be disrupted in sex offenders with ID. The development of attachment styles is a prominent feature for many theorists and for most of the variables (such as childhood abuse) the results on offenders with ID are consistent with the mainstream population.

The literature on stigma and negative social comparison only services to reinforce the importance of these phenomena in this client group.

One of the main variables cited in both the Integrated Theory and the Quadripartite Theory is that of isolation. Lack of interpersonal skills through adolescence and young adulthood may result in some men avoiding social situations and increasing their personal isolation. Lengthy periods of time alone may allow the individuals to foster deviant sexual fantasies and maladaptive sexual schemata which increase the possibility of a sexual offence. With repeated, ordinary social contact, any propensity to develop these maladaptive sexual schemata will be hampered by constant pro-social influences which constitute repeated 'reality checks'. These are not major significant events but rather, constitute mundane and ordinary social contact. Even with greater periods of isolation, developing males will continue to strive to fulfil basic human needs. Therefore, as Switzky (2001) and Reiss (2001) have made clear, they are likely to fulfil these basic needs in maladaptive, antisocial or asocial ways. Garlick, Marshall and Thornton (1996) in a study of mainstream offenders, found loneliness to be a feature prior to incidents of inappropriate or violent sexual behaviour.

One study on offenders with ID is particularly relevant to this hypothesis. Steptoe *et al.* (2006) reported some interesting findings when they compared a group of 28 sex offenders with ID and 28 members of a control group. They used a measure of quality of life (QOL) (Life Experience Checklist (LEC); Ager, 1990) and a measure of significant relationships (the Significant Other Scale; Power, Champion and Aris, 1988) to assess relationships, QOL and community engagement in these groups. They found that although the sex offender group participants reported the same opportunities as other participants, they seemed to choose to take advantage of these opportunities less often than the control participants. Their scores on the LEC scales of opportunities, leisure and relationships were consistent with the control group but they reported less engagement with these opportunities. This suggested a higher level of isolation in this client group. In addition, they appeared to have more impoverished relationships than the control group as measured by the Significant Other Scale but reported being quite content with this more restricted range of relationships. This led to the conclusion that while sex offenders might appear lonelier and more isolated than other groups of individuals with ID, this may reflect a more self-contained way of life. Therefore they are fulfilling human needs in a more self-contained, relatively independent manner.

Further evidence for the maintenance of subjective well-being in the face of developmental and environmental adversity is provided in the writing of Cummins and colleagues (Cummins and Lau, 2003a,b). In their studies, these authors have found that people strive for an optimum level of subjective well-being (SWB). Significant life events, both positive and negative, may have an impact on SWB but a variety of human functions will operate to adjust to adverse (or positive) circumstances to create a homeostasis in maintaining SWB. Cummins and Lau (2004) draw on a wealth of research which supports this phenomenon. The basis for their research is the field of ID and they note that improvements in QOL resulting in moves from institutions to community homes are likely to produce increases in SWB in the short term. However, over longer periods of months, individuals adapt to their new circumstances and their levels of SWB revert to the homeostatic norm which is around the 70–80% level of any scale ranging from 0 to 100. A similar phenomenon is seen when external conditions provide more impoverished circumstances. As long as conditions are not so bad as to provide homeostatic defeat, then SWB will revert to this optimum level of 70–80% of the scale. This is convincing evidence, coming from an authority in the area of QOL and ID, supporting the notion that men with ID can quite quickly adapt to circumstances of isolation which in turn can interact with other variables and inappropriate sexual drive and maladaptive developmental experiences to fulfil human needs and allow the emergence of maladaptive sexual schemata. Therefore, disruptions to attachment to society are unlikely to reduce subjective well-being.

Commitment. As I have mentioned, commitment refers to the rational aspect of individual appraisal in relation to the loss they will experience if they are arrested and convicted of particular acts. This has specific links to the concept of a threat threshold which I have taken from the Quadripartite Model and employed extensively in the previous section of the current model. A distorted perception of the importance of society's laws or a lack of commitment to their relevance will contribute to the perpetration of sexual offence. The concept of commitment also refers to the predicted personal loss that may be experienced. When people live in relatively impoverished circumstances with fewer interpersonal resources, the loss may be considered correspondingly lower.

Involvement. Involvement with society is one component of control theory which has attracted a great deal of empirical support. Increased unemployment and lack of commitment in relationships are repeatedly associated with increases in criminal behaviour. Unfortunately, they are also implicated as a specific feature of the population of people with ID. There is an extensive literature on supported employment, the reason for which is that people with ID tend to have lower rates of employment, increased levels of social deprivation and greater disengagement with the general aspects of society (Emerson, 2007). While, for the vast majority of individuals with ID, these obstacles to involvement do not produce antisocial and criminal behaviour, when lack of engagement is allied to other factors such as sexual drive, lowered threat threshold, developmental disruption, poor relationship skills and so on, it is likely to become an even more important factor. It is clear to me that at a very simple level, people will do things during the day. If they are not engaged in pro-social activities, then they may well engage in antisocial activities. It is one of the simple, fundamental principles on which our own community forensic service is based. We strive to provide people with things to do and encouragement to engage. These may be supported occupation, day service activities, educational placements and other pro-social activities.

Belief. Control Theory suggests that most individuals accept that the laws of society are a reasonable framework for community cohesion. Therefore, we are willing to abide by these laws in order that society will function. One further aspect of the Cummins and Lau (2003a,b) model provides a mechanism by which it is possible for men to detach themselves from such belief. In order to maintain SWB, we all employ a cognitive buffering system. This system includes perceived personal control, maintenance of self-esteem and optimism. These concepts represent a set of cognitive schemata which enable the individual to adjust to developmental experiences and environmental circumstances in order to maintain SWB. Maladaptive adjustments through this buffering system for sex offenders with ID may occur irrespective of the laws of society and lower the individual's belief in the conventions of society in order to maintain SWB in the face of environmental and developmental experiences. This, in turn, will have an effect on their perception of the threat threshold in the context of the perpetration of sexual offence. In this way, a range of concepts relevant to people with ID will have a specific impact on the behavioural routines, cognitive scripts and cognitive schemata of sex offenders with ID in relation to their interpersonal interactions and, ultimately, inappropriate sexual behaviour.

Community Engagement and Quality of Life

Control Theory suggests that we should promote methods that will increase attachment, commitment and engagement to society and its social values as a major strand for treatment for all offenders including sex offenders. Therefore it is not only important to investigate strategies for self-restraint and promote extensive techniques for self-control and cognitive restructuring at crucial points in the offence cycle, it is also important to promote greater commitment and engagement in society. In the field of IDs, this is common practice. There is a wealth of literature on the provision of accommodation with varying levels of support, the development of leisure opportunities and the organisation of supported employment for this client group. We should take advantage of this favourable position of being able to focus on societal engagement as a specific theoretical and practical method for the treatment of sex offenders. Because these practices are so widespread with this client group, this approach has been used frequently. However, until the Lindsay (2005) paper, its theoretical importance had never been elucidated explicitly. It is also clear that the theoretical importance of human values and QOL has been made explicit for mainstream sex offenders in the form of the GLM. QOL of Offenders should become a central issue in treatment. If the individual has, for example, an impoverished QOL, with low levels of personal relationships, lack of pro-social influences, poor community integration, and impoverished housing, then would predict, on the basis of this theoretical model, that it would increase the likelihood of sex offending and recidivism. All of these factors will allow disengagement from society, lack of commitment to society and a lowering of the level of belief in society's conventions and laws. Correspondingly, cognitive buffers which maintain homeostasis in relation to SWB will promote alternative, possibly maladaptive cognitive schemata and sexual fantasies which will accommodate sexual drive and adverse developmental experiences.

One further important ramification of this analysis is that placing people in secure accommodation, away from society is precisely the wrong thing to do and will simply encourage disengagement and lack of commitment in society's mores, functioning and activities. Institutions develop idiosyncratic cultures and are likely to become more divorced from the day-to-day values and conventions of society. Therefore, in the spirit of the Counterfeit Deviance Hypothesis, they are less likely to promote behavioural, relationship and cognitive skills which will adapt to the community. Unfortunately, such a course of action is increasingly seen in services where individuals with forensic difficulties are sent to secure institutions. Although such therapeutic solutions might be useful for the self-restraint aspects of treatment, segregation is the antithesis of the social engagement/QOL component of this treatment model. For a relatively small number of individuals, this may be the only solution. Their offending may be of such a serious, persistent and driven nature that the prospect of societal integration cannot be envisaged. However, the revised treatment model proposed in this chapter would state that we should be aware of the explicit anti-therapeutic nature of such placements as a management solution.

A further practical consequence of this model for treatment is that QOL becomes an important consideration for the effective treatment of sex offenders with ID. QOL should not be considered in terms of physical and material surroundings only (although these are undoubtedly important, Emerson and Hatton, 1994) but, in terms of pro-social influences and community integration. Community integration, perception of community connectedness and SWB are also important in the assessment and treatment of sex offenders with ID. The main self-perception variables for offenders with ID are related to friendship, engagement with occupational and leisure activities, a sense of being part of a community in which the individual is valued and the maintenance of constant opportunities for ordinary pro-social influences. Correspondingly, that community should be a normal part of society with its shared social values.

The fact that there can be homeostatic defeat in SWB is an important treatment consideration for sex offenders with ID. Cummins and Lau (2004) have written that when external events cause a failure in homeostasis with a significant reduction in SWB, the various cognitive buffers will adapt to allow the person to move towards the maintenance of an optimum level of SWB. When a sex offender is apprehended by the police and is introduced into the criminal justice system, it is my experience that the SWB undergoes catastrophic failure. In almost every assessment I conduct on sex offenders, if I complete the Brief Symptom Inventory, they report elevated levels of depression. Invariably the interviewee will relate these negative feelings to the criminal justice procedures. This is an opportunity for treatment. I make extensive notes at these points so that I can re-invoke the feelings of homeostatic failure in subsequent treatment sessions. This provides another factor which can motivate the individual to maintain an offence-free lifestyle, thus avoiding a recurrence of these reductions in SWB. It is important to keep references which are as graphic as possible to aid the individual's memory. The research of Cummins and Lau (2003a,b) confirms that individuals will employ a range of psychological processes to resurrect and maintain homeostasis in SWB. In other words, they will forget how bad they felt and the effect the process had on their feelings of well-being. A further implication of this research is that it is important, if possible, to take advantage of the criminal justice process. Firstly, it reinforces the reality of the threat threshold and the extent to which society condemns sexual offences. Secondly, it provides the opportunity to take advantage of homeostatic defeat as a future motivational factor.

As we have seen in Chapter 3, research employing comprehensive treatments that have included attention to QOL have, incidentally, reported good outcomes. Griffiths, Quinsey and Hingsburger (1989) and Haaven, Little and Petre-Miller (1990) reported comprehensive treatments with no re-offending. In our own reports which included cognitive behaviour therapy for sexual offending issues in addition to occupational and educational placements (Lindsay *et al.*, 2002, 2004b, 2006c) we have reported significant reductions in the rate of offending when comparing pre and post-treatment periods. Sturmey (2004, 2006) has written that non-specific aspects from these procedures might account for the reduction in recidivism. The current model suggests that the organisation of occupational and educational placements is specific to therapeutic techniques from which one would theoretically expect therapeutic gains through the mechanisms of commitment to and engagement with society.

Conclusion

I have linked theories of sex offending in mainstream work to a comprehensive model which includes motivational factors in the aetiology of sexual offending and wider psychological and sociological factors which will affect the individual's engagement with society. The model draws on research on sex offenders with ID, research on sex offenders in general and previous theories of sexual offending. It recognises the importance of sexual drive and inappropriate sexual offending on the basis of large-scale research studies and the employment of this concept in the Quadripartite Model. I have addressed adverse developmental experiences which are central concepts in the Precondition Model, Quadripartite Model and Integrated Theory and which have an extensive research base in the field of ID. I have employed the concept of the threat threshold, forwarded in the Quadripartite Model and specifically supported by research in ID, the Counterfeit Deviance Hypothesis, control theory, and research on subjective social well-being incorporating homeostatic defeat. Personality factors, cited in the Quadripartite Model, have been shown to be as important in the field of ID as they have in mainstream offenders. External and internal inhibitors (Precondition Model) are clearly important in sex offenders with ID and specifically relevant to the threat threshold. Emotional regulation and impulsivity have also been found to be salient in this group although, in relation to isolation, cognitive buffers interact with these aspects to promote social well-being through the possible triggering of sexual fantasies and maladaptive sexual schemata. It is important to address all of these aspects during treatment for sex offenders with ID and methods to address these issues form the subject of the following chapters.

Addressing these specific offence related issues is one main arm of treatment. Treatment should also address the way in which sex offenders engage with society this will involve attempts to make an impact on personal living circumstances and QOL. I have demonstrated the way in which identification and engagement with society is a crucial aspect of treatment and the way in which sex offenders evaluate their relationships and QOL should constitute the other major strand of treatment. Therefore, we should promote occupation, education and leisure activities. This is far from an easy task, requiring the organisation of these activities so that individuals can have a group of friends and acquaintances whose values will continually impinge on their own. Not only will this provide specific benefits in terms of engagement to society but also, direct links to gains in personal life can be made during psychological treatment sessions. If we can encourage clients to strive to maintain relationships, interests and so on, it is possible to use this reference as an incentive to the promotion of techniques of self-restraint, altering cognitive distortions, identifying important points in the offence cycle and so on. In this way, these twin theoretical foundations of treatment are clearly linked in practice. On the one hand, changes in sexual and social behaviour improve QOL and engagement while, on the other, the maintenance of a better life can be used as motivation to reflect on the possibility of losing it if the person offends again. These concepts are fairly simple in theory but in practice require a great deal of organisational effort across disciplines and systems.

The obvious crucial caveat to encouraging a commitment to society is that society itself must be protected by monitoring and management of sex offenders. Therefore, while we are considering the improved and increased engagement with society for our clients, we must always bear in mind the risks inherent in each situation. These risks must be managed and reduced through external controls and monitoring and the promotion of self-restraint and self-regulation in the man himself. These considerations are not confined to sex offenders with ID. They are also paramount in work with mainstream sex offenders and GLM (Lindsay, Ward and Morgan, 2005; Chapter 18). The complex balance between encouraging individual self-restraint and allowing individual human rights while protecting the safety of others is one that is familiar to all who work with sex offenders. At all times, considerations of safety, appropriate supervision and adequate monitoring should be held alongside efforts to promote identification with society.

Part Two

Treatment Considerations

Chapter 7

Introduction to the Treatment Programme

This programme has been developed over the years according to the various principles outlined in the introductory chapters. These principles and the research which has contributed to them or is derived from them are crucial to the development of this programme and to the continued effectiveness of any treatment programme. Some of the underpinning principles have already been discussed extensively in the introductory chapters; others, for example the central importance of motivation, will be discussed and illustrated with reference to their relevance in this programme and they are listed below:

- Cycles of offending.
- Pathways to offending.
- Approaches developed through cognitive therapy.
- The importance of motivation.
- Perspective taking and victim empathy.
- Self-regulation and self-restraint.
- Relapse prevention.
- The Good Lives Model and Quality of Life.

The principles remain the same although the methods vary considerably adapted to suit the client group. This programme has been developed for implementation in a community setting. Therefore, it is designed to enable the clinical team to implement it in circumstances where there is likely to be a higher rate of referrals of sexual offenders and sexual abusers. However, I have also adapted it easily for use in maximum security settings and the programme is sufficiently flexible to be used across a variety of situations. It has been validated by an external agency for use in the State Hospital. Therefore, it is designed to be applicable across a range of settings.

The Treatment of Sex Offenders with Developmental Disabilities William Lindsay
© 2009 John Wiley & Sons, Ltd

Getting Started

In my experience, getting started is often one of the most difficult stages for any group of facilitators embarking on the delivery of a treatment programme. There are often a series of doubts on whether the individuals selected are appropriate for group treatment, whether or not the individuals chosen will work together as a group and, perhaps most importantly, doubts about whether 'we' as facilitators have sufficient skill and knowledge to conduct the programme. Two things are essential before beginning. The first is that facilitators should have a good knowledge of sex offender treatment and its applications with men with ID. The information is available through books and articles in academic journals and the chapters of this book pull together the available literature, incorporating it into treatment methods.

The second is to have at least one individual in the treatment team who is very familiar with people with ID. It will become clear throughout this volume that language and concepts must be simplified in order to ensure understanding and participation of group members. While, intuitively, this may seem a relatively easy skill, in my experience it is extremely difficult for facilitators who are used to expressing themselves in a 'normal' fashion to alter their use of language in order to make it more easily understood. Our interpersonal style comes to us so automatically that it is very difficult to make the appropriate adjustments and alterations. I have seen individuals with 20 years of experience who seem unable to ensure that they are understood. This is a crucial prerequisite because there is no point in implementing a treatment programme if the group members find it difficult to participate for reasons of communication.

It is difficult to monitor constantly your own utterances – but that is important. It becomes second nature to avoid difficult words and to simplify concepts. It is important that facilitators try to guide the discussion and promote group cohesion rather than give an explanation of concepts by themselves. I have been invited to sit through treatment sessions where the facilitator gives a 5-minute explanation of certain concepts while writing key points on the flipchart. It seems clear that few group members will understand what is being explained and, since few will be able to read, they are unlikely to recognise or remember the five or six key points. Afterwards, my natural response (for me this is a common response) is to ask group members 'what was the last five minutes about' or 'can anybody tell me what the key points are'. Generally, only one or two participants can provide an answer. On one occasion, after I had attended a group which had been going for 2 years, I felt the need to ask, 'What is this group about?' Only two of eight participants could tell me that it was a sex offender group or that the material dealt with was related to sex offending. These illustrations underline the importance of communication. It is axiomatic that without effective, simple communication, group members will be unable to participate fully with the group process.

It is generally recommended that a sex offender group runs once or twice a week for 18 months to 2 years. Running sessions twice weekly will, obviously, considerably shorten the amount of time to complete the programme. In an early study (Lindsay and Smith, 1998), we compared those individuals who had been treated under a 1-year probation sentence to those individuals who had been treated under a 2- or

3-year probation sentence. Essentially, we were comparing those individuals treated for 1 year against those who had been treated for at least 2 years. Although the sample sizes were very small (seven in each group), those treated for 1 year showed significantly poorer progress on every measure both at the end of treatment and at 2-year follow-up. After this review and subsequent similar reviews, I came to the conclusion that treatment for 1 year was a waste of time. The reason for this is outlined in Lindsay *et al.* (1998b). It is quite common for participants to show a high level of treatment resistance in the first few weeks or months of treatment. This issue will be dealt with under motivation (Chapter 6). Therefore, the first 3 months of treatment may be taken up with dealing with resistance to treatment. There then might follow 5 or 6 months of good therapeutic contact in which one can deal with issues of disclosure and begin to review the cycle of abuse, cognitive distortions, and so on. However, by about 9 months treatment, the individual realises that as long as they attend the group, they will fulfil the conditions of their probation or contract and their motivation to engage with the process week by week can reduce correspondingly. As a result, the final 3 months may be lost because of a reduction in motivation to engage. Therefore, 1 year of treatment may represent 6 months of actual engagement with the treatment processes. Obviously, this would not happen with lengthier periods of treatment, which allows for a lengthier period of engagement with the treatment process. As we have also seen in the earlier chapters, the importance of a lengthy period emphasising issues of self-regulation and restraint is likely to be crucial in relation to the *counterfeit deviance hypothesis*.

Outline of Basic Methods

Simplification of communication

Although it has just been mentioned in the previous section, effective communication cannot be stressed enough. It is important to develop a habit of monitoring the communication within each group session. Therefore, facilitators should not only think about the message which they are trying to convey at any given moment but also monitor the way in which it is being conveyed. This dual process is not a natural process and therefore is not easy at the initial stages of treatment. However, it develops with practice.

As will be illustrated extensively later, one important way of promoting understanding is to facilitate the development of treatment concepts through group members' responses. This requires extensive reliance on Socratic methods which shall be explained later. It is not uncommon for one of the participants to use a relatively complex word. For example, 'We're just making justifications for our offences.' The facilitator could respond with a statement such as 'justification – that's a good word. Can anybody tell me what justification means?' After one or two individuals have defined *justification*, the facilitators could ask, 'So what is Brian meaning when he talks about justification for offences?' In this way, the word is defined, participation of other members is encouraged and the statement is used to discuss the importance of cognitive distortions in relation to sexual offending.

Ownership

One of the basic aims in a sex offender programme is to promote clear appropriate ownership and cohesion among group members. One way to promote this sense of ownership is to use the induction sessions at the very start of the group to encourage participants themselves to set rules, the modules and the agenda. Facilitators should also encourage the participants to do all of the recording for group sessions. In this way, they themselves can develop some sense of ownership over the group and it also gives a clear message that these sessions are somewhat different to other teaching or occupational sessions which they may have experienced previously. For example, sex education sessions tend to be more didactic in nature. Throughout this book you will see illustrations of the way participants have recorded group sessions. The example on Figure 7.1 shows the way in which participants have recorded group rules.

Group rules

There are a number of issues involved with this approach. The first one is that, because of the intellectual limitations of the participants, the rules should be extremely simple. Generally, I confine the principal rules to two – attendance and confidentiality.

Attendance. As we shall see in subsequent sections on motivation, it is extremely unusual for any participant to want to attend a sex offender's group. The reluctance to attend is normally unequivocal in that individuals will say quite explicitly that they are only here because they have been forced to come, they may say, 'I have come here this time but if I don't like it, I'm not coming back' or 'I have decided to come for a few sessions and then that's it.' This attitude should not be regarded as an obstacle to treatment but rather an asset. In the field of intellectual disability, we are so used to acquiescence that a strong resistance to attendance shows a healthy emotional response to the process. As facilitators, as soon as we have a strong emotional response, we can employ it over the course of treatment. In fact, as has been mentioned, treatment is likely to last for at least 2 years and so attendance is one of the non-negotiable rules. It may be that participants, at the outset, say they will not comply with this requirement for extended attendance. Facilitators should immediately embark upon an exploration of the benefits of attendance and the consequences of non-attendance. This discussion can be recorded by one of the group members on a flipchart by simply splitting the page into advantages of attendance and consequences of non-attendance. It is perfectly acceptable, indeed preferable, if these records are recorded through drawings rather than words. For example, the advantages might be maintaining home placement, maintaining a considerable degree of freedom in the community, being allowed continued attendance at clubs and being allowed continued attendance at occupational or educational placements. Consequences of non-attendance might include continued escorting at home and in the community, a return to court for non-compliance with conditions of probation, losing educational placements or even losing the domestic placement. Group members are likely to mention other personal advantages and consequences related to attendance. All of these can be recorded on the flipchart. In the end, the arguments will be organised

GROUP RULES

1. No talking about the group outside the group 4 WALLS
2. No bulling in till this person is finshing talking
3. No swerening in the group
4. KEEP going to ALL the groups on a Tuesday moring
5. No riseing you voice in the ~~group~~ group
6. NO HORSE PLAY NO TOUCHING OTHERS
7.

Figure 7.1 Example of group rules

in favour of attendance but the individual participant should be allowed to make his own decision. As with other exercises throughout this book, once the pro-social decision is made, facilitators should emphasise the extent to which the participant is making their own decision and praise and encouragement should be extended for making a socialised decision which is consistent with the expectations of society and the individual's personal community.

Confidentiality. Confidentiality is emphasised for two main reasons, the first of which is the normal requirement for confidentiality in any psychotherapeutic group. The second reason is, for me, as or more important. Over the last 20 years, attitudes towards inappropriate sexuality and sexual offending have become more censorious and hardened to the extent that vigilante activity is common. If anyone were to realise that a group of sex offenders were meeting in a specific building every (say) Monday afternoon, then the danger of a number of individuals gathering outside the building at that time for the purposes of vigilante activity would be considerable. It may be that a number of service users use the building for other reasons and it is likely that the vigilante activity would be extended to everyone since, obviously, no one knows what a sex offender 'looks like'. Indeed, vigilante activity is often so ill-informed that people may turn up on another day entirely showing verbal and physical violence towards service users and staff alike. Similarly, if one group member begins to talk about another group member outside of sessions, he may put that individual in danger. For these reasons, confidentiality is of the highest importance. All of this information should be presented to group members through Socratic methods. Some of them are likely to have had experience of vigilante activity already and will be quite willing to share their experiences with the group. In this way, the importance of confidentiality can be described by group members rather than facilitators. Group members can be more graphic, explicit and clearer in their mode of expression than facilitators can be in putting these messages across.

Individual groups may have further rules which they wish to incorporate into the induction sessions. I, myself, keep the rules to two main ones and perhaps another couple if absolutely required. Facilitators should guard against having too many rules such as no interrupting, no shouting, no swearing, no accusing other people, no fidgeting, no standing up, no arguing, and so on. While they do make it clear that appropriate, civil behaviour is required, too many rules can become confusing and might dilute the importance of the first two. It may be appropriate to include a rule concerning behaviour such as 'no swearing'. If there are specific issues which are important within any particular setting, then this should be incorporated into the group rules.

Generally, participants are fairly sensible with the rules and modules which they wish to establish or suggest. They will understand that dealing with sexuality is important; they can be led to the conclusion that understanding how the victim feels is important; thinking about sexuality is crucial; relationships, what led you into offending, how you are going to behave in the future and risky situations are all important. All of these can be accepted and will be included in the programme. However, it is possible that one member of the group might be quite outrageous to the rules he wishes to establish or the modules which he wishes to cover. It should be reflected to the group to show that they have the collective authority to establish a sensible agenda. If such an individual were to continue with an overbearing and bullying manner, trying to force other members to comply with outlandish suggestions, then the group leaders would have to intervene saying that they would not allow one individual to direct progress of principles of a group. This would certainly work against the principle of ownership but would be required in such an exceptional circumstance. In my experience, this has not happened to an extreme extent.

An issue which acts as something of a counterweight to the previous paragraphs is that I am not so naive as to think that participants do not see through this 'ownership' principle. They can clearly perceive that the setting characteristics mitigate against participant ownership. Group leaders have set the group up, they have directed the general topic for the group, they have an idea of the timescale, they have set a weekly time and place and they clearly have a prior knowledge of sex offender treatment principles in practice. All we are doing here is trying to promote some sense of control on behalf of the participants. In addition, facilitators should establish that the methods used will not be didactic, but rather will be Socratic. During these induction sessions, there may be clear statements from group members reflecting this effect such as

'How am I meant to know what the rules are, you should be making the rules.'
Or 'I don't know what we should be dealing with in this group, you tell me.'

An example of group rules developed by participants can be seen in Figure 7.1. This example, as are all the examples in this book, is a reduced photocopy of a flipchart sheet completed by participants during the induction phase. The figure demonstrates that recording is done with both words and pictures. The drawings help those individuals with no reading skills to contribute to and understand the requirements of group membership. The two essential rules of attendance and confidentiality are included.

Socratic methods

As a basic principle when working with clients with developmental and intellectual disabilities, facilitators should attempt not to employ any didactic methods. In other words, try not to tell participants anything. Instead, facilitators should follow a line of Socratic questions to elicit the information from participants. In this way, group members will generate the appropriate information themselves and are more likely to retain the information. This approach can be extremely difficult at the beginning of treatment because participants will expect the group leaders to outline the procedures, methods, modules, group rules, and so on. Some participants may be worried about making mistakes, 'giving the wrong answer', 'doing the wrong thing' or 'making a fool of myself'. Socratic methods can be used in a supportive manner but the group leader has to try and resist an urge to conform to expectations that they will lead or direct sessions in the expected didactic manner. If the methods can be established early on in the programme, it will reap benefits as it progresses.

Socratic methods encourage or induce the participant to follow through the arguments themselves and review the pieces of evidence available to them. For this reason, the methods are also called inductive (inductive reasoning). This forces the individual to think about the issues and arrive at a socialised cognition or principle by themselves. By doing this, they are more likely to retain and internalise the information because they have arrived at it by their own inductive reasoning. Not only do they know the socialised principle, socialised cognition, socialised behavioural routine, and so on, but they have also worked out themselves why this principle or cognition is desirable and more adaptive than other ways of thinking or behaving. The method is doubly difficult when facilitators are also reviewing their own interaction style for its cognitive and linguistic simplicity. While use of this method on a single occasion would have little effect on anyone, its repeated use week after week, month after month through the duration of any programme is likely to promote two basic therapeutic mechanisms:

- The first is the fundamental principle of cognitive therapy. Participants review the evidence for underlying assumptions and schemata which they have about themselves and the resulting cognitive distortions and self-statements which arise from the underlying schema. By repeated review and questioning of the evidence, they are encouraged to understand that previous schemata and underlying assumptions are likely to have supported the perpetration of sexual offences (see later sections for examples). They will certainly have endorsed cognitive distortions which in turn will have contributed to the pathways to offending and cycles of offending. Participants, being encouraged to work this out for themselves through Socratic questioning and inductive reasoning, are more likely to internalise these therapeutic messages and are more likely to adopt socialised adaptive schemata and resulting cognitions.
- A second therapeutic gain is that individuals develop a response set and habit of questioning their own standpoint and motivation. This is precisely the habit which we wish to promote in any day-to-day situations which might involve risk of recidivism.

Examples of Socratic methods will be seen throughout this manual and already we have seen the way in which they are used from the outset to establish group rules and ownership of procedures. Prior to starting any sex offender programme, facilitators can practise Socratic methods with each other by role-playing some of the examples outlined in later chapters.

Use of role-play

People with ID relate well to role-playing. It can produce powerful emotional and behavioural responses and facilitators should be aware that these reactions may emerge. For example, when we are conducting alcohol treatments, we invariably set up the basic aspects of a pub in which the person has to ask for a non-alcoholic drink. There will be a table representing a bar, a few glasses and someone behind the bar. I have seen some participants becoming so embarrassed about asking for a non-alcoholic drink in this role-played setting that they can refuse to do it or begin to sweat with the effort of asking for a non-alcoholic drink. In anger management treatment, participants have become quite aroused in response to role-played anger provoking stimuli. These reactions can come as a surprise to facilitators since the role-played situation is so obviously different from the real situation. However, it does have some of the salient aspects and can produce significant responses.

Role-play is used frequently in sex offender treatment across a number of modules. It is used in a number of different ways both informally and formally. There are examples of formal and informal role-plays throughout this manual.

An informal role-play is one which would happen on the spur of the moment. A fairly frequent example is the role-playing of an administrative group. This may be a multidisciplinary community team, a panel considering supported housing, a parole board or a clinical team meeting in a ward. A usual situation would be one where a group member is complaining about the decision of a carer not to allow him to do certain things or the decision of a multidisciplinary team to postpone a change in living circumstances for the individual. The group leaders can immediately arrange the situation to illustrate the way in which decision making is made at every level. Group leaders can make a decision to designate the individual in question as the chairman of the multidisciplinary panel or, depending on the personalities of individual group members, they can designate another individual as chairman of the panel. It can be illuminating when the individual is role-playing someone who has the power to make decisions about himself. Group members can then be designated the role of social worker, community nurse, psychologist, psychiatrist or other relevant professionals. It is often safer and less threatening to group members if one of the group leaders takes the part of the client/participant. Arguments and issues can then be put to 'the chairman' of the panel concerning the issue in question. They may consider the individual is a risk in relation to the activity that is under discussion or they may consider the individual's risk in relation to the change in life circumstance. Either way, they will make recommendations to 'the chairman' on how he should decide regarding the participants future. 'The chairman' then has to make decisions about 'the client' based on these various assessments concerning their risk. It is likely that the other participants will make a decision which will minimise risk. The group leaders can go to each participant and ask them to make a decision based on information which is well known about the participant. For example

FACILITATOR: Now John, you are the social worker and you have to make a decision on whether or not Alex here should be allowed to go to a nightclub on his own. You know that he has four previous charges of indecent exposure and in this group he has said that he has touched females in nightclubs. He has been going to sex offender treatment for nine months and he wants to begin going to nightclubs on his own again. What recommendation would you make? What would you decide?

ALEX: I don't think he should be going to nightclubs yet on his own. He might re-offend.

FACILITATOR: He's been going to sex offender treatment for nine months, how much do you think he's changed.

ALEX: Well, he might have changed a bit but I don't think he's changed enough and I would be worried he would re-offend.

FACILITATOR: Okay. Now Peter, you have been manager at Alex's home for two years and you know how he is behaving and managing. You have to say something to the meeting about what you think should happen. Alex wants to go to the nightclub now.

PETER: Well he's been okay and he's been not any trouble at home. But he was
              drinking last week and I think he should wait for a few weeks before he
              goes anywhere like the nightclub.

Similar information would be given to the other participants in the role-play and it
is likely that they would give a conservative recommendation to 'the chairman'. 'The
chairman' has then to make a final decision on whether to allow 'the client' to go to
a nightclub. It may be that one of the participants or indeed 'the chairman' makes
a decision or recommendation that 'the client' should be allowed to enter the risk
situation. In this case, facilitators can then remind the individual that they have a duty
of care to society and if 'the client' re-offends, they may be considered culpable for
their decision. In addition, they might be reminded that their job is partly dependent
on successful outcomes in treatment, and if they make a decision which is considered
risky by a future review, it may jeopardise their employment. In this way, individuals'
decisions can be placed in much wider contexts.

A typical result of a role-play such as this is that 'the chairman' is placed in a
quandary. He wants to make a decision which will allow 'the client' to go to a
nightclub but he begins to realise why others are making conservative decisions which
prevent him doing as he wishes. The role-play has an outcome on several levels.
The first is presenting a series of arguments which the offender has to consider in
addition to his own wishes. The second is that, for the whole group, it begins to
promote perspective taking. It encourages consideration of the fact that other people
have opinions based on issues which are relevant to them and which are not known
to the offender. They will make decisions on the basis of these other issues. This
encouragement of perspective taking will have ramifications for future modules on
victim empathy. Further advantages of role-play such as this are that they are fun,
spontaneous and they break up the normal process of groups.

A second major type of role-play is the formal role-play which is organised and
planned in advance. A series of formal role-plays can be seen in the victim awareness
section of the programme. These can be organised to illustrate specific points or to
demonstrate specific types of experience. The main value of them is that the group
member himself is placed in a position where he might gain some experiential insight
into the issue of topic at hand.

Role-play can feel embarrassing and even threatening to both the group leaders and
the group members. Group leaders should rehearse role-plays prior to the beginning of
sessions. It would even be an advantage for facilitators to practise some administrative
role-plays prior to beginning the induction sessions. This allows them to become more
comfortable and familiar with the methods. It also ensures that they have some idea of
the process and experience of this particular role-play before they engage with clients.
It is helpful if one of the facilitators has more extensive experience and knowledge of
a role-play.

The use of metaphor

Metaphor is often used in therapy to illustrate particular points. It is considered to be
a helpful method which allows participants to discuss the relevant principles related

to a particular psychological problem without what might be considered the personal threatening context of the real situation. Therefore, it is an example which one can review, dissect and consider in abstract rather than the real situation. However, it will be directly relevant to the real situation to the extent that it shares the same underlying principles or illustrates one particular principle or issue. The current sex offender programme is infused with this method. It is much easier to extract and illustrate cognitive distortions, underlying assumptions and schemata, cycles of offending, behavioural routines and feelings of physiological excitement or arousal through illustrations which are not each participant's index offence. All of these factors can be drawn out when reviewing other types of crime such as car theft or alcohol or drug abuse. Group leaders must be careful to guide the inductive reasoning towards the principles which he or she wishes to draw out of the exercise. In this way, principles can be established in a free, less threatening setting prior to moving on to the way in which these issues are relevant to sexual offending in general and each participant's offence history, in particular.

As the programme develops, it becomes possible, relatively quickly, to use illustrations and metaphors that are extremely close to the index offences. Therefore, the hypothetical situations can be sexual offences which will certainly be similar to the offences of particular participants. However, because they are hypothetical and illustrative, they still remain relatively safe situations to discuss for group members. If group members were to begin modules by discussing individual's particular offences, then the unfolding of basic schemata, distorted cognitive frameworks, interpretation of sexual drive, and so on might become quite threatening and even confrontational to particular individuals. By presenting a hypothetical situation, discussion and review are easier. It may be that one particular participant, for whom the example is particularly relevant, perceives the similarity between his own offence and the hypothetical offence and become somewhat uncomfortable with the analysis of the incident. However, this will not be true for the other group members who will discuss the example quite freely. Given that the hypothetical example or illustration becomes so close to an individual offence, it might be considered that it is no longer a metaphor but rather a parallel illustration. Nevertheless, given that it is not the specific offence and is a hypothetical illustration, it allows the similar principles to be extracted without the individual participant becoming defensive about their own actions or offences.

Moving from general illustrations (metaphor) to specific offences

This is a very frequently used technique for eliciting cognitive distortions, identifying behavioural scripts, identifying cycles of offending and promoting cognitive challenge. It relies on the group leaders having a comprehensive knowledge of each individual's offence history and a thorough knowledge of the group programme. Normally a discussion of hypothetical incidents, problem solving scenarios and exercises to elicit cognitive distortions will be conducted after disclosure phases where each participant has reviewed their index offence and other relevant offences in their history. Therefore, group leaders will be able to guide the inductive process towards the establishment of a set of principles which they feel are relevant to offences in general and, perhaps one participant's offence in particular. They can then move the focus of the session from consideration of the hypothetical situation towards consideration of the participant's specific offence. There are examples of this process later in this programme but one illustration from a group session can be seen below.

The group has been discussing the hypothetical situation of a man in a pub feeling sorry for himself because of his life situation (details had already been described in the group session) and becoming drunk. He feels sexually aroused and sees one particular woman whom he finds attractive and who is also drinking quite heavily. He follows her up the road and sexually assaults her. The details of the situation are much more extensive when they have been discussed in the group but this particular situation is analogous to an offence committed by one of the group members (Bill):

DAVID (a group member):	That guy might have come out the house thinking that he wanted to have sex and he couldn't get his courage up.
FACILITATOR:	That's interesting David, you think he was already wanting to have sex before he even got to the pub?
DAVID:	Yes, he might have wanted to chat somebody up but felt he wasn't very good at it so he would have to think of some other way to get women.
FACILITATOR:	So why would he have gone to this pub?
DAVID:	Well he might have known that women were there and got drunk and he would be able to have a drink himself and get some courage up to approach someone or sexually assault them.
FACILITATOR:	So what would you call that?
DAVID:	What do you mean?
FACILITATOR:	Well, is he deciding in the house; is he making a choice earlier on that's going to lead to a sexual offence?
OTHER PARTICIPANT:	Is that one of those decisions and he's kidding himself on.
FACILITATOR:	What do you mean he might be kidding himself on?
OTHER PARTICIPANT:	Well, he thinks he's not making a decision but he is making a decision because he's deciding to go to the pub where he knows there's women.
FACILITATOR:	So what would that be called, making a decision like that?
OTHER PARTICIPANT:	Would that be grooming or what did you call it? Yes, would that be grooming?
FACILITATOR:	Well, it could be a grooming situation.
DAVID:	Getting himself into a place where he might attack somebody. Or he knows a woman's going to be there.
OTHER PARTICIPANT:	Well, he could chat her up or if he had to, he would attack her. Like sexually assault her or rape her.
FACILITATOR:	All right, well that's good. You're all correct. You've thought about it well but it seems to me this is quite the same as what you did Bill. Didn't you go drinking in a pub and then see a woman who you sexually assaulted when she was walking home.

BILL:	Well that's happened but I didn't see her and think I was going to assault her. My case is different.
FACILITATOR:	Okay, you are saying you didn't see the woman and you didn't plan to sexually assault her. But here (points to the flipchart) the guys are saying that this man maybe went out the house thinking he was looking for a woman. Was that in your mind when you left the house that night?
BILL:	No, it just happened on the spur of the moment to me.
FACILITATOR:	Well, I wonder what other people think of that.
DAVID:	You said this guy (points to the flipchart) was setting it up so that he had a chance to sexually offend but Bill said it just happened on the spur of the moment.

Bill has revealed several possible cognitive distortions in this passage. He has said, 'I didn't see her and think about sexual assault.' 'It happened on the spur of the moment.' These statements might be true but they may also be cognitive distortions which have the theme of 'I'm not the kind of person who would plan to sexually assault someone.' This in turn suggests that Bill has a self-image and basic cognitive schema which do not consider himself as a sexual predator (I don't go out to sexually assault women). However, through the Socratic process and by generalising the hypothetical example to Bill's specific offence, it has been possible to elicit these cognitions and then invite cognitive challenge from other members of the group. In this way, Bill's cognitions are being challenged directly through the use of metaphor and subsequent discussion of the hypothetical example. The fact that he denies these cognitions and the further possibility that his denial may be justified is quite in order within the context of sex offender treatment.

Because they are knowledgeable about the theoretical framework of sex offender assessment and treatment, facilitators may consider that going to the pub was an explicit strategy for finding a woman with whom he could have sex (approach explicit offender), or an active but maladaptive strategy to avoid offending (active/avoidant offender) (see also Chapter 11). Throughout the process, they are collecting information to aid further assessment and future treatment and management. The exercise explores the role of cognition in the cycle of offence and goes on to challenge the individual on the extent to which these cognitive distortions have played a corresponding role in the cycle of their own offence. The topic will be revisited repeatedly and further repeated challenges will be made on Bill's cognitive framework and possible distortions. The exercise educates participants on the role of cognitive distortions in the cycle of offences and invites them to begin to consider their own thoughts and attitudes in relation to sex and sexual offending.

Recording

In relation to the issue of ownership, recording and methods of recording have already been mentioned. As a general principle, group members should make all the records during the group sessions. Clearly, facilitators can make their own records and notes after groups finish. It had been thought previously that having group members write or draw on the flipchart would emphasise any literacy deficits or inequalities resulting in embarrassment for particular individuals. However, both in hospital and community groups, we have not found any adverse consequences from having group members record either the collective record of the session or individual disclosure reports. Generally, the records are made in simple line drawings. Where a particular individual is having difficulties with certain words to label the drawings, he is generally quite happy for others to help him spell it out. Occasionally, some individuals are quite proud of their skills in artwork while others are quite proud of their ability to spell. In a closed group, where all of the participants are learning the methods together, early in the induction, during the *'getting to know you'* exercise, the group leaders can draw some basic information about themselves on the flipchart. By keeping to drawings and some basic English, the precedent is set for simple direct information to summarise a session. If there is one group leader who is particularly poor at drawing (I, myself, am quite astonishingly poor) then he or she can be encouraged to draw some aspects of their life activities or interests. Once again, it is better for facilitators to practise this prior to the session. Having participants keep their own records on the flipchart is more immediate and direct than having group leaders record information. It has several advantages:

- By generating and recording group processes such as the induction process and the group rules, ownership is promoted.
- If the participant himself draws the main points of his own index offence and account, he cannot later deny that he said certain things or that the group leaders misunderstood when he was drawing on the board. This issue is again one of ownership but, in this case, it is personal ownership. The same is true for drawing life maps, time lines, eliciting cognitive distortions and projecting future lifestyles.
- Flipcharts from the previous session can be used to review the extent to which participants can recall information from the previous session. This is done simply by placing the flipchart back on the stand and asking participants what they can recall about the previous session.

Note on format

Each module is split into several exercises. This term is preferred to sessions. The reason for this is that each exercise will take different lengths of time and will not be confined necessarily to a single session. One or two exercises will take a very short time indeed, perhaps half an hour to go round the whole group. Other exercises may take the same number of sessions as there are group members. There is no expectation that any one module will take a finite number of sessions, although it is likely to take around 18 months to 2 years to cover all of the modules at a rate of one session per week. Less if two sessions are conducted per week.

As group leaders become more experienced, it is occasionally relevant to mix aspects of future and previous modules into a particular session. Thus, it may be appropriate and specifically relevant to spend time on relationships and attitudes while conducting other modules. Although there is a specific module on disclosure of offences, I always think that as facilitators we are constantly reviewing an individual's offence and, if there is an opportunity to gain further information about cognitive distortions related to an offence or behavioural scripts related to an offence, then we will return to disclosure as part of another module. Because of this, it is important to have an understanding of the whole of the programme prior to beginning any group sessions. In this way, aspects from future modules can be incorporated into earlier sessions if they are specifically relevant and vice versa.

This programme can act as a guideline which can be followed very closely or, once facilitators are more experienced, quite loosely. It is not my intention to be utterly prescriptive concerning the format of any sex offender group. As group facilitators become more experienced, they will begin to add material which is relevant to their own participants. They will also add material which is relevant to their own situation, be it in community settings, community houses, supported accommodation, low secure or other custodial settings. All of this is quite in order and should be done within a multidisciplinary context. It may be that group leaders feel some aspects of this programme are not relevant at all to their participants or would be construed as inappropriate by their participants. Once again, it is quite in order to delete exercises or a series of exercises because it is not felt by the facilitators to be relevant. However, facilitators should caution against not wishing to engage in certain aspects because they feel embarrassed themselves about doing it. Dealing with aspects of sexuality, role-play or disclosure exercises can be embarrassing, uncomfortable and personally disquieting. Sex offender treatment can be personally difficult for facilitators and this should be discussed openly during the support sessions which facilitators will have. These issues are outlined in more detail later.

An open 'rolling' programme

Over the past 15 years or so, I have employed an open 'rolling' programme approach whereby the sex offender treatment has been conducted continuously. Individuals join the programme following assessment and will leave when they have completed their individual treatment targets or when the clinical team agrees that it is appropriate for them to finish. If a participant is on a Probation Order, they will usually leave at the end of their probation period. This approach has a flexibility which allows treatment to accommodate to a range of individual requirements and also has specific strengths in terms of the group dynamic. Firstly, clients do not have to remain on a waiting list for lengthy periods of time waiting for a new group to start. They can begin treatment after the completion of their initial assessment. As will be made clear throughout the description of this programme, assessment is a continuous process but there is a clear initial assessment phase when background interviews are conducted, risk assessments are compiled and initial psychometrics are completed.

A major strength of this approach is that participants who have been in group sessions for lengthy periods of time can support new members when they begin. During initial disclosure phases, more experienced group members will invariably empathise with the new member engaged in disclosing their offence accounts. They show this support explicitly with statements like, 'We all found it difficult when we were talking about our offence'; 'You might as well get it over with because you'll feel better when you've finished'; 'Everybody finds it difficult and I got really angry when I had to talk about it'; 'I wanted to just forget about it and not talk about it but it's better if you just get it over with'. I have also found that this support and encouragement speeds the initial disclosure process considerably. When we began, we found that some participants could spend weeks and even months refusing to talk about their offences (Lindsay *et al.*, 1998b). The encouragement and support of experienced group members is much more powerful than the support of facilitators. The result is that no individual in the past 10 years has refused to talk about their offence for more than 2 or 3 weeks. Normally, once facilitators have decided to start the process with an individual, the resistance to disclosure will be overcome in a session or two. The support more experienced members give to new members can be impressive.

A further aspect of a rolling programme is that it improves responsivity to urgent issues. Where an individual has a particular lifestyle issue or a particular issue relevant to sexual offending, this can be dealt with during the session. New members are able to observe the way in which more experienced members are dealing with other aspects of their programme such as victim awareness or the cycle of offending. They will automatically and vicariously learn how to organise relevant information for the time when they will be called upon to deal with these aspects of the programme. This certainly facilitates the treatment process.

When I have started a new group with the intention of developing it into a rolling programme, there is often concern on the part of facilitators and group members when the time comes to introduce a new sex offender. The concern is that group cohesion and trust have developed between facilitators and participants and that a new person may disrupt this cohesion. It is also the case that facilitators may be becoming more comfortable with the methods of the programme and the introduction of a new member will disrupt this flow, requiring a different set of skills which will incorporate the dual purposes of beginning treatment with the new participant and continuing treatment with existing members. In practice, I have only had difficulty on a few occasions and it is always in relation to the anxiety generated in a new person. On one occasion, the new member found it so anxiety provoking to join an existing group that it proved impossible to incorporate him at any time. We had to make alternative arrangements for his treatment. On other occasions, we have overcame the problem by allowing the new member to have individual time with one of the facilitators while the group was continuing and then introducing him gradually to the main group. While he was being introduced, we ensured that no highly confidential or personal information was being discussed in case our attempts were unsuccessful. Therefore, there was no possibility that he would know highly confidential information about other individuals while not being a fully integrated member of the sex offender group. Although these cases stand out as having required significant changes in the process, it is quite common, especially at the initial stages of treatment, for an individual participant to have some time with one facilitator in order to be supported while coming to terms with group treatment. On some occasions, an established member who can provide additional mentoring and support has accompanied the new member and facilitator.

The programme continues throughout the year and, as has been mentioned, participants are required to attend every session. One of the messages, which can be incorporated into this arrangement, is that required attendance means that participants lose some of their freedom as a result of committing the sexual offence. They do not lose as much freedom as they would have done had they been admitted to hospital or prison but they lose some of their freedom on the day of the group session. This acts as an example for losing freedom in other ways which will be required through aspects of their own personal self-regulation or risk management, such as not using public transport when school pupils are going home, not going to parties where alcohol is present or avoiding public parks. Generally, we run with a number of facilitators which allows the group to continue during holiday time, other leave time or when facilitators are required to attend other duties. Over the years, the only days when the group has been suspended are the public holidays around Christmas and New Year. However, because of the risks associated with that time of year – parties, increased use of alcohol, family gatherings, and so on – I always conduct a group session between Christmas and New Year, if possible. During this session, I will make these risk factors quite explicit as the reason for running the session. This can also be done in sessions prior to this time of year.

Clients will normally remain in treatment until therapists feel they have achieved the treatment goals or until probation ends. Since probation is normally for 3 years, the period of treatment is adequate (see Chapter 4; Lindsay and Smith, 1998). Increasingly, the clinical team involved with the person will ask that the client remain within the group while major changes are occurring in their life even although they have achieved their treatment goals. The most usual example is that the client is moving to new accommodation but it could also be related to other major changes in their life. The rolling programme allows sex offender treatment to accommodate to these general requests.

Staff Support

One of the essential considerations in sex offender treatment is regular staff support and monitoring. A significant component of treatment is repeated disclosure of offences and incidents which involve sexual abuse of adults and children. Of necessity, these accounts are detailed and personal and they can be upsetting or disquieting for facilitators and therapists. It is usual for us all to become upset by some of the accounts and even after two decades of working in the field. I still become disquieted by the deep and permanent sadness of some stories. It is important to monitor facilitators' feelings routinely. Facilitators can react to any aspect of the programme including the disclosure accounts, the victim empathy modules, exercises on the cycle of offending, covert sensitisation on sexual fantasy or pornography. We have regular meetings after each treatment session in order to review the material that is being dealt with, personal reactions to any aspect of the session, group members' engagement with the material and individual progress. Although all these aspects are important, facilitators' personal reactions to the material that has been dealt with are the most salient at that point. Other aspects can be discussed in other planning sessions, if possible. In other settings, sessions from an independent counsellor are made available to facilitators so that they can discuss any personal reactions to the material, independent from other facilitators. While not all services feel that this is necessary, it is certainly an arrangement that is in place from time to time in certain areas. Facilitators might only see the person once every 2 months or so, or not at all, but the service is available.

There is no expectation that all care staff should be able to cope with this kind of work. Some people find the discussion of sexual offences to be sufficiently upsetting that they cannot concentrate on their work for the rest of the time. I have known two individuals who were reasonably keen to begin working with sex offender groups but soon found the material being dealt with oppressive. It was quite in order for them to move on to other areas without any implication that they were unable to cope. It is simply that some people are not cut out for this kind of work. Others have said that they felt comfortable doing a placement for 6 months and that they understood well the necessity for the work but that they were pleased to be moving on and would not like to work in this area for any extended period of time. Once again, this is quite acceptable. I prefer people to be honest about their reactions rather than concealing them and becoming increasingly uncomfortable. Other facilitators have been highly valued members of the clinical team for 4 or 5 years and at that point have said that they have had enough. Even when they are continuing to work in the service, 5 years is a significant amount of time to contribute to a sex offender treatment programme and there should be no expectation that a facilitator is required to continue in the programme for the length of the time that they are in the service. We simply have to recognise that the work can be personally draining. Understanding, mutual support and routine team meetings are extremely helpful in mentoring facilitators through any difficulties and there should be no expectation that they will continue this work for extended periods of time.

There is a developing literature on staff well-being and burnout (Skirrow and Hatton, 2007). It is likely that the well-being of staff will have an impact on their effectiveness as therapeutic and social supports to offenders (Hastings, 2002) and so it is important to consider the feelings and well-being of staff who work with offenders and sex offenders. The literature generally suggests that those experiencing the greatest levels of stress and burnout are staff who work with individuals who exhibit violent behaviour and aggression (Taylor, 2002). In a study of care staff in residential settings for offenders with ID, Rose and Cleary (2007) reported that they found no consistent evidence that care staff exposed to high levels of challenging behaviour were more fearful about work-related violence. However, it remains the case that staff burnout is related to exposure to violence and, crucially, lack of support from management (Hastings, 2002). Although staff may be exposed to aggression and violence in some settings for individuals with ID, they will not usually be exposed to information of a sexually abusive nature. Neither are they likely to observe sexual abuse. In this regard, group facilitators are in a unique position in ID staff groups. By its very nature, sex offender treatment will expose them to stories of sexual abuse against adults and children and one might extrapolate that if violence and lack of support cause burnout, similarly exposure to stories of sexual abuse accompanied by lack of support may induce burnout and low staff morale. Therefore, it is extremely important to consider issues of support for facilitators of sex offender treatment.

I would make a clear recommendation that when sex offender treatment is being organised within an establishment, one of the first considerations should be that time must be given for discussion among facilitators and mutual support. During these sessions, they can explore their feelings towards the material being discussed and review ways in which they each deal with it. It is also important during these sessions to plan and organise subsequent sessions, review materials, review participants' reaction to material and review progress.

It is not the purpose of this book to make an extensive review of staff support issues. There are several chapters and books (e.g. Perini, 2004; Mosher, 2009) which deal extensively with these important issues. Any interested reader should follow-up this material.

Chapter 8

Promoting Motivation

Motivation is not a specific treatment module. There is no expectation that facilitators will spend a block of sessions attempting to increase motivation. Instead, motivational sessions are generally spread throughout the treatment programme when the facilitators identify an opportunity to increase motivation. I often think that we are in constant search for opportunities to motivate change in a socialised direction. This is because very few of the individuals who are referred to treatment will have any motivation whatever to even attend the sessions let alone engage in the process. This is not specific to sex offenders with ID. In general psychological therapy with people with ID, there is often little motivation to make personal changes. This is not to say that clients lack motivation or aspirations, but these aspirations are generally focused externally rather than internally. Therefore, clients may wish a change of domestic arrangements, easier access to their finances or 'to get the social worker/community nurse off my back'. It is less common for clients to perceive the focus of their psychological difficulties within themselves, for example a problem with their anger control or difficulties with their budgeting priorities. Therefore, we cannot assume any motivation to change when clients are first referred for sex offender treatment. However, if we can manage to arrange that the person will attend, then we have the opportunity to work on their motivation.

One of the basic motivational principles has been outlined by Lindsay (2005) in his theoretical exposition of the underlying basis for sex offender treatment with this client group. Previously, in Chapter 6, it was noted that two fundamental tenets underpin treatment. These are, firstly, dealing with the personal psychological issues associated with the sex offence such as cognitive distortions, cycle of offending and victim awareness, and secondly, the promotion of engagement with society with subsequent exposure to pro-social influences, attachment to the beliefs of society and engagement with occupational activity. In terms of motivation, the latter is crucially important. When working with sex offenders with ID, I often think of a line in Bob Dylan's

The Treatment of Sex Offenders with Developmental Disabilities   William Lindsay
© 2009 John Wiley & Sons, Ltd

Like a Rolling Stone: 'When you ain't got nothing, you've got nothing to lose.' By developing clients' engagement with society, we can begin to enrich their lives to the extent that there are tangible benefits in remaining offence free and continuing access to community opportunities. At the outset, it should be noted that these attempts do not always work – some clients continue to resist attempts to engage them in education, occupational and social activities. However, it is important to make links with the appropriate agencies such as local college courses in special education or local disability employment agencies. In this way, with appropriate cautions and observation, this higher quality of life experience can be used in treatment during motivation exercises which encourage the client to maintain these socialised experiences through an offence-free lifestyle. This is entirely consistent with the Good Lives Model discussed in Chapter 5.

There are a number of specific exercises which can be employed when facilitators recognise an appropriate opportunity. Group leaders have to be flexible in their use because some are more appropriate to certain settings than others. For example, community groups may have a number of individuals on probation while groups run in a secure hospital are likely to have most individuals on sections of Mental Health Legislation or Guardianship Orders and groups run in prison for low functioning offenders may have differing lengths of sentence with the prospect of post-release monitoring. Therefore, different groups will have different reference points for some of the motivational exercises and facilitators will have to review the exercises and adapt them to be relevant to their particular setting.

Exercise 1: Reviewing Statutory Penalties

In the services in which I have been involved or acted as a consultant, we usually encourage the various authorities to prosecute offences for clients through the appropriate legal channels. This has a number of advantages, both in terms of encouraging motivation and establishing the basic context of treatment. If an incident is prosecuted through the legal system, treatment is conducted within a social, societal context. The incident has been placed under public scrutiny, and society, in the form of the court, has decided the outcome. It is likely that the individual will have been placed on probation and may also have a treatment order. In this case, the facilitators have also entered into the societal context by contracting with the court to provide the treatment. In that sense, both the client and the group leaders have entered into a contract with society which results in the treatment sessions. If the client complains about having to attend, they cannot direct the criticism at the facilitators. Instead, the facilitators can simply point out that the complaint should be addressed to society, in the form of the court. Treatment is firmly placed in a social context and the aims of treatment are placed within society's values.

On the other hand, if group members are required to attend through the imposition of Mental Health Legislation, then a specific medical practitioner or clinical team can be viewed as the focus for the requirement to attend. The dialogue can then change from facilitators simply fulfilling their part of the contract to facilitators being seen as part of the agency which have caused the changes in the client's life. Although the following is a caricature, it serves as an example of the way in which such a dialogue can progress:

CLIENT: When am I getting off my order?
FACILITATOR: When you've improved and got better.
CLIENT: But I have got better.
FACILITATOR: Well maybe you should ask Dr William, your psychiatrist.
CLIENT: He says that it's up to you to say when I've got better.
FACILITATOR: Well you haven't improved enough.
CLIENT: Yes I have improved enough, I think I'm much better.
FACILITATOR: No you haven't improved enough.
CLIENT: Well I am not going to re-offend so I must be better.

It can be seen that placing treatment within a societal context will completely alter the basis for attendance and delivery. During discussions in this motivational exercise, facilitators can also point out that, as part of the contract, they have agreed with the court to deliver treatment. If they do not fulfil this, then the client will be able to go back to court and point out that the contract is not being honoured because the facilitators have not fulfilled their requirements. Therefore, attendance at treatment and provision of treatment share the same statutory basis.

In a sex offender group run in the community, this can be a powerful motivational tool. When an opportunity arises, group leaders can conduct a reasonably quick review of the different bases on which group members attend. Half may be attending because of probation while others may be attending because their carers have said that the only way they will guarantee placement is if they attend a sex offender group. During such a discussion, the individuals who are on probation are likely to make it clear to others who have not been through the court system that they are extremely fortunate to have avoided the process. They are also likely to compare offences (if this is conducted after the disclosure phases) and express the opinion that these individuals should have gone through the court processes because of the severity of their offence. Facilitators can harness this opportunity to emphasise the importance of remaining offence free in order to avoid any legal processes or further legal processes. It is also likely that certain group members will have experience of prison and some will certainly have had experience of the police cells. It is then possible to compare probation and group treatment against the restrictions of custody as group members describe their experiences in custody. The main aim of these discussions is to emphasise that while clients have certain restrictions upon their life such as group attendance and compliance with treatment arrangements, in most ways they are able to continue with their lives. If they had received a custodial disposal, this would have placed far greater restrictions with a much poorer quality of life.

Exercise 2: Comparing Prison and Probation

Materials: flipchart and pen

This is a more formal means of conducting the review exercise. The flipchart page is split into two with one half representing prison and the other half representing probation. Group members are then asked, 'What is good about prison?' 'What is good about probation?' On a second sheet, clients are asked, 'What is bad about prison?' 'What is bad about probation?' Figure 8.1 shows the outcome of such a session with the left-hand portion representing responses to the questions 'What is good about prison/probation?' and the right hand 'What is bad about prison/probation?' As can be seen, group members were quite perceptive about the value of probation and other non-custodial arrangements, identifying a number of relevant issues. Firstly, they identified the counselling and self-development aspects of probation and treatment with statements like 'You get help; you talk about things; you think and learn'. They also identified the maintenance of freedom saying, 'You get more freedom; you're not locked up,' with the corresponding continuation of the individuals normal life, 'you can go home.' They also identified the self-restraint, socialising aspects of probation and treatment with the statement 'keep out of trouble'. All of these are accurate perceptions of the function of probation and treatment. It was somewhat surprising to facilitators during this particular session that group members identified no advantages of prison whatever. Other groups have identified that a prison sentence is often shorter and 'you get it over with'. However, more recent changes in sentencing structure for sex offenders may have altered this perception.

On the section on 'What's bad about prison/probation?', some group members have been quite graphic about the drawbacks of prison. They have identified the boredom of confinement in statements such as 'locked up for 23 hours; don't get out; no freedom'. They have also identified the prospect of vigilante activity with the statement 'get your head kicked in because of sex offence'. While this kind of statement may seem anti-therapeutic, it is the reality that all sex offenders, even those with ID, are acutely aware of the negative views expressed by society towards sex offending and the possible consequences of vigilante activity. It is, therefore, an aspect of the process which group members will discuss quite freely (this is discussed in more detail below). The group members also note the poverty of the regime in prison with another reference to vigilante activity: 'Food is not so good. Put odd things in your food.' They have also referred clearly to lack of contact with relatives and loved ones: 'Don't see family often in the nick.' Interestingly, presumably in contrast to the comments regarding probation, group members will often mention the lack of support and therapeutic input in prison. It is certainly the case that if individuals are in for a relatively short period of time, it is unlikely that they will receive sex offender treatment. This particular group was also able to identify drawbacks experienced while on probation. These were generally related to the imposition of requirements with the following statements: 'You've got to go, you don't get so much freedom, holidays (you can't go on holiday without informing your probation officer), rules (there are rules you have to follow).' They have also noted that there are difficulties with the therapeutic process with comments such as 'You're in the hot seat, you don't forget about your sex offence'. 'Hot seat' is a term which some groups have used to any activity where the group member is placed in an uncomfortable position such as disclosing their offence, being challenged about their cognitions or having to consider how their victim might feel. Interestingly, this particular group have expressed the opinion that by receiving probation, the offender has 'got off

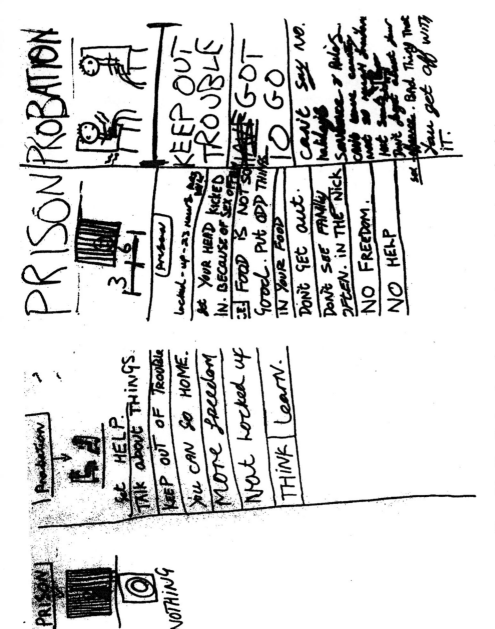

Figure 8.1 Two flipchart sheets from an exercise comparing prison and probation

135

with it'. Therefore, they see probation and treatment as a more lenient disposal than custody.

In general, this exercise simply emphasises the benefits of probation as a motivation to remain offence free.

Exercise 3: Review Community Reactions

This can either be done through discussion or by writing personal experiences on the flipchart. Community reactions to sex offending are always negative and this exercise serves as a motivation to avoid negative experiences by maintaining socialised relationships and socialised routines. Several group members are likely to have had vigilante experiences, even at a relatively low level. These will involve being called 'a beast' or 'a pervert' in the street. While these are less serious, they are still likely to be extremely frightening for the individuals involved. They can be discussed within the group in terms of both the personal anxiety which they arouse and as an example of society's view of sexual offending. While this may appear anti-therapeutic, it is realistic and protective. Increasingly, society holds vindictive views towards those individuals who commit sexual offences and it is important that group members are aware of these feelings. However, this group exercise not only makes them aware of the phenomenon but also employs it as a motivational technique. Within any particular group, facilitators will be able to discuss personal experiences of group members but the following are examples of vigilante activity experienced by members of groups which I have run:

- Threatening phone calls to the client and his family members.
- Having 'beast' and 'pervert' across the front of the house in red paint.
- Having the family car vandalised.
- Being forced into a side street and attacked.
- Having one's relatives attacked.
- Having the house fire-bombed.

I have listed these somewhat dramatic incidents to emphasise that, as a motivational exercise, this aspect of therapy is protective towards clients. If they maintain offence-free, socialised patterns over months and years, these incidents will not recur. In fact, when a sex offender group has been running for a lengthy period of time, there will be examples where individuals have been accepted by society and even accepted by those who have previously expressed the insults. These examples can also be used to reinforce the value of change.

Exercise 4: Employing Group Processes

This is an exercise which is common to all psychotherapeutic groups. Group members will become very aware of the consequences of behaviour which is consistent with sexual offending and correspondingly aware of the benefits of socialised behaviour or self-restraint with respect to sexual problems. Where an individual has demonstrated self-restraint in a risk situation or, better still, taking steps to avoid a risk situation, this can be discussed within the group setting with praise and encouragement. Facilitators can also reflect from one example where an individual has avoided risk to another group member where they may have been in a situation without avoiding risk or might hypothetically get into such a situation. Again, the successful example can be used as a motivation for future examples for that particular client and for other clients. Other chapters in this book have several illustrations of the way in which facilitators can move from one client's situation or hypothetical situation using them to review other clients' experiences, offences or future situations. The same process can be conducted when clients have behaved in a way that might be considered consistent with sexual offending without showing the appropriate restraint or avoidance of risk.

One example was a report of a group member who had been seen waiting at a bus stop opposite a primary school. It was on the road from the treatment centre into town but he would have had to walk some distance from either to wait at that stop. When we discussed the report, other group members mentioned that he had walked down the road on several occasions and so it was likely that he had walked to that bus stop a few times. This led to the following exercise which can be adapted to a range of situations.

Exercise 5: Review and Imagine the Consequences of Behaviour Consistent with Re-Offending

A group member was asked to consider what would happen if someone (e.g. a neighbour) saw him loitering at the bus stop outside a primary school. Typically, when a group member is confronted with behaviour that might be consistent with offending, he is likely to be resentful and argumentative in his response with statements such as 'I can wait at any bus stop I like'; 'It's none of her business, she should mind her own business and stop looking out her window'; 'All I am doing is waiting for a bus, I'm not causing any trouble'. Such responses should not be seen as a problem for facilitators; in fact, they are a good start for the beginning of the inductive process. Through the Socratic dialogue, the group member can be taken through the following sequence:

- What happens if the neighbour called the police to say that a man is loitering at the bus stop outside the school?
- The police will come and question him.

At this point, the client may continue with his robust responses saying 'I'm doing nothing wrong, the police can just mind their own business'; 'The police are not going to bother because I am not doing anything'.

- What happens when the police ask his name and phone in for information from their central computer records?
- When they get to the information about his name and previous offence, do they still have an incident where a man is standing at a bus stop?

Through this exercise, the other group members will contribute to the inductive process helping the client to the conclusion that the police now have a situation where a man with a record of sex offending is loitering outside a primary school. They are likely to contribute to subsequent processes of apprehension, driving to the police station and being interviewed by the police. Facilitators should not lose sight of the fact that the purpose of the exercise is to increase motivation towards socialised routines and self-regulation of sexual impulses. The client may construe such a discussion as a punishment but emphasis should be placed on alternative socialised routines with their consequent positive outcomes as well as the negative outcomes of behaviour consistent with sexual offending.

Exercise 6: Review Progress

Materials: flipchart and pen

This is an exercise which is an amalgam of several suggestions by group members over the years. It began by group members rating each other's progress with a scale of 1:10. It developed eventually by a suggestion by one client that it would be better to consider their progress in terms of 'climbing up a ladder'. We therefore adapted the review to include 10 steps with the bottom of the ladder representing no progress and the top of the ladder representing excellent progress. Each group member then has their progress reviewed by the others and they each give him a place on the ladder. All of the scores (1–10) are then averaged with a final place. In this way, all group members are allocated a place on 'the ladder'. Figures 8.2 and 8.3 demonstrate the results of such exercises.

Figure 8.2 demonstrates the way in which each individual's ratings of other group members are recorded by one group member who is able to write the numbers. Group members do not give themselves a rating. Each individual's progress is discussed with a review of successes and problems they have experienced in the last few months. It is likely that preferences and disagreements which have arisen previously between group members will be reflected in the ratings. However, the purpose of the exercise is not to arrive at an exact valid reflection of progress, it is more to discuss and reflect on developments with the added incentive of peer review. Once all the ratings have been completed, the facilitators can explain the function of an average rating and help group members to arrive at an average rating for each individual.

The relative placing can then be reviewed by the group and, if necessary, appropriate adjustments can be made so that a group decision on each member's progress is arrived at. The facilitators and participants can then discuss the reasons why certain individuals are at a low point on the ladder and what they might do to enhance their

Figure 8.2   Example of group evaluation of each member

139

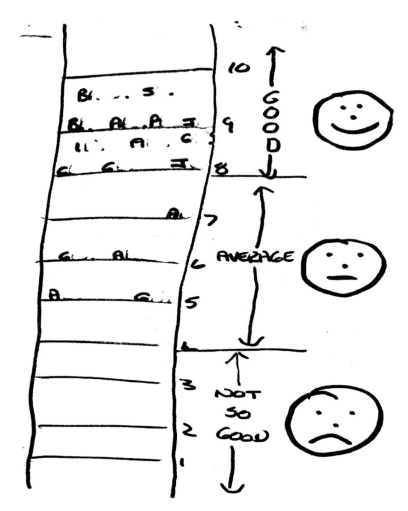

Figure 8.3 Each group member placed on 'the ladder' allowing comparisons and discussion of progress

progress. This is usually a very enjoyable exercise which not only motivates individuals to improve their place on the ladder but also helps motivation to engage in group treatment itself. The exercise can be repeated at appropriate intervals with reference to the previously constructed ladder. Advancement and deterioration can then be included as a further aspect of the exercise. It should be emphasised that the form of this was suggested by group members and it may be that in other groups, another structure of peer evaluation might emerge. Further uses of this method and its results can be seen in the Chapter 20 on evaluation.

Exercise 7: Organising Special Events

As part of the motivating and socialising process, we have become accustomed to organising lunches or some other special event at appropriate points. I began the practice in the early years of programme development when the first client came successfully to the end of his probation. We organised a lunch to celebrate his success and I was surprised at the positive effect it had on group members. It was one of the first indications of the extent to which some clients' social lives are impoverished and any social event is a highlight. Group members have to be washed and dressed appropriately for this event and facilitators emphasise that they will not be able to go if they are not washed with clean clothes. The extent to which group members respond has been surprising.

On a practical note, it is of importance to have an adequate number of escorts and at least one male member of staff. We always go to a pub for lunch and while it would be inappropriate for formal escort to the toilets, the male member of staff will always go back and forward to the toilet as group members wish to go. In our experience, group members are invariably appropriately behaved but I am sure any observers in the pub think I have a particularly weak bladder on these occasions.

These events develop into significant aspects of the therapeutic process. Group members will ask with enthusiasm if they are likely to have an outing when they finish and various menus will be discussed in sessions prior to the outing. All of this increases the motivation to engage with the therapeutic process and is likely to promote self-esteem in relation to achievement in social settings.

Use of relatives and significant others

This is not an exercise specific to the group programme itself; however, it is important to engage relatives in promoting and supporting group attendance, motivation and co-operation. It is also important to engage relatives and carers in the knowledge of risky situations and how to avoid them. I have experience of relatives who are implacably opposed to intervention, either through the legal system or through the therapeutic systems. In the face of incontrovertible evidence and admissions concerning the perpetration of the sexual offence, some parents can say things like 'I know Alex is a good boy, he would never do that kind of thing'; 'He's told me he didn't do it and these girls must be lying'. Such attitudes can only serve to reinforce the offender's denial and undermine the therapeutic process. In all cases, we engage with the social workers and community learning disability nurses to inform families and carers about the general direction of treatment and the way in which they can help and support treatment. In a minority of cases, the community learning disability nurses or social workers are forced to challenge the families that if they continue with these attitudes which support denial or mitigation then they will undermine the group members engagement and progress through the system. Once again, it is helpful to emphasise that it is not the facilitators who are insisting on treatment or instigating the whole legal and therapeutic process. Rather, it is society and the form of the courts that have made the conditions and everyone else is serving to comply with these conditions.

Exercise 8: Incorporating News and Other Stories

Group members will be sensitive about news items related to sexual offenders or other stories they have heard about offending incidents. These can be employed in the same way as has been described previously under community reactions or imagining the consequences of re-offending. It is quite common for a group member to bring a news cutting along to a session and we can discuss the offence described and the judicial decision or potential decision. This can then be used as a metaphor or example of the process and consequences of such an offence and reflected in comparison with group members offences. It will then be used to increase the motivation to remain offence free and maintain socialised routines.

Exercise 9: People Get Chances in Life

This is a variant of the exercise of reviewing progress and is another way of reflecting advancement and deterioration. After a year or so of treatment, it is likely that group members will have been afforded opportunities to progress, for example enrolment in a college course, a relaxation in supervision, an employment placement or introduction to a social club. The way in which group members respond to these opportunities can be discussed. Most will have taken positive advantage of these opportunities while others may have caused problems related to their sexual offending cycles. Each individual can be discussed in the following terms:

FACILITATOR:	So, John got the chance and what happened when he got the chance?
GROUP MEMBER:	He took the chance and he did the best with it.
FACILITATOR:	Yes that's right, he took the chance and made the most of it didn't he?
GROUP MEMBERS:	Yes he did well when he got the chance.
FACILITATOR:	Now what happened with Ian when he was given the chance to go to college?
GROUP MEMBER:	Well, he went off to the toilet on his own when he knows he should have told people.
FACILITATOR:	That's right, so what happened when Ian got his chance?
GROUP MEMBER:	He blew it didn't he.
FACILITATOR:	That's right, so what can happen when you get a chance to do something with yourself?
GROUP MEMBER:	Well you can take your chance or you can blow it.
FACILITATOR:	That's right, so what's important when you get these chances?

By reviewing the group member's progress in this way, facilitators can highlight the importance of progress through successful engagement with opportunities which arise for them. Again, the aim of the exercise is to increase motivation to achieve successful outcomes and avoid risk situations.

Conclusions

Motivation cannot be conducted as an independent module. It permeates the whole of the programme and exercises can be repeated with different variations at appropriate times throughout the process. Some of the exercises, such as the peer review exercise, can be inserted as formal sessions at regular intervals. Others will arise spontaneously. It is important that facilitators are aware of the way in which they can harness certain types of material to generate a motivational exercise so that they are able to increase and maintain motivation as the group programme progresses. Often, I am of the opinion that, as facilitators, we are constantly searching for opportunities to increase motivation and, even it is only for a few minutes in a group session, we should take any advantage of any chance to promote motivation to change and to maintain socialised routines.

Part Three
Treatment Manual

Chapter 9

Induction, Setting the Rules, Explaining the Modules

Explicit aims
- To introduce everyone to the domestic arrangements.
- To introduce everyone to the format of the group.
- To introduce everyone to each other including the group leaders.
- To establish the purpose of the group.
- To establish the rules of the group.
- To establish the modules for the programme.
- To introduce the way in which the modular format will be pursued.
- To reveal some preliminary information about each individual in the group sessions, including the group leaders.
- To explain the nature of the group and how it will work.

Implicit aims
- To establish the principles and practice of participant ownership.
- To demonstrate through example the methods of Socratic questioning and inductive reasoning.

The induction phase of the programme is crucial. The first two or three sessions will establish the tone and process for the whole treatment programme. Because it comes at the beginning, it may be that group facilitators are less confident regarding the Socratic method. It is important that facilitators practice this before beginning and, if necessary, get help and instruction from colleagues trained in cognitive therapy. This manual describes a summary outline of the Socratic method and also includes several examples of the Socratic dialogue. Other texts (e.g. Wells, 1997) give extensive descriptions of the Socratic method with further examples related to different types of problems.

The Treatment of Sex Offenders with Developmental Disabilities   William Lindsay
© 2009 John Wiley & Sons, Ltd

Number of sessions. The procedures throughout this manual are arranged in exercises/ tasks rather than sessions. Experience suggests that the induction in a new group takes around two or three sessions to complete (a session being a morning or an afternoon). If a new person is being introduced to an established group, the induction will take around an hour or so. When a new member is introduced to the group, allow the participants to complete the induction with him (see section on rolling programme, Chapter 7). After that, he should be allowed to sit and observe the group without being invited to contribute too often. In this way, he can become familiar and more comfortable with the workings of the group. It is up to the group leaders to decide the appropriate point to begin to incorporate him more actively. With a new group, each participant will make contributions in equal measure or as equal as possible, given that each individual will have different levels of linguistic ability, differ in dominance and be differently outgoing.

Remember that everything, as far as possible, should be done through Socratic questioning. Facilitators should discuss the aims and have ideas on how they will arrive at the aims through inductive reasoning and encouraging group ownership. Begin by asking group members what they feel the purpose of this group should be and write the answers on the flipchart. As has been indicated earlier, it is somewhat disingenuous to proceed in this way because the general purpose has already been set either by the group leaders or by outside agencies. Therefore, the group is likely to know that the purpose is to address issues of sexual offending and to avoid re-offending. It is likely that there will also be group-specific goals such as moving from conditions of high security to lesser security or complying with the conditions of probation. One of the main purposes of these early sessions is to demonstrate the methods of Socratic questioning and inductive reasoning and establish the principles of participant ownership. This will be obvious through the tone set in these initial sessions. At this point, it is probably better not to have an exercise on why individuals are attending the group. This information is extremely personal and can be very embarrassing and emotionally charged for participants. Therefore, it is important to allow participants to become a little more comfortable with treatment processes before going on to exercises which begin to explore why participants are attending.

Exercise 1: Establishing the Purpose of the Group

Materials: flipchart and pen

A number of purposes will be suggested by group members which can then be dis- cussed, some of which will be retained, others might be dropped either because they are outlandish or because they are not germane to the core purpose of a sex offender group. These latter purposes can be dropped with the explanation that they might be important, and we hope that participants might achieve these goals along the way but they are not a core purpose. For example, participants might say they wish new accommodation or they wish to become less anxious. These are important personal goals but are not germane to the purpose of the sex offender treatment group. Others might say they wish to 'stay out of trouble' which can be explored in more detail as a legitimate goal for group members.

It is possible to be flexible and accommodating in establishing the purpose of the group. Participants may mention something like 'I would like to be able to talk to people more easily' or 'I would like to not be nervous when I meet people'. It is possible to broaden these out into aspects of lifestyle change which promote socialised personal routines which do not lead to offending. Facilitators should prompt each suggestion towards their pre-agreed purposes for the programme which will generally be to address sex offending issues, explore the cycle of offending, avoid re-offending and promote a socialised lifestyle incorporating non-offence related routines.

Exercise 2: Establishing Group Rules

This has already been reviewed in Chapter 7. Certain rules have to be established but would usually emerge from Socratic questioning. As has been mentioned previously, the crucial rules to establish are

- confidentiality
- attendance.

Others which may emerge as important include

- no aggression or violence,
- equality of participation,
- allowing people to speak.

These rules can be seen as they emerged from an inductive process in the previous example (Figure 7.1). In the same way as the purpose of the group has been established, the group can establish the rules. The same principles govern the establishment of group rules. As can be seen from Figure 7.1, the immediacy and language used when group members develop their own rules can be quite powerful.

Exercise 3: Reviewing Modules

There are two goals for this exercise. The first is to orientate participants towards the broad purposes of the programme and the second is to explain the modular nature of the programme to participants. It will be difficult for participants who are unfamiliar with group treatment or with sex offender treatment to think about issues to be dealt with during the programme but even those who are completely unfamiliar with the nature of treatment will come up with an idea such as 'I've got to keep out of trouble' or 'I've not to do anything again'. This can then be interpreted by asking the participant 'What do you think would be important to look at or deal with so that you stay out of trouble?' In this way, other ideas can be generated. In our experience, a list of topics will emerge which can then be grouped into modules which are covered in this programme. If two or three modules are missed, it is quite in order for the group leaders to say they would like to add these topics. This exercise emphasises the fact that a number of concatenous topics will be covered making up the totality of the programme. However, there is no need to be comprehensive or precise. The general orientation of the programme content is the main message to be imparted. Facilitators can prompt the participants towards the following modules which are incorporated in the programme:

- Talking about your offence (disclosure and account of the offence).
- What led up to the offence (cycle of offending).
- Thinking about sex (cognitive distortions and offence related cognitions).
- Keeping out of trouble (self-regulation, self-control and relapse prevention).
- Harm to the victim (victim empathy and perspective taking).
- Making friends and staying away from bad influences (appropriate pro-social influences and avoiding antisocial influences).
- Getting a girlfriend (attachments and relationships).
- Understanding about sex (sex education).
- What's happened to me in my childhood (abuse and the cycle of abuse).

Exercise 4: Introductions/Initial Disclosure

This exercise is started by the facilitators asking to find out about participants. The information imparted would be very basic such as where were you born, where do you come from, which town do you live in and perhaps (if it is not too sensitive) what school you went to. Each group member will write or draw something about themselves on a flipchart sheet. Ensure that each participant confines their information to only one page. This avoids huge disparities between participants with one person completing half a page and another going on to three or four flipchart pages. Facilitators should attempt to avoid any implicit or explicit dominance of any one group member. It is likely to happen simply because of the nature of people and their individual differences. However, group leaders should try to ensure that the methods themselves do not encourage dominance. At the end of the task, each individual will have one page of information containing their name, age and any other information they feel comfortable about revealing. At this point, they do not have to reveal anything about their index offence although several might. They do not have to reveal other non-sexual offences, although, once again, several might. Facilitators can prompt the participants to reveal where they come from, how many members are in their family, previous work or activities, interests and hobbies, experience such as holidays and weekends away and where they have lived in the past. One of the main purposes of this exercise is to help participants gain some experience on revealing information about themselves and writing it on the flipchart. The actual information revealed at this point is not so important.

Chapter 10

Offence Disclosure and Accounts

Aims

- To get a reasonably detailed account of the offence which can be used throughout the course of the programme.
- To get accounts of other related offences and incidents.
- To have an account of previous offences.
- To begin to establish issues related to the patterns and pathways of individual offences and offences in general.
- To establish the link between sexual feelings, cognitions, behavioural scripts and actions.

Things to be careful about

It is likely that participants will have been waiting for and would be anxious about this initial aspect of the programme. They will realise that they are going to be asked to disclose information about their index offence and some individuals will have been dreading it since they were first referred to the sex offender group. Generally, it is better to get this aspect of the programme into the therapeutic process as soon as possible so that the individual participant can lose these feelings of anxiety and apprehension. However, it is certainly the case that with a group of six or eight people, one person will have to wait for 6 to 8 weeks before they can even begin to disclose their offence (assuming that each offence disclosure takes one session). Facilitators should try to be aware of any unusual, excessive buildup of anxiety in any participants.

It is not uncommon for individuals to become angry during disclosure. It is likely that this is brought on by a mixture of anxiety, embarrassment, resentment about curtailment of lifestyle and worry that others will be extremely censorious when they hear the details of the index offence. This is one reason why some reference to swearing,

The Treatment of Sex Offenders with Developmental Disabilities William Lindsay
© 2009 John Wiley & Sons, Ltd

anger or violence may be mentioned in the rules. The anger should be dealt with in a supportive way with group leaders saying that they understand it is difficult to talk about these things because people get anxious and wonder what other folk think, that the exercise is important and that the participant is managing well. As the group develops, participants generally become more able to challenge each other and be supportive of each other. When new individuals begin the group (in an open, rolling group) and begin their disclosure sessions, other members can be encouraging and supportive with statements such as 'We know it is difficult because we've all done it' or 'I found it really hard but it's better once you've got it over with'. Such support can be prompted by facilitators with questions to existing group members such as 'Albert, can you tell us again how difficult you found it talking about your offence?'

Another issue to be careful about in this exercise is that participants should not feel that their index offence can be excused because it is less serious than someone else's. If there is any indication that such an attitude is emerging in relation to certain individuals, it should be reiterated that everyone has committed a sex offence and there are no sex offences which are acceptable to society. During the initial sessions, and indeed in subsequent sessions, it is quite common for one group member to criticise another because of the nature of the offence. For example, someone who has offended against adults may be critical of another man who has offended against children. On these occasions, it is quite common for facilitators to ask the question 'Are there any angels in here?' to which the answer is obviously 'No'. Occasionally, the answer might be 'Yes, but I haven't done anything as bad as that'. This is the kind of dialogue that might ensue:

PARTICIPANT: That was a terrible thing to do, my crime isn't as bad as that.
FACILITATOR: Well everyone in here has committed a sex offence.
PARTICIPANT: Yes, but there are sex offences and sex offences. Mine was nothing like that.
FACILITATOR: What do other people think? Do you think that there are any sex offences that are okay?
OTHERS: No they are all bad. It doesn't really matter, does it?
We've all done something that's bad.
Everyone's done something wrong.
FACILITATOR: That's what I think. I agree with you, is everyone here for the same reason?
PARTICIPANT: Yes, everyone's here for the same reason. We've all committed a sex offence.
FACILITATOR: So are there any angels in here?
PARTICIPANT: No, but my offence wasn't as bad.
FACILITATOR: Well, are there any offences that are okay?
PARTICIPANT: No, there's none that are okay.
FACILITATOR: So is everyone here for the same reason?
PARTICIPANT: Well I suppose so, everyone has committed a sex offence haven't they.
FACILITATOR: That's about it, I don't see any angels in here.

Clearly, the individual has not been convinced that the baseline of committing a sex offence is sufficient to establish equality, but the principle of equality has been reinforced.

Exercise 1: Graded Disclosure

Materials: flipchart and pen

In a completely new sex offender group, it is better to start with what might be considered 'graded exposure'. This carries on from the previous exercise in the induction phase in which individuals introduce themselves. There is a very specific reason for graded disclosure. If there are six individuals in a group, the first five may give full accounts of their offence while the final participant may refuse to do so. This places the first five in a vulnerable position with respect to confidentiality. If the final participant breaches confidentiality by recounting to external individuals, aspects of the offences committed by the other five, he can do it from the relatively safe position of not having revealed aspects of his own offence to the others. With a process of graded disclosure, group members can reveal information which is, at first, fairly innocuous (such as name, where you live, where you used to work, where you work currently and so on) and then move on to information which is more and more related to the offence itself. Therefore, individuals can reveal:

- When the offence happened.
- Where it happened.
- Age of the victim.
- Sex of the victim.
- How the incident was discovered.
- Who investigated the incident.
- Whether or not the police were involved.
- The extent to which it went through the judicial process.

This information is increasingly central to the offence itself but if individuals reveal this information first then they all remain, more or less, with an equal knowledge about each other. Only after all of this information has been disclosed would the facilitators go on to gain details about the specific index offence itself. In this way, no individual is particularly protected in relation to the others by not having disclosed information and no individual is particularly exposed in relation to the others by having disclosed everything about their offence while others have not.

Figure 10.1 shows graded disclosure, occurring over two sessions with six group members. As can be seen, aspects of where they live, where they went to school, their age, where the offence occurred, age of the victim and sex of the victim are all recorded on the flipchart. Participants all began by recording where they stayed and which school they went to and progressed through to recording that four offended against children and two against adults, five offended against females and two against males (one recorded index offences against both males and females). They also wrote the location of the offence during this exercise. Therefore, although specific details of the index offences are not revealed at this point, a great deal of offence-related information can be elicited. If one group member subsequently refuses to reveal details of their particular offence, facilitators can then reflect that they already know a fair bit about this particular offence from these graded disclosure exercises.

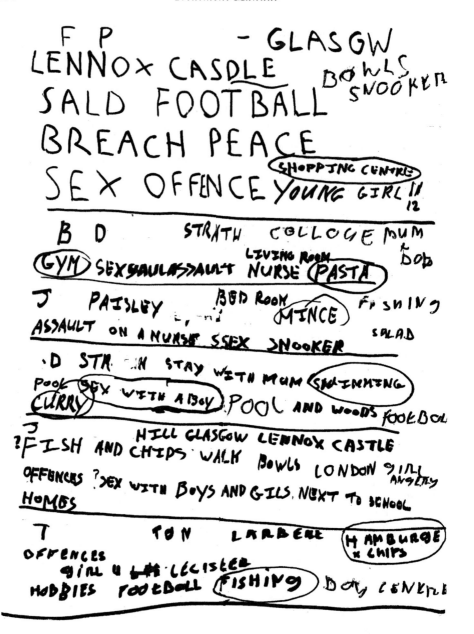

Figure 10.1 The beginnings of a graded disclosure exercise

Exercise 2: Offence Disclosure Accounts

Materials: flipchart and pen

Each individual will give an account of their index offence. This should be completed in as much detail as possible. Each participant can draw or write their index offence on the flipchart. Facilitators should take the participant through the sequence of events leading up to the incident, during the incident and after the incident. This information will be useful at a later date when reviewing pathways and cycles of offending.

It should be possible to draw out emotion and cognition at each point in the cycle. Therefore, the group leader can ask 'How did you feel when you were in the pub?' or 'What were you thinking when you were in the pub?' Remember to draw out information on the four channels of emotion – behaviour and action, physiology, emotion and cognition. Therefore, it will include the sequence of events and actions, the sequence of emotions associated with these actions, and the point at which sexual sensations and an adrenaline 'rush' emerged and the sequence of cognitions which accompanied the emotion, the feelings and the actions.

It may not be possible to draw them out in detail and it is counterproductive to challenge the emotions and cognitions at this point in the programme. For example, it would be common for a participant to say 'I was angry with her so I attacked her because of what she was doing'. Alternatively, an offender might say 'I was so angry with her mother that I don't want to hit women or attack women so I took it out on the daughter by assaulting her'. Clearly, there are cognitive distortions associated with mitigation of the offence and shifting responsibility on to the victim or to the victim's mother in these cases. It may be possible to make some comment or allusion to the cognitive distortions and excuses that the individual is making to themselves at that point in time. However, despite the natural inclination of facilitators to be amazed, indeed horrified by those cognitive distortions and despite the fact that they may wish to challenge them as soon as possible, it is better to leave the exercise on intensive challenging of cognitive distortions and thinking errors until later in the programme. At this point, the main aim is to get a reasonably detailed account of the chain of events during the offence. We do not wish participants to suppress their attitudes at an early stage in treatment; rather, we seek to understand as fully as possible their cognitive framework and schemata surrounding the offence.

During the later sessions of cognitive distortions and cycles of offending, the relationship between cognition, emotion, physical feelings and action will be explored in detail. During these sessions, a great deal of time will be given over to reviewing cognitions and personal excuses and, in turn, challenge these self-statements. However, at this earlier point in the programme, the important exercise is to elicit the sequence of events related to the index offence. This exercise will take at least one session for each participant. Because of the personal difficulties in recounting these incidents, participants will be reluctant to divulge detail and it may in fact take two or three sessions or even longer to gather all the relevant information. This can be done at a later date during later modules. As is mentioned previously, facilitators are likely to uncover information about the cycle of offending related to the index and other offences throughout the programme.

At regular points in this exercise, other participants can be invited to make comments on issues they would like expanded or issues about which they are puzzled and would like clarification. It is important that the disclosure sessions do not become a single person account of their own incident. If one individual is taking too long a time, the others may become distracted. Therefore, the facilitators should encourage the other group members to take an active role as the account unfolding, questioning pieces of information, asking for clarification, asking for additional information and so on.

It is usual for participants to address comments and questions about each other towards the facilitators. Try to develop the habit of reinforcing the question (if it is appropriate) and redirecting it to the person to whom it is relevant as follows:

ALEX:	Do you think he stayed behind so he could get to her on his own?
FACILITATOR:	That's a good question, Alex, but I don't know. Why don't you ask him?
ALEX:	Did you stay behind so you could get her on her own or your own?
PARTICIPANT:	No. No I did not.
FACILITATOR:	What do you think about that answer Alex, it was a good question, why did you ask it?
ALEX:	Well I think he was waiting to be on his own with her.
FACILITATOR:	Well ask him again and see what he says.
ALEX:	Were you waiting to be on your own with her?
PARTICIPANT:	No. I told you I wasn't.

This passage illustrates a number of points and methods which can be fostered by facilitators. The facilitator is encouraging group members to gain information from each other about specific aspects of a disclosure account. She is also emphasising the fact that each person's question and opinion are valued (as long as it is appropriate). Although the participant who is giving the disclosure gives a short, curt (and perhaps annoyed) reply, the facilitator is supporting the questioner. This support, conducted repeatedly throughout the programme, conveys the message that participants are not going to be able to intimidate others through being annoyed or implying that they might become aggressive. Such a defensive tactic will simply encourage further questioning. If the participant who is disclosing becomes overtly angry, the facilitator would then ask the other participants why he is becoming angry. The answer which is likely to be induced is that he is becoming annoyed because he does not want to discuss his offence. Using such redirection repeatedly also promotes group cohesion and demonstrates to participants that they are not only allowed to discuss each other's offences but also that it is encouraged.

When there are points in any individual's account that the facilitators would wish to register as general points, then it is quite in order to disrupt the flow and put a marker down for the future.

As an example, if two or three individuals had mentioned anger prior to the perpetration of the sexual offence and yet another personal account involves anger prior to the sexual offence, the group leader should pull out the commonalities in the following way:

PARTICIPANT:	I felt angry with the mother for what she had done and so I just waited until they went out of the house and then I thought I'll get her back through her daughter.
FACILITATOR:	So why didn't you just attack the mother?
PARTICIPANT:	Because I don't want to hit women and I'm not a violent man so I wouldn't do that.

FACILITATOR: So what did you do instead?
PARTICIPANT: Well I attacked the daughter instead because that would be getting her back.
FACILITATOR: So you felt angry at the mum and because of that you got her back by attacking her daughter.

Some more time is spent in developing detail on this sequence. In addition, the facilitator knows the emotion that other participants felt prior to their index offence and so she may broaden the discussion to draw out the commonality:

FACILITATOR
(to another
participant):   How did you feel before you attacked the woman in your hostel?

OTHER PARTICIPANT: Well I was angry with her because I felt sexy and she didn't want to go out with me.

FACILITATOR: So did you feel angry as well before you sexually assaulted her?

PARTICIPANT: Yes, I was really angry with her because I had asked her to go out and she'd told me to fuck off.

FACILITATOR: Remember that you're not meant to swear in this group but is that what she actually said?

PARTICIPANT: Well not at first, she told me to go away or she didn't want to go out with me and then she said it.

FACILITATOR
(to another
participant):   And when you attacked that bus driver, how did you feel before that?

PARTICIPANT: Well I wanted to kill her, I was so angry with her.

FACILITATOR: So you were angry before you attacked the bus driver.

PARTICIPANT: Yes, I told you I wanted to kill her. I was really angry with her.

FACILITATOR
(to another
participant):   And how did you feel before you followed that woman all the way out to New Town?

PARTICIPANT: Well I wanted to follow her because I wanted to have sex with her.

FACILITATOR: But after you had been in the club, how did you feel?

PARTICIPANT: Well I was angry with her when she told me to go away after I'd asked her if she wanted to go for a drink.

FACILITATOR: Yes, you said you'd danced with her and how many times did you ask her to go for a drink?

PARTICIPANT: Well I asked her a few times but she just told me to fuck off.

FACILITATOR: So how did you feel when you were waiting outside the nightclub?

PARTICIPANT: Well I was still angry with her.

FACILITATOR: So when you were following her out to New Town, how were you feeling?

PARTICIPANT: Well I was angry and I was feeling sexy as well.

FACILITATOR: So what's the same about all these different sex offences?

In this way, the group participants came to realise that anger can be a common theme amongst offences. It may be a motivation, an accompanying emotion or an enabling emotion, but it is a common theme. In the case above, it may serve as an excuse or cognitive distortion. The individual may have used the example of being angry with the mother in order to justify having sex with the daughter. In this way, the individual may be supporting a self-concept/core belief of 'I'm not a child molester'.

Case examples

Two case examples are presented to illustrate the way in which offences are likely to be disclosed during this module.

Alfred

Alfred took two sessions to disclose the information in Figure 10.2. The figure shows in the top that he was in a nightclub and asked a woman to dance. This part of the disclosure is marked by (A) in the figure. She told him quite explicitly that she did not want to dance with him whereupon he became angry, left the nightclub and waited across the street in a shop doorway for her to leave (B) in the figure. When she left, he followed her to the train station and got on the same train as she did (C). You can see the way he has drawn the woman at the front of the train and himself at the back of the train in order that he would not be seen (D). He said at the time he felt angry and sexually aroused. He followed her to her home (E) and waited outside all night. When she left in the morning, he broke into her home and stole several items for the purposes of masturbation. These included home videotapes (F) and clothing (G). He returned the following evening in order to watch her and masturbate. He also phoned her in the evening (I). He broke in again the following day and stole more items. He repeated the routine on the subsequent days and was eventually apprehended by the police and charged. The figure also shows that Alfred thought that they might develop a romantic relationship (J) and that he subsequently realised that she was not attracted to him (K). All of this detail is clearly depicted in the notes which he recorded throughout the session and these notes were used later in subsequent sessions on the cycle of offending and cognitive distortions.

Brian

The notes from Brian's disclosure session can be seen in Figure 10.3. He had been staying in rented accommodation and, for some time, had not been getting on with his landlady (A). One evening when he came home from work, he went to the pub with his friends and drank several pints of beer (B). He then went back to his accommodation where his landlady told him that she wanted him to babysit while she went out with her boyfriend to a nightclub (C). He then had to stay in and spent some time watching television (D) and becoming increasingly angry. He also said that he was watching pornographic programmes on television which raised his sexual arousal together with his anger. As the evening wore on he decided that he would check

Figure 10.2 Alfred's disclosure account

his landlady's children. He went upstairs and sexually assaulted the daughter aged 9 (F). He gave details about the sexual assault in that the girl woke and he eventually ejaculated on the sheets (G). He then walked out of the house and the incident was discovered when the couple came home. He was apprehended later by the police and charged with sexual assault. Details from the disclosure were employed extensively in later sessions.

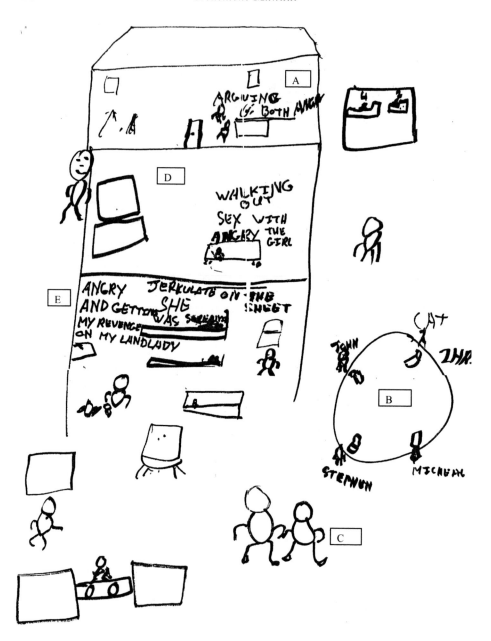

Figure 10.3 Brian's disclosure account

With a group of eight participants, this exercise may take 12 to 16 sessions. If facilitators feel that, because they are becoming more familiar and comfortable with the process, offence disclosure accounts from later participants are more comprehensive than disclosure accounts from earlier participants, then it is quite in order to go back to the earlier accounts and gain more information.

Exercise 3: Reviewing Commonalities

Materials: all of the previous completed flipcharts and further blank
flipcharts sheets with pens

Place all the flipchart sheets on the floor or on the walls around the room and encourage participants to review across all of the accounts, drawing out common themes. It is likely that facilitators will have to spend some time explaining the purpose of this exercise. Facilitators will have to simplify the meaning of the word 'similarities' and explain that she is interested in similar aspects of the offence while understanding the offences are not exactly the same. Participants are likely to say things such as 'But they are not the same they are different', 'But his was on children and mine was on women'. The facilitator can simplify the language and foster an example, such as 'Yes, I see that, but there are bits of the flipcharts which are the same. How many of you have written that you were angry during the offence?' The themes most likely to emerge are:

- Alcohol or substance abuse.
- Anger and hostile attitude.
- Cognitive distortions which might mitigate responsibility of the perpetrator.
- Cognitive distortions which minimise the responsibility of the perpetrator.
- Behavioural routines/scripts that will lead to offending.
- Sexual excitement.
- Use of pornography.
- Lack of consent.
- Use of force.

If this is the first treatment model which has been covered, it is likely that the analysis of common themes will be fairly simple. However, the principles of formulation and common themes can be established. In addition, it may also be that the principles of simple cognitive distortions being involved in the cycles of sexual offending and pathways towards sexual offending are also established.

In relation to cognitive distortions, Abel *et al.* (1989), in a factor analysis of the Abel and Becker Cognitions Scale, found six themes as follows:

- The sex offence helps the victim.
- Victims initiate the sex offence for their own reasons.
- Perpetrators initiate the incident for specific reasons.
- Victims show desire for sex with the perpetrator.
- Perpetrators can predict if they are harming the victim and whether or not the harm will last.
- The sex offence (e.g. sex with children) is or will be acceptable to society under certain circumstances.

These are relatively complex, nuanced basic schemata related to cognitions and they are unlikely to emerge as commonalities from the offence disclosure accounts gained in this module. However, it is worthwhile keeping them in mind during this exercise since, if they do emerge, they can be used in later modules. In our own research on

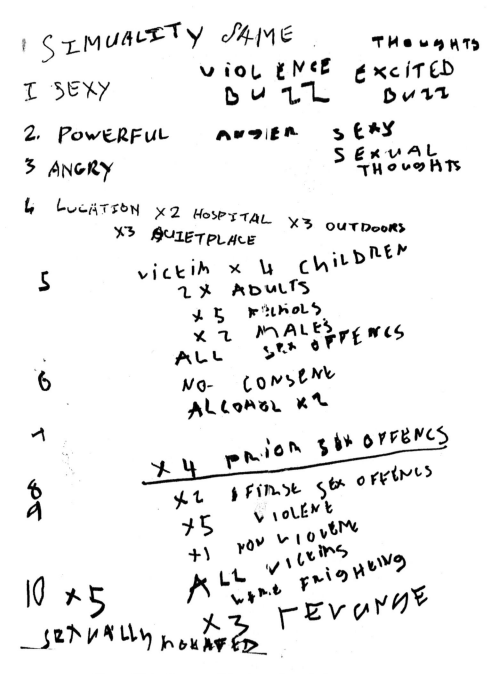

Figure 10.4 Commonalities drawn from disclosure accounts

cognitive distortions (Lindsay *et al.*, 2008b), in a similar factor analysis, we found two factors emerged strongly from cognitions scales. The first was minimisation of the offence. This includes thoughts that there was not too much harm done to the victim, that it was understandable under the circumstances, that victims laughed about it (minimised it) and the society accepts these incidents under certain circumstances. The second was a concept of mutuality. That victims initiated the incident, that the perpetrator initiated the incident, that victims enjoyed the incident and that victims might have gained something from the incident. Figure 10.4 is a record from a group which has reviewed the communalities among offence disclosure accounts. As can be seen, group members have made some fairly astute identification of some of the main similarities including the following:

- Violence.
- A sexual 'buzz'.
- Anger.
- Sexual thoughts.
- Feelings of power during the sexual offence.
- Lack of consent.
- Fear in the victims.
- The fact that the offence occurred in a quiet place.
- Some were motivated by revenge.

All of this material will be used in later modules when reviewing cycles of offending and identifying motivation for offending. The advantage of this exercise being linked to later exercises is that group members have identified this list of motivations, emotions, physical feelings and other variables by themselves.

Exercise 4: Returning to Disclosure

This is not really an exercise at all but simply a reminder that as the sex offender programme progresses, further information will emerge from discussions, role plays and various exercises which will add to the information gained during this disclosure phase. Therefore, facilitators should not feel too concerned if they think that the disclosure may not have been completely comprehensive. It is quite reasonable to come back to further aspects of disclosure if and when further information emerges. Often, it will emerge indirectly from an offhand remark by a group member. If this happens, try to deal with the information at an appropriate point in the group sessions. Place it alongside information which is already known to facilitators to emphasise to group members that one of the purposes of treatment is to build up a clearer picture of the offence and the various aspects and issues surrounding it.

Chapter 11
Allocating Offenders to Pathways

As we have seen in earlier chapters, the current literature on pathways into sexual offending and re-offending is applicable to offenders with intellectual disability and, in mainstream work, is being incorporated into treatment. However, it is difficult to allocate offenders to pathways prior to gaining significant amounts of information about their index offence and other offences. Therefore, at this point in treatment, having gathered information from disclosure sessions, facilitators should take some time outside of the treatment sessions to consider allocation of each offender to one of the offending pathways. This enables facilitators to review the disclosure information in detail and in a structure which will inform on the information to be gained over the course of the modular programme. It will also help in determining how that information will be used for each group member by providing an individual formulation for each participant.

It will be remembered that Ward and Hudson (1998) proposed four basic pathways for offending into which sex offenders could be categorised. These were split into two approach pathways and two avoidant pathways. The first is the approach/explicit pathway in which the individual has a clear, active wish to sexually offend and uses explicit plans and procedures to carry out the act. The approach/automatic pathway involves the individual engaging in over-learned behavioural scripts which result in a more passive set of routines which are consistent with sexual offending. The third pathway is avoidant/active where the individual attempts to control actively their thoughts and behaviour which might lead towards sexual offending but the strategies are ineffective and counterproductive leading to an increased risk of sexual offending. The fourth pathway is avoidant/passive where the individual may wish to avoid sexual offending or abusive incidents but lacks coping skills to prevent it from happening.

Illustrations are given below as examples of the way in which offenders with ID can be allocated to different pathways.

The Treatment of Sex Offenders with Developmental Disabilities   William Lindsay
© 2009 John Wiley & Sons, Ltd

An example of the avoidant/passive pathway: Colin

It will be remembered from the earlier chapters that in studies on sex offenders with ID which allocate individuals to pathways, few individuals were allocated to the avoidant/passive pathway. However, Colin was considered to have offended following an avoidant/passive pathway.

Colin has a stable family history and lived with his parents all his life. Colin is a 28-year-old man with an IQ of 68 (WAIS-III UK). He was a quiet man who had attended school for children with intellectual disabilities. He lived a very sheltered life with his parents and, after school, had not attended any day services for people with ID. He had gained two short work placements through his father but because of his slowness in completing tasks and his difficulty in understanding the requirements of the jobs, he had not been kept on longer than a few months. His mother had never worked and his father had not worked for around 10 years. They did have a holiday caravan in a nearby coastal town and they spent extended periods in the caravan. Colin's social contact was now confined to his mother and father, spending periods of time with them at home and in their caravan. He had little contact with people of his own age since individuals on the caravan site were either young teenagers on holiday, resulting in short periods of contact time, or retired couples there for extended stays.

Colin had never had a girlfriend and he began to worry excessively about his lack of sexual contact. He began having sexual fantasies and it disturbed him that his thoughts were about boys. He made attempts to stop thinking about boys in a sexual fashion but found that it was difficult to do so. At around the age of 25, he began following boys both at home and in the town with the caravan park. Following each episode, he reported that he felt terrible and thought that he was doing 'something really bad'. However, incidents increased in frequency and he began masturbating while he was watching the boys (as the incidents developed, it later transpired there may have been dozens of episodes). He began to move closer to the boys and utter obscene utterances to them such as 'Would you like to wank me off', 'I bet you get fucked all the time', 'You'll not wank me off but you'd wank anybody else off, wouldn't you'. These obscene remarks appeared to be part of his feelings of disgust at himself and his feelings of worthlessness. It was not until around 4 years after the onset of these incidents that one was witnessed and reported to the police and he was charged. Colin masturbated to fantasies of the incidents, although he tried not to because of his feelings of disgust. He had not come into contact with the intellectual disability services since school.

Avoidant/passive pathway

The avoidant/passive pathway is characterised by under-regulation and a desire to avoid sexual offending but a lack of coping skills to prevent it from happening (Ward *et al.*, 2004). The individual is likely to make negative self-evaluations, express a desire to avoid offending but seems unable to develop the skills and strategies which would help him avoid such incidents. Because these individuals are unable to develop appropriate skills, Keeling and Rose (2005) hypothesised that sex offenders with ID may be most likely to follow this pathway. As noted in earlier chapters, empirical studies have not supported this hypothesis. Colin certainly appeared to experience loss of control and following this loss of control, appeared to experience a great deal of disinhibition. These incidents were followed by negative appraisal and because of his feelings of inadequacy, his negative self-appraisal and his apparent inability to control his behaviour, we allocated Colin to the avoidant/passive pathway. It may have been that when he went for walks near his home or near the caravan, he was employing an active strategy to look for boys, but, by his account, it appeared that he was kidding himself when he went out for walks determined not to follow boys in the way he had done in the past. Of course, he invariably did fall into the behavioural routine of following boys and experiencing sexual arousal.

If one considers the risk factors associated with Colin's case, his score was medium risk on the Static-99. His sexual offence had been committed against an unrelated victim, a stranger and a male victim. However, he had no previous charges or convictions, was over 25 (thus reducing his risk on the Static-99) and his offences did not involve violence. He has never had a relationship but this item seems difficult to score in sex offenders with ID since so few have ever had a relationship for longer than six months, not because of their sexuality but because of their intellectual disability. In a series of comparisons of sex offenders with ID and other types of offenders with ID, Lindsay *et al.* (2004b, 2006c) have noted that extremely few individuals with ID have had even medium-term relationships where they have lived with a partner. It should be noted, however, that Colin admitted to having committed dozens of previous, similar incidents which had not been prosecuted. The police had apprehended him on a few occasions but had simply returned him to his supportive parents. Had Colin been normally able, it may well be that the police would have prosecuted the incidents.

Colin certainly has a number of dynamic factors which would increase his risk. There are a number of standard factors which are relevant to him including intimacy/relationship deficits, deviant sexual interest, social loneliness and problems with coping with his negative emotions. Colin also had a high level of resentment regarding sexuality, particularly related to his lack of sexual contact and extremely low self-esteem. This latter construct has been considered to be a particular dynamic risk variable in sex offenders (Thornton, 2002). Assessment using the Questionnaire on Attitudes Consistent with Sexual Offences (QACSO) found that Colin endorsed a high rate of cognitive distortions associated with sexuality with boys and women. Further exploration of these cognitive distortions suggested that they were associated with resentment regarding Colin's lack of heterosexual social and sexual contact.

This idiomatic formulation allows us to consider treatment targets which are specific to Colin and which can be addressed as part of group sessions and in addition to group sessions. Lindsay (2005) in his analysis of sex offender treatment for men with ID has written that treatment should focus on the dual aspects of the sexual offence itself and the individual's engagement with society in general. Clearly, Colin has specific deficits in relationships, loneliness and engagement with others. These variables, and this analysis of Colin's pathway, suggest that it is vitally important to address these issues in addition to dealing with Colin's attitudes and behaviour associated with the sexual offence. Colin clearly lacks strategies for coping with his sexual feelings and his behavioural routines which are consistent with the sexual offences. At the time of assessment, these behavioural routines were supported and endorsed by his cognitive distortions. Indeed, the cognitive distortions seemed to act as motivation for engaging in the behavioural routines consistent with sexual offending. A further goal of treatment is to deal with the negative self-evaluation that Colin places on all of this behaviour. At the time of assessment, the negative evaluation simply serves to promote feelings of worthlessness which in turn appear to continue the cycle of offending.

Avoidant/active pathway: Darren

Darren was a 30-year-old man with a measured IQ of 62 (WAIS-III UK). He was convicted of a severe, aggressive sexual assault on a female care worker in the home in which he lived. He had had a very disrupted childhood, coming from a disorganised family who were unable to deal with his behavioural problems. He had spent many of his younger years in residential schools and other establishments for children and adolescents with ID. On leaving school, he had been transferred back to his home area where he had been placed in a group home for young adults with ID. He had progressed well and had been transferred to an individual tenancy for 2 years but behavioural and sexual problems started to emerge and he was transferred to his current group home where he had lived for 3 years. The placement had not been particularly harmonious and Darren had continued to demonstrate some behavioural and emotional difficulties. He had been referred a number of times for psychiatric assessment and psychological treatment and had a range of support workers. He had four previous heterosexual relationships all of which had been actively sexual. One of these relationships, in his final school placement, had lasted for around 9 months. He had not had a relationship over the last 5 or 6 years since leaving his first group home to go into the individual tenancy.

Around 5 years before the incident, Darren began to identify himself strongly with a popular rap/hip-hop artist. He began to collect clothing and memorabilia about the artist and his bedroom was festooned with pictures, T-shirts and other items of clothing. He always dressed in shirts and jackets associated with the rap artist. Over the last year, he had begun to march up and down the corridor of the home wearing the clothing and shouting the violent songs. He fully acknowledged that this gave him feelings of power and invincibility. During these years, he had also begun to worry about having a sexual relationship. He began masturbating to sexual fantasies, pornography and thoughts of previous sexual relationships. There were records of him attempting to masturbate up to 10 times per day and worrying that he was unable to gain a heterosexual relationship. He began to worry about his sexual fantasies and masturbated excessively in an attempt to control his sexual feelings. He also increased his feelings of energy and power by listening to other American rap artists and listening to rave music. At one level, he seemed to thrive on the feelings which he derived from rap, rave music and pornography. At another level, he felt that he was controlling his sexuality and sexual feelings through the use of these stimuli. During this period, he also became attracted to a number of females, one of whom was the care worker. During the day of the assault, he began to have one of his regular fantasies concerning the care worker in which he had a relationship with her and she also enjoyed listening with him to the rap artist. The feelings of sexual frustration, power associated with the rap artist and wishes to have a relationship increased as the day progressed and towards the evening while he was masturbating he decided to sexually assault the care worker. He assaulted her violently in the dayroom and it required a number of other staff to stop him.

Avoidant/active pathway

The avoidant/active pathway is characterised by inappropriate regulation strategies whereby the individual attempts to control his sexuality through inappropriate means such as alcohol use or masturbation. These strategies generally do not work and may have the paradoxical effect of increasing sexual frustration and sexual risk. In situations which may carry a risk of sexual offending, the individual may employ these strategies which will increase the chances of an offence. Darren was clearly attempting to control his sexuality and sexual frustration through excessive masturbation. It may also have been that his relatively recent identification with a rap/hip-hop artist was a substitute for a sexual relationship in which he would cope with his emotions in a more adaptive fashion. However, the identification simply served to increase his feelings of power which in turn appeared to increase his feelings of sexual frustration and entitlement. Therefore, Darren appeared to employ active strategies to avoid coercive sexual encounters with women. After the incident, Darren was unable to control his anger even when apprehended by the police and taken to the station. However, by morning, he was contrite saying that he realised it was an awful thing to do and stating that he could not understand why he had acted in such a fashion. Over the following months, Darren continued to state that he understood it was a 'terrible thing to do'. His statements on the matter accompanied as they were by apparent feelings of deep dejection, seemed different to statements from other sex offenders when they place negative associations with the incident.

Risk assessment

Darren did have two previous offences where he had been verbally abusive to women. These incidents were not, at the time, considered to be sexual but may be re-appraised during sex offender treatment. He has also shown violence associated with the sexual offence and offending against unrelated victims. He has a history of disrupted relationships and behavioural problems as a child and as an adolescent. Notwithstanding the four heterosexual relationships he has had, there is some evidence of intimacy deficits in relation to his family and, more recently, in relation to peers. Therefore, there are a number of static risk factors which place Darren in the range of medium risk for future offending. In relation to dynamic risk factors, he has shown severe sexual frustration associated with feelings of empowerment and entitlement. This is a specific, individual confluence of dynamic risk factors in this case. However, assessment on the QACSO suggested that he had a very low level of cognitive distortions associated with offences against women or children. In fact, assessment placed all of his scores on the QACSO in a range lower than the means for non-offenders with ID. Extensive psychiatric assessment concluded with a diagnosis of bipolar disorder which was controlled with moderate levels of appropriate medication. (This diagnosis had been made some 2 years prior to the incident and his mood disorder had been well controlled on medication.)

The assessment of Darren's pathway and the risk assessment provide clear individual treatment goals for him. It also provides a series of idiomatic risk factors which should be considered in his future treatment and management. Feelings of empowerment, feelings of entitlement, excessive masturbation associated with sexual frustration and exaggerated concerns about establishing a heterosexual relationship should all be incorporated into sex offender treatment as part of the group processes. The modules on attachments and relationships, described later in this volume, were of particular relevance to Darren's treatment. Treatment should also employ his remorse concerning the incident and his apparent lack of cognitive distortions and attitudes supportive of sexual offending. In this regard, it is possible to focus on the dissonance between his behaviour, his feelings of power and entitlement and his relatively socialised attitudes towards women and children. Unusually for sex offenders with ID (as we have seen in the previous chapter on motivation), Darren was quite keen to attend for treatment.

Exercise 1: Beginning Pathways to Offending

Materials: flipchart sheets and pens

This is a simple beginning, to review the offence pathway of the individual participant. This exercise is a preliminary version of the final exercise on developing a life map and relapse prevention plan (Chapter 19). Begin with each individual listing good things and bad things that have happened to them in their life. This is done in a straightforward fashion by splitting the page into good on the left and bad on the right. With two or three facilitators, all the participants will be able to complete this at the same time. Each participant can then present their list and facilitators can involve the others by asking questions such as 'Can anybody see anything missing in this list?' 'What do you think is the most important thing about this list?' 'Do any of you have anything on your list that is not on this list?'

Figure 11.1 shows a list of good and bad things that Fred (see later) drew up in his life. It represents some anchor points which can be used to begin the life map exercise which allows the facilitators to introduce sex offending pathways to clients in a straightforward and meaningful manner. There will be a tendency for the group members to place their sex offence and other offending behaviour in the 'bad' list. However, it is important to establish at this point that the reason why they engaged

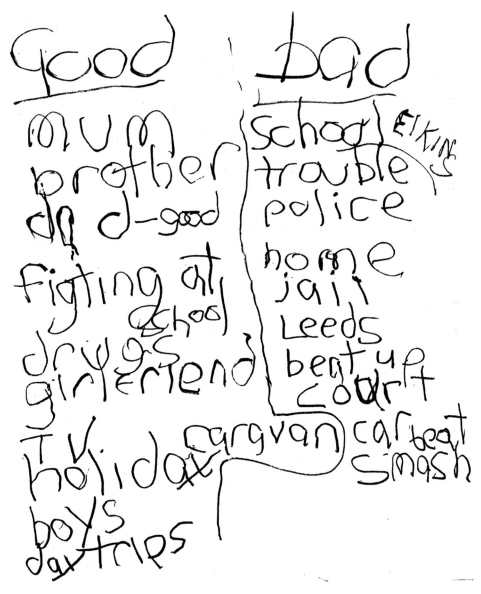

Figure 11.1 'Good things' and 'bad things' drawn up by Fred

in the offence was that it fulfilled a human need in their life at the time. Indeed, it is likely that such behaviour will continue to fill this human need unless it is addressed through sex offender treatment. Therefore, offenders will have to employ alternative self-regulation strategies to control these needs while facilitators are able to support them in fulfilling their needs in pro-social and acceptable ways. This is a crucial practical approach which emerges from the GLM and which is illustrated frequently throughout this and later chapters.

Exercise 2: Developing the Offence Pathway

Materials: flipchart sheet in landscape and pens

Begin this exercise by using a few of the important events listed by the participant. From the analysis completed by the facilitators, the main risk factors and the basic offence pathway should have already been drawn up. A timeline can now be constructed which incorporates the main risk factors and which illustrates the pathway to the index sexual offence and/or other sexual offences. Figure 11.2 shows a section of the pathway which Darren developed following his disclosure exercise. This clearly illustrates all of the risk factors which had been identified, including static and dynamic factors, and incorporates them into his avoidant/active pathway. The exercise also incorporates information concerning the detail of his index offence.

The figure shows that he identifies rap music, rap clothes, pornography and rave music as stimuli which induce feelings of power, anger and sexual excitement. This combines with 'thinking about females, lots of time alone, hiding in my room' which in turn leads to 'lots of masturbation'. In this way, Darren has generated an extremely pertinent and accurate formulation of the variables leading to his particular offence.

Approach/automatic pathway: Edward

As pointed out in the introductory chapters, research suggests that the approach pathways are more common in sex offenders with ID. Edward was a 28-year-old man with a measured IQ of 65 (WAIS-III UK). He was first brought to the attention of the forensic ID services when he was charged with breach of the peace after writing obscene letters to a member of staff in the local council offices where he organised his rent to be paid. The charges resulted in a 1-year probation order and he attended for a short period of treatment. Shortly after that, he was reported for following the shop assistant in his local grocery store when she was going home one evening. On this occasion, the woman turned to confront him and he ran off. However, the incident was investigated by the police and he was given a warning against his probation order. Although the period of probation finished, it became clear that he persistently followed women for voyeuristic purposes. He was extremely reluctant to attend for treatment and felt that since he was not touching the women, he was doing no harm by following them.

Edward had been brought up by his mother in impoverished circumstances. His father had left and his mother had two other children who were taken into care. Edward attended local schools for children and teenagers with intellectual disabilities and showed no behavioural problems. He was a fairly resourceful individual and on leaving school, organised his own council tenancy. He lived there on his own with no friends and visited relatives. Following his first offence, he became known to services but was extremely reluctant to engage saying that he was too busy. In fact, he slept for much of the day, watched pornographic videos and television during the afternoon and went out walking in the evening.

He was referred 1 year after the first probation order with a very similar offence of following women. On this occasion, treatment was more intensive and it became clear

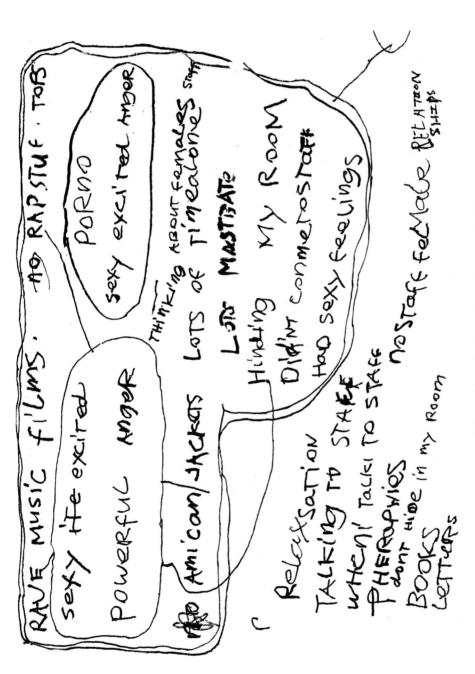

Figure 11.2   The avoidant/active pathway drawn up by Darren

173

that he had a variety of sexual fantasies, some of which were violent, that he would sit at home often watching ordinary television programmes but having sexual fantasies about the women in the programmes and then would go out for walks. During these walks, he might see a woman he liked and would start to follow. After 2 years of probation, he was once again caught following another woman and was charged and given a further 3-year probation order. His behavioural scripts and routines were pervasive in that he would go out walking any time from 7.00 pm until 5.00 or 6.00 am. He began to attend local all-night garages, 24-hour supermarkets and the early morning opening of newsagents as long as there were women whom he liked. He used many of these voyeuristic encounters in his masturbatory fantasies. The automatic nature of his self-regulation seemed obvious in the similarity and constancy of the behavioural scripts. However, latterly, there developed an active aspect of his night-time walking in that he began to realise that police were picking him up on CCTV. He noted the location of the cameras and started to walk streets which would avoid his detection on CCTV. His behavioural scripts began to impinge on the somewhat impoverished social life he led. He began to visit his uncle on so many occasions that his uncle told him to stop coming. When Edward continued to visit, his uncle got in touch with the police who then placed a restriction order on him and gave him a caution, resulting in a warning associated with his probation regime.

Approach/automatic pathway

Edward clearly has a number of over-learned behavioural scripts which are consistent with his voyeuristic sexual offending. These behavioural scripts and voyeuristic offences seem to feed his sexual fantasies which in turn strengthen the behavioural scripts and increase their frequency. His responses seem habitual and automatic, related to his daytime television activities, and although they may be under his control, he reported that he becomes agitated and angry when he is forced to stay in the house in the evening. There seem no higher level goals associated with his routines in that he simply watches television, becomes interested in sexuality with cognitions associated with voyeurism and subsequently acts accordingly. There seems little planning of his offences in that he begins walking and starts following whatever woman he sees and likes. Alternatively, he came across premises which were open all night and staffed by women. Edward reported no negative affect in relation to his voyeuristic behaviour; indeed the opposite seemed the case. He reported that he 'got a buzz' from these various activities and showed no wish to regulate or restrain the feelings of sexual excitement. He became recalcitrant and oppositional in the face of efforts to persuade him to comply with treatment. Indeed, over a period of 3 years, he complained about attending for almost every session.

Risk assessment

Edward has a number of static risk factors including the fact that he has a large number of prior sexual offences, a number of charges, convictions for non-contact sexual offences, sexual offences committed against unrelated victims and offences committed against strangers. There is also a record of prior treatment failure. He did not show any behavioural problems at school or as a teenager, neither has he shown any violent behaviour and so these do not constitute risk factors. During his first period of treatment, he was diagnosed as having bipolar mood disorder although this was not marked. It was, however, treated successfully with appropriate medication.

Edward also has a number of dynamic risk factors which are extremely important when considering his future treatment and management. He has problems with self-regulation in terms of his sexual behaviour and his general behaviour. He has never had close friends and continues to have deficits in his intimacy and relationships. Assessment on the QACSO indicated that he had a high level of attitudes consistent with sexual offending towards adult women, in relation to voyeurism, exhibitionism, dating abuse and stalking but not in relation to offences against children. His scores on the offences against children scale were consistent with non-offending men with ID. In addition, this positive self-appraisal and resistance to treatment intervention indicate that he has feelings of entitlement and justification with regard to his voyeuristic behaviour. His reluctance to attend treatment also reflects the fact that he avoids positive social influences.

This information has a number of treatment implications including the suggestions that Edward requires a high intensity of treatment focusing on his attitudes consistent with sexual offending, sessions focusing on the effect he has on his victims, procedures aimed at dealing with his feelings of entitlement, management procedures to disrupt his daily routines, altering his day/night routines so that he stays awake during the day and sleeps at night, increasing his pro-social influences and support networks in the community and promoting his general self-regulation and self-restraint. Edward is likely to be difficult to treat because he remains unmotivated, makes excuses for not appearing at treatment, is persistently reluctant to turn up for treatment, is reluctant to accept that he has a problem and does not accept that his behaviour might be harmful to others.

Approach explicit pathway: Fred

Fred is a 24-year-old man with a measured IQ of 66 (WAIS-R). He has been convicted of eight counts of sexual offences against boys. He came from a relatively stable background, having been brought up by both his mother and father with a younger brother and sister. His father worked as a deliveryman for a local firm. He attended local mainstream schools but had learning support throughout. There were no reports of behavioural problems but Fred himself reported a number of same sex relationships in secondary school. He also reported that in his late teens, he engaged in some prostitution activity. He was first arrested and charged with sexual assaults on three boys aged 10 and 11. He had gone to the depot of his father's firm where he knew young teenagers hung around in the evening and, on separate occasions, had induced the boys to masturbate him and perform fellatio on him. One of the boys informed his parents and the other two then came forward with similar charges. He received probation for this set of incidents but 1 year later, was charged with another five incidents, all of a similar nature with boys of the same age.

During assessment, he said that he would begin to feel sexual urges in the evening and decide to go down to the industrial area where the depot was, to see if he could find a boy who would have sex with him. Later, during treatment, it became clear that he offered inducements of cigarettes, alcohol and money for sex. On one occasion, he said that he had forced one of the boys to have sexual relations with him, although this had been dropped in the charges. When he became engaged in treatment services, it became clear that he was frequently seeking opportunities to have sex with other men and occasionally other women.

Approach explicit pathway

Fred's self-regulation strategies for achieving sex seem well organised and regulated. Despite the severe recriminations which followed the incidents and the legal processes which ended in a series of charges, he appeared to make no attempts to avoid sexual encounters with boys. Rather, he continued in the same directed and controlled pathway. While his plan for offending was simple and fairly regular, he continued, over a period of years, to manipulate victims so that he could gain sexual contact and sexual gratification. Fred seemed to have core cognitive schemata which motivated his sexual offending and supported his behaviour. His reasons for going to the distribution depot were quite explicit in that he wanted to have sex with the boys and, further, he had quite explicit strategies of offering inducements. He also knew the area very well and was familiar with places to go where he would be unseen. Despite criticism from family and social workers, he maintained a sense of entitlement regarding sexual encounters and his sexual behaviour. There was no hint of negative affect or even self-evaluation with Fred. His main affect during the assessment phases was anger and hostility towards the assessor to the extent that he refused to cooperate for weeks. He had specifically targeted both the areas he knew, an area which he knew boys frequented and had specifically targeted boys with a method he knew would be successful. He did not consider whether or not his sexual abuse of these boys was harmful. Instead, he seemed to be pleased that his method was successful, continued some aspects of it when engaged in treatment and showed anger when it was curtailed.

Risk assessment

Fred has a number of static risk factors including prior convictions for sexual offences, offences against unrelated victims, male victims and child victims. He also has multiple offences which, taken together, place him in the range of high risk for future offending.

In terms of dynamic risk factors, he has shown a persistent lack of concern for his victims accompanied by feelings of entitlement and high self-esteem. He has shown persistent deviant sexual preferences for young males. Assessment on the QACSO revealed a high level of cognitive distortions on every scale indicating considerable disregard for others across all victim types. Though there were no records of him offending against women, his cognitive distortions supporting rape and sexual assault against women were high along with his attitudes supporting offences against children. Interestingly, although he had experience of same sex relationships, his cognitive distortions supporting sexual offences against men were also high. His hostile attitude arising from the curtailment of his sexual offending is also a dynamic risk factor. When he had previously been given a probation order for the first discovery of sexual offences, he had continued to offend thus breaching the conditions which constitutes another dynamic risk factor. This latter point converges with his feelings of entitlement and his anger concerning the curtailment of his activities.

Treatment can focus on these risk factors and pathways to offending. His lack of empathy for victims and apparent inability to take the perspective of others is a clear treatment goal along with his belief that sexual activity with boys is not harmful. Indeed, he seems to hold a range of beliefs supporting sexual offending including mitigation of the incidents, placing responsibility on the victims, denial of harm to the victims and personal entitlement for sex. It was his contention that the boys were willing to have sex with him. These are a set of core cognitive schemata which must be addressed through extensive, intensive treatment. Ways should also be found of engaging him with the community. He has never worked since leaving school and has had no non-coercive sexual relationships. Both of these pro-social aspects should be involved in the treatment provision. Treatment should also address the extensive cognitive distortions reported by Fred.

It is interesting that neither Edward nor Fred were willing to report the details of their sexual offences. Ward, Yates and Long (2006) in their treatment manual related to the self-regulation model of the offence process have written that since the approach explicit offender does not generally regard their behaviour as wrong, they are likely to admit freely to the details of their offences. Both examples reported here were reluctant or unwilling to report details. It was the view of the assessor that this was due to two reasons. Firstly, they did realise that their behaviour was wrong and were unwilling to invite censure from individuals in authority. A second factor for their reluctance to recount details of the incidents was their anger at having these activities discovered and stopped.

Edward and Fred completed the same initial pathways into offending exercise described previously for Darren. On the top of the flipchart sheet, they placed good things in their lives and on the bottom of the sheet placed bad things in their lives. He viewed several aspects as negative in the weeks prior to offences and in the weeks during the re-offences. The negative aspects were lack of relationships and sexual frustration in addition to being caught and given probation. This exercise is fairly straightforward and begins the concept of a life map or timeline which starts in the individual's past but moves on to incorporate the Good Lives Model with possible pathways into the future. It should be noted that Edward's self-regulation pathway had a number of self-evaluations leading to offending which he construed as negative. He considered his lack of relationships and his sexual frustration as being big problems in his life prior to the offence. This is the significant difference with Fred's offence pathway. However, these illustrations demonstrate the way in which the fairly complex notions of self-regulation pathways and approach/avoidance goals can be simplified for sex offenders with ID and incorporated into their treatment programme.

Chapter 12

Cognitive Distortions
and Attitudes

Cognitive distortions and attitudes which support sexual offending are considered fundamental to the processes in which offenders deal with their internal inhibitions and establish a series of thoughts which might be considered permissive of or consistent with actions which result in sexual offending.

The introduction to this manual refers to a number of research studies and theoretical models which illustrate the centrality of cognitive distortions in the cycle of offending and pathways to offending.

Aims of the module

- Established the link between thinking, emotion, bodily sensations (sexual arousal) and action.
- Establish the function of cognitive distortions in the perpetration of sexual offences.
- Review the types of cognitive distortions – minimisation, mitigation, denial, entitlement and so on.
- Place cognitive distortions in personal cycles of offending.
- Examine the contribution of cognitive distortions to seemingly irrelevant decisions (SIDs).
- Review the personal social context which permits the development of cognitive distortions, for example isolation, antisocial influences.
- Review the personal social context which inhibits or discourages the development of cognitive distortions, for example appropriate relationships and attachments, prosocial influences.
- Review SIDs in risky situations and personal offending situations.

The Treatment of Sex Offenders with Developmental Disabilities   William Lindsay
© 2009 John Wiley & Sons, Ltd

- Review alternative socialised thinking and its relationship to offence cycles, pro-social behaviour, emotion and physiological arousal.
- Review the ways in which cognitive distortions shift responsibility from the offender to others, including the victim.
- Review the way in which cognitive distortions have shifted the responsibility in each participant's offence cycle.
- Use general and hypothetical situations and individual participant's offences to establish the way in which socialised thinking places responsibility with the perpetrator (individual participant).
- Continually challenge these cognitive distortions and inappropriate attitudes.

Not all of these will be relevant to each offender. These aims will be organised below into exercises and session formats. It is likely that facilitators will continue the programme by adhering to session formats. However, it is quite feasible that certain sessions will merge into each other. Once again, it is important that the facilitators are sufficiently familiar and flexible with the programme so that they can employ topics and methods from other sections which may be relevant to the on-going material being dealt with. For example, when reviewing types of cognitive distortions, it would be quite in order, if it was felt relevant and appropriate by the facilitators, to spend some time examining the contribution of cognitive distortions to SIDs. Similarly, when reviewing the place of cognitive distortions in the cycle of offending and noting the point at which a SID is being employed in the cycle, it would be appropriate to rehearse the kind of cognitive distortion which is relevant at that point. In this way, each of these session topics is likely to be relevant to the other.

Notes on language

These are some of the phrases clients have used which have helped to simplify the language in sessions.

Cognitive Distortions. Thinking errors, twisted thoughts, wrong ideas, wrong thoughts, crazy thoughts and danger thoughts.

SIDs. Looks like it's a spur of the moment but it is not; I thought it wasn't planned but it was; I thought it just happened but maybe I planned it.

Physiological Arousal. How your body feels; a buzz; feeling sexy; getting sexy; a rush; up for it.

Emotional Feelings. When dealing with emotional feelings, the facilitators should talk about concrete examples such as depression; anger; happiness; frustration; feeling uptight and so on.

Behavioural Script. Just doing it without thinking; You've done it so often you don't even realise what you are doing; You just do it and you don't even think about it; If you really thought about it then you might stop yourself.

Exercise 1: Establish the Link Between Thinking, Emotion, Physical Sensation and Action

In research and theory on emotion, the links between the channels of emotion and sensation, physiological arousal and action are well established. For example, in relation to anxiety, the emotion of anxiety may be associated with cognitive distortions which are consistent with anxiety, for example 'This is hopeless, I'm not going to manage this', physiological sensations (an increase in adrenaline) and actions consistent with anxiety, for example 'escape from the situation'. To establish these links, this exercise begins with simple associations and then moves quickly to examples related to sex offending. The mismatch of cognitions, arousal and action will be initially confusing to participants with ID. It is therefore important to finish this session with a quick review of examples related to sexual offending.

Materials: flipchart and pen

First, construct some simple associations using familiar everyday situations. It is straightforward to begin with the physiological sensation of hunger. The facilitator could begin the session by asking the question 'What do you think about when you feel hungry?' It is likely that a series of thoughts and actions will be elicited from the group. The facilitator can then go through each suggestion asking, 'Now is that something you would think or is that something you would do?' In this way, the separation between the physical sensation of hunger, the thoughts associated with the physical sensation and the subsequent actions can begin to be separated. A number of different sensations can then be employed as further illustrations. Encourage the group members to generate as many examples as possible related to thirst, itching, pain, discomfort and so on. The important thing is to establish the links between cognition, arousal and behaviour.

The exercise can then continue by linking certain emotions and cognitions with bodily sensations and action. So the facilitator can introduce the next section by asking, 'What happens to your body when you feel angry?' Once again the group responses are likely to include a mixture of action and physiological sensation. The facilitator can then ask, 'Is that something you feel or is that something you do?' Again, the associations between physiological arousal, emotion and action are being established. The exercise can continue with a range of emotions including anxiety, depression, frustration, jealousy and so on.

In order to complete the exercise, the association between sexual thoughts, feelings and actions should be reviewed. The facilitator would ask, 'What happens when you get sexy feelings?' In my experience, it is more likely that group members will respond with actions such as 'masturbation', 'have sex'. It is likely that facilitators will have to ask specifically 'What do you think about when you feel sexy?' Again, the connections and associations between bodily sensations, thinking, emotion and action are being drawn out in relation to the specific issue of sexuality.

Exercise 2: Behavioural Scripts

This can be a short exercise and is designed to establish that there are a number of things which we do automatically. Facilitators should generate a number of examples of the way in which we do things without thinking consciously about them. These can be very simple like sitting down to somewhat more complex examples such as opening doors, putting on a CD or operating a television. More complex examples still are riding a bike and driving a car. Very few group members are likely to drive but they might have experienced getting on a bus and arriving at the destination without being aware of the intervening travel time.

There are two main ways in which behavioural scripts can surprise us. The first is engaging in an automatic routine and forgetting the motivating cognition. Therefore, we might find ourselves in a room or looking in a certain place and forgetting the original reason for going there. The second is engaging in an automatic routine with no memory of having done so. Therefore, we can find ourselves going to work or getting the bus into town with no memory of travelling along a certain piece of road. The most obvious example is driving but since few participants drive, walking, cycling or getting on the bus are appropriate examples. (Using the bus can only be used as a loose example since it is a passive activity while driving a car is an active activity. There are enough similarities to use it among other examples.) This exercise establishes the actuality of behavioural scripts and automatic routines which are concepts that will be employed throughout the programme.

Exercise 3: Dysfunctional Associations

Parts of this exercise can prove difficult for participants and some may become annoyed. Building on previous exercises, draw up functional associations between physiological sensations, thoughts and action.

For example: hunger (physiological sensation), cognitions (I think I'll have a sandwich) and action (eating something).

Needing the toilet (physiological sensation), I need to go (cognition) and going to the toilet (action).

Figure 12.1 shows three flipchart sheets from this exercise, conducted in a single 2-hour session. On the first sheet, participants generated a number of bodily sensations, cognitions and actions in relation to hunger. All of these were functional and consistent, for example physiological sensations (belly talks, tummy rumbles), intervening cognitions (thinks - that smells good) and actions (eat, have some food). On the second sheet, participants generated a number of bodily sensations, cognitions and actions in relation to going to the toilet, for example physiological sensations (bursting, wriggling, I can't hold it in), intervening cognitions (I need to go) and subsequent action (relieve yourself, do it in the bushes). On the third sheet, they then generate dysfunctional cognitions and actions related to hunger and going to the toilet. During this session, some participants may express the opinion that the exercise is ridiculous. As they juxtapose the wrong action onto the bodily sensation,

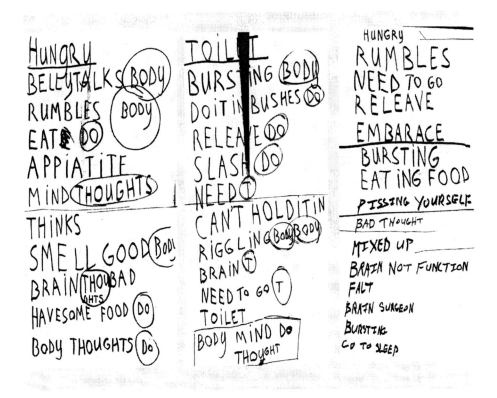

Figure 12.1   Flipchart records from a session on dysfunctional associations between cognition, behaviour and physiology

they may express confusion and even irritation or annoyance. The third sheet on Figure 12.1 demonstrates the dysfunctional associations in relation to hunger. Participants have generated physiological sensations (tummy rumbles) associated cognitions (I need to go) and dysfunctional actions (relieve yourself). They have also written that this dysfunctional association would cause embarrassment. Similarly, they have noted the dysfunctional associations in relation to going to the toilet with physiological sensations (bursting), a dysfunctional thought (I need to eat food), with a subsequent dysfunctional action (pissing yourself). They have also written on the sheet their views on these associations indicating that they understand the dysfunctional nature of the inconsistency between physiological sensation, cognition and behaviour (bad thoughts, mixed up, brain not functioning, you need a brain surgeon). Facilitators can then move on to the physiological sensation of sexual arousal, the inappropriate cognition of having sex with children or attacking women and the dysfunctional behaviour of sexual assault. Finish the session by using the confusion and irritation generated by the dysfunctional combinations of hunger and going to the toilet (and vice versa) to generate dissonance between the fact that they may be irritated by these dysfunctional associations but are quite comfortable with the dysfunctional associations between sexual arousal and their particular sexual offence. The following transcript gives an idea of how the dissonance might be employed:

PARTICIPANT ONE:	That is ridiculous, nobody would go to the toilet if they feel hungry.
PARTICIPANT TWO:	Yes you would have to be crazy, you would have to be out of your mind if you were going to feel hungry and want to eat and then go to the toilet.
FACILITATOR:	I am just trying to show you what happens when you get it wrong between how you feel and what you do.
PARTICIPANT ONE:	Yes but if you need to go to the toilet and then you went to the kitchen and had something to eat, you would wet yourself. That would be a really stupid thing to do.
PARTICIPANT TWO:	Yes, you're right, I'm trying to point out how people can do stupid things.
PARTICIPANT ONE:	Yes that would be ridiculous to eat something if you needed to go to the toilet. You would feel like a fool in the kitchen.
FACILITATOR:	Okay so you all think these are really stupid things to do but what if the thing you do is feel sexy? What should you do when you feel sexy?
PARTICIPANT ONE:	What do you mean? What's that got to do with it? If you feel sexy then you could play with yourself.
FACILITATOR:	But all of you are here because when you have had that feeling, you know, feeling sexy, that's not what you did was it? What was it you all did?
PARTICIPANT TWO:	What do you mean?
FACILITATOR:	Well when each of you felt sexy did you do something that was okay?
PARTICIPANT THREE:	No we didn't do something that was okay, we did something that wasn't okay, we did something that was bad didn't we.
FACILITATOR:	Well what was it you thought when you felt sexy, what were you thinking after you felt sexy when you wanted to approach those boys Fred?
FRED:	Well I felt sexy and well mmh I think I see what you are getting at.
FACILITATOR:	Well Fred what am I getting at? You felt sexy and then what happened?
FRED:	Well I don't know what happened, maybe I thought about the boys?
FACILITATOR:	That's exactly right, well done Fred. So was it a sensible thing to think about the boys when you felt sexy?
FRED:	No I don't suppose it was.
PARTICIPANT TWO:	You mean the way you think makes you do something sexy when you feel sexy.
FACILITATOR:	Yes you're dead right, that's it.
PARTICIPANT ONE:	Well I don't think that's right, I think that woman was still asking for trouble by the way she dressed.
FACILITATOR:	But you were feeling sexy so was it a sensible thing to think about attacking her?
PARTICIPANT TWO:	Well I don't think it was sensible but I don't think she was sensible.

These examples show different ways in which participants can assimilate the information. Some might assimilate it by beginning to understand the relationship between dysfunctional thoughts and sexual feelings. Others might simply give an indication that their basic schemata about themselves are being questioned. For Participant Two, although he maintained his basic schema concerning the sexual assault, it is clear that he was making a start on questioning his own assumptions. This is all one would expect at this early stage of treatment.

Exercise 4: Introduce Emotion as a Cognitive Dimension

This exercise emphasises the importance of emotion in the associations between behaviour, cognition and action. Functional associations have already been dealt with in previous exercises and on this occasion, dysfunctional cognitions can be linked to bodily sensations to produce dysfunctional actions. The following are a few examples but facilitators can generate examples that are more appropriate to group members. These can be role played to add to the discussion and interest.

Example 1. You are walking into a shop and another customer coming out bumps into you. You have a dysfunctional thought (he did that deliberately) which leads to dysfunctional emotion (anger and irritation). The dysfunctional thought and subsequent emotion lead you to a series of dysfunctional actions (shouting at the individual and other forms of verbal abuse). With someone who is quick to anger, this could become a behavioural script where they become irritated when anyone accidentally bumps into them.

Example 2. You are tired when you get home late from your work placement or the training centre. You cannot be bothered making a meal and have a dysfunctional thought (I need a drink). This leads to a dysfunctional action (drinking alcohol) which in turn produces a number of dysfunctional emotions (pleased at doing something to counteract the tiredness, feeling that this is really working and decide to have another drink, becoming annoyed at yourself for starting drinking alcohol again when you are trying to stop).

Example 3. You are working quite happily at your placement when one of the supervisors comes along and makes a comment about something that you have missed. This leads to a dysfunctional thought (he's getting at me, he doesn't like what I am doing), which in turn leads to a dysfunctional emotion (becoming annoyed or angry at the supervisor). This results in a series of dysfunctional actions (going in the huff, stopping working and walking away annoyed or shouting at him).

Facilitators can generate other exercises which they feel may be more appropriate to the participants in their own group. They should also decide what is the most appropriate language to use for dysfunctional thoughts, dysfunctional emotions and inappropriate actions. Guidance on possible phrases to use can be seen earlier in this chapter. This exercise can also generate a great deal of discussion.

Exercise 5: Sexual Arousal and Dysfunctional Cognitions

This is a simple exercise following on from the previous one. Having established the context of dysfunctional thought and dysfunctional action, it should be relatively easy to generate dysfunctional thoughts and dysfunctional actions related to feelings of sexual arousal. Allow the group to generate a number of dysfunctional thoughts which might arise from sexual arousal and then to generate dysfunctional actions which might occur as a result of the dysfunctional thinking. It is likely that participants will generate thoughts which they may have experienced in the past. A range of situations and examples can be seen in Appendix 1.

Chapter 13

Problem Solving Scenarios and Exercises Which Challenge Cognitive Distortions

Cognitive distortions are central to this sex offender programme and much of the material deals with the way thinking and attitudes mitigate or minimise the sexual offences. The aim of this section of treatment is to undermine fundamentally these cognitive schemata which men hold. It is completely understandable, from a number of viewpoints, that men hold such schemata. Firstly, from the point of view of the Good Lives Model, it is part of human nature to pursue human goods which make our lives more fulfilled. Our self-concept will support the pursuit of these human goods, and in order to maintain a positive self-image, they must adopt a series of attitudes and thoughts which support the pursuit of human goods in this way. Secondly, and relatedly, none of us wishes to think that we are 'a bad person'. Therefore, if we have engaged in one or more sexual acts which are morally reprehensible, then we are likely to develop a series of cognitions which mitigate or moderate our culpability in relation to these acts.

This mitigation will be related to the act itself (it's not so serious), in relation to the situation (it is understandable under the circumstances), in relation to others involved in the situation (they are as responsible as I am), in relation to its relative severity (other people do things much worse than I do), in relation to oneself (I only do it when I'm feeling bad – its not really me) or in relation to intent (I didn't mean to do it). All of these represent cognitive distortions which, to a greater or lesser extent, most of us employ in certain situations. A common example is the attitudes and cognitions that we would employ to defend ourselves when breaking the nationally agreed speed limit for cars. Another example would be using IT equipment at work to an extent that it exceeds any agreed limits (one member of an IT Department told me that the most common web site visited in the NHS is eBay and this is clearly not work related). In this respect, sex offenders are no different and employ a series of cognitive distortions which ultimately serve to maintain self-esteem in the face of palpable negative evidence.

The Treatment of Sex Offenders with Developmental Disabilities   William Lindsay
© 2009 John Wiley & Sons, Ltd

Various authors (Salter, 1988; Marshall, Anderson and Fernandez, 1999) have outlined the types of cognitive distortions which sex offenders may hold in relation to women and children. These cognitive distortions, in addition to maintaining self-esteem and self-image, reduce inhibitions prior to committing an incident, mitigate responsibility for the incident and may contribute to minimisation in post-incident evaluation. They fall into the following categories:

1. *Denial of an offence.* This is fairly common at the beginning of assessment and treatment but can be maintained for significant periods throughout treatment. In this cognitive distortion, the offender simply denies that any sex offending incident occurred. The denial can be in the face of incontrovertible evidence. One participant continued to deny the offence occurred for several months in the face of two identity parades in which he was positively identified and several witness statements from children detailing the offences. An offender may hold on to one detail which he knows is inconsistent with him having perpetrated the offences; for example, in this case, one witness mentioned that the perpetrator had a tattoo, and despite the weight of evidence, the client held onto the fact that he did not have a tattoo and therefore he could not have committed the offences.

2. *Denial of intent.* Here the client may accept that a sexual offence occurred but indicates that his intent was not to offend but rather to engage in some other activity. In one case, the offender had been babysitting two nieces of 8 and 12 years of age. He accepted that he was in bed with them and that he had been rubbing his erect penis against the girls but explained that they had been difficult during the evening and rather than chastise them or smack them to calm them down, he had put them to bed and got into bed alongside them. Therefore, he explained that he had not intended to offend sexually but was trying to control boisterous and difficult girls. In another case, a man with arthritis in his hands explained that while he was fixing a girl's bike, his hand slipped and went between her legs. It was his habit to fix children's bikes (grooming) and he accepted that he had touched the girl inappropriately but had explained that his arthritis had caused the spanner to slip while she was standing next to the bike. In this way, these men had accepted that the incident had occurred but denied that their intent was sexual.

3. *Mitigation of responsibility through victim action.* This is a more general form of cognitive distortion and questions reflecting this concept form the core of questionnaires evaluating the extent to which men may hold such attitudes. Examples take the form of men who feel that women who dress in short skirts or tight clothing are 'asking to be sexually assaulted'. It is not uncommon for men who offend against children to endorse the attitude 'children do sexy things to turn men on'. In one extreme case, an offender told me: 'Girls should be taught in school that if they have sex with men, the man is going to get into real trouble. Look at me – I'm here in prison and these girls are still walking about and nothing happened to them.' This man had a measured IQ outside of the Learning Disability range (WAIS-R IQ 81) and so his distorted viewpoint could not be accounted for by his

degree of intellectual disability. More moderate instances of cognitive distortions which move responsibility onto the victim are quite common.

4. *Minimisation of the incident.* These are, once again, frequent core beliefs regarding sex offending incidents. Generally, they form several of the questions in an inventory of cognitive distortions. Men may hold cognitions such as 'it's alright to follow women and masturbate, as long as you don't touch them', or 'it's alright to masturbate in front of children as long as you don't touch them', or 'staring at women and starting to feel sexy is not really an offence'. As has been indicated previously, men may reduce the importance of even serious offences by comparing them to what they consider to be more serious offences. Therefore, offenders against adult women may feel that their offence was not serious when compared to offences against children.

5. *Mitigation through mutuality.* This is similar to the cognitions which place some of the responsibility on to the victim but, in this case, the offender considers that the victim enjoyed or benefited from the incident. Therefore, he may hold the attitude that 'children enjoy having sex with men' or 'once we started having sex she obviously enjoyed it'. The offender may also feel that the incident was educational or maturational for the child or adolescent. Therefore, in some way, the incident has been mutually beneficial.

6. *Mitigation of responsibility through life events.* Here the offender may blame stress in other areas of their life for placing them in a situation where they have chosen the option of committing a sexual offence. Therefore, they may blame stress at work or stress in the family for placing them in the situation or frame of mind that caused them to perpetrate the sexual offence. This is not a common group of cognitions expressed by sex offenders with ID.

7. *Denial of a normal state.* With this set of cognitive distortions, the offender may blame stress, depression, mental illness or intoxication through alcohol or drugs for placing them in a frame of mind in which they would even consider committing a sexual offence. Although this is not common in offenders with ID, there have been a few occasions where clients have blamed intoxication with alcohol as the reason for the perpetration of sexual offence. In these cases, the offender holds a cognitive distortion something similar to 'I'm not the kind of person who would do that – I only did it because I was drunk' or 'If I stay off drink, I'll never do that again', or as an excuse for avoiding the consequences of the incident, 'I don't need to come to your group – I just need to stay off drink and I will be fine'.

Exercise 1: Problem Solving Scenarios. Non-sex Offending Example

This particular example can be done through role-play or can be completed using a flipchart. Because so many of the exercises in this manual are completed using flipchart and pen, it is better to use role-play wherever possible. In order to give the participants ideas on how to role-play the problem solving scenarios, it can be a reasonable plan first to write down the ideas on a flipchart.

Example on Alcoholism/Problem with Alcohol

Materials: flipchart and pen. Space for role playing

A man is doing himself harm by drinking too much. He drinks beer and whisky every night until he is reasonably drunk. The alcohol intake is affecting his work in that he is late for work, cannot concentrate, makes mistakes, is irritable and short-tempered with his workmates and gets grumpy towards the end of the working day because he wants to get to the pub. It is also affecting his life at home where he is irritable with the children and has frequent arguments with his wife. She criticises him for his drinking and makes suggestions about how he should stop. She says he should not go to the pub as often and should stop drinking so much during the week. He gets into arguments at work and his friends criticise him for mistakes he is beginning to make. He can also become very argumentative with his friends when they are drinking or going out at the weekend.

He does not accept that his problem is due to alcohol and thinks it is possible that he might drink a little too much.

One of the group members can record the cognitive distortions on a flipchart. Using Socratic questioning, try to get the group to generate as many cognitive distortions as they can think of. The following are some examples:

Denial (there is not a problem)
I don't drink any more than anyone else.
I have read that alcohol is good for you.
I drink a fair bit but I don't drink too much.
I might drink a bit much but I am fit and healthy.

Minimisation
It's not so bad: It's not a big problem.
I might drink a bit too much but I still hold down a job okay.
I drink too much but I can handle it.
Sometimes I do go over the score but not always.
I only drink too much at the weekends and I'm not working.
My drinking is causing me a few problems but no more that anyone else.
I've got a bit of a problem but I work harder than anyone else.

Entitlement
I work hard, I deserve a drink.
Every man is entitled to go out and have a drink if he wants it.
I'm not going to listen to her and let her criticise me, I'm entitled to have a drink.
I've got plenty of money; no one is going to stop me drinking.

Mitigation (shifting responsibility onto others)
Anybody who listens to my wife arguing like that would need a drink.
She drives me to it.

The boss is always on my back and so when I get out of work I need to go to the pub. The other guys at work are so critical that it would make anyone go for a drink. I've got a really stressful life and I need a drink to cope with the stress.

Mitigation of responsibility (blaming others)
I wasn't going to drink tonight until my supervisor started getting on my back. I was going to have a quiet weekend until the wife started her usual nonsense. Why do my friends get onto me like that? I need a drink.

In previous exercises, the facilitators have linked cognitive distortions to behaviour, arousal and emotion. They have also pointed out the role of cognitive distortions in the cycle of offending. This is a further objective for this exercise.

Role playing it

One of the facilitators should take the role of the main character. Group members can be workmates, friends, children or a spouse (this may be embarrassing for group members). The aim is for the lead individual to maintain his cognitive distortions in the face of evidence presented by others in his life.

Exercise 2: Problem Solving Scenarios Involving Sex Offending Situations

Materials: flipchart and pen

Apportioning responsibility

This is the first in a series of exercises which directly draw out cognitive distortions related to sex offences. There are a series of scenarios, all of which can be used for similar purposes (see Appendix 1). One of the important aspects in many of the scenarios is the somewhat uncertain nature of apportioning blame. This is organised intentionally to draw out cognitive distortions which participants may hold. In fact, facilitators should always understand that the exercise is moving towards the fact that the perpetrator, and no one else, is always responsible. Other people may have a duty of care or responsibilities of friendship which they have not fulfilled completely but they are not responsible for the sex offence.

Each scenario can be completed in two ways. Either the whole situation can be read out by a facilitator or one of the group members, if they have literacy skills, or it can be drawn on the flipchart as individual sections of the scenario are revealed. I prefer the latter but either is possible.

Scenario

Mr and Mrs Smith and their daughter Jane are on holiday at the seaside. One day they go for a walk and see a play park. They go into the play park and Jane starts playing on the swings. Mr and Mrs Smith sit talking and watching Jane but start to get bored.

They see a pub across the road from the play park and decide to go for a drink. They tell Jane to stay in the play park and keep safe. They then go over to the pub and have a drink. John is out for a walk, passes the play park and sees Jane on the swings. He goes into the play park and starts talking to Jane. He takes her into the bushes and sexually assaults her.

The facilitators should then ask who is to blame for Jane being sexually assaulted. Responses can be recorded on the flipchart as shown in Figure 11.1. The following is one way of presenting the scenario:

FACILITATOR: Now today we are going to do a story about a girl and her parents on holiday. Who is going to draw it?

DARREN: I will draw it on the flipchart.

FACILITATOR: Okay, what is the girl's name?

ANDREW: It could be Jenny.

FACILITATOR: Okay, draw Jenny, Darren, and what age is Jenny?

COLIN: I think she is nine years old.

EDWARD: 14.

FACILITATOR: These are both good ideas, Colin said she was nine, let's go with that. Jenny is nine years old. What's her mum and dad's name?, Brian?, Mr and Mrs what?

BRIAN: Gray.

FACILITATOR: Okay we have got Mr and Mrs Gray and their daughter Jenny and you should draw them in a play park Darren, that's good. Now, Mr and Mrs Gray get fed up and they see a pub across the road so draw a pub Darren.

EDWARD: They shouldn't be going to the pub when the wee girl is in the play park.

FACILITATOR: But that's the story so now Mr and Mrs Gray are in the pub having a drink Darren. Good. Now draw a man walking past the play park, what's the man's name?

ANDREW: His name would be Paul.

FACILITATOR: Okay, Paul walks past the play park and sees Jenny and goes in and starts to talk to her. So draw Paul in the play park as well.

COLIN: But where are the mum and dad?

BRIAN: They are in the pub, they shouldn't be in the pub. They should be with Jenny.

FACILITATOR: Now Paul takes Jenny in behind the bushes and sexually assaults her, so draw the bushes and Paul taking Jenny in. Good. Now, I would like to ask each of you, who is to blame for Jenny being sexually assaulted? Ok, let's start with you Colin.

In this scenario, there are built-in ambiguities of responsibility. The parents are being deficient in their duty of care and as can be seen in Figure 13.1, several of the men feel that they are responsible for the sexual assault. Two feel that the child should not have gone with the man and because she did so she is responsible. This discussion should focus on which of the three is thinking about sex. Facilitators can review what Jenny is thinking about. Facilitators can review what Mr and Mrs Gray are thinking about and they can also review what Paul is thinking about. It will become clear that Paul is the only one who is thinking about sex. Therefore, although there

Figure 13.1 Records from the problem solving scenario on responsibility for the offence

are ambiguities, the discussion should finish with everyone agreeing that Paul is to blame for committing the sexual offence. The conclusion will always be that the sex offender is the only one responsible for committing a sexual offence. This exercise can easily take 30 to 45 minutes to complete.

Supplementary/Additional Exercises

Once it has been established that Paul, the sex offender, is responsible for the incident, it is possible then to reflect on the initial responses from the participants. Several of the participants will have placed responsibility with either Jenny or Mr and Mrs Gray. At this point, it is possible to ask each participant why their locus of responsibility has changed from, for example, Mr and Mrs Gray to Paul. In this way, participants can reflect on the fact that they may have mitigated the responsibility of the sex offender by placing it on one of the other parties. The dialogue might be as follows:

> FACILITATOR: Okay Colin, you said that Mr and Mrs Gray were to blame before we started didn't you? and now you say it's Paul, so why have you changed your mind.
>
> COLIN: Well I don't know I just thought that Mr & Mrs Gray were to blame.
>
> FACILITATOR: Yes but you just thought about it and said that Paul was to blame and I think you're right Paul is to blame but I am interested to know why you thought Mr and Mrs Gray were to blame at first and why you have changed your mind?
>
> COLIN: Well now I think that Paul is to blame because he did the sex offence.
>
> FACILITATOR: That's right. Paul is to blame because he was the one who did the offence.

It is fairly obvious that the level of analysis is not sophisticated in this section. However, the important point is that the participant has been encouraged to reflect on the fact that he minimised the sex offender's responsibility and has now correctly located responsibility with the sex offender. It is possible to go round the group in the same way reflecting on why certain members have changed their mind. It is also important to congratulate those individuals who have located responsibility with the sex offender all the way though, for example:

> FACILITATOR: Andrew, you have stayed with Paul all the way through, you thought that Paul was to blame at the beginning and you still think that Paul is to blame – well done.

On the other hand, occasionally one of the participants may persist with responsibility on one of the other parties. Facilitators can employ group pressure to encourage this participant to continue to reflect on his location of responsibility.

> FACILITATOR: So Darren, you still think Mr and Mrs Gray are to blame because they went to the pub? What does everyone else think about Darren's choice?
>
> EDWARD: Well he is just wrong because Mr and Mrs Gray did not commit the sex offence did they?

FACILITATOR (redirecting the statement):	Well don't tell me, tell Darren.
EDWARD:	You're wrong because Mr and Mrs Gray did not commit a sex offence it was Paul who committed the sex offence.
DARREN:	Yes but they shouldn't have gone to the pub.
EDWARD:	Yes but they still did not commit the offence, it was Paul!
FACILITATOR:	What does anyone else think about this?
BRIAN:	I don't know why he still thinks it was the mum and dad because Paul did it.
FACILITATOR:	Don't tell me, tell Darren.
BRIAN:	The mum and dad didn't commit the sex offence, who committed the sex offence? – Paul!

It may be that Darren does not change his mind but notice how the facilitator is engineering the group to challenge his cognitions. Notice the facilitator is encouraging the group to challenge each other rather than make these challenges through the facilitator. As has been mentioned in the methods section (Chapter 6), this is a technique for developing group processes.

Further Supplementary Exercise

The second supplementary exercise which can be conducted after the initial analysis of the problem solving scenario is to use the scenario as an example or a metaphor with principles related to certain individuals on offence. Perhaps to use the word metaphor is too strong in this case since the example is often so close to one or two participants' actual index offences. However, because it is not the index offence for any particular individual, it seems much easier to discuss, and group members are more willing to express opinions and attitudes in relation to the hypothetical situation. It is now possible to use the conclusions of the scenario to challenge individual members' attitudes related to their own index offence. A typical example would be as follows:

FACILITATOR:	Fred, you thought that Jenny was to blame here because she went away with Paul and you said that maybe Paul had given her sweets or something to go into the bushes, is that how you feel about the boys you offended against? Do you think it was their fault that they went with you after you gave them something like cigarettes?
FRED:	Well I changed my mind about that and I thought that Paul was to blame in the end.
FACILITATOR:	Yes I know you thought Paul was to blame in the end but at first you thought Jenny was to blame so I'm wondering if you thought that the boys were to blame because they went away with you?
FRED:	Yes but I'm not talking about that we're talking about this on the board.
FACILITATOR:	Well that's true we are talking about what is on the board but we're always talking about each person here. Can anybody tell me why you are here?
ALEX:	Because we have done sex offences.

FACILITATOR: That's right. So why doesn't Fred want to talk about his here?
EDWARD: Maybe he doesn't want to talk about it because that is what he did think.
               Maybe he thought the boys were to blame.
FACILITATOR: Well don't tell me, tell Fred what you just said.
EDWARD: Fred, maybe you don't want to talk about it because you did think that
               the boys were to blame?
FRED: This is nothing to do with you this is private for me.
FACILITATOR: No. It's not private once you have been to court and – well your case was
               in the paper wasn't it and if it's in the paper that's not private is it?
FRED: Well I just don't want to talk about it?
FACILITATOR: Does anyone have any idea why Fred doesn't want to talk about this?

In this way, the group process can continue with some challenge on Fred's cognitions in relation to his victims. The fact that Fred is resisting both the challenge to his cognitions and talking about his case at all is a positive sign. It certainly indicates that he is not acquiescent to therapeutic assessment and treatment processes and his degree of discomfort suggests that the challenge to his cognitions may be forcing him to defend a basic schema related to his perception of these incidents, and perhaps to his GLM. The fact that we appear not to be having much impact on this basic schema at the moment is of little importance. For each group member, we will return to these cognitive challenges on numerous occasions over months.

Exercise 3: Offences Related to Adult Women. Eliciting and Challenging Cognitions

This second example has similar ambiguities concerning the purpose of responsibility. However, the situation is different and directed towards offences against adults.

Scenario

A woman is waiting at the bar in the pub for her friend to arrive, she is wearing a very short skirt and she is looking forward to going out with her friend Jane. Her friend is late and while she is waiting she has a look around the pub. She notices a good-looking man at the other side of the pub between her and the door. She keeps looking at the door for her friend to come and looks just past the man. The man notices that she keeps looking over towards him. He thinks that she must fancy him and he definitely fancies her. Eventually, she decides that her friend is not going to arrive so she leaves the pub. He decides to follow her and when he gets the chance he goes up to her and asks if he can take her to another pub. She is surprised, shouts at him to go away but he attacks her and sexually assaults her.

This exercise is conducted in the same way as the previous one. Figure 13.2 shows the record on the flipchart recorded by one particular group. The facilitator would begin with something like:

FACILITATOR: Now today I would like to do a story about a woman in a pub so can
               someone draw a woman in a pub?

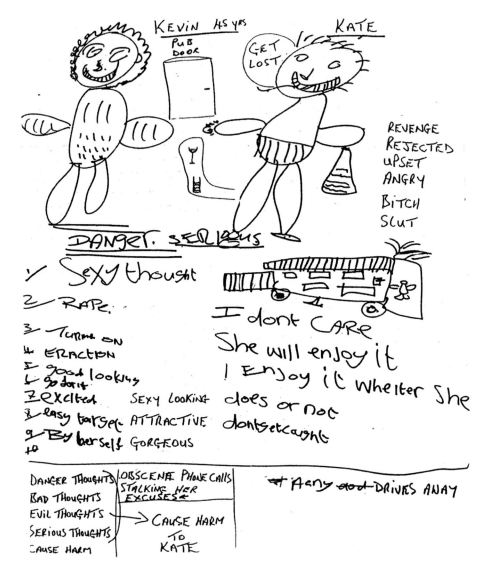

Figure 13.2 Flipchart record from the second exercise on responsibility for offences against women

FACILITATOR: What's the woman called, do you think?

COLIN: Kate.

FACILITATOR: Fine, okay. Now will you draw a man in the pub and give him a name as well.

The facilitators in this exercise have developed the process further than allocating blame. Here they have begun to extract the sequence of events leading up to the incident as perceived by the perpetrator. Therefore, we are beginning to look at the cycle of abuse and these cycles can be related to appropriate group members. In response to Socratic questioning, the group members have attributed a number of thoughts to *Kevin*. These are that *Kate* is 'sexy looking, attractive, gorgeous'. They have then attributed a further series of thoughts and intentions as he follows her and as he initiates the sexual assault, 'rape her, rob her, pawing her, stalking her' and one individual has made an extreme attribution that he is thinking about 'killing her'. They have also attributed his motivation in that it is related to his feelings that she is 'sexy looking', that he has 'sexy thoughts', and as a result of the woman telling him to 'get lost', he is 'upset, angry, feels rejected and wants revenge'. Group members have then put a valency on these thoughts saying that they are extremely negative, 'danger thoughts, bad thoughts, evil thoughts, serious thoughts, cause harm, cause harm to Kate'. Therefore, the importance of cognitive distortions within the cycle of abuse is being established and both the cognitions and abuse cycle are being viewed extremely negatively. These exercises will continue repeatedly.

As with the previous example, some of the details would be added by group members themselves. Some group members may feel that Kate is to blame for wearing a short skirt and looking at Kevin, some may feel Jane is to blame because she did not turn up and others will think that Kevin is to blame because he committed the sexual assault. Occasionally, in these scenarios, all the group members immediately place the responsibility on the perpetrator. In this case, the facilitators can immediately move to the cognitive challenge of individual participants in the following manner:

FACILITATOR:	Okay George, you said that Kevin was to blame here because he was the one who followed Kate up from the pub and committed the offence. But that's exactly what you did isn't it? You followed a woman home from the pub and sexually assaulted her in the street. So if you think that Kevin is to blame here and you think it's a wrong thing to do, why did you do exactly the same thing?
GEORGE:	Well I was drunk so I wasn't quite sure of what I was doing.
FACILITATOR:	Yes, but did you think the same things as Kevin. Did you think that she was attractive and gorgeous and sexy looking.
GEORGE:	I can't remember coz I was drunk but I must have thought she was good looking.
FACILITATOR:	So did you have sexy thoughts and follow her because you wanted to have sex with her?
GEORGE:	Well, I was drunk so I don't know. I can't remember.
FACILITATOR (to the whole group):	George followed this woman up the street after he had been in the pub and says that he might have thought she was good looking. So what does anybody else think he was doing?
OTHER PARTICIPANTS:	Well, he must have wanted to have sex with her. I think he was wanting to rape her. He would have been wanting to get her into a quiet place and have sex with her.
FACILITATOR:	Well George, everyone else thinks you wanted to have sex. Did you wait until you got into a quiet place because no-one saw you did they?
GEORGE:	I suppose I must have done because that's what happened isn't it and it was my fault, but I was drunk.

FACILITATOR:	But Kevin's been drinking as well hasn't he? So why are you so clear that he is to blame? Do you think that you were definitely to blame when you assaulted that woman?
GEORGE:	Yes, I think it was my fault and I got caught.
FACILITATOR:	So if you think it was good that you got caught, why did you go home and change all your clothes?
GEORGE:	What do you mean change all my clothes?
FACILITATOR:	Well, when you got home that night you changed all your clothes and when the police found you, you were wearing completely different clothes. I wonder why you did that?
GEORGE:	Well that's because I wasn't wanting to be caught wasn't it.
FACILITATOR:	Are you saying you definitely knew it was wrong when you did it?
GEORGE:	Well I didn't think so at the time but I can see now how bad it was.

In this way, the facilitators can challenge each group participant who has a relevant index offence. George's index offence is particularly relevant but Darren's offence where he was following women has sufficient similarities to allow a cognitive challenge along the lines of

FACILITATOR: Now Darren, you've said that Kevin is to blame here for following Kate and sexually assaulting her but you keep following women around town so who is to blame when you follow these women?

Here we can see that as long as the scenario has some relevance to the individual's offence, it can be used as a metaphor or example illustrating the principles of the offence. If the facilitators can then think of something to add to the scenario which increases the ambiguity, it may be possible to increase the pressure on participant's decision making. For example, once these cognitive challenges have been completed, the facilitator could add

Okay, let's say Kate didn't get a fright and tell him to go away, let's say that she did go to the pub with him and have a few drinks and then he walked with her back to her flat but she didn't want him to come in. If he tried to sexually assault her then who would be to blame?

Now that the pattern has been established, the relevant interpersonal themes can be continued as follows:

Okay, you still all think that Kevin is to blame but what if Kate said would you come in for coffee and they start kissing on the couch and he asks her for sex but she says no she wants him to go. So now Kate has met him, gone drinking with him, gone out with him, gone back to her flat, had coffee and been kissing with him. Would she be to blame now if he sexually assaulted her?

Now that the pattern has been set for group members to allocate blame to the perpetrator, it is likely that they will continue in this manner, however, one or two might waver. This is an opportunity to establish the principle that no matter what happens, the perpetrator is always to blame for a sexual assault.

Throughout the course of the programme, there are many sections that deal with cognitive distortions and attitudes towards victims. Appendix 1 contains several straightforward examples or more complex ambiguous examples which can be employed at these points in the programme.

Exercise 4: Cognitive Distortions Related to Victim Motivation and Mutuality of the Incident

The next exercise demonstrates the way in which facilitators can challenge the attitude that victims want to engage in a sexual incident. This is linked to the last example when we say that some of the group members thought that the child was to blame for going with the man and for one group member being interested in sex.

Materials. A picture or scenario of a man reading a story to a child. One of the pictures in the Kempton Life Horizon Slide Series (Sex Education for the mentally retarded) is a good stimulus. However, the exercise works just as well with a picture from a magazine or as a problem solving vignette drawn on a flipchart.

Vignette

Craig is looking after his young niece Gemma. After tea, Gemma often likes listening to a story. Uncle Craig asks Gemma if she wants to sit on his knee while he reads her the story. Gemma gets quite excited when Uncle Craig reads her favourite story (Thomas the Tank Engine) and she bounces up and down on her uncle's lap. Uncle Craig enjoys Gemma bouncing up and down on his lap and begins to get sexual feelings. He begins to get an erection. Once the 'Thomas the Tank Engine' story is finished, Uncle Craig asks Gemma if she would like to hear another story.

The scenario should either be drawn on a flipchart or developed from the Life Horizons slide or any other similar appropriate picture which the facilitators can find. No matter which way the picture is shown to participants, the session would begin as follows:

FACILITATOR: What's happening in this picture?
EDWARD: Well he's reading her a story.
FACILITATOR: That's right, so anything else happening in this picture?
ALEX: She's just on his knee listening to the story.
FACILITATOR: And is she enjoying herself listening to this story?
COLIN: Yes, she's enjoying herself and so is he.
FACILITATOR: What's he thinking about whilst he is reading the story?
ALEX: Well, he might just be reading the story or he might be thinking about having sex with her.

FACILITATOR: Okay, so he might just be thinking about the story and does anyone else think that he might be thinking about having sex with her?

DARREN: Yes, he might be thinking about that because she is on his knee.

FACILITATOR: So what would be happening to him here, whilst she is on his knee?

ALEX: Well he might be thinking about sex and he might be getting a hard on.

FACILITATOR: Okay, so he might be getting an erection, what's she thinking?

BRIAN: Well she might be thinking about having sex with him.

KEVIN: Don't be ridiculous, she's just a wee girl she wouldn't be thinking about having sex with him.

FACILITATOR: Well Kevin I'm just interested in what people think about the girl just now. So does anyone else think that this girl is thinking about sex with the man?

EDWARD: Well, she might because she is smiling and she is jumping up and down on his knee.

ALEX: Well I don't think she wants to have sex with him but I think he wants to have sex with her.

It can be disconcerting for facilitators when these stark, uncluttered cognitive distortions emerge in response to a simple, relatively neutral picture. I call these 'jaw dropping moments' but facilitators do get used to it. However, to be fair to participants, the demands of the session are set up to permit and even encourage such attitudes to emerge. Everyone knows the session is to address issues of sex offending, they have all disclosed information about their sex offence, they will have discussed each other's sex offences in detail and will also have reviewed other scenarios dealing with offending. Therefore, the demand characteristics are very clearly related to sex offending and cognitive distortions. Therefore, when the facilitator asks 'What is the girl thinking?' the scene is set to allow such attitudes to emerge. At this point, it should be established quite clearly which of the group members have endorsed the attitude that a 6-year-old girl is thinking about sex. These individuals should not be able subsequently to deny that they had originally expressed this attitude because the core of the technique is to employ, once again, the cognitive dissonance between a socialised attitude and an attitude consistent with sexual offending. Facilitators should now use the Socratic process to establish that the girl is not thinking about sex but the man is. They might go back to an hour before the picture in the following manner:

FACILITATOR: So what was the girl doing this afternoon?

COLIN: I think she was probably playing with her friends.

FACILITATOR: That's fine, so she was playing with her friends, was she thinking about sex when she was playing with her friends?

DARREN: No she wouldn't be thinking about sex they would just be playing.

It is likely at some point in the Socratic process that one group member will express the opinion that she is thinking about sex. This should be dealt with by comparing her considerations of sex with the man's/perpetrator's considerations about sex. For example

EDWARD: Well yes she might be thinking about sex because they get sex education at school and so they might think about sex.

FACILITATOR: Yes they do get sex education at school don't they? What kind of things do they get in sex education?

EDWARD: Well they get taught about men and women and how to make babies.

FACILITATOR: Did any of you get sex education at school?

ANDREW: Yes, we got sex education in high school.

FACILITATOR: So stuff you got at sex education like how to make babies and the difference between men and women and what men and women do when they have sex?

ALEX: Well we got that but I don't know if we got so much about how to have sex.

FACILITATOR: Well fine, let's say this girl has had sex education and she has had something on how people have sex, would that make her want to have sex with this man?

EDWARD: No, it wouldn't make her want to have sex, it might just make her interested in sex education.

FACILITATOR: When kids get sex education, do they get told how strong a man feels when he wants to have sex? Do they know how strong his feelings are?

ALEX: No I don't think you get anything to do with that, it's just about making babies.

FACILITATOR: Do they get told how strong men's sexual urges get? Do kids get any idea about how strong your sexy feeling was when you committed your offence?

ALEX: No they wouldn't get anything about that.

FACILITATOR: So if they were talking about sex education would they be talking about men getting really strong feelings for sex and wanting to have sex?

ALEX: No, they wouldn't talk about anything like that.

FACILITATOR: Okay, so when this girl is playing with her friends, would she be thinking about sex in the same way as the man would be thinking about sex?

ALL: No, she wouldn't be thinking about that, that would be nothing to do with it.
                   They wouldn't even be talking about sex if they were playing.

FACILITATOR: Right, are they thinking about different things? So what would happen next, after she was playing with her friends?

COLIN: Maybe she would be called in for her tea.

This process might take around 15–30 minutes as group members, by their own inductive reasoning, come round to the conclusion that the girl is not thinking about sex but the man is. This socialised conclusion is then confirmed with each group member. At this point, the facilitators can employ the dissonance between the original cognitive distortions and the socialised attitudes that they have now induced through the Socratic dialogue. She can then employ this dissonance to challenge the original cognitions as follows:

FACILITATOR: Now you're all saying that the girl is not thinking about sex and I think you're right. Colin, you have said that six year olds don't think about sex and I think you're right about that as well. Girls and boys don't think about sex at that age. So this girl will not be thinking about sex when she is on her uncle's knee and listening to a story but I don't understand why two of you – you Brian and you Darren – you both said that she was thinking about sex when I asked you at first. Now I think you're right when you say that she isn't thinking about sex but why did you say at first that she was thinking about sex?

DARREN: Well I don't know why because she might be thinking about sex.

FACILITATOR: No, you've worked it out now and you've worked out that she is not thinking about sex. But why did you say at first that she was?

BRIAN: Well you're just getting me mixed up because that's what you always try and do.

FACILITATOR: Well I'm not trying to get you mixed up but I am interested in why you have changed your mind, or why you thought that at first?

BRIAN: Well that girl isn't thinking about sex but other girls might be thinking about sex.

FACILITATOR: So you think that this girl might be different from other girls? Why would she be different from other girls?

BRIAN: I don't know why she would be different; you're just trying to get me all twisted up.

As you can see from this extract, Brian has not been willing to change his cognitions to a socialised framework; however, as in previous examples, the exercise has led him to challenge his own cognitions which appear to have placed him in a position of some discomfort. Again, it is important to reiterate that the cognitive schema which supports his self-image and self-esteem in relation to the sexual offence will be difficult to alter. Reasons have already been laid out at length on why they will be difficult to alter. However, once again, we can see he is beginning himself to question the logical basis for these schemata and the attitudes which arise from them. These fundamental beliefs will be repeatedly challenged over the course of sex offender treatment. Other pictures such as a couple walking in a park, a couple meeting on the street, a couple sitting in a café or other fairly natural relationship scenes can be used in the same way. More explicit scenes such as a man pulling a woman behind a wall or a bush or a man exposing himself to women can also be used in the same way. Many such pictures can be found in the Life Horizons series or in magazines. A reasonable alternative is to draw the picture on a flipchart, especially if the facilitators have available to them someone who is good at drawing.

Exercise 5: The Cognitive Distortions of Offenders. The Cycle of Offending and Abuse

This is another series of exercises, lasting over several sessions, in which the facilitators might choose scenarios which are consistent with group members' offences. In this way, the cognitive distortions in each group member might be elicited in a relatively non-threatening fashion so that they can be both added to the disclosure information and incorporated into the final relapse prevention exercise. Most of the scenarios can be used for this exercise since there are no requirements for making decisions or choices between possible solutions. In this exercise, we start with the sexual offence and work backwards. The offence could be against a child when the offender is babysitting, against an adult female when the adult is at a shopping centre, an exposure offence in a public park or a stalking offence in a local town. The essential aspect of this exercise is that facilitators encourage group members to elucidate the way in which cognitive distortions promote the cycle of offending.

In order not to describe another scenario in this text, the illustration used is the example where the young girl is sexually assaulted in the park while her mother and father are in the pub. Figure 13.3 shows the same scenario but most of the considerations are from the point of view from the offender.

Once the basic components of the vignette are drawn (in this case with different names), the exercise can review the cycle of offending including SIDs, cognitive distortions and behavioural scripts. In this exercise, we begin with John getting up and deciding to leave the house. The Socratic dialogue would continue as follows:

FACILITATOR:	You remember this story don't you? So what I want to know is, John gets up, why does he decide to go out of the house?
ALL PARTICIPANTS:	He might want to get something for his lunch? Maybe he wants to go for a walk or he could be feeling sexy so he wants to go and see if he can find a person or the child.
	No I think he probably wants to go for the paper or something.
	No he might be feeling sexy so he wants to go out.
FACILITATOR:	Could he be thinking all of these things at the same time?
EDWARD:	No, he'll just want to go for the paper or something for his lunch.
BRIAN:	Well he could be thinking he could go out for something and if a chance comes along he'll take it or he could be feeling sexy and he just wants to go out and see if he can find the girl.
FACILITATOR:	I think you're right with all these things, he could be doing any of them. And Brian you think he could be going out but if a chance comes along he'll take it?
BRIAN:	Yes, he's going out to see if he can get something but if the chance comes along he's going to see if he can have sex with the girl.
DARREN:	Well I think he's just going out looking for sex.
FACILITATOR:	Is that what you do when you leave the house Darren? Sometimes do you feel sexy and you just go out and follow women and think about sexy things?
EDWARD:	Oh you've put your foot in it now Darren.
PARTICIPANTS:	All laughing.
BRIAN:	Darren has put himself in the hot seat. You're in the hot seat now.
FACILITATOR:	No-one is in the hot seat I'm just interested if Darren leaves the house and thinks about having sex and so he follows women. Darren, do you know you're going to follow women when you leave the house?
DARREN:	Well sometimes I do and sometimes I don't. Sometimes I just go walking and I see someone.

Figure 13.3 Reviewing cognitive distortions of offenders against children

FACILITATOR: It sounds to me like you're saying that you go for a walk and half of you knows that you are going to look for a woman to follow.

DARREN: (getting annoyed) Well I did say that it is true sometimes so I don't know why you keep going on about it.

FACILITATOR:	I wonder if anyone can say why Darren is getting annoyed and angry?
DARREN:	I'm not getting annoyed I just want you to shut up.
FACILITATOR:	Well it looks to me like you're getting a bit annoyed and I was just wondering if anyone else knows why you might be getting annoyed?
COLIN:	I think he's getting annoyed because he knows he does think about it before he goes out the house.
FACILITATOR:	Well don't tell me, tell Darren.
COLIN:	Darren, are you getting annoyed because that's what you do when you leave the house?

It can be seen that by using the hypothetical vignette in this way, possible attitudes related to sexual offending can be extracted quickly. This allows the facilitator to move easily from the hypothetical situation to specific situations and begin to challenge the motivation and attitudes of particular group members. It is not unusual for participants to become agitated and even angry during sessions such as this. As has been explained earlier, these cognitive challenges strike at some of the main supports that individuals maintain for their self-esteem and self-image. It is therefore unsurprising that participants wish to defend their self-image. The fact that individuals become angry should be considered positive. It is a possible indication that the cognitive challenge is having some impact on the self-schemata which maintain the sex offending routines. However, the facilitator should be careful to keep these processes under control. If one participant has been challenged for 10 or 15 minutes then, if the opportunity arises, it is appropriate to move the processes onto another participant. Allow the first individual to have a rest and become engaged in the process once again rather than being the focus of the challenge. This is one enormous advantage of group treatment over individual treatment. Lindsay *et al.* (1998c) compared the treatment of two participants, one with group therapy and one with individual therapy. They commented that individual therapy frequently resulted in a continuing challenging dialogue between facilitator and client from which there was no easy avenue of respite. This is not the case in group treatment where the facilitator can decide that one particular individual has been challenged sufficiently for the time being and can move on to other related matters or another participant.

This particular exercise will now move on to *John* walking around the streets. The facilitator will challenge certain issues which will come up in the initial statements of participants, for example, if he is simply going out for a newspaper or to buy his lunch, why doesn't he just go to the shop and return home. Through the Socratic dialogue, participants are likely to accept that he should have gone to the shop and returned home and those group members who suggest that he would be going out for a non-sexually related purpose would be challenged by the facilitator. Group members would come to the conclusion themselves that if he was thinking that he was simply going out for an innocent purpose, this itself is a cognitive distortion in that he was simply making an excuse for himself to walk the streets in search of a victim. In fact, he was planning the sexual offence or the opportunity to commit an offence. These conclusions would then be used to challenge specific participants for whom this scenario was particularly relevant. Examples of this process have already been illustrated.

As the exercise moves on, we will then elicit the cognitions that *John* has when he sees Jane, the little girl. In Figure 13.3, group participants have written the thoughts which he might have on the flipchart. Group members have attributed a number of cognitions to *John* including SIDs 'what will I do, I'll go to the park', cognitive distortions 'sexy feelings 50–50, I won't get caught, she enjoys it and won't be hurt' and approach cognitions 'she's by herself, easy prey, I'm going to have sex with the six year old, go for it'.

Once again, the opportunity arises to reflect on whether or not any of the group members have had these thoughts during their index offence or other offences. Group members are likely to deny that they had these thoughts in which case there is an opportunity to ask them which thoughts or cognitions they did have to maintain the sexual offence. It is unlikely that they will be forthcoming in the initial stages of the process, but as the exercise is repeated from a number of different perspectives, these motivating and sustaining cognitions emerge. Facilitators should bear in mind that the processes are not quick and it is highly unlikely that any sex offender will offer their motivation, planning and cycle of offending related cognitions at early stages of treatment. It is only after weeks of repeated, related exercises that change will begin to be noticed.

Finally, a valency has been placed on *John's* thoughts by the various participants. It can be seen that they have labelled them 'crazy thoughts, bad thoughts, sexy thoughts, evil thoughts, danger thoughts, mad thoughts, twisted thoughts, terrible thoughts'. They are also clear that these cognitive distortions serve as excuses to justify the sexual assault. Here we have an example of the way in which group members can be far more graphic and direct in their language than facilitators can be. It is unlikely that facilitators would call such cognitive distortions 'evil', 'crazy' or 'bad'. They are blunt, graphic descriptions. Facilitators might take such an opportunity to distance the cognition from the person. It is common during sex offender therapy to say something like 'You may have done bad things but that doesn't make you bad people'; or 'Yes, these might be evil thoughts but I don't see evil men here, so how have you got into that situation'. In this way, throughout the initial and middle stages of treatment, the facilitator is continually gathering information and priming the Relapse Prevention, Good Lives section of the programme. In this final section, we will be looking at future pathways in which the participant gains human goods and subsequent self-esteem/self-image from pro-social influences, actions and behaviours.

Exercise 6: Reviewing Scenarios from the Victim's Perspective

The methods which serve the processes of this exercise are the same as the previous exercise but the purpose is completely different. A series of exercises such as this can be completed in close proximity to the previous series of exercises in order to employ the dissonance in perception, cognition and expectation between the perpetrator and victim. This exercise can also be employed in the victim awareness module.

Any of the scenarios in the appendix can be used, there is no requirement for any ambivalence in the apportioning of blame as there has been in previous exercises. However, if one of the scenarios is used where there might be some uncertainty, the

Figure 13.4 Flipchart record of the exercise on victim perspective and the disparity with offender's perspective

facilitator can reflect back to previous sessions where certain participants may have felt that the victim shared some of the blame. It can also be helpful to use a scenario with which group members are familiar. However, this is not a requirement. The main purpose of the exercise is to emphasise that the victim is not thinking about sexual assault and has no responsibility in the preparation of the sexual offence. The second aim is to point out that the perpetrator may have cognitive distortions concerning the victim's feelings.

Figure 13.4 is the record from a session demonstrating the exercise. The scenario is a simple one whereby a man babysits a young girl and while they are watching television he sexually assaults her. The group can be given some ownership of the material by naming the individual, choosing the television programmes, deciding on their positioning of the room and even deciding where the sexual assault occurs (in front of the television, in the bedroom or elsewhere). Part of the dialogue would begin as follows:

FACILITATOR:	Right. So we know who everyone is now. You decided that Jill's mum and dad are leaving some lemonade and some sweets so that Jill can have them while she is watching television with Bob. Is Jill looking forward to Bob coming round?
ALL PARTICIPANTS:	Yes she is because she thinks he is a nice man.
	Yes, because she feels safe with him.
	Her mum and dad have left some lemonade so she is going to have that with Bob.
	Yes, she's looking forward to watching her favourite programme.
FACILITATOR:	So is she thinking about sex when her mum and dad goes away and Bob comes round?
BRIAN:	No, don't be stupid, she's not thinking about sex.
EDWARD:	Why would she think about sex? She's only seven years old.
FACILITATOR:	No, that's good. So you've decided that she's not thinking about sex but she is looking forward to all sorts of other things when Bob comes to babysit. No that's fine. Now when mum and dad go away what will happen now? Fred, you haven't said anything in a while, what do you think is going to happen when mum and dad go away?
EDWARD:	Well I think that she will be...
FACILITATOR:	Now Fred hasn't spoken for a while so I want to know what he has to say, Edward you ask Fred what he thinks will happen when mum and dad go away.
EDWARD:	Fred, what do you think is going to happen now?
FRED:	Well they're just going to sit down and watch television aren't they?
EDWARD:	That's right.
FACILITATOR:	And what is Jill thinking Fred?
ALL:	Well she's not thinking about sex.
FACILITATOR:	Well I want Fred to think this through, Fred, what is Jill thinking when they sit down to watch television?
FRED:	Well she might be thinking about the programme or thinking about having some cakes.
FACILITATOR:	Good. Well done. I think you're right, I think that is what she would be thinking about. Fred – would she be thinking about having sex with Bob?
FRED:	No, she wouldn't be thinking about that.
FACILITATOR:	Good, I think you're right. Why wouldn't she be thinking about having sex with Bob?
FRED:	Because she's too young.
FACILITATOR:	Yes, good that is one reason, can you give me another reason?
FRED:	Because she wants to go to bed and she just wants to sleep.

FACILITATOR:	Yes that would be another reason because at bedtime children just think about bed. Can you give me another reason?
FRED:	I can't think of any other reasons, she's just not thinking about sex.
FACILITATOR:	Can anyone else give me a reason?
ALL:	Well she might be thinking about having a story.
	She wants to watch television.
	Maybe she is thinking about her supper or the sweets and juice that mum and dad left.
	She's too young to think about sex.
FACILITATOR:	Yes, all of these things are right, are you managing to get them on the blackboard? Can you tell me what the reasons are?
FRED:	I didn't hear everything but she's not thinking about sex.
FACILITATOR:	Yes you're right about that, that's good. Edward, you tell them the reason you gave about why she isn't thinking about it.

As these various aspects are elicited, it will take a while to note them on the flipchart, slowing the pace of the session considerably. There are two basic methods being demonstrated here. The first is reviewing the reasons behind the socialised cognition. Therefore, it is not sufficient for Fred to acknowledge that Jill is not thinking about sex, the facilitator wishes to explore the reasons why the 7-year-old girl would not think about sexual matters. The second is that it was fairly obvious that Fred was unable or unwilling to furnish a number of reasons concerning the fact that 7-year-olds would not think about having sex with men. The facilitator has elicited these reasons from other group members and will now ask each of them to reiterate the reason not to the facilitator or other group members, but to Fred. The facilitator will then ask Fred to repeat each reason as follows:

FACILITATOR:	Edward, you tell Fred what you thought the reason was that girls wouldn't think about sex.
EDWARD:	I think she's just thinking about her supper and her juice.
FACILITATOR:	Okay, don't tell me, tell Fred.
EDWARD:	Fred, she's just thinking about her juice and her supper.
FACILITATOR:	Fred, what did Edward say to you?
FRED:	She's just thinking about having her supper.
FACILITATOR:	Well done, that's right, she is just thinking about her supper. Now you tell Fred what you said Darren.

In this way, the facilitator is trying to enable the men to understand the victim's perspective and is also trying to ensure that they internalise and retain the information. The session will then go on to examine the victim's feelings when she is watching television beside the perpetrator and her feelings of shock and especially incomprehension when he begins to make sexual remarks and sexual advances. The Socratic dialogue continues in a similar way and all of the information is recorded on Figure 13.4. The exercise may finish by reviewing the victim's feelings if the perpetrator threatens her about revealing the information to her mother and father.

This will continue in the same way as other previous exercises with the facilitator using the exercise as an example or metaphor for participants own offences. Therefore, he/she might ask, 'Fred – do you think any of the boys felt this way when you offended against them?', or 'You threatened the boys after your offence so how do you think they felt when you threatened them?' Therefore, the hypothetical example and the conclusions drawn from it are made personal and relevant to the individual group participants.

Exercise 7: Personal Accounts and Related Cognitive Distortions

At this point, facilitators can revisit the disclosure accounts of each group member's index offence and, indeed, their other offences. By this point, facilitators should have some knowledge of the cognitions which individual group members may have had during the cycle of their offending both before the incident, after the incident, and between incidents if appropriate. It is now possible to link up the hypothetical scenarios, the problem solving exercises, the way in which these exercises have been linked with individuals own offences and the current exercise on cognitions within each offenders cycle. In this way, cognitive distortions are placed in personal cycles of offending, and the contribution of these cognitive distortions to SIDs in these offending situations is examined. The cognitive distortions are likely to be varied in terms of minimisation and mitigation but, at the end of the exercise, participants will realise that they serve as 'excuses'.

Conclusions

Cognitive therapy is a guiding set of principles for many sections in the programme. This chapter has dealt primarily with cognitive distortions which mitigate responsibility for the offence, justify the offence or minimise the consequences of offending. Along the way, I have dealt with ways in which these methods of cognitive therapy can elucidate information in relation to the abuse/offending cycle and victim empathy. Once these cognitions have been elicited in relation to the offence cycle and victims, they can then be used to challenge whether or not offenders employed such attitudes and thoughts in their own offence cycle. In this way, the cycle of offending can be investigated in more detail as we shall see in Chapter 15. Similarly, once the thoughts and feelings of victims have been considered during these cognitive exercises, facilitators can set up enquiries with each group member on how they think that their victims felt. Therefore, these cognitive exercises are one of the central principles to the whole process of the programme. It is certainly worthwhile for facilitators to spend some preparatory time practising the way in which they might use the various exercises within different parts of the programme. Time spent preparing before sessions and between sessions will allow facilitators to feel more confident in eliciting cognitions, linking the elicited cognitions to the offenders own offence and their offence cycle, and challenging the thoughts which they have had during the offence cycles and thoughts about victims.

Chapter 14

Personal Physical and Sexual Abuse

This section of the programme addresses a pervasive issue in the field of sexual offending, that of physical and sexual abuse in childhood. It is one of the most commonly noted developmental issues in reviews of sex offenders' histories and as such should be addressed at some point during the programme. My own preference is to place it at a break somewhere in the middle of the extensive period containing sessions which challenge cognitive distortions. Alternatively, it can be placed at the beginning or end of the section of cognitive distortions. When reviewing the developmental experiences and comorbid psychopathology of sexual offenders, Fago (2006) writes that 'probably the single most common comorbidity that has been identified in sex offenders of all ages is a history of previous sexual victimisation. This finding is so intuitively reasonable that it has led to a general acceptance among clinicians and investigators that previous sexual victimisation provides a primary pathway to future sexual offending' (p. 195). However, he goes on to review a number of studies which demonstrate that reported sexual abuse history in sexual offenders is highly variable.

In an earlier study of 13 offenders against girls, Johnson (1989) reported that all 13 had been sexually abused in their own childhood. Pithers *et al.* (1998) studied 72 children with sexual behaviour problems and found that 59% of the boys and 63% of the girls were victims of both physical and sexual abuse. However, some evidence suggests that personal sexual abuse may not be as pervasive in sex offenders. Fago (2003) in his own study of 72 sexual offenders found that 13 (18%) had themselves been sexually abused. He compared this result to national statistics on sexual abuse in childhood and concluded that it was not markedly different from estimates in the general population. Ray and English (1995) found that 90% of the sex offenders in their sample had been the victims of physical and sexual abuse, although they reported that in an earlier study (uncited) they found that only 6% of 89 children in their sample had been sexually abused. Therefore, there are considerable differences among studies on the prevalence of sexual abuse in sex offenders' histories.

The Treatment of Sex Offenders with Developmental Disabilities   William Lindsay
© 2009 John Wiley & Sons, Ltd

As noted in the introductory chapters, the experience of sexual and physical abuse in childhood has been seriously considered as a major aetiological factor in the development of a propensity towards sexual offending in all areas. However, support for a direct link between being abused and becoming an abuser is not strong since significant numbers of individuals who have themselves been abused do not go on to sexually abuse others. In fact, in one prominent study (Cycle of Abuse, 1996) in which boys who had been sexually abused were followed up prospectively, there was no difference between the cohorts who had and had not been sexually abused in the numbers going on to commit sexual offences. This would certainly reinforce the conclusion that a significant number of boys who have been sexually abused in childhood do not go on to perpetrate sexual offences on others. However, it does leave us with the conundrum of why so many sexual offenders report having been abused in childhood. Authors do not generally address this inconsistency but, rather, suggest that sexual abuse in childhood is one pathway to sexual offending. Fago (2003) suggests that comorbid neurodevelopmental deficits may act as a catalyst and further pathway to sexual offending. Once again he notes that the reported incidence of the diagnosis of comorbid neurodevelopmental deficits is highly variable from 7% to 82%. Cantor *et al.* (2005), as already mentioned in the introductory chapters, although not dealing with the issue of pathways into sexual offending directly, have suggested that low IQ itself and a corresponding neurodevelopmental perturbation may be a factor in the development of propensities towards offending against children.

In general work dealing with mainstream sexual offenders, mentally disordered sexual offenders and sexual offenders with ID, I have come across a view (which is expressed neither cynically nor in a condemnatory fashion) that a sex offender may report personal sexual abuse in the hope that it is considered a mitigating factor in their own offence. Some may report personal abuse when it has not occurred in order to be viewed in a more sympathetic light. Such an effect would increase the incidence of reports of sexual abuse. In sex offenders with ID, I feel that the calculation involved in this kind of disclosure makes it unlikely that such an effect would be a major influence on reported incidents.

More likely is the fact that a significant number of clients come from abusive backgrounds where violence is not uncommon and sexual boundaries are much less tightly drawn. Therefore, it may not be uncommon for adult family members to have been themselves abused by the adults in their lives, and within the family such relationships, while not being condoned, are not considered unusual. In these families, sexual abuse may be more likely to occur but may not be reported to the authorities.

This would lead to an effect which would influence the prospective study conducted under the auspices of the House of Representatives (1998). In that prospective study, boys who were admitted to accident and emergency services for reasons of sexual abuse were compared to boys who had been admitted for general medical reasons. However, for a boy to appear at accident and emergency for reasons of sexual abuse, carers would have to view the abuse as clearly abhorrent and a medical emergency. In families where boundaries have been less clear over generations, this is less likely to be the case and boys abused in such families may be less likely to appear in accident and emergency services. Therefore, they would not be included in the cohort of boys who had been sexually abused. This does not reinforce the 'abused to abuser' hypothesis but rather suggests that alternative mechanisms of social learning may exert an influence.

As reported earlier, Lindsay *et al.* (2001) compared sexual offenders and non-sexual offenders on their experience of sexual and physical abuse in childhood. They found a higher rate of sexual abuse in the histories of sexual offenders when compared to non-sexual offenders and a higher rate of physical abuse in the histories of non-sexual offenders when compared to sexual offenders. Clearly, sexual abuse is a significant variable in the history of sex offenders with ID but is neither a sufficient explanation nor an inevitable developmental experience. Most of the individuals who committed sexual offences had not themselves been sexually abused in childhood.

These considerations provide an important context for this section of the programme which reviews the influence of sexual abuse on sexual offending. Generally, issues of personal sexual abuse are dealt with in individual sessions which might run concurrently with the group sessions. Individual sessions can deal with the personal details of the experience of sexual abuse and the psychological consequences. A number of aspects may emerge from these individual sessions which the client may not wish to be shared with other group members. The first issue which is likely to emerge is the extent of the anger which the client feels towards the perpetrator. This can come as something of a surprise to the facilitator since the abuse perpetrated against the client is often very similar to the abuse which the client perpetrated against their own particular victim. However, the anger should first be dealt with in individual terms. It is an understandable and adaptive response in the circumstances. Facilitators can review the extent of the client's anger, the impact it has had on their own personal development over the years and the impact it has on their current adjustment.

A second issue, related to the last, is the link between the anger felt by the client/offender to their own abuser and the emotions of his own victim towards the client/offender. This can be a powerful review of circumstances since, because of perspective taking difficulties in the client group, they may not have considered this synergy prior to the sessions. A third consideration is to review the details of sexual abuse experienced and relate it to their own developing sexuality. The experience of an abusive sexual relationship is likely to result in psychological disturbance, apprehension and anxiety about developing social and sexual relationships. Significantly, it may also influence low self-esteem and depression through self-recrimination and feelings in the client that they may have instigated the incident or incidents or, at least, did not do anything to prevent them. Here the issues of power differential between the adult and the child will be explored. However, following the exploration, it is inevitable that the power difference will be reflected in the client's own offence. It may be that initial sessions dealing with personal abuse may finish with the client focusing on their own experience of abuse with statements such as 'yeah, I know it was bad what I did, but he shouldn't have done that to me and I'm not going to stop being angry about that'. However, the individual sessions can concentrate to a greater degree on the personal experiences and sequelae of abuse rather than dealing with the sex offender issues.

The fourth aspect of individual sessions on sexual abuse, which has emerged in my own experience is that some offenders may say that they did indeed initiate the incident. Some have also suggested that they returned to the situation on a number of occasions in order to continue the experiences. In this context, I have employed similar exercises to those mentioned in the previous chapter on cognitive distortions. The particular issue of relevance is that although children may have some notion of the conduct of sexual intercourse through their sex education classes, they have no conception of the strength and force of a man's sexual appetite. A child's understanding of sexuality is completely different from an adult's perception and understanding. The adult will be aware of the unacceptable nature of the abuse, they will be aware that the child is an easier target for sexuality than would be an adult, they will be aware that they will not have to negotiate a sexual encounter to the same extent with a child as they would with an adult, they will also be aware of the range of possible sexual interaction, all of which will not be the case in the child. Therefore, for a number of reasons, if the client indicates that he feels he made sexual approaches to the adult, his understanding of what these approaches entailed would be entirely different from the understanding of the perpetrator of sexual abuse. Therefore, the client himself, although he may feel he holds some of the responsibility, can, through the Socratic process, come round to the view that as a child, he held no responsibility whatever. Once again, this discussion may have repercussions for his perception of culpability in his own offence.

A final point which can be dealt with during individual sessions and in group sessions is the extent to which the experience of sexual abuse or physical abuse can be used as a mitigating factor for the perpetration of sexual abuse. For the purposes of sex offender treatment, the main message is that although there are a number of sequelae of personal sexual abuse which will be addressed during treatment, it cannot be considered as an excuse for committing a sexual offence.

Group Exercise 1: Types of Abuse and Consequences of Abuse

Materials: flipchart and pen

In this exercise, group members are asked to write or draw the different types of child abuse which they can think of. Figure 14.1 shows that this particular group has arranged the different types of abuse around a central common core of '*child abuse*'. Through the Socratic process, they have produced a number of types of abuse including 'violent, sexual, neglecting abuse and verbal abuse'. They have then gone on to produce the kinds of sequelae which they imagine or have experienced. The predominant response for this group was 'angry – punch walls; thinking about it makes you angry'. It can be seen that during this phase of this particular group, they mentioned anger, 'commit suicide', and ways of dealing with abuse 'carry on with life, move on, put to back of mind and deal with it, speak to people – counselling sessions'.

Figure 14.1 Reviewing types and consequences of child abuse

Although this information is quickly reviewed in an analysis such as this, it may take 30–60 minutes to deal with during a group session.

In this session, once suicide had been mentioned, other group members added to the flipchart with some of their own experiences of wishing to be alone and sadness, 'sad, depressed, alone'. This individual also mentioned the common reaction in children of wishing to maintain the secret for fear of personal reprisal, 'keep it to yourself'. Helpfully, he also added two depictions of depression and anger.

Although it was not a particular goal of this exercise, the group members themselves have mentioned that one should not employ personal child abuse as an excuse or reason for perpetrating a sexual offence. Therefore, this has also been placed on the flipchart. In fact, they have mentioned the possibility that a sex offender may try to mitigate his own responsibility by invoking the experience of personal abuse in childhood, 'try to get off with it'. While this has not been emphasised as part of this session, since it was discussed, it was placed on the flipchart. The main purpose of the session is to review the personal experience of sexual abuse. One aspect which was not reviewed during this session was the correspondence between the sequelae which group members may have experienced, such as anger, depression, anxiety about disclosure, wish to isolate and so on, and sequelae which their own victims might have experienced. This could be done as a further extension of this exercise with a Socratic introduction such as

> FACILITATOR: You've done really well here because you have brought out a whole load of different types of abuse and the kinds of things that people can feel after they have been abused. You've said that people will feel angry, depressed, sad, they want to be alone and they worry about being blamed. So how do you think your victims would have felt?

In this way, facilitators can develop the exercise into aspects of victim empathy by asking each group member what they think their victim felt at the time and over subsequent weeks or months.

Exercise 2: The Abused to Abuser Cycle

Materials: flipchart and pen

In this exercise, the 'abused to abuser' cycle is reviewed. It has a number of similarities to the previous exercise in that the different types of abuse may emerge and personal reactions to abuse may also be expressed. However, the group members will generally finish the exercise by concluding that the offender himself is responsible for the incident and he should not invoke any mitigating factors of personal abuse when considering his own responsibility.

Figure 14.2 shows the flipchart records from such a session. The individuals in this case have identified two types of abuse, sexual and violent at the top of the page, and have drawn a number of depictions of each type of abuse. Following that they have placed the emotion of anger experienced by the victim and have suggested that the victim may grow to perpetrate a violent offence or a sexual offence in order to 'get my own back'. However, they have also inserted quite clearly that the perpetrator is always the guilty individual and that using memories of personal abuse as a mitigating factor constitutes an excuse which is unwarranted. Once again, although the information can be reviewed very quickly in a paragraph such as this, the actual exercise

Figure 14.2 Flipchart records from an 'abused to abuser' session

will take around an hour. The main message from these exercises on sexual abuse is that although an individual may experience behavioural, emotional and social consequences as a result of sexual abuse, they should be dealt with individually and for that person. They cannot be considered as reasons for mitigation for committing sexual offences on another victim. The responsibility for the sexual offence lies with the group member.

Chapter 15

The Cycle of Offending

All of the modules and exercises completed up to this point have been contributing to information which facilitators can use in developing each offender's cycle of offending. Therefore, during preparation sessions, facilitators may have already drawn up some fairly clear outlines of the offence cycles for each participant. As the facilitators move the process forward and as the group process elicits information from each participant, a clearer picture of each offence cycle is developed. All of this information will contribute to the relapse prevention module at the end of the programme. Despite the fact that previous sections may have added to knowledge of the offence cycle that this module can draw upon, it is worth reviewing explicitly at this point in order to ensure that it is completed adequately.

Exercise 1: Reviewing the Disclosure Accounts

Materials: previous information regarding disclosure and a flipchart and pen

Each group member has already given an account of their index offence and may also have given accounts of other previous offences. Facilitators will have at least one and perhaps a few flipchart sheets which give detailed accounts of individuals' index and other offences. For this exercise, these should be sellotaped to the wall or placed on the floor as reminders about the information each offender has already disclosed to the group. During the disclosure phase, another exercise was conducted in which commonalities were extracted from each of the disclosure accounts. These commonalities included violence, sexual excitement, anger and emotional disregulation, sexual thoughts and cognitive distortions and fear in the victims. One of the important aspects to draw out from this exercise is the extent to which the offender planned the incident. We have seen previously, during the exercise on reviewing the

---

The Treatment of Sex Offenders with Developmental Disabilities William Lindsay
© 2009 John Wiley & Sons, Ltd

sex offending scenario from the perpetrator's perspective, that motivation, cognitive distortions and planning have been reviewed fairly extensively in relation to the hypothetical scenarios. During these exercises, the feelings, motivations, thoughts and actions attributed to the offender in the scenario have routinely been linked to group members' offences with questions regarding their motivation, thoughts and so on. It cannot be emphasised enough that there is a strong continuity running across modules. Modules are not discreet but rather information is being gathered about each individual which will be relevant to subsequent modules and the final relapse prevention process.

During this exercise, it may be better to deal with only one offence disclosure per group member. If one member has committed four offences with four disclosure accounts, then the whole lengthy session could be taken up with a discussion of a single person's offence cycle. Depending on how the session goes, this could have two negative effects. Firstly, the spotlight is on one person for the whole period and they may become uncomfortable with pressure being put on them for such a length of time. Secondly, other group members may become distracted because of the relative lack of input they are being called on to contribute.

Gary had already disclosed information on two sexual assaults on women. The first was during an evening when he had gone to a pub in a main town 20 miles from his home. He had spent a couple of hours on his own in the pub drinking beer and had seen a number of women come and go. It was his habit to go to this town to drink but he said that on this occasion he had a higher level of sexual arousal. He spent the time drinking and trying to pluck up enough courage to approach one of the women to begin a conversation. Eventually, he said that he saw a good-looking woman and approached her. He asked her if he could buy her a drink and she refused. He then went back to his place in the bar and continued drinking. While he was drinking he ruminated on the rejection, developed feelings of anger and wished for revenge. She stayed with her friends until the pub shut and he continued drinking. They then left and he followed them whereupon they split up and started to walk home their separate ways. He followed this particular woman and sexually assaulted her in the street. It was between 12:00 p.m. and 1:00 a.m. and the street was extremely quiet. Figure 15.1 has two sections. The section on the left hand side shows some simple aspects of the offence cycle in Gary's case. It records that he has travelled to a town reasonably far away in order to commit the offence ('pub far away'). In a subsequent session, we returned to this disclosure account to review in detail his thoughts during the day about what he was going to do that night and why he went to the city 20 miles from his home town when all he was planning to do was going to the pub. He was questioned in detail about his motives as follows:

FACILITATOR: I am wondering why you wouldn't just go to a pub in Hometown when there are loads of pubs there you could have gone to. Why did you want to travel to the city?

GARY: I was just going out for the Friday night and I wanted to go somewhere different.

FACILITATOR: What does anybody else think about that. Why would Gary go to the city rather than one of the pubs in Hometown?

DARREN:	There is plenty of pubs around Hometown, it's big enough. There must be dozens of pubs.
FACILITATOR:	Maybe you should ask Gary why he didn't go to one of these pubs.
DARREN:	Gary, why didn't you go to one of the pubs in the high street, because there's lots around there?
GARY:	I'm fed up with these pubs. I wanted to go to the city and go somewhere different.
BRIAN:	Maybe he was thinking that it would be easier for him to get caught and people would know him in Hometown.
FACILITATOR:	That is a very good thought Brian, why don't you ask Gary.
BRIAN:	Were you worried you would get caught because you were wanting to attack a woman and people would know you?
GARY:	No I wasn't going to attack somebody I was just wanting to go somewhere different.
FACILITATOR:	If Gary was thinking about attacking a woman, why would he have gone to the city?
BRIAN:	Well, he would be worried that people would know him and he might get caught.
GARY:	Well I wasn't thinking about it and I wasn't worried about getting caught, so don't you accuse me of something that I wasn't doing.
FACILITATOR:	We are not accusing you Gary. You don't have to get angry. We are just wondering about what was happening before you offended. Gary, you tell me if somebody was thinking about attacking a women and went to the city instead of their own town what would they be doing?
GARY:	Well they would be worried about getting caught.
FACILITATOR:	So what would that be called?
GARY:	What do you mean?
FACILITATOR:	Does anybody else know what that would mean if somebody went to the city because they knew what they were going to do and didn't want to be caught?
DARREN:	Well they would be planning what they were going to do and worried that they would get caught.
FACILITATOR:	That's right. They would be planning their offence and thinking about how to not get caught.
FRED:	That's called grooming, when you are thinking about it. You are grooming the situation and making sure you don't get caught.
FACILITATOR:	That's a good word. Grooming. Does anyone know what grooming means?
FRED:	Well, grooming means that you're making a plan of how to offend. Sometimes you groom against children and you get their trust.
FACILITATOR:	Yes, that's one kind of grooming and what would be the other kind that Fred just talked about?
FRED:	Well, you're looking at the situation to see if you'll get away with it.
FACILITATOR:	That's interesting. Looking at the situation to see if you'll get away with it. What does that mean Edward?
EDWARD:	Well, it means you don't want to get caught I suppose.
FACILITATOR:	Does anybody want to get caught when they commit a sex offence?
ALL:	No, don't be stupid.
FACILITATOR:	So does that mean everybody would plan what they are going to do?

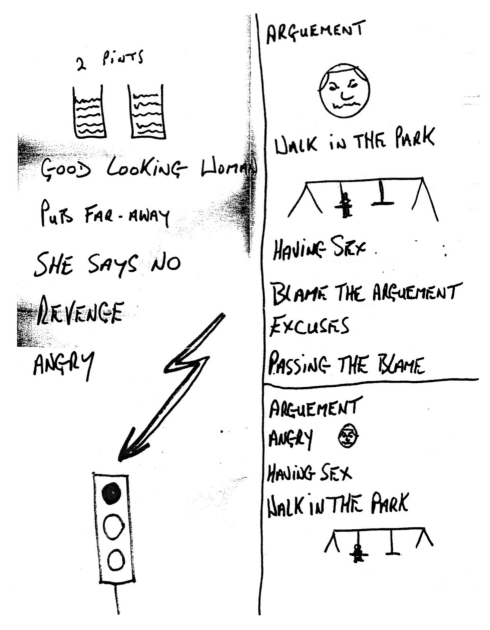

Figure 15.1　Gary's offence cycle

There then ensued a discussion about planning, grooming and the cycle of offending. This has two functions – it allows Gary to get a short rest from the disclosure and challenging process and it also introduces and reinforces concepts related to the cycle of offending which will prime all group members for the module. It also makes it clear to Gary that, although he denies it, the group suspect that he has developed some outline plans for, at the very least, a sexual approach to a female. Further evidence for this can then be reflected back to Gary. He said that he had been looking at some women over the course of the evening and had been trying to pluck up courage to talk to them. This would suggest, again, that he had some intention of making contact with a female that evening.

When he eventually did approach someone in the bar, she refused his offer of a drink. He then allowed feelings of revenge and anger to develop which eventually led to the sexual offence. We were then able to discuss these emotions from a number of perspectives. Firstly, we discussed the extent to which it was appropriate to become angry because someone refuses to accept a drink from a stranger. At this point, it is possible to role-play the pub and a scenario where one of the group members asks another if they want a drink, when it is part of the role-play that they are strangers. The following short extract is taken from such a role-play. All the participants are role-playing themselves but they are pretending that they are strangers. Brian and Edward are standing at the bar and Gary is role-playing himself on his own in the bar. Gary approaches Brian and asks him if he wants a drink:

GARY:	Can I buy you a drink? Would you like to chat?
BRIAN:	No.
FACILITATOR:	Gary, why don't you ask him again and ask him if he wants to talk?
GARY:	Okay. Would you like to have a drink and have a talk?
BRIAN:	No. Go away.
GARY:	Okay.
FACILITATOR:	Okay, well done guys. Brian, how did you feel when Gary came up and asked you if you wanted a drink. He's a complete stranger so how did it feel when he came up to ask you?
BRIAN:	I thought he was off his head. Nobody would come up and ask you if you wanted a drink if you didn't know them.
FACILITATOR:	Okay, so would it have been different if you had been a girl Brian?
BRIAN:	No, I don't think so. I just wouldn't have wanted to talk to him. I'm talking to my friend.
FACILITATOR:	Yes, that's right, you're talking to your friend so you wouldn't want a stranger to come up to you.
BRIAN:	No.
FACILITATOR:	How did you feel Gary when Brian told you to go away and he didn't want a drink?
GARY:	Felt okay. I wouldn't ask a man if he wanted a drink.
FACILITATOR:	Right, so why would you go up to a strange woman who was talking to her friend and ask her if she wanted to drink?
GARY:	Well that's what you do isn't it, you just go up to girls and ask them if they want a drink.
FACILITATOR:	Fine, but Brian said he didn't want a drink and told you to go away so did you get angry with him?
GARY:	No, of course not.
FACILITATOR:	So why did you get so furious with the woman in the pub?
GARY:	I don't know, I just did.
FACILITATOR:	Was it okay to get so angry?
GARY:	No, obviously.

It is unusual for any of these role-play or discussion sessions to be particularly significant on their own. However, the constant, persistent repetition of various messages, presented from different points of view, during different discussions and during a range of exercises, builds up to contribute to a complete picture of the offence cycle and risk factors. This particular discussion went on to illustrate that the female was not being unreasonable, that Gary was planning at least some aspects of his sexual offence, that his anger response was inappropriate and that his victim had done nothing to instigate the incident. We discussed whether or not Brian had instigated a violent incident by refusing a drink from a stranger. The obvious conclusion was that he had not and this was then reflected on the extent to which Gary's victim had instigated the incident. Following on from this, it was concluded and emphasised that his feelings of revenge were a series of cognitive distortions justifying and minimising the incident. Therefore, a cycle of Gary's offending was being built up which included distal planning (deciding to go to a pub 20 miles away), an active self-regulation strategy of going to a pub in order to meet a female, a strategy for heterosexual contact which included approach goals (at an early point in the evening this was not necessarily for sexual offending), the use of alcohol as a proximal strategy to overcome inhibition, the specific approach towards 'a good-looking woman', emotional disregulation following rejection, thoughts of revenge which constituted a series of cognitive distortions which were used to justify the offence, mitigate his own responsibility and place some of the responsibilities on to the victim and the eventual approach/explicit strategy employed in the 60 minutes prior to the offence taking place. All of this information was then placed in Gary's relapse prevention strategy. It is interesting that he placed a red traffic light at the foot of the account. This was taken from some of the relapse prevention information which is described in Chapter 20.

The second section of Figure 15.1 describes another offence which happened in a local park. Once again, the offence was committed against a woman in her early 20s. In this case, Gary had had an argument with his father prior to the offence taking place. During his offence disclosure account, it was clear that he had used the argument as justification for the sexual offence. Once again, anger had played a significant part in the cycle. During the discussion, the commonalities between the two offences and others' offences were drawn out. Importantly, the role of anger was cited across different offences. A number of men had interpreted their anger as justification for offending against the victim. In this case, the anger is not directed at the victim, as it was in the previous example; this time it was directed at his father. He has acknowledged that he has interpreted the argument and employed it to generate cognitive distortions excusing himself for the sexual offence with the words 'blame the argument, excuses, passing the blame'.

The first time he listed the sequence he recorded that he went for a walk in the park in response to having an argument with his father. He said that he went for a walk to cool down and then saw the woman sitting in the park. At this point, he said that he began to have sexual thoughts and employed the cognitive distortions, based on the argument with his father, to justify approaching the woman and attempting to sexually assault her. Following a discussion about the incident, it became clear that the sexual thoughts occurred at an earlier stage in the cycle and that the planning was significantly different. In the lower part of the section in Figure 15.1, he places his thoughts about having sex, after the argument and before the walk in the park. His anger at his father prompted sexual thoughts and he then developed a hasty plan of going to the park with the possible opportunity to have sex. This was a highly significant change in his account of the offence cycle. The change meant that he developed the sexual thoughts and the plan for a sexual assault in response to anger and resentment at his father. Therefore, as Marshall and Barbaree (1990) hypothesised, he appeared to be using sex as a coping mechanism for emotional regulation. This is an important difference from the point of view of his relapse prevention plan. It means that when he experiences anger, irrespective of the situation, he may begin to develop sexual thoughts, justifications for a sexual assault and a rudimentary plan for sexual gratification. It changes his self-regulation assessment from an approach/automatic assessment where he engages in a behavioural script such as going for a walk and happens upon an opportunity for sexual offending to an approach/explicit offender whereby he develops an active plan to offend sexually in response to an adverse emotional experience. Facilitators should be sensitive to this information, incorporating it into relapse prevention plans and self-regulation strategies.

Exercise 2: Using the Timeline to Develop the Offence Cycle

In Chapter 11, we have already seen the way in which the timeline can begin to illustrate the offence cycle. In the case of Darren (Figure 13.2), he identified a number of factors which promoted feelings of anger, power and sexual excitement. He attempted to control these feelings through isolation, masturbation and an increasing use of sexual fantasy. Timelines are used extensively in treatment and are built up over the course of the programme. They will be described in detail in Chapter 20, and at this point Figure 15.2 illustrates the way in which they can be employed to illustrate the cycle of offending.

The case of Alfred has already been described in Chapter 10. In Figure 10.2, his disclosure account is analysed. Figure 10.2 shows that he was at a nightclub, asked a woman to dance, felt resentment when she refused, waited until she left the nightclub, followed her home on the train and later broke into her house to steal items for masturbation. Subsequently, he returned to phone her and break in again.

Figures 15.2 and 15.3 show sections of his timeline in temporal order which were incorporated into his relapse prevention programme and which illustrate his cycle of abuse. Group members experience positive events at the top of the timeline and negative events at the bottom of the timeline. He also writes that he was feeling under pressure. In the earlier section (Figure 15.2), he wrote that he was drinking increasing amounts of alcohol 'drinking lager, sherry, gin and lime'. He was spending money in amusement arcades and was unable to pay his bills. He therefore felt under pressure from a number of sources. He was not able to pay his fuel bills, he was breaking into houses and was worried about detection by the police and at the foot of Figure 15.3 writes that youths were breaking into his own house and 'they wrecked the house'.

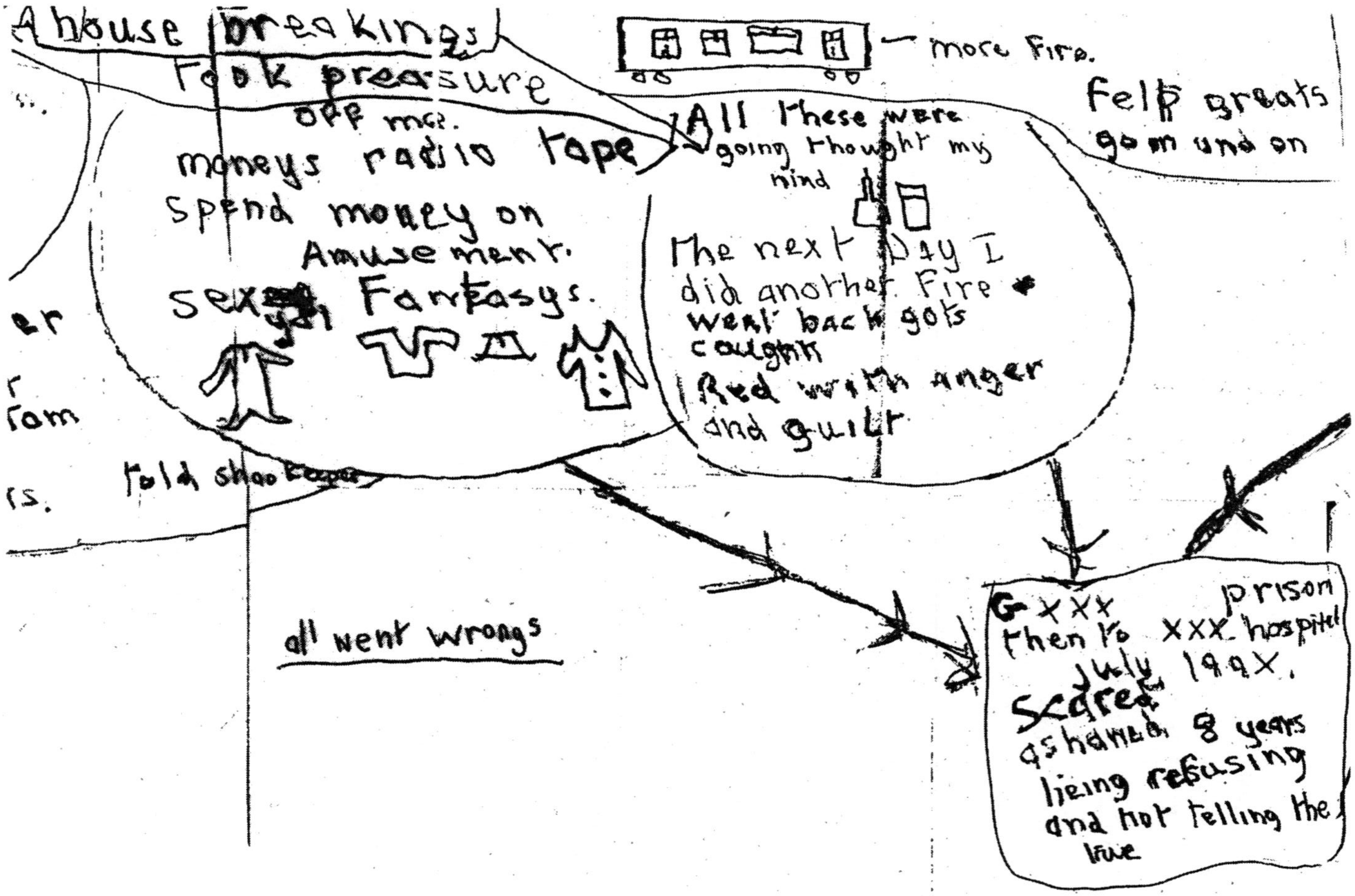

Figure 15.2 Alfred's timeline used to understand the sequence of offending

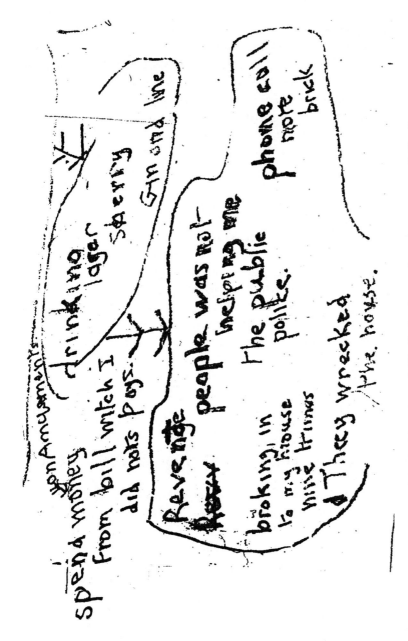

Figure 15.3 Another piece of Alfred's timeline to show the sequence of offending

229

From this information, we can gather a number of risk factors which were incorporated into the cycle of offending. He lived on his own and reported that vandals were breaking into his house. He was isolated, lacked pro-social influences and was developing feelings of anger and revenge into the perceived inactivity of the police. Therefore, isolation, emotional disregulation and cognitive distortions leading to justification were important aspects of the cycle. Figure 15.2 indicates that he began to resolve these problems by breaking into houses stealing 'money, radio, tape' and then spending this money in amusement arcades. He writes that he 'felt great' and says that he could 'go on and on'. He also reports that he was developing sexual fantasies and has drawn women's clothing which he was also stealing. The excitement and acquisitions gained from housebreaking produced an enormous sense of well-being which he used to cope with his negative feelings of isolation, anger and stress. At this point, he also notes that he was setting fires. This series of crimes contributed massively to his GLM and sense of well-being. They fulfilled many of his human needs which in turn provided motivation for him to continue. Following Figure 15.3, we inserted his sexual offence disclosure account (Figure 10.2). In this way, the disclosure account is incorporated physically into the timeline which begins in childhood and is projected into the future. Therefore, Alfred's sense of well-being, the excitement he gained from housebreaking and setting fires and the way in which these actions fulfilled his human need to deal with feelings of anger, helplessness, isolation and revenge all fed in to a feeling of entitlement which led on to the sexual offence. In many ways, the patterns of breaking into houses, going on trains to distant locations in order to set fires, stealing items of value and clothes for sexual gratification, and the developing sexual fantasies all contributed as distal factors leading up to his sexual offence. The sexual offence is physically placed into the timeline at the appropriate point. In this way, the sections on offence disclosure, relapse prevention, allocation to pathways and cognitive distortions are all incorporated into the cycle of offending and then into the Relapse Prevention Plan for each participant.

Exercise 3: Intervening and Altering the Offence Cycle

This exercise can either be done after the group member has completed his account of the offence pathway or, if the group is closed, after everyone has completed their offence cycle. It is a fairly straightforward exercise whereby the group discuss the timeline with the prospect of making alterations in order to change the outcome. These alterations will be individual to the group member and so there are many, many examples. Minor changes to routine may take the form of using a different bus stop which is not adjacent to a school. It may involve walking a slightly longer distance but the reduction in risk is significant. The group member might be encouraged to take a different route home which avoids a park or pathway, which might constitute the kind of circumstances which invited the prospect of indecent exposure or public masturbation. In another case, we altered a man's daily routine so that he stopped taking an early bus into town when he was going to work placement and sessions with his social worker. In this case, we suspected that he was spending the extra 30 minutes in town following women and thinking about public masturbation or an indecent assault. We used specific, immediate communication with his family to ensure that he remained at home until an appointed time whereupon he took the bus and went straight to whatever appointment he had. These are examples of relatively minor changes in routine which reduce the chances of an offence occurring. In other cases, the changes in routine are mandatory. Some men are banned through a Restriction Order from going to certain places where they have committed offences before. One example is when an individual is prohibited from going to a shopping centre where he has been convicted of approaching strangers in the toilet or masturbating in an open cubicle. Therefore, there are a range of ways in which routines can be altered in order to lower the risk of an offence.

In other cases, major life changes will have to occur to change the offence cycle. In one case, we discussed the importance of an individual changing his weekend routines entirely and stopping going to parties with his relatively wide circle of friends. In this case, the individual had been convicted of several counts of public masturbation and, in one incident, a fairly serious matter of stalking, indecent exposure, public masturbation and panicking a mother and daughter. There had been a very high density of incidents over a period of around 6 months and a restriction had been placed on the person that he should stay away from females who were not known to him. However, he had a wide circle of friends and knew many women of his own age whom he saw frequently at parties they went to every weekend. He reported having sexual feelings when he was at these parties and, following group discussion, it was decided to be extremely important for him to avoid these situations in order to avoid the development of powerful sexual desires.

Unfortunately, in cases such as this, the extent of the risk exceeds the importance of achieving human goods in the form of attachments and relationships, through attending these events. Therefore, his quality of life was reduced considerably by avoiding parties at the weekend. However, it was necessary in order to disrupt the cycle of offending. It was also the fact that he did not do anything during the day and we began to promote attendance at work placements which were supervised by training staff and educational staff. In this way, we placed extended periods of pro-social contact which was directed at skills acquisition in place of the intense, loosely structured social contact of regular weekend parties. As we shall see later, it is often the case that we will be quite explicit with offenders that the pro-social alternatives we discuss and advance for the attainment of human goods and improvement of quality of life will not be as exciting as the methods they have used in the past. The excitement that offenders experience in relation to offending incidents is often described as being very intense. Car theft, excessive drinking, drug abuse and situations involving sexual offending are described with such vividness and excitement that we are quite explicit (and realistic) in saying that the ways we suggest of achieving human goods in a socialised manner will not have the same 'buzz'. However, they are much less likely to lead to offending.

It is also necessary to alter the offence chain when emotional disregulation is evident. Therefore, with Gary in the previous case, the importance of anger regulation is analysed. Because, in our own area, we have developed a comprehensive forensic learning disability service, it is fairly easy for us to refer an individual with a specific anger problem to an appropriate anger management group (Lindsay, Allan, Parry *et al.*, 2004). However, it is clear from Gary's case that no matter who was treating him, the importance of anger, feelings of revenge and alternative coping strategies for dealing with his anger would be extremely important. He required an alternative strategy for dealing with anger in order to disrupt the cycle of offending. It is important to consider coping strategies for emotional regulation as a means to disrupt the cycle of offending.

In this way, changes in routine, alternative behavioural scripts, protective attitudes and cognitions, changes in decisions, alternative ways of dealing with emotional regulation, new coping skills and different ways of dealing with sexuality will all alter the chain of offending. The facilitators should also emphasise that one change in the chain might alter the outcome but it is important for the offender to stick with these changes, continually rehearse them and incorporate them into general lifestyle rather than veer back into the offending chain once again.

General Considerations in Altering the Offence Chain

When reviewing the individual cycles of offending, facilitators can consider the theories of sex offending in order to place each participant's offending in a logical context. This will be done more extensively in the final section on relapse prevention but, as has been said repeatedly, each of these modules builds up a picture of the individual offender and all of this information will be employed in the relapse prevention programme and the GLM. In Chapter 6, a number of concepts were involved which contribute to sexual offending, and I will review their place in the offence cycle.

Motivation. Several of the theoretical models cite sexual arousal and inappropriate sexual preference as part of the motivation. Addressing this factor might be made quite explicit with measures to circumvent the situations which will promote sexual arousal. Examples have already been given such as avoiding a bus stop outside a school, stopping going to parties, going for a different bus and so on. Distraction techniques have also been discussed in relation to arousal (see Chapter 17). Even when men find it extremely difficult to suppress their sexual arousal to inappropriate stimuli, we can promote self-regulation and avoidance of inappropriate situations and settings.

Developmental factors. Once again, the various developmental factors which might promote cognitive distortions and attitudes supporting offending can be dealt with directly during treatment. The points in the offence cycle where they are activated should be analysed repeatedly with clear, persistent messages on the extent to which they are inappropriate. At the same time, facilitators can promote the adoption of socialised appropriate attitudes which will disrupt this cycle.

It has been mentioned repeatedly that the development of new problem solving skills is an important part of treatment. This will allow the offender to make alternative choices at crucial parts in the sequence of offending. These might be decision making skills about routines or new skills for emotional regulation which circumvent maladaptive problem solving leading to sexual offending. These new skills and ways of dealing with situations will also disrupt the cycle of offending.

Reducing internal inhibitors. Once again the importance of cognitive distortions and the influence they have on justifying the individual's behaviour is an important consideration. It cannot be emphasised enough that attitudes which allow each man to continue with the cycle of offending should be addressed and at the very least undermined. These may be relatively minor and might constitute seemingly irrelevant decisions. These seemingly irrelevant decisions are employed frequently in the Relapse Prevention Model of treatment which, as has been described earlier, relies heavily on the addiction literature. In this, small decisions which appear relatively benign or neutral of themselves contribute to a pattern which leads to offending or relapse. Facilitators should be alert to these relatively minor attitudinal factors which may in fact contribute to the overall cycle of offence. Another obvious example of ways in which internal inhibitors are reduced is the use of alcohol or drugs. This can be drawn out clearly from most group members' cycle of offending.

Overcoming external inhibitors. These may emerge quite clearly from the cycle of offending in that the offender has induced children with sweets, alcohol, cigarettes or other gifts. These can be changed quite explicitly in the changes to routines. In other cases, it may be somewhat more subtle. Some offenders may continually go to pubs alone in the hope of finding women who have had too much to drink. In this way, they may implicitly be looking for women who have a lowered resistance due to their alcohol intake. In a few cases which I have dealt with, this has emerged as treatment progressed, although the man himself has not appeared to realise that he is looking for drunk women. If we think about the recent publicity on excessive alcohol use in young women, it seems that some men may be alert to the sexual opportunities afforded when women have had so much alcohol that they are no longer in control of sound judgement. At its extreme, there are reports of men giving women stupefying drugs in order to eliminate the control they have over their consent to sex. While I have not come across such an extreme example in men with ID, there have been a few examples of individuals looking for women who have been drinking excessive amounts of alcohol. A further way of reducing external inhibitors, more common in men with ID, is looking for isolated areas where victims might be walking. There have been several examples given previously of finding victims on isolated paths, parks, quiet streets and so on.

The threat threshold. The reduction of internal inhibitors, external inhibitors and any increase in personal arousal will affect the threat threshold. This is likely to be an important part of the cycle of offending in that at the point of offending, the group member will perceive the threat to be low enough that the sexual incident is worth the risk. Facilitators should support the individual in increasing the threat threshold while reducing the personal motivation for fulfilling human goods through sexual offending. This programme is replete with ways of doing this.

QOL and the GLM. We will review these issues further in the chapter on relapse prevention but the point here is to improve the group members' QOL by reducing isolation, increasing contact with the community, increasing commitment to routine socialised activities and improving pro-social influences in order to improve the sources of human goods available to the offender. Supporting the person in the development of a better quality of life will not only improve fulfilment and reduce isolation, it will also be a source of motivation to maintain that better life and, as a result, is likely to increase the threat threshold to avoid a drastic reduction in QOL. While these may seem complex theoretical notions, they are in fact very simple. Driving a car is a highly valued activity for most of us. It is an activity which improves QOL through increases in our freedom, allows us to make greater choices and is valued in the community. If we have 12 points for speeding, we lose our license. Once a driver acquires 6 points on license, the threat threshold for losing it increases and, I would imagine, most become much more alert to speed limits. Although the case of sex offending is more complex in its organisation, it has similar conceptual simplicity.

Conclusions

This module can be conducted at various points in the programme. It may be that for some participants it is more appropriate to place it earlier than others. Because of the intellectual variation between participants, it may be that some take much longer than others. It is quite appropriate to split the group or take a group member for an individual session in order to construct aspects of the offence cycle. This can then be brought back and explained to the rest of the group who can then express their views and offer contributions and additions. The significant aspect is that each group member is gaining a clear picture of the cycle of events which progress towards the commission of a sexual offence.

Chapter 16
Victim Awareness and Empathy

There are a number of cognitive distortions and basic beliefs about sexual offending which are inextricably related to views about victims and victim empathy. It is important to review these issues and challenge any basic beliefs which the offender has concerning the victim. Therefore, the objectives for this module are to increase the understanding which the offender has in relation to the victim and to undermine any distorted beliefs they may have about the effect of the offence on the victim. Specifically, the objectives are as follows:

1. To undermine any belief that the offence was in any way beneficial to the victims.
2. To undermine any concept of mutuality the offender may have in relation to the specific offence.
3. To increase the offender's understanding of the actual effects on victims. These include behavioural, cognitive, emotional, developmental and social effects.
4. To increase facilitators' understanding of the offender's empathy deficits.
5. Address the identified empathy deficits.
6. Increase pro-social behaviour with regard to understanding victims.

There has been a great deal of research investigating the importance of empathy training in the place of empathy deficits in sex offender treatment. Marshall *et al.* (1995) developed a model of empathic response which has four stages – recognising the other person's emotional state, an ability to see things from the other person's perspective, developing a compassionate response to their emotional feelings and taking action to ameliorate their distress. They felt that it was important to incorporate assessment and treatment of empathy deficits into any sex offending programme. Jolliffe and Farrington (2004) have reviewed studies which investigate the assessment and training of empathy in a range of different types of offenders. They noted the difficulty that certain offenders have in understanding the concept of empathy and they also note the corresponding difficulty in treating empathy deficits. Knopp, Freeman-Longo and Stevenson (1992) reported that over 90% of programmes for offenders in North America include empathy training as a principle component.

The basic principle behind empathy training is the view that a lack of victim empathy allows an offender to eliminate or avoid any 'anxiety, guilt or loss of self-esteem' (Abel *et al.*, 1989, p. 136) following the perpetration of an offence. If he is able to avoid taking the perspective of the victim or avoids trying to understand the way in which the incident has affected the victim and their family, it allows the offender to defend the self against responsibility for the effects on the victim and his or her circumstances. The lack of victim empathy encourages feelings of entitlement and discourages any self-doubt concerning the perpetration of any offences. Clearly, the purpose of the module is to make inroads into these basic beliefs and cognitions.

Exercise 1: Group Discussion and Simple Role-Play on Why Empathy is Important

Materials: flipchart and pens

As the discussion unfolds, it is appropriate for one of the group members to write or draw the main points on the flipchart.

It is the case that sex offenders with ID can be puzzled by the concept of empathy during the initial parts of the discussion. In my own experience, some individuals in mainstream sex offender groups can also lack an initial understanding of why these issues are important. Group members may not display empathy and may only have a vague notion of the concept. The discussion will focus around perspective taking abilities and their importance. Several of the men may have specific empathy deficits as has been suggested by Marshall, Anderson and Fernandez (1999). These can take the form of specific deficits in relation to their own victims rather than general empathy deficits. Therefore, an offender may not evidence a generalised lack of empathy or perspective taking but might show a lack of understanding of what their own victim or victims experience during their offences. It is undoubtedly the case, however, that ID makes perspective taking more difficult. In their review, Jolliffe and Farrington (2004) concluded that the ability to demonstrate empathy was related to IQ to the extent that the relationship between low empathy and offending disappeared when intelligence and socio-economic status were controlled for.

The group discussion should include the following issues:

- What is empathy?
- Why is empathy important?
- What do victims feel – what kind of damage can be done to a victim?
- How can group members consider the thoughts, feelings and emotions of their victims?

Once a general discussion on feelings of victims and damage to victims has been initiated, the facilitators can review specific damaging experiences which the victim is likely to have. Physical damage is the most obvious aspect of victim experience and several offenders can consider that there has been little damage to their victim because they were not physically harmed. All aspects of emotional, psychological, cognitive and relationship damage to the victim should be covered including the following:

- Emotional damage at the time.
- A breach of trust which can last for years through the individual victim's life.
- Post-traumatic experiences.
- Adverse developmental progress and maturation as a result of the sexual offence and abuse.
- The effect on emotional development.
- The effects on future interpersonal relationships (linked to the issue on trust).
- Effect on sexual development.
- Ability to establish trust in emotional relationships.
- Effect on the wider social network including family and friends.

Proctor and Beail (2007) studied empathic responses in 25 offenders and 25 non-offenders, all with ID, and found that the offenders with ID had better empathic responses than the non-offenders. Their conclusion was that the results suggested that empathy training was not indicated for the offenders since they had a better empathic response. However, an alternative conclusion might be that since they have such a basic level of empathy, there is much to build on during treatment in efforts to support them in understanding the full implications of the offence for the victim. This in turn might be an additional factor promoting self-regulation and motivation to avoid future offending. In addition, since Jolliffe and Farrington (2004) found a relationship between low empathy and IQ, there do seem to be persuasive arguments for enhancing victim empathy during group treatment to counteract this general lack of empathy.

Discussions on empathy and perspective taking can begin by reviewing whether or not each person has the same view of the room in which they are sitting. Clearly, this is not the case and one or two individuals can be asked to describe the perspective of someone across the room from them. They should be asked to do this without turning round so that they can begin to gain an understanding of how difficult it is to see things from another person's point of view. The discussion can then move on to interpersonal situations. Each individual can be asked how another person is feeling with possible examples from previous group sessions when something has happened to a particular member and the group tried to understand how they felt. This will also begin to clarify why it is important to understand the feelings of other people which can then lead on to understanding feelings of victims.

Part of the discussion might relate to how people feel when they are assaulted. Group members may have a greater understanding and empathic response to physical assault from another man than they are able to gain with a sexual assault. The group can discuss how they would feel if they were physically assaulted. The emotional repercussions of physical assault can be explored and then related to sexual assault. For example, if a physical assault were to happen in a certain area of town, at a certain time of day, in a certain building or whatever, group members can be asked how they would feel about going back to that area of town or how they would feel at that time of year. This can then be related to a sexual assault and the group can review how a victim would feel if they were back in the same area in which they had been assaulted. In this way, the effects of the assault can be broadened from physical harm to emotional consequences.

At this point, a series of simple role-plays can be enacted, some of which might be specifically relevant to individual group members. The facilitator can turn round and stare at one group member for as long as possible. Different group members will report different feelings but some will certainly report feeling very uncomfortable at being stared at. This can be immediately reflected by asking the group members how women might feel when they are being stared at or followed. It is likely that group members will conclude that they feel similarly uncomfortable.

Another role-play which we have used occasionally is relevant to men who stalk women. Facilitators ask the group member to walk around the room and follow closely behind him. The group member will immediately stop and look at the facilitator asking, 'What are you doing?' The facilitator simply says, 'Nothing – just keep walking.' As the offender continues to walk around, the facilitator continues to follow closely behind. This will produce some light relief and amusement to the group but the group member involved will continue to turn round saying things like 'Why are you doing this? What are you up to?' The facilitator should keep saying, 'I'm doing nothing, just keep walking.' The facilitator can use an innocent expression and tone of voice to emphasise the fact that 'the stalker' continues to proclaim his innocence. However, the group can discuss the role-play making it obvious that the particular group member has clearly felt uncomfortable because he kept turning round and asking the facilitator, 'What are you up to? What are you doing?' The group member himself might accept that he felt uncomfortable. This example can be related to how a victim feels but it should be stressed that the situation for victims is much more serious and they will feel a great deal more threatened and uncomfortable. Facilitators can say something like 'So, you felt uncomfortable in this situation and what I was doing was just silly, following you around the room. You know you are safe because you are here and you know everybody. But you still felt uncomfortable so how do you think women would feel when they are outside and don't know who you are and they don't know the people around?' Therefore, the discomfort in the relatively benign role-play situation is being compared to the much greater discomfort experienced by victims.

Another role-play, along the same lines as the previous examples, is when a facilitator sits beside a group member and touches them on the arm constantly. Over a short period of time, this can become irritating or, as in the above example, the group member might start asking the facilitator what they are doing. The feelings of annoyance, which are certainly legitimate, can then be related to the feelings of victims when they are being touched in a much more severe and serious fashion. Before beginning this role-play, ensure that the group member knows what is going to happen.

Exercise 2: The Four Stages of Empathy. Role-Playing

Marshall and colleagues (1995) have identified four processes which make up empathic responses. These are emotional recognition, perspective taking, emotional replication and decision making. In my experience, it is difficult to convey the four stages of empathy to men with ID. Alternative ways to describe the stages would be: try and understand how someone else feels; try and see things from their point of view; try and feel how someone else is feeling; do something helpful. However, one has to be careful with group members since this last point could be focused upon and used as an instruction for approaching women and 'doing something helpful'. It has not happened to me in 20 years of working in this field but I could imagine a group member approaching a woman in the street to help her with her shopping or her children and then justifying this by saying that he had been instructed in the group to 'do something helpful' when he saw others having difficulty. While facilitators should have these four stages of empathy as a framework for conducting sessions on perspective taking and victim empathy, intervening with victims in a 'helpful manner' should not be encouraged.

Perspective taking and some aspects of emotional replication can be dealt with in the role-plays and discussions conducted during the previous exercise. The role-plays described in this exercise are fairly straightforward with each group member role-playing an emotion and other guessing what it is. There should not be any expectation that you cannot role-play the same emotion as a previous group member. It is likely that the first group member will role-play sadness since this is the easiest to do and if others feel awkward with the role-play exercise, they should understand that they can role-play sadness again. Possible role-played emotions include the following:

- Sadness
- Happiness
- Anxiety
- Anger
- Frustration
- Embarrassment
- Contentment
- Fear
- Jealousy
- Puzzlement/uncertainty.

If the group is familiar and comfortable with role-playing, then facilitators can write the emotions on pieces of paper which can then be randomly drawn from a hat. In this case, group members role-play the emotion which they have picked. They can use non-verbal cues only and then verbal cues or both. If group members are not particularly good at identifying emotion, facilitators can praise their efforts for role-playing and for identifying at least the difference between positive and negative emotions. It is likely that most group members will be able to recognise happiness/contentment/feelings of well-being/love as opposed to fear/anxiety/anger/frustration/jealousy. However, with verbal cues, it is more likely that group members will recognise the different emotions. Group members should be able to move from their seat while doing the role-play if they want.

Exercise 3: Discussion Exercises on Role-Play and Offending Situations

A range of offending situations can be discussed to review how the victim is likely to feel. Group leaders can develop situations according to the needs of offenders. However, the following situations are suggestions which would be understood by most group members:

- You have had a drink with a friend on a Saturday afternoon and you are walking home. You are having fun and feel great. Your friend says, 'Let's steal a car' and you think it's a great idea. You go to the local supermarket, see a car on the edge of the car park, smash the window, jump in and take the car. Riding it round on a Saturday afternoon with a drink feels great.

Discuss this situation in terms of how the woman feels when she comes out of the supermarket with a full trolley and looks for her car. Does the thief think about her emotions? She will be uncertain where the car is parked, she will look round with self-doubt about what has happened, finally understanding that her car is not there. What are the emotions she feels? What has happened to her plans for the day and the rest of the week? How will this affect her in the longer term?

- Other situations involving theft can be used such as one's feelings when a television, CD player or DVD player is stolen. How do you feel when your house is broken into?
- Situations involving aggression can be discussed. As with previous examples, there are a range of situations which can be reviewed such as walking home after going to the pub on a Friday night and being assaulted by a gang of youths. What would you think when you are walking home? What would you think when you see the youths? What would be your feelings when the youths confront you? What is the immediate damage and what is the lasting damage?

This discussion will raise similar issues to previous exercises and the review of other types of situations should always be related back to sexual situations.

- How does the victim feel in a situation of sexual assault? What does the perpetrator feel in a situation of sexual assault? If he understood how the victim felt, would he continue the sexual assault?
- What does the child feel in a situation involving sexual abuse? If the sexual offence does not involve overt physical violence, what are the effects on the child? What are

their immediate thoughts in relation to the interpersonal situation, trust, emotional responses and cognitive responses? What will be the developmental effects in relation to all of those aspects? Discuss the longer lasting effects on the victim and their family.

Exercise 4: Videotaped/DVD Accounts of Sexual Assaults

There are a number of recorded videotaped/DVD accounts of sexual assault which are available from a range of different agencies. There have also been episodes of all the 'soaps' in which sexual assaults have occurred. Reviewing recorded videotapes/DVDs allows the group members to comment on the victim's experience in the same way they have done discussion exercises. All the points made for previous exercises are relevant to this exercise. These videotapes/DVDs can generate a great deal of discussion among group members and are likely to emphasise the importance of effects on victims. Once again, it is possible to make links between individual offences and the victim's accounts on the videotape/DVD.

Exercise 5: Empathy Deficit Role-Play

By this time, there will have been a number of discussions on empathy and the importance of victims' feelings. There will also have been reviews on the feelings of friends and family and the effect of the offence on them. In this session, explain that it will be focused around a role-play of a specific group member's offence. It is important to explain that you understand this might be difficult for the individual involved and that he will require support to deal with the feelings it might arouse. Explain to group members that they will be asked to take roles during the session and that there are rules.

Rules of the role-play. When the facilitator says 'Stop!' everything must stop. Anyone can stop a role-play for a good reason, for example, if they are feeling a bit upset or do not understand what is going wrong. If anyone asks to stop for a good reason, this will be accepted. There will be no physical contact during the role-play, touching will only happen when the facilitator says so and only if it has been agreed beforehand.

The role-play itself can involve a number of things related to the particular victim in the offender's incident. It might be the victim themselves, a relative or a friend. Explain that it is very important to try and think about how your victim feels or how the particular relative feels. The following example is taken from a role-play of an incident where a group member sexually assaulted a young shop assistant on a quiet morning when the shop was empty.

Setting the scene. The offender's name is Harry. It is the night after his offence and he is going to play the victim. She is at home with her husband and her family and they are making the tea. Her children are upstairs watching television and her husband is in the kitchen making the tea.

One of the group members can take the role of the husband and a further two will take the role of the children. Ask the group member to describe the room, the furniture, where is the door, what they are doing, and so on. The group member chooses a name for his victim, a name for the husband and names for the children. The session continues as follows:

> FACILITATOR: Now Harry it is really important for you to try and think about how 'Alice' feels while she is home that night. What are you doing just now when you are Alice?
>
> HARRY: I am making the tea and I am worrying about the kids – if they're safe.
>
> FACILITATOR: How old are the kids?
>
> HARRY: I don't know.
>
> FACILITATOR: Well, you are about 25 so your kids will be quite young won't they?
>
> HARRY: Yes. Maybe they're only four or five.
>
> FACILITATOR: So, it's good to be worried about your kids, but why are you worried about them on this night?
>
> HARRY: Well because someone just attacked me and I am worried about everyone now.
>
> FACILITATOR: That's good. So, you are not just worried about yourself you are worried about your kids' safety. Fred – you are the husband 'Alistair' so how do you feel about what has happened when you are talking to your wife tonight?
>
> FRED: I am really worried and angry.
>
> FACILITATOR: So why are you worried and angry?
>
> FRED: Well I'm worried that Alice is going to be safe and I'm angry that someone would attack her so I want to go and get the guy.
>
> FACILITATOR: So you feel angry and worried Alistair and Alice, you feel worried for the safety of your children. How do you feel inside?
>
> HARRY: Burning, I'm burning inside.
>
> FACILITATOR: Burning? Can you tell me what that means, you're burning?

As has been mentioned in Chapter 7, people with ID can enter into role-playing enthusiastically. Occasionally, they seem to forget that even a simple situation is being role-played rather than a reality. Therefore, individuals are likely to engage with these role-plays with some conviction. They can be quite powerful in generating an initial understanding of the way in which victims feel. Occasionally, as indicated in the extract, unusual responses emerge such as a feeling of 'burning'. These should be analysed before going on with the action in the role-play. There may also be a degree of nervous laughter during role-plays and group members should be assured that this is understandable. The facilitators can then explore the various victim emotions with a range of questions which either can be put directly to 'Alice' or can be given to 'Alistair' with prompts to ask Alice such as

How did you get to work this morning?
How did you feel when you were on the bus going to work?
How did you feel when you opened the shop and you were in it?
How did you feel when you saw a man come into the shop?
What was it he did to you?
How upset did you get?
How did you feel after it happened?

What did he do afterwards?
What did you do for the rest of the morning?
How do you feel now?

There are a large number of areas that can be explored during these role-plays. Facilitators can go on to review how the victim will sleep that night, what they will do the next day, what they will do in 3 months, how they will consider returning to the same situation, and so on. Facilitators can then explore the same kinds of issues with family members, husbands, children, parents, and so on. Following the role-play, facilitators should prompt as much discussion about the exercise as possible. They should also be aware of any emotional responses in any of the group members. It is important to reduce any anxiety that might have developed and this can be done through a group relaxation exercise if it is felt that the discussion is insufficient.

Exercise 6: Further Role-Play Exercises on the Same Situation

There are a large variety of situations that can be role-played around most offending in-cidents. In the example above, a role-play could be set up where the victim is returning to work for the first time with the group member role-playing the victim. The victim could be in the street with her partner or husband and sees the group member walking the other way. In this case, the feelings and actions of the victim and the partner might be explored. In other role-plays, a child or adult victim may be given information that they suspect a sex offender has moved into a nearby house. Role-plays can involve child victims getting older and entering into relationships. All of these should be scripted by facilitators prior to introducing them to the group. They can all promote understanding of how victims might feel as a result of the sexual offence. They also ensure that the wider context of effects on victims is considered by all group members.

Possible Role-Plays

- The group member has made a sexual assault on a 13-year-old girl. Role-play her beginning college at the age of 18 years. One of her college tutors, who is significantly older than her and is short of time at a meeting, suggests they meet over lunch. The participant has to attempt to experience the emotions of the victim as she is asked to meet this man outside of class time. What would the effects of the sexual assault be on this encounter?
- Same offence as above. Participant is asked to experience the thoughts of the victim 10 years later when she is reading the paper and sees that the perpetrator has committed another sexual assault and has been committed to prison.
- This role-play can be related to any offence. Role-play how the victim feels if the social worker tells him or her that the offender is being released from prison on condition of release and is returning to the same town.

- A sexual assault on an 8-year-old girl or boy. Role-play how the victims' parents feel about their children including the victim. How will the parents respond in terms of their views of other men, their feelings of protection towards their children or their anger towards the perpetrator. What will be the long-term result of changes in parenting practices. This role-play can be conducted from either the mother or father's point of view.
- In relation to stalking offences, the group could role-play how women feel walking the street following an incident of stalking. Also role-play how they would feel about walking in the park, on a beach, and so on.

Group facilitators should discuss possible, relevant role-plays prior to group sessions. They should be scripted roughly so that facilitators have some idea about the direction they will move the role-play and the questions they will ask concerning each role-play.

Conclusions

Victim empathy can be a powerful tool in developing a generalised awareness of the effects on victims in men who have probably never considered the issue previously. It is an important aspect to deal with from the point of view of developing further factors that might promote self-regulation. There are so many aspects of victim empathy that it would be possible to spend months going over various role-plays, discussion points and issues specific to each offence and it is quite easy to become 'waylaid' by this section. There are a number of points to emphasise. Once the principle of perspective taking and the effects on victims is established, there are probably diminishing returns from going over and over the issue. Therefore, facilitators should decide on a finite amount of time to spend on victim empathy issues and a finite number of exercises for each group member. Issues of victim empathy should be kept in mind so that if a suitable and appropriate opportunity occurs during another part of the sex offender programme, then a victim empathy role-play can be quickly arranged in order to reinforce the messages that the incident will have a profound effect on the victim. These more spontaneous role-plays will not have the form of the organised, scripted variety described in the later exercises in this section. However, they could include the discussions and 'stalking' type role-play where the group member walks round a room and is followed by a facilitator. These can be both amusing and instructive in the way in which they make group members mildly uncomfortable and force them to reflect on the victim's feelings.

Chapter 17

Use of Pornography and Dealing with Sexual Fantasy

The role of pornography and sexual fantasy in the development of sexual offences and sexual offending interests is contentious. Deviant sexual fantasies are alarming when revealed by a convicted sex offender. The difficulty is that we do not know how many men have deviant sexual fantasies. Seto, Cantor and Blanchard (2006) and Seto and Eke (2005) conducted studies into use of Internet child pornography and found that only 1% of those individuals went on to commit contact sexual recidivism. The state of opinion concerning pornography is similar. We do have an idea on how many sex offenders use pornography generally, and in the commission of sexual offences. We have little idea on the equivalent use of pornography in non-sexual offenders. For this reason, I will outline some of the small amount of literature which is available on both pornography and sexual fantasy.

For some time, several people working with sex offenders have thought that pornography may exert some influence on the rate of sexual crimes. The first possible mechanism is that pornography may create a social climate conducive to rape or offences against children that facilitates an individual to commit a sexual offence. The second mechanism may be that pornography directly affects certain individuals, increasing sexual interest and drive and thereby increasing motivation to commit a sexual offence. However, Marshall (2000) has written that sexual offenders are not a homogeneous group and it is likely that different individuals will respond differently to the various forms of pornography. In addition, we have a fair idea that the base rate for use of pornography in the general population must be very high, given the success of the porn industry. One important issue to remember is that in all studies information on rates and types of pornography use has been collected through self-report. It is unlikely that non-offenders will be truthful about their pornography use. On the other hand, sexual offenders only become participants in studies once they have been identified and are therefore a specially selected and biased group. Marshall (1989b) reported information on frequent current use of pornography. Twenty-two per cent of rapists,

The Treatment of Sex Offenders with Developmental Disabilities William Lindsay
© 2009 John Wiley & Sons, Ltd

26% of child molesters and 13% of non-offenders were classed as frequent users of pornography. Therefore, sexual offenders reported a higher use of pornography, but it was still the case that three-quarters of the sex offenders did not report frequent current use. A few of the sex offenders frequently used pornographic images that matched their offence category. He also reported that 35–38% of the sex offenders said that exposure to pornography did, on at least one occasion, serve as an instigator to offend but in all cases the instigating pornographic images depicted adult consenting sex. He concluded that '[t]he inference … from the available literature is that pornography exposure may influence (not solely cause) the development of sexual offending in some men, but for most, its use is simply one of many manifestations of an already developed appetite for deviant sexuality' (p. 74). He felt that counselling sex offenders about the wisdom of continued use of pornography and the relationship of pornography to the risk of a future sexual offence seemed eminently sensible. He did not recommend attempts to impose complete restrictions on access to pornographic images since the evidence did not support such an action and pornographic images are ubiquitous.

Langevin and Curnoe (2002) classified the use of pornography into four areas: self-stimulation, grooming the victim, later stimulation and monetary gain. In relation to self-stimulation, they reported a number of studies where the use of pornography among sex offenders was higher than that among non-sex offenders. However, the number of sex offenders using pornography in their cycle of offence was generally around 25–35% (in line with the results from Marshall, 2000). In relation to the use of pornography to groom victims, they reported one study where 10–15% of paedophile offenders showed pornographic magazines or videos to their victim as part of the grooming process. They reported certain cases where pornography was used as self-stimulation by individual offenders after they had committed their offence. They also hypothesised that members of 'sex rings' may take photographs of children for later marketing for financial gain. In their study, they compared sexual offenders against children, sexual offenders against adults, incest offenders and miscellaneous sexual offenders (exhibitionism, voyeurism, etc.). They found that pornography played only a minor role in the commission of sexual offences. Only 17% of all cases used pornographic material in a way that was clearly connected to the sexual crime in question. Their study suggested that possession of pornography, *per se*, did not lead to the commission of sexual crimes. The majority of those who did use it committed offences against children. Another notable finding was that one in three offenders who actually used pornography were taking pictures of the children.

Production of pornographic materials and a possible link to sexual offences creates a link between pornography and sexual fantasies. The available evidence would place the link in the area of offences against children. However, Langevin, Lang and Curnoe (1998) found that even men who persistently offend against children also had fantasies about non-deviant sex with adult women. In their study of 201 sexual offenders and controls, they found that only one-third of the sexual offenders reported having deviant sexual fantasies. The non-sexual offenders reported having more sexual fantasies in general than the sex offenders, which is somewhat surprising given the natural reluctance of non-offenders to admit freely to sexual fantasy. They felt that, in general, sexual fantasy probably did not have a general aetiological importance in sex offenders but may be important in individual cases.

Dealing with Pornography and Sexual Fantasy

Dealing with pornography and sexual fantasy during sex offender treatment can be difficult for a number of reasons. We have stopped using disclosure of sexual fantasy as a method during group treatment. There is no empirical reason for stopping. It is based on a feeling that the group dynamic and interest when members are describing sexual fantasies feels different than when they are describing their index offence. Index offences are generally public events. They may have been described in court and even reported in the newspapers. They have been publicly punished or at least censured and the events are clear with a sentencing outcome. Sexual fantasy does not have the same public scrutiny. They are private events with no outcome beyond personal sexual gratification. Although there is often little difference between sexual fantasy and a sexual offence, there is a clear difference in the extent to which they have been publicly examined and censured. For this reason, I am uncomfortable about the description of sexual fantasies during group sessions. There is more prurient, voyeuristic feel about group interest when sexual fantasies are being described than is the case when index offences are described.

For the reasons outlined above, we often deal with sexual fantasy during individual sessions. This may not be a large number of sessions but two or three may be necessary. Facilitators should watch for the possibility that an individual offender is trying to shock them with the nature of the fantasy. Another point to be careful about is that the offender simply lies with an anodyne fantasy. It is difficult to decide if any of these processes are occurring because, by its very nature, a fantasy is a private event.

As has been seen from the previous short discussion of the literature on pornography and sexual fantasies, it is difficult to determine to what extent these processes are linked to the sexual offending itself. Therapists have to work out for themselves or work out in clinical teams the extent to which they feel pornography or sexual fantasy is related to any individual man's sexual offence.

Exercise 1: Discussion about the Link Between Pornography and Sexual Offending

This is simply a discussion about the way in which men use pornography and the way it may be related to sexual offending. Facilitators should be aware that it may be linked in individual cases. Points to bring out are the following:

- Some men definitely do use pornography in the cycle of sexual offending.
- It is worthwhile having a discussion on whether or not group members feel pornography might encourage a sexual offence where it would not otherwise have been committed. Conversely, the discussion might include the consequences of avoiding pornography. One issue that could be explored is whether or not avoiding pornography results in an increased use of sexual fantasy in the absence of pornographic stimuli.
- Pornography is widely available and group members should discuss the way in which they will control their use of pornography in order to prevent events which might

lead to sexual offending. This might include a discussion on where and when it is appropriate to use pornography. When would be the most dangerous/risky times to use pornography? When would be the safest times (if there are any) to use pornography?

- In discussions on the use of pornography and its relationship to sexual offending, facilitators should be aware of offenders who employ avoidant goals. The evidence suggests that most offenders with ID employ approach goals but one of the classic avoidant/active strategies is to use pornography in a misguided attempt to reduce the chances of future sexual offences.
- The use of pornography is ubiquitous among men and only a few commit sexual offences. Therefore, there is no clear link between pornography and sexual offending.
- Various different kinds of images are construed as sexually stimulating by different men. Some group members have told me that simple pictures in the local paper of children receiving school prizes can be sexually arousing. The underwear sections of mail order catalogues are often referred to as having sexually arousing images. Late night television programmes often have reasonably sexually explicit material. It will be impossible to control all the sexually stimulating images available to group members and so facilitators should not worry about making an exhaustive review of images.
- The information on the relationship between the use of adult pornography and offending against children is worth exploring. Many men may feel that the use of adult pornography will prevent them from thinking about children. While adult pornography is widely available and its use cannot be controlled, group members should be aware of any possible link between the use of 'any' pornography and offences against children.
- Group members should be made aware of the relationship between the production of pornography and offences, that is, men who take pictures of children (outside family and friends) may be more at risk of committing a sexual offence. This is the one area about which I, myself, am sensitive. I make attempts to prevent group members taking pictures of children which could later be used for masturbation. This can be very difficult when the pictures are of their own younger siblings, younger cousins or nephews and nieces. Individual judgements with the support of a clinical team are required in these cases.

Exercise 2: The Link between Sexual Fantasies and Sexual Offending

In this case, the conversation is likely to take the form of a discussion on the role of sexual fantasy in the commission of sexual offences. One does not have to go into detail concerning individual group members' sexual fantasies in order to conduct these discussions. However, it will be useful for the facilitators to have an idea about the role of sexual fantasy in each group member's cycle of sexual offending. It is likely that some group members will at least have rehearsed the offences prior to the incident. This may not be in specific detail but it is likely to have been done on a general level. For example, an individual who offended in a voyeuristic fashion against women may have done so on several occasions and may have masturbated to personal images of some of these voyeuristic incidents. These sexual fantasies are based on previous experience and may facilitate future voyeuristic offences:

- Some offenders are likely to have a sexual fantasy directly related to their sex offending incident. In our experience, this sexual fantasy can last for years with similar potency. During group sessions, it will become clear, even through oblique references and tangential statements, that some of the men still think about their sexual offence or offences quite clearly. One might suspect that the clarity is maintained by its role in sexual fantasy and masturbation.
- During the discussion the group can review the way in which sexual fantasy may promote the cycle of sexual offending.
- The discussion should explore ways in which men can suppress sexual fantasies and the way in which they can break any cycle through suppression of the sexual fantasy.
- The discussion can also review ways in which men can distract themselves from the sexual fantasy.
- The group can review certain aversive techniques in general (without going through specific sexual fantasies in detail) during their discussion. If the facilitators have previously gone over the sexual fantasy in detail with offenders on an individual basis, they may have used some aversive techniques during these sessions. These can be referred to during group sessions but generally would be conducted on an individual basis (see later).
- It is likely that during the group discussion, participants will discourage each other from engaging in sexual fantasy and several of them will make the point that sexual fantasies will promote personal feelings of sexual arousal and encourage the individual to rehearse the sexual offence in imagination. They will quickly understand that this rehearsal may encourage or at least facilitate the offender in a repeat of the offence. During the discussion, group members will support each other to suppress such rehearsal and its link to the cycle of offending. Therefore, it is likely that the outcome of these discussions will be to suppress or divert the fantasy.

As part of this discussion, facilitators can explore the relationship between pornography and sexual fantasy. Most members of a sex offender group will already understand the link between pornography, sexual fantasy and sexual offending. By discussing these issues, we are not placing any ideas into their consciousness. However, on this occasion, it may be that some sex offenders will deny any link between pornography and sexual fantasy. Several do not report a connection between pornography, sexual fantasy and sexual offending. Nevertheless, it is worth exploring in much the same terms as the previous exercises with similar issues:

- Is there a link between pornography, sexual fantasy and sexual offending?
- Does pornography encourage fantasy and offending?
- Is sexual fantasy connected to other issues in the individual's life rather than the use of pornography?

- Would avoidance of pornography discourage the use of sexual fantasy?
- The evidence which we have linking pornography to sexual offences and by implication sexual fantasy suggests that the use of some pornography may be linked to deviant fantasies. The link is unlikely to be specific for individual sex offenders. By this, we mean that offenders against children, for example, do not appear to relate only child pornography with child offences or child sexual fantasies. Rather, some child offenders may use adult pornography in their cycle of offences, presumably to heighten sexual arousal.
- Perhaps, the main reason for exploring these areas is to increase the awareness and understanding of the role of sexual fantasy in the cycle of sexual offending and what strategies they can employ to deal with it.

Some men may use sexual fantasy and masturbation as a 'faulty solution' when feeling angry with others. This is consistent with the Marshall and Barbaree (1990) analysis that some men use sex and sexual assault as a coping mechanism for solving problems in their life. When they feel angry with others or feel they have been dealt with unjustly, they may turn to sexual fantasy and masturbation. Therefore, the group should discuss the importance of adaptive coping skills in these situations rather than using sexuality as a coping mechanism which might prime the individual for sexual assault. There was no doubt, from the example of Gary in Chapter 15, that following an argument with his father he turned to sexual thoughts as a coping skill.

Exercise 3: Aversive Conditioning in Imagination

Aversive conditioning in imagination is a cognitive behavioural technique which is generally conducted, if at all, in individual sessions. Occasionally, I have used it in the group setting to reinforce certain aspects of the technique but it is usually an imaginal procedure. The technique is not confined to dealing with sexual fantasies and it is often used as an aversive technique in cognitive or behavioural scripts or routines which might lead to sexual offending. In this section, I will describe different ways in which aversive conditioning can be used.

There is a significant caution associated with this technique. Occasionally, certain sexual fantasies are themselves so vile and aversive that, in my opinion, inserting a punishing event or stimulus into the technique may be irrelevant or self-defeating. Where sexual fantasies involve pain, injury, mutilation, and so on, it may be pointless to insert a mild aversive event. It may even increase the sexual excitement of the fantasy. This is extremely unusual in men with ID but I know of no research to support this point of view. An alternative view is that placing a mild aversive event such as the appearance of a police vehicle would indeed function as a disincentive in the same way as it does with less deviant sexual fantasy. I am simply pointing out that, when using this technique, a therapist should be alert to the possibility that the procedure may increase the excitement of the sexual fantasy.

Another serious consideration with this technique, as with all sex offender treatment, is that if the facilitator or therapist is uncomfortable with the material being dealt with, then they should not begin. If this discomfort happens as the session continues, then he or she should stop the session. All of these are the normal precautions one would take with sex offender therapy and, particularly, work on disclosure, child sexual abuse and sexual fantasies. The material itself can cause therapists and facilitators real discomfort and, if this discomfort becomes acute at any point, therapists should discuss their feelings and responses to the material during supervision. Supervision and therapists' responses to the material have been dealt with in Chapter 7.

Aversion in imagination

This technique involves developing some detail about the individual's sexual fantasy. In one case, a client had a sexual fantasy about hiding in the woods and watching two pre-adolescent girls walk past. He maintained that he did not imagine them undressing but simply imagined them walking past him while he was hiding in the woods. He found the repeated use of this sexual fantasy could be sexually stimulating and it was one of his masturbatory images. Once a degree of detail had been taken from the offender, I inserted an aversive event into the cycle. He was in the bushes watching the girls when, unknown to him, he was spotted by a large man walking through the woods with his dog. He comes over to him and shouts at him, 'What are doing – you are looking at these girls you pervert – don't you move or I'll get my dog onto you.' As a variation on this aversive addition to the sequence, one could use a gamekeeper coming across the individual as he watched the girls. These aversive images were continually placed in the sequence of fantasy and, by his reports, considerably reduced the potency of the sexual fantasy. Indeed, he asserted that once the image of the man with the dog or the gamekeeper had been placed into the fantasy, he found it difficult to stop it coming into the sequence of events. In some ways, it seems similar to the phenomenon of being asked not to imagine 'a blue polar bear'. As soon as you are asked not to imagine a blue polar bear, the image comes to mind.

Another example was a client who imagined having sexual intercourse with his sister. He had not offended against his sister but early on in treatment it became clear that it was one of his sexual fantasies. Again, we gathered detail of the sexual fantasy – it was in his own bedroom, it was in the afternoon when there was no one else in the house, and he had certain routines associated with music for encouraging his sister into his bedroom. During the sequence, when his imagined relationships with his sister were becoming more and more intimate, we inserted a police raid on his bedroom. Two policemen burst into his bedroom to arrest him. Once again, this imagined aversive consequence to the sexual fantasy proved effective.

It is often possible to check the extent to which the offender is able to imagine the event and the aversive consequences. For example, when the policemen burst into his room, we can then go through a series of events which continue the aversive nature of the fantasy and allow us to check the extent to which the offender is able to imagine the scene. This can be done through a series of questions. If the police are handcuffing, on which hand do they place the cuffs? When they take him downstairs from his bedroom, how do they go down? We would expect the offender to explain that either he goes down first while cuffed or the policeman goes down first. When they go into the car – how do they get into the car? We would expect the offender to explain the awkwardness of getting into a car while cuffed. In this way, we can make some simple checks on the extent to which the individual is able to imagine the various sequences of events.

In both of these examples, the outcome was successful. Both individuals reported the elimination of the sexual fantasy and, in the context of the wider comprehensive treatment, neither has re-offended. For the first individual it is 8 years since the offence and for the second it is 12. Therefore, over lengthy follow-up periods, treatment has been successful in both cases.

Aversive consequences of offending

This technique can also be used in relation to potentially offending situations. In one case, a client had sexually assaulted a woman in the street. This had happened on three occasions. He had followed women until he felt there was an opportunity, approached them and made a sexual assault. In every case, the women had pushed him away but all of the offences had been reported to and investigated by the police. During group sessions, he described how he had seen another woman at a bus stop and had found her sexually attractive. As he was standing behind her at the bus stop, he felt that he wanted to touch her. This was the first part of the behavioural sequence which led to one of his previous sexual assaults. He had wished to touch a woman outside a shopping centre and then had followed her to her car and sexually assaulted her. He said that he had not touched the woman at the bus stop because it had been on a busy high street, a number of people had been watching and the public nature of the situation had encouraged self-restraint.

We were concerned that the self-restraint had been imposed externally rather than internally and we began a short sequence of aversion in imagination during the group. We asked him to imagine, once again, the scene where he was behind the woman at the bus stop. On this occasion, however, the street was empty and there was no external disincentive for him touching the woman. We then asked him to imagine moving closer to the woman and placing his hand on her shoulder. At that point, we asked him to imagine a hand being placed on his own shoulder by a large policeman who was asking him what he was doing. In fact, there were two policemen behind him, who had seen him and were apprehending him. It was clear from the way in which he was imagining the sequence of events that the aversive consequences were having an impact. His face was quite calm and relaxed as he went through the sequence until he was told to imagine the policeman at his shoulder. By his facial expression, it was apparent that he was surprised.

For this sequence, it was possible to conduct the aversion in imagination in a group setting and other members of the group then placed a great deal of detail on the sequence which added to the aversive nature of it. They made a number of suggestions about him being handcuffed, taken to the police station, waiting for interrogation, being placed in the cells, undergoing a police interrogation, and so on. Another group member then suggested that the two policemen might be in the car at the other end of the street unknown to the offender. They then discussed the fact that it is impossible to be aware of where the police are at any one time and whether or not you are being watched in the course of committing a sexual offence. They then discussed that if members of the public, other than the police, happen to see you then they may engage in vigilante activity. Sexual offenders are extremely aware of the possibility of vigilante activity being directed at them and this, in itself, acts as an imagined aversive consequence. In the community groups which I run, offenders are also extremely aware of CCTV and the fact that any of us can be picked up on CCTV if we behave illegally. In this case, group members inserted CCTV detection into the sequence with the police arriving on the scene very soon afterwards having been alerted to the incident by the camera.

It can be seen from these examples that aversive conditioning in imagination can be used with certain sequences of deviant sexual fantasy. However, to reiterate, group facilitators must be extremely cautious in the use of these techniques. As has been indicated at the beginning of this section, group discussion of sexual fantasy may have a different valency since it has not been censured by society in the way that index offences have been. It may also be disturbing for group facilitators and if you feel uncomfortable with the material, then stop.

Exercise 4: Suppression of Sexual Fantasy

This exercise is easier and more comfortable than the previous exercises. It once again takes the form of a discussion about ways in which men can suppress sexual fantasy and divert their thinking onto other things. It may be done in conjunction with the earlier exercises and is relevant for all sexual fantasies. It is not necessary to go into detail of the sexual fantasy in order to conduct this exercise. It is simply a discussion of ways to suppress or divert thoughts. The kind of ideas which emerge might include

- Go and do another activity such as playing on the computer.
- Engage in some physical exercise such as going to the gym.
- Engage in a household task.
- Train yourself to think of anything else that interests you, for example, football, money, another sporting activity, and so on.
- Go and read the paper.
- Do something else around the house.
- Make sure you are taking your medication (antidepressant medication, antipsychotic medication, anti-anxiety medication).

Do not engage in offending behavioural scripts or maladaptive coping routines such as the following:

- Go and have a drink (alcohol) to try and control it.
- Go for a walk which previously has been part of the offending routine.
- Masturbate to the deviant fantasy in order to 'get it out of your system'.
- Take recreational drugs to try and forget about it.
- Watch pornography or violent films to try and get it out of your system.

All of these discussions can use the Socratic method so that group members themselves can produce the material which will be used as recommendations for future protection against the use of deviant sexual fantasies.

Conclusion

This chapter has outlined a number of methods which can be used to deal with pornography and sexual fantasy. Some of these can be used in-group settings but generally they would be used in individual sessions. It is likely that a few sessions will be given over to each client to review their sexual fantasies and masturbatory practices. In this way, fantasy can be covered without making public too much individual detail.

Chapter 18

Attachments and Relationships

This chapter on attachments and relationships will draw heavily from the theoretical model outlined in Chapter 6 and on the GLM. The basis of these models is the importance of people achieving a quality of life and primary human goods which include relationships, feelings of achievement through employment and leisure and a reasonable degree of community engagement. One of the requirements of an adequate quality of life is a range of good relationships on which one can depend and which contribute towards self-image and self-esteem. This in turn depends on the ability to make attachments and maintain these relationships. Another crucial aspect of the development of adaptive relationships is that they provide constant pro-social influences and constant 'reality checks' against the emergence of asocial or antisocial attitudes which might arise through isolation. The other side of these principles is that offenders may have developed self-esteem and self-image through a distortion of their attachment and relationships. Therefore, they may have relied on social interactions which promote antisocial behaviour and crime. It is quite easy to envisage the way in which self-image can develop through an exciting sense of relationships which promote joy riding, drug abuse and other types of offending. An individual may develop prestige and self-esteem through stealing for others or helping others in theft. Therefore, there are two aspects which can be counteracted by the development of pro-social, ordinary relationships – distorted attitudes and cognitive schemata that can develop through isolation and distorted attitudes and schemata that can develop through antisocial influences.

The GLM suggests a number of ways in which individuals can achieve human goods through the distorted means of inappropriate sexual behaviour and sexual offending. Closeness, human relationships, a sense of achievement and mastery can all be achieved through inappropriate sexual behaviour with a minor or through coercive and violent sexual behaviour with adults. Clearly, this is a maladaptive process but it is important for sex offender treatment to tease out the way in which these antisocial and illegal sources of human goods have contributed to the offender's development over the years. This is an important exercise in the context of these theoretical models and can be done in conjunction with various other sections of this programme. The module on relapse prevention employs the technique of a timeline or life map. This is explained in detail and is not reiterated here. However, the importance of the timeline is that it attempts to separate out enjoyable experiences in the person's history whether or not these have been illegal and negative experiences in the person's history.

There is no assumption that good experiences will be pro-social. This would be an inappropriate perception and is not the basis of the argument laid down by the GLM. Many of the experiences which individuals have enjoyed in the past and which have contributed significantly to their self-esteem, self-image and QOL will be antisocial experiences which have led to the break-up of relationships, disruption of educational experiences, disruption of developmental experiences and, ultimately offending. Therefore the offenders will place in the 'good' area of the life map, such experiences as disrupting the classroom in school, the excitement of giving cheek to the teachers, stealing cars, engaging in inappropriate sexual behaviour at school and in young adulthood, drug taking, feelings of power and invulnerability through steroid use and excessive exercise and so on. These are all real examples of powerful developmental influences which have contributed towards individual's life model prior to offending. While we, as professionals, would interpret these experiences as antisocial and maladjusted, they have been experienced as exciting and enjoyable and have fulfilled the human needs in the person's life.

One particular aspect should be mentioned at this point which I have noted more frequently in mentally ill, mainstream sexual offenders than I have in sex offenders with ID. However, it does occur in sex offenders with ID and should be considered to a greater or lesser extent in individual cases. Isolation has been noted frequently as an important variable by previous researchers and theorists and is fairly common in offenders with ID. However, a few sexual offenders with ID have recounted repeated episodes of isolating themselves and developing resentment to individuals in their lives, and this has taken a central position for lengthy periods of time. In extreme cases, they have begun to develop sexual fantasies and have sought out isolation in order to fantasise about deviant relationships such as sex with children. This has been true for individuals living in the community who have recounted during sessions the way in which they would isolate themselves for variable periods from a few hours to a whole day while they engaged in sexual fantasy. One individual recounted the way in which, when he went to prison, he requested isolation in order to be able to engage in repeated masturbation and aberrant sexual fantasies. This is a unique case but does illustrate clearly that the issues of pro-social attachments, relationships and social interaction are of paramount importance. If one isolates oneself from normal social interaction, opinions, attitudes and general dialogue, it is fairly easy to develop a distorted view of people, society and the nature of interactions and, finally, the nature of appropriate sexual contact. Those of us who work with sex offenders have seen the way in which these distorted views of the world have developed and are seen by particular individuals as appropriate. The phenomenon is not as extreme as the case described above, but it occurs to a lesser extent with many cases.

Abel *et al.* (1989) conducted an extensive piece of work on attitudes consistent with sexual offences against children. In their analysis, one of the factors to emerge was the view that society does or will condone certain sexual offending incidents. This is consistent with evidence on the basic principle that certain developmental experiences produce a distorted sense of self and a distorted view of the world which may condone inappropriate behaviour or sexual offences. Given these distortions in cognitions and distortions in perception of normal relationships, in particular sexual relationships, the offender may then put some of these views of the world into action resulting in a sexual offence. The following methods are aimed at remediating these attachment and relationship distortions and promoting ordinary friendships.

Obstacles to Development of Relationships and Attachments

The development of relationships is one area in which fostering quality of life and the GLM maybe considered to run counter to the 'Risk-Needs Model'. The Risk-Needs Model (Andrews and Bonta, 1998) suggests that intervention should reduce the number of risks and all of the therapeutic focus is on risk reduction. This is quite appropriate and has produced more powerful and successful methods of sex offender treatment over the last 15 years. The difficulty in developing appropriate relationships is that we, as therapists, automatically review each relationship situation for access to victims and increase of risk. If one considers any situation in which the sex offender may establish attachments and relationships, the nagging feeling of increased risk is always in the background.

In the development of these methods, we have adopted the approach of discussing the obstacles at length as we move through a timeline. In this way, the various exercises employed in the attachment and relationships module is often woven through lifestyle change and relapse prevention. It is common, during the development of an individual's life map, to give over a whole session to discussing the range of possible relationships and attachments for the person in question. This is quite in order but slows down the treatment process considerably. The life map itself can take up to six sessions and if it is further delayed by sessions given over to discussion of attachment (or occupation/leisure as will be seen later), one can see that this whole process begins to take a lengthy amount of time. Time is a major consideration when mapping out the course of treatment and it helps to conduct some individual sessions to speed up the process. The various obstacles to the establishment of relationships and attachments will be outlined in one of the exercises to follow.

Reviewing the Individual's History for Positive Developmental Experiences and Attachments

As has been explained above, as part of the exercise in tracing the timeline of developmental experiences, antisocial influences on development will emerge. In addition, it is likely that a number of pro-social and positive experiences will also emerge. Often the offender will mention certain pro-social family influences, enjoying sporting activity with friends or family, enjoying normal social interaction with workmates for periods of time, enjoying part-time activity with a family member or friends such as working in gardens, achieving mastery at certain activities (e.g. being a good swimmer or runner) or engaging in less social activities such as reading or playing chess. It is worth noting that in most of the cases we have treated, the group member mentions a family holiday as a particularly memorable, enjoyable and pro-social experience. This can be true even if there is only one short example of a family holiday. However few pro-social influences there have been, it is important to extract these and emphasise their value for past development of the individual's sense of self and future development. Reinforce and build upon any interests, strengths and relationships the person may have had. Chapter 20 contains examples of the way in which these experiences can be identified.

Exercise 1: Establishing Positive and Negative Contributions towards the Individual's Life Model

This exercise is part of the lifestyle change and relapse prevention module. It will contain a range of developmental experiences and developmental influences which have contributed to the individual's sense of self. As the person traces through their life, facilitators should bring out the positive and negative influences that have contributed towards offending. To reiterate and emphasise, the important issue is that certain antisocial influences will have been extremely enjoyable and exciting and will, therefore, be placed in the 'good' areas of a life map. Clearly, there will also be experiences in the 'bad' areas of the life map. These may include bereavements, losing friendships, being bullied, being found out in relation to antisocial behaviour and so on. One thing to look out for during this exercise is the extent to which 'bad' experiences such as being bullied have in turn contributed to the development of antisocial solutions which the person has employed as a negative self-resource, such as isolation or fantasies of revenge. These forms of maladaptive problem solving may feature as developmental coping skills.

Examples of experienced positive influences contributing to an individual's life model

Pro-social Experiences

- Family attachments.
- Particular friendships which have developed sociable routines and influences.
- Holidays.
- Periods of employment.
- Appropriate adult company – both male and female.
- Specific interests such as computers, reading, films.

- Any activity which has led to a sense of mastery – this would include sporting activity or some activities which the person has been good at school. It could also include reading or knowledge of computers.
- Living in a place where the individual co-operated and enjoyed the company of their neighbours.
- Specific pro-social engagement with a relative, for example going to football matches with an uncle or going fishing.

Negative Influences

- Enjoying isolation.
- Enjoying truanting.
- Enjoying disrupting school activities.
- Enjoying aberrant sexual fantasies and making time for them.
- Excitement of drug abuse or alcohol abuse.
- Aberrant relationships promoting crime such as car theft or stealing.
- Feelings of mastery in relation to a range of situations, for example feeling powerful when intoxicated, maladaptive or antisocial support of a football club, feelings of power in relation to violent films or violent pop music, excessive physical exercise, unusual clothing such as uniforms.
- Feelings of rejection or revenge.
- Use of aberrant pornography.

This list is extensive but it is not exhaustive. There are always individual items to emerge from cases. With a recent case, it emerged that a major motivating influence for an individual and influence which developed their self-esteem was following women repeatedly and then returning home to masturbate over fantasies about these individuals whom he had followed an hour before. It is clear that this is a fairly long exercise which may take a single individual a session as they move through their life map. However, commonalities can be drawn between group members and a number of individuals can complete the same exercise at the same time.

Exercise 2: The Difference between Romantic Relationships and Platonic Relationships

This is a fairly straightforward exercise introduced under the title 'Who could be your girlfriend and who would not be your girlfriend'. Figure 18.1 shows the outcome of such a discussion. On the left of the figure, group members have made a list of places where they might meet a friend and activities they might do with them. At first they have listed that a special friend might be their brother, cousin or sister. However after discussion, these have been deleted as the group members themselves are led, through Socratic process, to understand that these individuals would never enter into a romantic relationship. They then continued the list to say that they could meet them

Figure 18.1   Discussion on romantic and platonic relationships

in college or a special needs club or day centre. As activities to do together they have included eating, swimming, bowling, sports, shopping, talking, going to a disco or walking. On the right of the figure they have included individuals who would not constitute romantic relationships.

This is a straightforward exercise conducted with the next exercise, and the outcome is seen on both figures.

Exercise 3: Obstacles to Establishing Relationships

It is an automatic reaction for us, as sex offender therapists, to think about risk factors as soon as any developments in attachment or relationships are mentioned. Tony Ward and myself (Lindsay, Ward and Morgan, 2005) presented to a conference a list of factors that we had come across in our discussions of obstacles. It is very unlikely to be an exhaustive list.

Some of the suggestions contained in this exercise will be uncomfortable for people reading this manual. It is important to remember that human beings are social and that they will strive to develop relationships and attachments. If they do not develop pro-social relationships and attachments, then they will do it in an antisocial fashion. It may feel uncomfortable even thinking about asking an offender to try to develop a relationship in any situation. However, it is always better to begin these personal developments while the offender is in treatment and while they are being monitored closely through the probation service, supportive clinical teams, community staff and so on. If we do not begin this process while they are in treatment with us, it will begin when they leave and they are no longer under our system of monitoring. This is a much worse solution. Additionally, it presents a risk to those of us who are engaged in therapy, monitoring and support. One of the aspects we are, understandably, apprehensive about is that if something untoward does happen, such as an incident of inappropriate sexual behaviour or even a complaint about allowing sex offenders into social situations, we as a clinical team or therapists or support officers or probation officers will be criticised. Therefore any engagement in therapy which promotes QOL or processes which are consistent with the GLM should be conducted with the knowledge of a wider clinical team. The various options and obstacles are as follows:

- If the sex offender wants to go out with somebody at the day centre, social centre, learning disability or aftercare centre, professionals and support workers will begin to consider that the offender is choosing this person because he or she is a vulnerable adult. The main issue from the point of view of the model is to discuss the topic with the emphasis on transparency and openness when the sex offender begins to think about establishing new relationships. The discussion will be based on the assumption that two individuals have ID and may be vulnerable. Unfortunately, for those of us who work in the area, most people meet their partners through their day activities. If your day activity is going to college then you are likely to meet a partner at college. The same is true for people who work for the same firm, work in the same establishment, go to leisure and social clubs and so on. Therefore, individuals who go to day centres or learning disability clubs or any other form of aftercare/out of hours activity, are likely to meet someone there.
- Going out with somebody in the neighbourhood. The main thoughts of those supporting the offender will be similar to those considered above in that we will wonder whether the person the offender has chosen is vulnerable, whether they have children or whether the other person is in some way being used as a conduit for access to victims.
- If the person with whom the sex offender considers developing a relationship is younger than them, we will begin to wonder if this is a predatory relationship.
- If the person with whom the sex offender wishes to start a relationship is older than them we will review whether or not this is 'a bit weird' and an indication of a deviant sexual preference for older women.
- Using the Internet and dating agencies is mentioned increasingly in any discussion of how to meet an appropriate partner. People with ID are increasingly aware of and using chat rooms and Internet 'relationships'. As we can seen in Figure 18.2

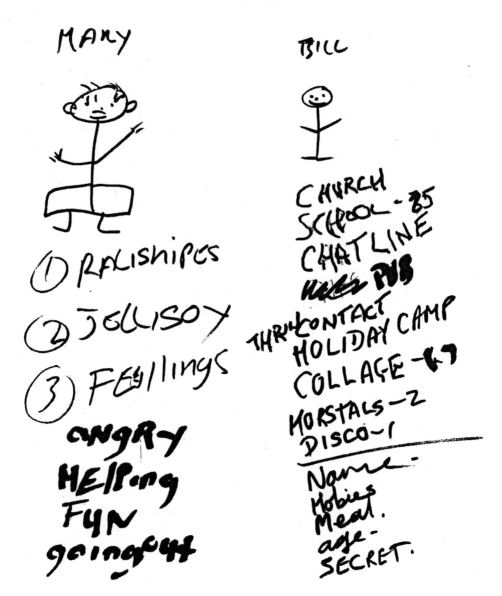

Figure 18.2 Establishing relationships

'chat-line' was the third suggestion. Not many group members will have access or a wish to use these agencies. However one or two might and the automatic concern is that the offender may be looking for an unsuspecting victim. The easiest thing for the sex offender therapist to do is to discourage the offender from establishing a relationship in this way. However if we are going to do this, we should consider an alternative such as the more realistic experiences outlined on Figure 18.2 – that is, in situations where group members meet other people under pro-social circumstances.

• Introduce training to develop relationship and social skills in-group members. When we do this, one of our thoughts is that it will be easier for the group members to groom victims. Therefore, we should always be explicit about our concerns regarding the development and promotion of appropriate relationships.

It can be seen that once we as therapists and facilitators begin to review the development of relationships and pro-social influences, we automatically view things through a sex offender lens. We first consider the risk factors. Having said that, this is a healthy sceptical view of the way in which group members might develop relationships and can only be construed as protective both towards the client and any potential victims. However, it should not interfere with the way in which these discussions and possible exercises take place. Individuals are social and will begin to develop relationships. We can either do this under our supervision, or wash our hands with these developments and allow them to happen once the offender has left the service. If we do this, we are increasing the risks and hazards as will be outlined below.

Figure 18.2 shows the results of a discussion on offending. The group was asked to consider a relationship between two people whom they named Mary and Bill. The discussion included a number of aspects on relationships and on the right-hand side of the figure they produced a list of places where men might meet a girlfriend. These included church, school, a chat-line, a pub, through a mutual friend, a holiday camp, college, a hostel where they stayed and a disco. The discussion focused on the possibility that a common place to meet someone and begin a relationship would be in a pub. In my experience, this is quite usual in a range of mainstream and ID sex offender groups. Meeting someone in a pub is a frequent suggestion. We then asked where group members had met any girlfriends they had had in their lives. There were seven examples of meeting someone at college, five at school, two in a hostel and one in a nightclub/disco. This is quite common. In fact, when I do this exercise in workshops, the majority of individuals have met their partners through work or leisure activities. It is less usual to meet a partner as a stranger in a pub. It is important to explore the most likely places where group members will establish relationships. When they are in treatment and in contact with services, it is possible to support them in these important personal developments.

Exercise 4: Relationships Are Very Hard Work

This exercise takes advantage of a discussion which will arise naturally as part of the module process. It would normally come into place as we consider future developments, lifestyle change and relapse prevention. There may have been in the offender's past an expectation that relationships should happen in a fairly straightforward and automatic fashion. Since people are all social by nature, and so many people have relationships, it may be understandable to develop an expectation that relationships are fairly straightforward. Attempts should be made to explore these attitudes with group members both from the point of view that this expectation was never correct, and from the standpoint that now the individual has a sex offending history, it will be doubly difficult. This discussion can also occur in conjunction with Exercise 2, in that there are a number of obstacles to relationships and difficulties with a variety of situations. There are a number of issues to discuss and the following list is not exhaustive:

- *At what point in a new relationship do you say that you have committed a sex offence?* Some individual group members will feel that it is impossible to come out with this statement 'I'm a sex offender'. There are no easy answers to this; it is a matter of exploring the issue. The main point is that the person will have to disclose that they have committed a sexual offence in the past.
- *How will the other person react when told the individual is a sex offender?* It is almost certain that in any sex offender group, a number of the members will have had experience of rejection and this is a situation where the offenders are setting themselves up for rejection. Therefore, a fear of rejection at any stage in a relationship should be explored as a realistic possibility. Where individuals have anger and revenge as part of their offence cycle, it is particularly crucial to analyse these reactions.
- *Relationships involve reciprocity, change, adaptation and accommodation to each other.* These are very difficult issues to come to terms with in the abstract. Figure 18.2, on the left- hand side, shows some aspects which different group members have written on their thoughts concerning relationship experiences. They have written 'relationships, jealousy, feelings, angry, helping, fun, going out'. Here, there is a recognition that relationships can be difficult in that they can produce jealousy and anger as well as nurturing feelings of mutual activity, fun and mutual support.

In several instances, group members may have been in hospital or supervised accommodation for many years. They may have developed an idealised idea of what a relationship involves and how a relationship is likely to develop. It is important to stress, quite specifically, that relationships involve arguments and accommodation to each other. These mixed emotions are likely to occur from the very first meeting to relationships which are longstanding. For example, if the other person accepts that they are going out with a sex offender and is willing to accommodate to that, what accommodations are required by the sex offender? It is worthwhile exploring the disclosures that the other person might make to review the extent to which individuals may be asked or required to accommodate to another partner. One of the dangers of these discussions is that they may become very focused on the group members themselves. For this reason, facilitators can emphasise that group members will have to accommodate to certain characteristics of a possible partner with which they may be unhappy. Facilitators can review, prior to each planned session, the possible accommodations that group members might have to make. For example, the other person has a physical disability, they like to do an activity which the offender dislikes or would wish him not to drink alcohol. The other person may wish the offender not to engage in a preferred activity more than a specified number of hours, for example only use the PlayStation for one hour a day:

- *How will they cope with arguments and disagreements?* Facilitators can come up with a range of situations where there might be arguments and disagreements. It should also be noted that during the disagreements the fact that the group member is a sex offender might be flung in their face as a recrimination.

- *Sex will not be easy.* Given that sex offending is an important aspect in the person's history, it will be a salient issue both for the group member and any possible partner. Discussion can focus around a number of issues including the development of a sexual relationship, how one broaches the issues of sex and how does one deal with the possibilities of impotence. Some group members will be on medication which interferes with their sexual potency. Others may experience anxiety and fear of failure. Following these discussions, it is important to explore the issue of reciprocity. The person's partner may not wish to enter into a sexual relationship.

- *Would you take time to get to know each other?* Although most group members would say that they would take time to get to know the individual, it should be pointed out that some support workers may feel that, by taking time, the sex offender is grooming the person. Again, all we can do is be explicit about these perceptions and discuss how they might be dealt with, both at a personal level for the offender and within any clinical or support team. It is another example of the way in which appropriate relationship building can be viewed through a sex offender risk lens.

- *Would you want to have sex as soon as possible?* The discussion around this issue would be the same as the discussion around the previous point. How would the individual himself feel, how would any potential partner feel and what would be the views of support workers. Many clinical teams would view an urgency to have a sexual relationship as one step away from sexual offending. It is likely that any possible partner would view similarly such an urgency as one step away from sexual offending.

Hazards in the relationship module

Because of the negative nature of these discussions, it is a serious hazard that complete pessimism will develop about the prospect of establishing attachments and relationships. The emphasis is on the difficulty and the perception of others that development of relationships is increasing risk factors. At various times during discussions, I have heard individuals say 'This is far too hard, I think the real advice is don't try to have a girlfriend' or 'She won't want to know us because we are all sex offenders'. The negative perception is understandable but should not be allowed to continue.

A more serious hazard inherent in the attachment and relationships module is the continuation of the view that any development of relationships is a risk factor. If we allow the sex offender to continue in the perception that it is too difficult to establish any relationship and become pessimistic about any prospects, the conclusion will be that they should not try. The various obstacles presented in the exercises should not be allowed to prevent discussion or promotion of the issue. If we were to accept that offenders should not join dating agencies, should not go out with other people with ID because they might be vulnerable, then we are cutting off all the possible avenues available to anyone in establishing relationships. The logical conclusion of this continued endeavour to reduce the risk factors is that the offender himself will become increasingly isolated and will become a celibate loner. We know from the literature on risk factors that for sex offenders, becoming isolated, lonely and cut-off from relationships is an extremely potent risk factor which will promote a range of other risk factors including resentment, development of aberrant sexual fantasies, a lack of pro-social influences and allow the offender themselves to develop a private distorted world view of the way in which relationships occur. In fact, this is the precise opposite of the GLM and fosters impoverished relationships and poor QOL. The offender will develop human goods from resentment, isolation, solitary activity and deviant sexual fantasy. Therefore, if we refuse to acknowledge the importance of GLM and the importance of developing appropriate attachments and relationships, we may actually be inadvertently, and with the best of intentions, increasing the risk. This is the most persuasive reason for introducing discussion, review and promotion of attachments, relationships and social skills into sex offender treatment.

Conclusions

Relationships and attachments are fundamental to human existence. We all strive for relationships and if they are not achieved in a pro-social manner, they are more likely to be achieved in an antisocial manner. As facilitators, we are naturally wary of promoting relationships in-group members since we automatically consider the risk factors in interpersonal situations. However, by denying and restricting relationship contact, we may be inadvertently increasing risk by promoting isolation. For the advancement of any individuals' GLM and improvement in their QOL we should consider realistic ways of establishing relationships which are relatively low risk. It is certainly the case that a nurturing relationship will be valued by the group member. Maintaining a valued relationship is another motivational factor for avoiding offending and recidivism.

Chapter 19

Lifestyle Change and Preventing Relapse

Much of this module is spent in explicitly reviewing ways in which the individual can engage with society, develop realistic adaptive relationships and generally employ pro-social influences for an offence free lifestyle. The method was developed for two main reasons. The first was a wish to incorporate theoretical developments of the Good Lives Model and the quality of life arguments outlined in Chapter 6. The second was a dissatisfaction with the 'old me – new me' or 'old me – future me' exercise which I had employed extensively and adapted from the UK Home Office Sex Offender Treatment Programme (Beech, Fisher and Beckett, 1998). The exercise has been a very helpful starting point in helping participants to consider their previous life which included a range of risk factors (old me) and a future life which would be both offence free and aspirational (future me). However, it draws participants into two response styles which interfere somewhat with the realistic consideration of previous lifestyles, future lifestyles and the possible transition. Firstly, there is a tendency to emphasise the negatives in previous lifestyles, considering abuse cycles, offence-related cognitions, catastrophic decisions and offence-related behavioural scripts and routines. There is a tendency to disengage cognitively and emotionally with this previous lifestyle under the heading 'old me'. Individuals would assert that they used to behave and think in such a fashion, that they have now learned how to act differently and will never resume these patterns again. I found this as true for men with ID as it was for mainstream sex offenders. Similarly, 'future me' starts when they are discharged from treatment or another service. Participants occasionally have an almost magical view that everything will change and that their lifestyle will not lead them into risky situations, antisocial influences, relationship difficulties and so on. There is a determination to stay free from any kind of future offence-related cycles almost to the detriment of realistic appraisal.

The second, related difficulty with this exercise, is the unrealistic aspirations that individuals will occasionally give to themselves in relation to 'future me'. Living in a

The Treatment of Sex Offenders with Developmental Disabilities William Lindsay
© 2009 John Wiley & Sons, Ltd

house in the country, adopting pets and establishing normal, long-term stable relationships are common aspirations. However, as emphasised in the previous chapter,
there is often a lack of understanding of the extent to which such aspirations are difficult to establish and similarly difficult to maintain. The procedure described in this
chapter was an alternative approach taken from other aspects of general psychotherapy
and is a life map/timeline approach.

Aims of the Process

The aim of this series of exercises is to help the individual to develop a realistic
appraisal of their personal history and to develop realistic plans for the future, drawing
on previous strengths and abilities together with the principles gained from all other
aspects of the programme:

- To gain a realistic appraisal of previous life using a life map/timeline.
- To realise explicitly previous sources of human goods and self-esteem.
- To continue that life map/timeline through into the future.
- To avoid unrealistic conceptual splits before and after the current treatment.
- To identify high-risk situations which are likely to increase the chances of offending.
- To link the various offence cycles with high-risk situations.
- To reinforce the personal and social requirements of avoiding high-risk situations
  which will result in an offending pathway.
- To promote pathways to fulfil human goods, increase quality of life and establish a
  personal GLM.
- Establish links between an adaptive lifestyle, personal GLM and offence free routines,
  behavioural scripts, cognitive schemata and so on.
- Review methods of maintaining motivation for pro-social influences, engagement
  with society, a pro-social lifestyle and an improved quality of life.

Exercise 1: Beginning the Life Map

Materials: Flipchart pages for each participant and a pen for each participant

Although this chapter puts all the life map exercises together, it can be more appropriate to begin the exercise earlier in an individual's treatment. In some instances, it
is better to begin the first two life map exercises at the point of offence disclosure. In
this way, the participant begins to build up their relapse prevention programme from
the very beginning of treatment.

To get started with a life map, each individual should write good things and bad
things that have happened to them in their life. This is done fairly simply and quickly
by splitting the page with good on the left and bad on the right. Some participants will
generate an exhaustive list while others a fairly impoverished list. They then present
their flipchart work to the group for some discussion. There can be a tendency for

group leaders to ask most of the questions about good/bad lists and this may be inevitable. Try to involve the rest of the group with questions such as 'Can anybody see anything missing on this list? What do you think is the most important thing about this list?'

In this way, a list of salient events in the individual's life can be generated. Commonalities can be drawn out from the various lists in participants' lives as interesting generalised risk variables or sources of human goods. There will be a tendency for some participants to place their offending as a bad thing in their life. This will generate discussion about why individuals offend and the positive motivation for offending. Some will realise quickly that offending itself is enjoyable, exciting and a way of fulfilling a human need. These can then be transferred to the 'good' side of the list. The purpose of the exercise is to generate sources of fulfilment whether or not they are pro-social or antisocial. Bad experiences may constitute risk factors, threats to self-esteem or points of homeostatic defeat in subjective well-being. An example of this exercise has already been discussed in Chapter 11 (Figure 11.1).

Exercise 2: Constructing a Life Map

Materials: Flipchart pages (landscape) and pens

The life map is now depicted by a timeline. The list of good experiences and bad experiences should now be incorporated into the timeline in addition to other more neutral experiences. Because each participant has already drawn up a series of good experiences as well as problems and bad experiences in their life, it is unlikely that it will develop into an 'old me' exercise. There will be aspects in the timeline which we will wish to maintain and build upon as future sources of human goods. The list of good and bad experiences can act as anchors for the timeline.

We do not want the individual to be given an early response set or expectation that is one of the pitfalls of relapse prevention where we are looking for a negative appraisal of the person's prior life. As Ward and Gannon (2006) have put it, we do not wish the participant's previous life to be construed as 'bundles of risk factors'. Rather, we wish each person to revise significant events in their lives with a timeline which represents positive events at the top and negative events at the bottom. As with previous exercises, this can be done with words and pictures. The life map should continue from birth through childhood to the present day and will project alternative pathways into the future.

Figure 19.1 shows the beginnings of a timeline for one participant who committed a high density of offences through the ages of 16 and 17 years. The figure indicates a number of sources of human goods which are both pro-social and antisocial. The pro-social sources are helping his mother, developing mastery through swimming, gardening, keeping occupied and fishing which he has noted as 'relaxing and peace'. The antisocial sources of human goods are clearly noted in stealing which he has said felt good in itself and attracted attention, and the inappropriate sexual behaviour which caused 'a big buzz, sexual feelings, thought I wouldn't get caught, felt good'.

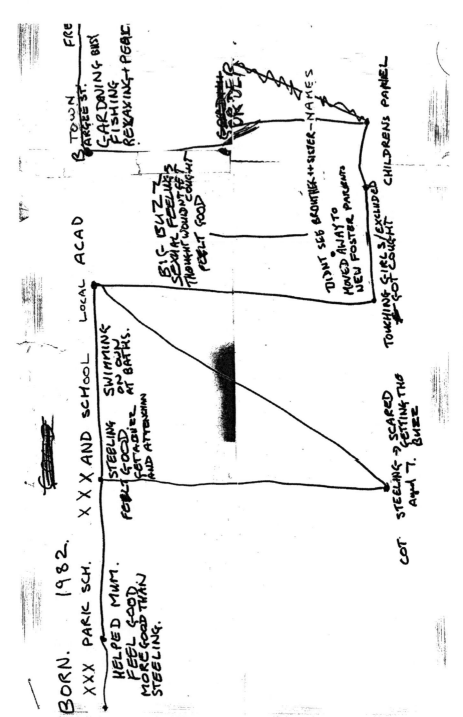

Figure 19.1 Ian's timeline

Interestingly, he has made the point that contact with his mother felt better than stealing, although stealing gave him 'a buzz'. In this way, he is beginning to identify the ways in which different sources of fulfilment provided a different quality of experience. The figure also shows negative experiences, threats to his self-esteem, possible points of homeostatic defeat and longer lasting disruptions to his relationships. He reports, 'I got caught stealing – scared, excluded (from school), got caught, didn't see brother and sister, moved away to new foster parents, Children's Panel (the legal forum for child offences in Scotland).'

Already we have a number of aspects which can be incorporated into treatment. Contact with his family, occupation in the form of gardening and leisure pursuits in the form of fishing and swimming can be considered as future sources of human goods. Swimming is a difficult activity for consideration by facilitators or a clinical team because of the proximity of so many semi-naked bodies. However, sufficient safeguards can be built in to consider the other pro-social sources of fulfilment, improvement of quality of life and establishment of relationships. On the other hand, the 'buzz' from stealing and sexual assault have also been significant sources of fulfilment. At appropriate points in the treatment programme, facilitators should stress that it is difficult to find a pro-social substitute for this huge feeling of excitement. In fact, for most sex offenders, they will not experience this feeling again. However, in this way they will be the same as the rest of society where few men experience these huge levels of excitement generated by one incident or a series of incidents. In fact, when these levels of excitement are generated through intense social contact, substance abuse and the like, they often produce antisocial consequences such as fighting, drug overdoses or other personal catastrophes. Because of this, most of us adapt to a life without short-lived periods of massive excitement. When this issue is discussed in a group setting, adaptive suggestions and conclusions will always be drawn. Facilitators should then judge the extent to which individual participants are receptive to these messages.

The figure also shows periods of threats to self-esteem and homeostatic subjective well-being which might produce emotional disregulation and certainly produce a more impoverished quality of life and relationships. He reported being scared when he was caught stealing and noted, as negative experiences, being excluded from school and appearing before the Children's Panel. Facilitators can attempt to help men re-enact the feelings they had at the time as a motivation to avoid experiencing them again. He also noted disruptions to his relationships with his family when he was moved to a new foster home. This was because he offended against one of the girls in his previous foster home. Facilitators should discuss the impact of these disruptions on relationships, using them as motivation to change in order to establish the relationships once again. In this way, attachment and quality of life become central to each individual's consideration of his offence pathway and the wider impact which the offence has had on his life.

Figure 19.2 shows the same process but on this occasion the individual completing the timeline has much poorer literacy skills. He drew all of his main experiences with a minimal use of labelling.

Jason was a 56-year-old man who had completely different experiences from Ian. The section of the timeline is taken from the middle of his childhood where he had

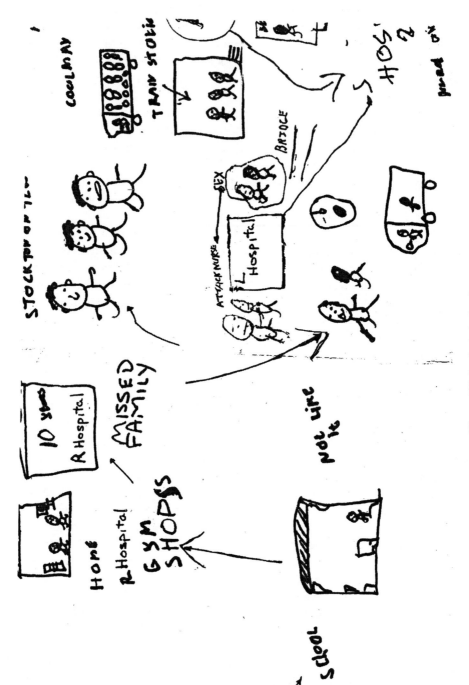

Figure 19.2 Jason's timeline

been admitted to a long stay hospital for people with learning disabilities as a child. He had been disruptive at school and had disliked it (drawn on the bottom of his timeline). He was then transferred to hospital which he said had more enjoyable activities than being at school. He said he enjoyed 'the gym and going to the shops'. However while there, he missed his family. In the next section, he has drawn a short holiday which the family organised in Stockton-on-Tees. Although this is a short few days in his life, it is an interesting aspect of this exercise that even short family holidays are often remembered vividly and fondly by group members as significant sources of human goods. These periods which are away from normal family pressures and which afford fairly constant contact with family members are obviously valued by all of us as periods where we experienced good relationships. At the foot of this section of his timeline, however, he has drawn his father beating him with a stick and these experiences of abuse in childhood are clearly remembered as vividly and are significant contributions to a highly negative quality of life and emotional disregulation. The figure then goes on to depict two periods of employment, one helping with coal deliveries and one in the local train station. In the middle of the timeline, a little out of sequence, he has drawn his first sexual offence which was a sexual assault on a female after he had followed her for a period until she had gone under a local railway bridge. He was then transferred to hospital where he records committing a sexual assault on a nurse. This further illustration of the construction of a timeline shows the way in which pictures can be used predominantly. Despite his intellectual limitations (Jason has a measured IQ of 58 on the WAIS-III UK), he could remember clearly the meaning of each drawing since it depicted important aspects in his life.

Figure 19.3 illustrates the basic plan of the life map from birth to the time of offending which has been illustrated in previous chapters. Previous figures have indicated that these plans are more complex in practice but, basically, events and experiences which have been enjoyed are placed at the top of the life map and events and experiences which have been bad and have not been enjoyed are placed at the bottom. This is carried out sequentially through the individual's life, which sets up the habit of reflecting

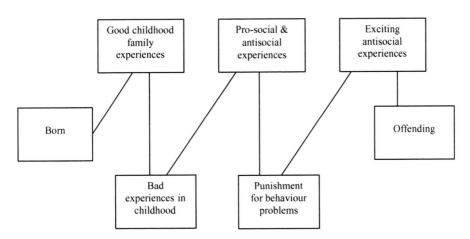

Figure 19.3 Basic life map plan indicating sources of human goods leading to offending

on experiences linking together as a temporal pathway. In this fairly straightforward manner, the fundamental principles of various theoretical structures are incorporated from the beginning. Aspects of GLM which have been a source of human goods and promoted quality of life are incorporated. In the days and months leading to the offending incident or incidents, the self-regulation offence pathway will be drawn up. The cycle of offending including emotional disregulation, sexual arousal, planning offences, cognitive distortions, use of pornography and so on will also be included. There is no assumption that the good things which have happened in the offender's life will be pro-social. GLM focuses on the pursuit of human goods whether they are pro-social, developed from positive experiences and positive self-resources (PSR), or antisocial, developed from antisocial experiences or negative experiences and negative self-resources (NSR), and all of these will be placed on the life map along the top of the pathway.

Exercise 3: Inserting the Disclosure Account into the Timeline

This exercise has been described in previous chapters. Figure 15.2 was analysed for the way in which Alfred's behavioural scripts, routines and cognitive schemata combined with his sexual drive and risk factors to construct the cycle of offending. His offence disclosure account, seen on Figure 10.2, was then incorporated into the timeline as a continuation. Therefore, his childhood, offence cycle and disclosure accounts were combined to build up his life map incorporating many of the factors discussed in this programme. These included sources of human goods, both pro-social and antisocial, disruptions to his subjective well-being, threats to his self-esteem, emotional disregulation and risk factors. The life map then includes ways in which these distal and developmental factors evolve into behavioural routines and scripts which correspond to developing world views and cognitive schemata. These routines serve the function of fulfilling human goods, and maintaining subjective well-being and quality of life in a maladaptive fashion consistent with the perpetration of a sexual offence. Although the methods are time consuming and painstaking in their execution, they provide a practical method of enabling and supporting the group member to consider all of these complex factors in a personalised straightforward fashion. They provide both meaning and continuity to the person's developmental experiences and enable him to consider his sexual offending in his own developmental context. It also provides a graphic vivid depiction of his life map, offence pathway and offence account which he can keep for later review.

Exercise 4: Projecting the Life Map into the Future

This exercise involves projecting two alternative pathways into the future – an offence free pathway and an offending pathway. The exercise draws on most of the previous material as being dealt with in treatment. There is likely to have been a section which included discussion and role-play on relationships and attachments. Realistic opportunities for relationships and attachments will now be inserted into each individual's life map for the future. The various administrative role-plays that have occurred are also very relevant at this point. In earlier chapters, I have discussed the way in which clinical team meetings, annual reviews and even community protection reviews which pertain to each individual can be role-played in the group setting. These often have the individuals themselves as the 'chairman' of the panel and one of the facilitators role-playing the particular group member. The decisions which have arisen out of these will generally have taken into account all of the relevant risk factors. These decisions will be an important framework for future projected pathways. Discussions and role-play exercises on risk factors, cycle of offending, offending pathways and dealing with cognitive distortions will all be relevant to future negative, risky, offence pathways. Developmental experiences are important in this exercise. Salient experiences in the individual's past have already been inserted into their timeline, and these can then be taken from past events and transposed into suitable adult appropriate activities which may be a similar source of human goods. Pro-social experiences can be projected into the future offence free pathway while antisocial experiences, which have contributed towards human goods in the past, can be projected into the future offence pathway.

Figure 19.4 demonstrates this exercise in a simplified fashion. For this offender, a future offence free life plan incorporated pro-social influences, contact with family, engaging in occupational activity and continuing to manage his risk. He then added to his future pro-social pathway by suggesting that he re-engage in hobbies of cycling and football while maintaining all of the sources of human goods which he had established. At the same time, we can see a differential, negative pathway clarifying the effects of falling back on the antisocial sources of human goods such as brooding, isolation, child pornography, alcohol and lack of activity. This would result in the excitement he achieved from offending. In turn, this would lead to the resumption of his self-regulation pathway of 'active/approach'. In this way, therapy can focus on providing the internal and external conditions required to assist in achieving personally valued and socially acceptable human goods.

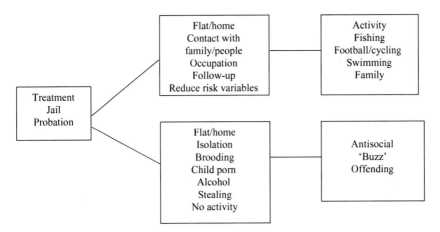

Figure 19.4 Future projected pathways – an offence free, pro-social pathway and an offending pathway

Kenneth was a 28-year-old man who had committed three sexual assaults in a manner entirely consistent with the principles of the GLM. In fact, his case is not unusual in contemporary services where the distinction between staff and residents is (quite rightly) de-emphasised. Staff make attempts to support clients on a more informal fashion, during leisure and recreational periods in addition to advocating for clients. As a result, some men with ID begin to feel that female staff members may develop more than professional attachments and start to consider romantic relationships. Kenneth had attempted to establish a romantic relationship with three members of staff over a period of around 8 years. During the earlier exercises, we had established a number of risk factors and human needs including a strong wish for a relationship, anger at being denied the relationship when he approached a female he liked, feelings of resentment and increasing levels of depression which combined with the resentment and anger to produce a sexual assault. In this way, he was similar to Gary, the previous case in Chapter 15 who sought relationships with females in pubs.

Figure 19.5 shows the splitting of future projections into a protective pathway and an offending pathway. I have chosen this example because it is messy and gives an idea of how this exercise works out in practice.

Kenneth was currently in a local hospital and had undergone 2 years of sex offender treatment. On the left-hand side of Figure 19.5 he has written that he wishes to continue enjoying going to the gym, working in the gardens, working with occupational therapists and other staff and attending the group for inappropriate sexual behaviour. He has projected that pro-social lifestyle onto his life when he moves to supported accommodation noting that he will continue with pro-social activities and treatment in the form of anger management and treatment for sexual offences. Towards the end of the offence free pathway he acknowledges both the importance of remaining in contact with community nurses and social work staff and that it is crucial to continue a dialogue with staff about his progress. Significantly, he has written that if he enters into a relationship, it is likely to be with another service user.

At the foot of the figure he has outlined clearly his offence pathway. It begins with depression and anger directed at females which he notes as a danger sign. Following that he has acknowledged the importance of relationships. On the one hand, if he accepts help in forming these relationships this will lead to a pro-social offence free pathway. On the other hand, he writes that he is 'frightened I mess up' which then projects into an offending 'relationship with staff' which, if it follows his historical pattern, is likely to result in a coercive incident. He, himself, has written 'relationship with staff' in the offence pathway. Perceptively, at the end of the figure he recognises the risk that he might 'fancy staff'. As these feelings progress he has written below that entry that he might want a relationship, want sex, become angry because of the probable rejection, will attack the individual involved, be charged and attend at court. He has labelled this pathway as 'bad'. Whereas moving up from the entry 'fancy staff', he has written 'talked to staff, social workers, community nurse' and has seen this as a protective pathway, labelled 'good'. In this way, the future pathways are set out clearly and are labelled as risk, offending pathways and offence free pathways.

Not all future projections are as complicated as that seen in Figure 19.5. Figure 19.6 shows Ian's future pathways which are much less cluttered. His offence free future

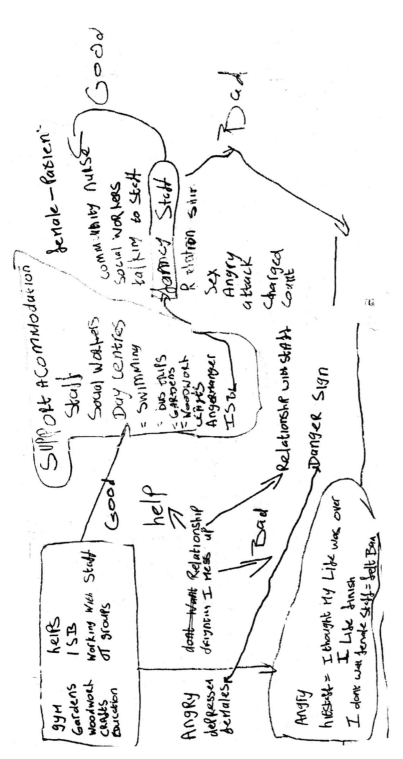

Figure 19.5   Kenneth's future offence free and offending pathways

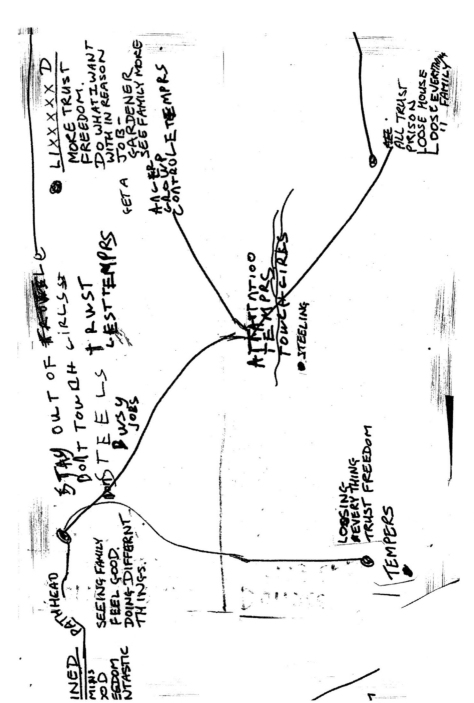

Figure 19.6 Ian's future offence free and offending pathways

278

pathway begins with the present where he is 'seeing family, feeling good, doing different things' and continues with him 'stay out of trouble, don't touch girls, don't steal, (maintain) trust, (maintain control of his) temper and busy jobs'. At the bottom of the figure and in the middle of the figure he notes two pathways which would lead to offending. The first is related to his temper which was a major feature in his case. With continued frequent loss of temper he is noted 'losing everything, trust, freedom, tempers'. In the second offence pathway, in addition to temper, he has added 'touched girls, stealing'.

Part of the exercise is to allow the group member to consider what he would do if he begins to experience these feelings and recognise various risk factors. From these hypothesised incidents, he has drawn a protective pathway with an anger management group and temper control. This offence free pathway includes staying in his current accommodation, 'more trust, freedom, do what I want within reason, get a job, gardener, see family more'. On the other hand, the offending pathway is drastic with a loss of all trust, loss of his accommodation, losing his family and other important things in his life.

One of the difficulties with these pathways is that they are written and many of our clients do not read or write. In most of the relapse prevention pathways, we would insert pictures and figures from standard programmes such as Boardmaker or Clipart. Since these are copyrighted, I have not included them in the figures. However, facilitators can insert them at appropriate points as memory aids.

These can be fairly time consuming exercises and facilitators may wish to conduct part of it during individual sessions. The finished timeline can then be brought back to the group for discussion. Other group members have the opportunity to add information which may be relevant from their own case or which they remember about the individual who is presenting. In an open group, these exercises can prime individuals who have been in treatment for a shorter time to think about their own relapse prevention plans.

Exercise 5: Prompts against Risk – The Traffic Light System

A traffic lights analogy is familiar to most individuals who work with people with ID. Red traffic lights are used to illustrate a number of things which should be prevented, which the individual should control, risk factors and general negative events. Green traffic lights on the other hand indicate acceptable behaviour, risk free situations, pro-social influences and general positive events. During group sessions, we have employed traffic lights in order to provide a quick, illustrative valency to various emotions, behaviours, situations, relationships and so on. The group members themselves suggested that they have a card which they might carry in their wallet and look at from time to time if they feel they may be approaching a risky situation. On one side of the card is a set of traffic lights with the words *stop* against the red light, *think* against the amber light and *walk away* against the green light. The illustration on the other side should be an image which will remind the individual of the group sessions and the importance of self-regulation. However, group members understandably did not wish

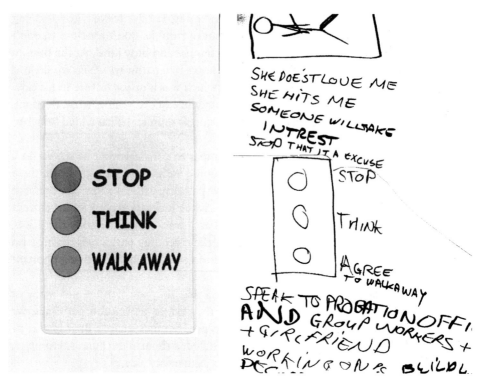

Figure 19.7 An illustration of the use of the relapse prevention card

the image to suggest anything to do with sexual offending. They were concerned that if it was stolen or seen by someone else, that the other person should not have any idea of its relevance. For ourselves, the only constant aspect to group sessions which did not have any obvious relevance to sexual offending was a picture of the author looking particularly severe. This was incorporated on to one side of all the relapse prevention cards. The relapse prevention card and its use can be seen in Figure 19.7.

Figure 19.7 shows the way in which one group member employed his relapse prevention card on one incident. He said he was sitting at home thinking of a relationship which had finished recently and he was becoming increasingly depressed with thoughts such as 'She doesn't love me, she hits me, someone will take an interest'. He then looked at his relapse prevention card which he said stimulated a number of adaptive solutions such as 'Speak to probation officer and group workers'. It is a fairly graphic illustration of the way in which a relapse prevention card can be used occasionally by group members.

Conclusions

This approach has two basic strengths. Firstly, the continuous nature of personal development is emphasised. There is no obvious point at which 'old me' makes a clear split from 'future me'. Since different individuals may choose different points to split their timeline, it will be emphasised that there are no clear dichotomous phases to anyone's life. Secondly, both strengths and weaknesses are reviewed in relation to their past and the future. In this way, positive aspects of the individual's previous life can be emphasised and extracted with a view to building on this strength and developing it into a more pro-social and adaptive coping lifestyle. Strengths can be incorporated into future engagement with society and adaptive relationships. It continues to employ risk factors from the past and project them into the future with clear pathways to offending. Also, facilitators and group members can discuss and illustrate ways of moving out of an offending pathway and back into an offence free pathway.

Chapter 20

Evaluation of Progress

It is of enormous benefit to maintain regular review and evaluation of each individual's progress through treatment month by month. Treatment tends to last a long time and there may be a number of individuals requiring monitoring, progress reports, end of treatment reports and so on. If the group is open and 'rolling' then different individuals will complete treatment at different times. If facilitators keep a regular note of progress, orientation towards the group, compliance with treatment methods, confrontation or cooperation week by week and the benefit they have derived from each of the module topics, it is much easier to go back over the information and incorporate it into reports. The methods I will review in this section are monitoring treatment orientation, peer review of progress, psychometric assessment and recording re-offending.

Several authors have developed a range of methods for monitoring aspects of the treatment process. In their evaluation of the prison sex offender treatment programme, Beech, Fisher and Beckett (1998) reported on a range of measures used which included measures of cognitive distortions and justifications for sexual offences, self-esteem, emotional loneliness, assertiveness, locus of control, victim empathy, attitudes towards treatment, participant's perception of the value of the programme, participant's perception of the relationships within the group and their views on relapse prevention. In all, they report on 25 different measures each of which assessed one or more of these factors.

This is too much for sex offenders with ID for two reasons. Firstly, the complexity of the information will overload participants and they will become frustrated and even annoyed with all of the diverse assessments. At worst, they may end up answering in a random fashion 'just to get it over with'. Secondly, it has to be remembered that all assessments with participants with ID are done through structured interview. Because of the literacy deficits inherent in each participant, it is never the case that facilitators will be able to distribute questionnaires and have them returned completed. Facilitators will be required to read every question, explain it, explain the possible answers, support the individual in their thought processes without influencing their answer and record the response. To do this with 25 separate questionnaires would be onerous indeed and to do it repeatedly would be an enormous time commitment not only for the facilitators, but also for participants. At initial assessment, I would routinely complete a number of the assessments, described in Chapters 2 and 3 and which correspond to the categories of dynamic risk outlined by Thornton (2002). These would include measures of emotional regulation such as Brief Symptom Inventory, the Beck Anxiety and Depression Inventories, Novaco Anger Scale, the Dundee Provocation Inventory and a measure of locus of control. I would also employ measures of cognitive distortions and attitudes such as the Questionnaire on Attitudes Consistent with Sexual Offences (QACSO) and the Victim Empathy Scale. An assessment of sexual knowledge would also be important in contributing to an individual formulation. Self-management and self-regulation can be assessed with the Barratt Impulsiveness Scale while sexual preference and sexual drive are generally assessed using interview and a review of the individual's offence history. While these assessments and others like them can be repeated after a significant period of treatment or at the end of treatment, it would be extremely time consuming to use them as indicators of progress. Therefore, the assessments described here are generally quick evaluations or somewhat time consuming but germane to treatment.

Monitoring Treatment Orientation

Treatment orientation and compliance can be recorded with a few notes after each session. However, I have developed a short scale of Personal and Sexual Dynamic Risk (PSDR) based on the Short Dynamic Risk Scale (SDRS) developed by Quinsey (2004). The SDRS contains eight items each of which is rated on a five-point scale from no problem to severe problem. The items assess the extent to which the person takes responsibility for their behaviour, shows coping skills, demonstrates anxiety or frustration, demonstrates anger or loss of temper, is verbally aggressive, shows lack of consideration for others, shows poor housekeeping skills and poor self-care skills. Quinsey (2004) reported that SDRS was very easy for staff to use and highly predictive of future aggressive incidents. In our own studies (Lindsay *et al.*, 2008b) we found that the SDRS predicted violent incidents with moderate accuracy (auc = 0.73) and it was as predictive as any other static or dynamic assessments used. As mentioned previously, it is very easy to obtain and administer.

The PSDR is a similar short nine-item scale, completed by facilitators, which reviews three areas of functioning: group participation, impact and understanding of the material and self-regulation. It can be seen in Figure 20.1.

The PSDR can be filled out regularly while facilitators are discussing individual progress. It can be seen that there are three items on group participation including the participants' understanding of the material being dealt with, whether or not they are avoiding participation through absence, lateness, refusal to contribute or attempts to 'be invisible' or being angry and confrontational. There are three items on the way

For each item, circle one number which describes the way in which the client has been in the recent past. The recent past can be his response to the last two or three group sessions, his general behaviour over the last week or month and his interpersonal behaviour towards others in the last week or month. Ratings should not be made over a period of longer than a month. If the client has no problem or adequate skills in the area then circle 0, numbers 1, 2, 3 and 4 indicate increasing severity of that problem.

1. Takes responsibility for offending. A rating of 0 indicates that he takes full responsibility for his offending, understands that he placed himself in risk situations, employed risky routines or took advantage of a risky situation. A rating of 4 means he does not acknowledge his own responsibility, feels that the situation or others, including the victim, were to blame. Intermediate ratings indicate he takes partial responsibility.

0	1	2	3	4
No problem		Moderate Problem		Severe Problem

2. Perspective taking, consideration of others and victim empathy. A rating of 0 indicates that he shows a reasonable understanding of victims' experiences, shows an understanding of others' feelings and is co-operative with others' wishes. A rating of 4 indicates he is unconcerned about victims, shows no consideration of others and demonstrates a lack of perspective taking. Intermediate ratings indicate partial understanding.

0	1	2	3	4
No problem		Moderate Problem		Severe Problem

3. Sexual self-restraint and coping skills. A rating of 0 indicates that he has good coping skills for risk situations, takes steps to avoid risk situations and shows good sexual self-restraint with appropriate sexuality. A rating of 4 indicates that he has problems with sexual self-restraint, takes advantage of inappropriate opportunities for sexuality, and seems to have poor coping skills in interpersonal situations. Intermediate ratings indicate degrees of coping skill.

0	1	2	3	4
No problem		Moderate Problem		Severe Problem

4. Angry and unco-operative during the group. A rating of 0 indicates that he is motivated and appropriately engaged in the material dealt with by the group. A rating of 4 indicates that he is hostile, unco-operative and disruptive during group sessions.

0	1	2	3	4
No problem		Moderate Problem		Severe Problem

5. Avoids participation. A rating of 0 indicates that he is active, appropriately engaged and co-operative during group sessions. A rating of 4 indicates that he avoids sessions by saying he is ill, arriving late, or sits quietly trying to be "invisible".

0	1	2	3	4
No problem		Moderate Problem		Severe Problem

Figure 20.1   Personal and Sexual Dynamic Risk (PSDR)

6. Understanding of material. A rating of 0 suggests that he has a good understanding of the material, is able to retain the material (given the limitations of his intellectual disability) and uses the information. A rating of 4 indicates that he cannot or refuses to understand the material, is unwilling to try to accept there should be continuity between sessions and has no interest in remembering previous sessions.

0	1	2	3	4
No problem		Moderate Problem		Severe Problem

7. Self-care and personal hygiene. A rating of 0 indicates that his self-care and personal hygiene are appropriate. A rating of 4 means that he attends group sessions and other sessions unkempt, clothes unwashed, unshaven and with poor hygiene.

0	1	2	3	4
No problem		Moderate Problem		Severe Problem

8. Lifestyle regulation. A rating of 0 means well regulated, attends placements, courses and appointments, good relationships. A rating of 4 indicates poor routines, poor sleeping pattern, irregular meals, antisocial relationships or isolation, substance abuse.

0	1	2	3	4
No problem		Moderate Problem		Severe Problem

9. General coping skills. A rating of 0 means he copes with social situations, daily living and occupational placements reasonably. A rating of 4 indicates he has trouble coping with interpersonal and daily living problems either through frustration and hostility or anxiety and avoidance.

0	1	2	3	4
No problem		Moderate Problem		Severe Problem

Notes:

Figure 20.1   (*Continued*)

that the individual is incorporating the material into their social and sexual functioning. These are whether the person takes responsibility for their offending, whether they are demonstrating perspective taking and consideration for others and whether or not they have developed sexual coping and self-regulation skills. There are then three items on lifestyle change and relapse prevention which are lifestyle regulation, poor self-care and personal hygiene and general social and life coping skills. Each of these items is very much a summary of the area involved but that is not to say that it will be insensitive to progress. In their landmark evaluation of relapse prevention treatment for sex offenders, Marques *et al.* (2005) found that a similarly simple, regular review of treatment engagement and progress was highly predictive of outcome and recidivism. Therefore, the PSDR can be used regularly to update treatment progress and general progress.

    It should be remembered that these reviews will not always be valid indicators of the way a participant is progressing. In one case, I and my co-facilitators had thought that a participant was progressing excellently. He was certainly understanding the material we were dealing with and was cooperative in the group without being either ingratiating or demonstrative. We felt he was taking responsibility for the incidents which he perpetrated, reported good self-regulation skills and seemed to understand how victims might feel (given the limitations on perspective taking placed on all of our participants through their ID). He had a very regulated lifestyle living with his parents, was attending all of his appointments with probation, job agencies and ourselves and was reported as cooperative in all of these situations. For his annual review, I wrote that treatment was progressing satisfactorily, he was completing the exercises, he continued to be sociable and regulated and that I was comfortable with his progress.

While we were conducting these reviews and while I was writing my positive report, he had organised his attendance at the job agency in such a way that he arrived in town half an hour early and followed women around. A couple of weeks after I sent the report he offended by approaching a woman in her car and attempting to put his hand up her skirt. This episode served to illustrate that even the most experienced clinicians, with the support of an experienced clinical team, can be made to look ridiculous in individual cases. The outcome was negative in two ways in that it must have been shocking for the woman involved to have a man approach her and behave in this manner. It also suggested that his self-regulation style continued to be approach automatic rather than one of self-restraint. The positive aspects were that we as a staff team were required to reflect on the way in which we evaluated this individual and made a detailed multidisciplinary review of his routines.

Throughout the rest of his treatment period, we were able to emphasise the fact that although he appeared to be doing well, it was impossible to say because we had thought this previously and had been completely wrong. In the session after the offence we discussed, in addition to the details of the incident, the fact that he had let himself and his family down (back to square one), misguided and misled the other participants, may have placed the reputation of group treatment in jeopardy since the incident would be prosecuted and the court would come to know that he was engaged (unsuccessfully) in treatment, and had made the senior facilitator look like an idiot. In these discussions, it is important, but difficult, for facilitators to make attempts to keep the atmosphere supportive rather than accusatory. In this case, it was probably helpful that the senior facilitator was sanguine about looking like an idiot (it was not the first time and will not be the last). When asked about why he had not mentioned his offending routines in the group, he said that in order to avoid others finding out 'I would lie through my teeth'. We were able to use this statement frequently both with him and others during subsequent sessions when questioning group members and the individual concerned about their routines.

Peer Review of Progress

Over the years we have had a number of suggestions from group members on how to review each other's progress. These began with each group member rating the other on a scale of 1 to 10 with the eventual adoption of a suggestion by one individual that we should have a ladder which group members can climb as an indication of their progress. The ladder has 10 rungs with the first meaning poor progress and the tenth rung suggesting that the group member has climbed through the various stages and is doing extremely well.

Figure 8.2 is one illustration of such an exercise and Figure 20.2 is a similar, different illustration of group evaluation using the same method. Group members first discuss the individual's progress in the manner that all sessions are conducted. Once the discussion has taken place, each group member gives the individual a rating. Different group members will have a different style of rating with some tending towards extremities, while others might rate mostly at the upper end of the scale. Once the group members have finished rating the individual, it has become our custom to have the facilitators then rate the person on the same scale.

Table 20.1 shows the average ratings for 18 participants. The first column represents average peer review scores and the second column is average staff review scores. It is fun to calculate the relationship between staff and peer ratings using Spearman's correlations and in various exercises we have found a Spearman's correlation between the two sets of scores of 0.89, 0.78, 0.81 and 0.72. This suggests that there is a strong relationship, with large effect sizes, between the perceptions of staff and other group members of each individual's progress. It is likely that this relationship is influenced by the discussions on group members but we have found that, even when discussion has not been extensive, a strong relationship still exists. Therefore, peer reviews may be reasonably consistent with staff views of progress. There will of course be individuals for whom there are large discrepancies between peer review and staff review. There will also be instances where staff differ considerably in their assessment of an individual. There will certainly be huge differences in individual group member's ratings of a peer which are often influenced by likes and dislikes. However, it is interesting that despite these individual discrepancies, the overall averages seem to maintain a relationship. This exercise can be done whenever facilitators feel it is appropriate.

Frequently, group members will remember their previous peer assessment. They may not remember the exact number but will remember roughly where they have been placed 'on the ladder'. It is unfortunate but they may be very disappointed if their rating is lower than their previous assessment. Deterioration or improvement can be discussed in-group sessions in a number of ways. It may be a reality that the person has in fact been managing less well and the ratings reflect this. Facilitators might also review the reliability or unreliability of these assessments in the light of the fact that there may be new members in the group making their ratings from a different perspective. Some group members may be experiencing personal difficulties which have an effect on their ratings in general.

Revision of Modules and Topics

Revision is conducted as a matter of course throughout the programme as a result of the constant repetition of material. However, I have got into the habit of conducting

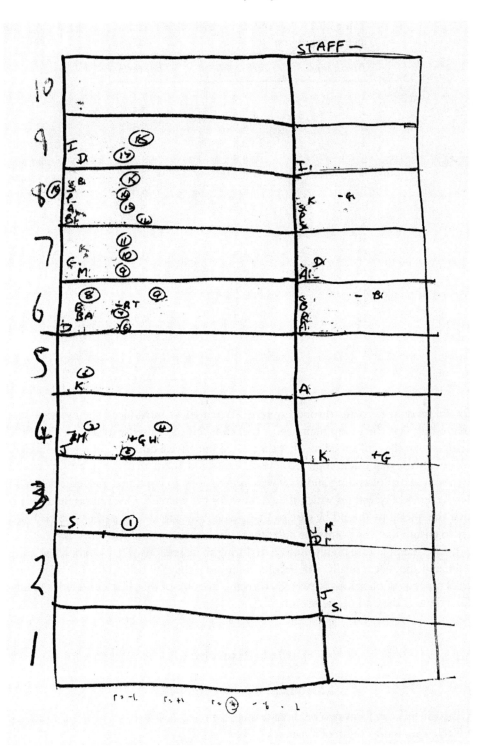

Figure 20.2 An example of group ratings on 'the ladder' with staff ratings added to participant ratings

Table 20.1   Peer and staff ratings of each group member's progress

Participant	Peer ratings	Staff ratings
1	9.4	9.1
2	9.1	7.5
3	8.9	8.5
4	8.8	8.4
5	8.5	8.3
6	8.2	5.0
7	8.1	6.5
8	7.5	8.5
9	7.4	6.7
10	7.1	7.1
11	6.5	6.1
12	6.5	6.4
13	6.1	3.1
14	5.1	4.1
15	4.2	4.1
16	4.2	3.2
17	4.1	2.2
18	3.1	2.1

formal revision exercises through quizzes. When I first introduced the exercise, it is interesting that the group members at that time felt such a sense of ownership of the sessions that they informed me that they could not have a quiz since the sessions were to do with sexual offending. However, I reassured them that the questions would be about sexual offending and they were quite happy to continue. Facilitators should have a series of questions which they can use for the exercise. One important aspect is that the questions should be easy so that participants are able to gather points. I also try to ensure that the points for different teams remain around the time.

  Group members are highly motivated during these sessions. They can become quite animated and, occasionally, will become annoyed if they fall behind the others in their total number of questions answered correctly. Because of this, it is a good idea to aim for a draw at the end of the session.

Quiz Exercise

Materials: flipchart and pens

- Participants can form two or three teams.
- Each team has to think of a name.
- Each team should decide on a spokesman/leader.
- Each team should be encouraged to discuss the questions before answering so that they agree on an answer.

- It is worthwhile having a few rules such as no shouting out the answer, no accusations of cheating to be made, it is a team effort, it is only a game.
- Teams can be asked alternate questions or both teams can answer the same question without being told whether or not it is correct until both have given their answer.
- Points are awarded for each correct answer.
- The facilitator has the final say about whether the answer is correct or incorrect.
- One of the team members can mark on the board, points for each correct answer.

As a derivative, or during the course of the quiz, teams can think up questions to ask the other team. This adds further competitiveness and contributes to group cohesion. Occasionally, teams are unable to give a correct answer for their own question. Group members will enjoy the quiz while concentrating on the material being reviewed. Facilitators can develop their own sets of questions but example sets can be seen in Appendix 2.

Psychometric Assessment

Because treatment relies so heavily on cognitive methods with a corresponding analysis of cognitive distortions, I assess attitudes towards offending at 3 to 6 monthly intervals. I use the QACSO which has been reviewed in Chapter 2. The QACSO presents a number of statements consistent with offending and the respondent is asked whether or not they would endorse the statement. The greater the number of statements endorsed, the higher the score. Because it relies heavily on psychometric interpretation, there are restrictions on the use of the QACSO. Like other psychometric instruments, such as the Wechsler Adult Intelligence Scale, the administrator is required to have undergone a certain level of training in psychometrics and to have an appropriate qualification (such as chartering by The British Psychological Society). The QACSO has eight scales, seven of which are related to particular areas of sexual offending. The scales are rape and attitudes to women, voyeurism, exhibitionism, dating abuse, stalking and sexual harassment, homosexual assault and offences against children. It has been standardised in two studies (Broxholme and Lindsay, 2003; Lindsay, Whitefield and Carson, 2007) and there are norms for sex offenders with ID, other types of offenders with ID, non-offenders with ID and mainstream, non-offending males. There is a social desirability scale which is empirically derived and consists of five questions which are ostensibly similar to all of the other questions in the instrument. However, the psychometrics of the social desirability scale indicate that most of the men across all of the standardisation groups endorsed most of the items. Therefore, although these items seem as socially unacceptable as items in the other scales, most men endorsed them. As a result, if a respondent does not endorse these items, the administrator should review their general responding with some circumspection.

Each of the scales on the QACSO has a number of statements representing cognitive distortions that might be considered to be supportive of sexual offending, minimisations or justifications for sexual offending. On the rape scale, endorsement of the question 'Do women make too much fuss about sexual assault?' indicates a minimisation of the offence. On the voyeurism scale, endorsement of the question 'If a woman is wearing a short skirt, does it mean that she wants men to look up it?' suggests mitigation for the offence in that the victim is perceived as partially complicit in any incident. On the exhibitionism scale, the question 'Do most women laugh about being flashed at?', would also indicate minimisation while on the dating abuse scale, the question 'If you don't ask a woman to have sex will she think that you don't like her?' would suggest justification for an incident. On the offences against children scale, rejection of the question 'Do you think sex with children does harm if the adult is gentle?' indicates a perception of mitigation under circumstances of non-contact offences. In this way, the QACSO reviews cognitive distortions from a number of points of view.

By conducting repeated measures, assessors can review an individual's progress through the treatment programme. The figures on Table 20.2 are taken from a man who committed a number of offences against male and female children. The columns represent the seven scales of the QACSO, total score and the social desirability score. The rows represent the points of testing which were around 6 months apart. I have not reported total score previously but Rose *et al.* (2002, 2007) and Murphy *et al.* (2007) found that total score was sensitive to change. On a number of the scales, this group member's scores were consistent with the average scores of sexual offenders with ID. Importantly, they were also at least one standard deviation above the average scores for the other standardisation groups. He endorsed a significant number of attitudes consistent with offending in the areas of voyeurism, exhibitionism, stalking, homosexual assault and offences against children. His responses were below the sex offender average on the scales of rape and attitudes to women and dating abuse.

Table 20.2 Case A. Questionnaire on attitudes consistent with sexual offending

Scale	Baseline	6 months	12 months	18 months	24 months	30 months	36 months
Rape and attitudes to women	2	2	2	2	1	1	1
Voyeurism	5	6	3	5	4	6	3
Exhibitionism	4	5	3	1	0	1	3
Dating abuse	3	4	2	2	1	1	0
Stalking and sexual harassment	4	7	4	7	1	0	1
Homosexual assault	3	3	1	0	0	0	0
Offences against children	6	8	5	5	3	1	2
Total score	27	35	20	22	10	10	10
Social desirability	5	5	4	5	3	3	5

Note: The table shows the repeated measures at initial assessment (baseline) and subsequent 6 monthly assessments after treatment has commenced up to 36 months. Seven scales for offending situations are shown in addition to total score and the social desirability scale.

On total score, his responses were just under the average for the reference group of sex offenders. Importantly, his social desirability scale indicated that he was not attempting to respond in a socially conformist fashion. In other words, he did not appear to be telling the assessor what he thought might place him in a positive light.

He was reassessed 6 months after the onset of treatment and his responses illustrate a pattern which is not uncommon in participants. He endorsed a slightly higher number of attitudes than he had at baseline. This was true for the scales of voyeurism, exhibitionism, dating abuse, stalking and offences against children. The main hypothesis for this effect of an increase in cognitive distortions is that group members realise that their attitudes are not being censured by facilitators and, during group sessions these various beliefs and opinions are explored through the Socratic process. Therefore, any inhibitory effects which might have been present at initial assessment, are now lessened. It will also be the fact that the group member will be more comfortable talking about these issues and may be more frank about their views. Despite the possibility of an inhibitory effect at initial assessment, he has still endorsed a significant number of cognitive distortions.

Thereafter, treatment seems to have had a fairly orderly effect on his thoughts and attitudes with a steady reduction in his endorsements over the next 2 years. It may appear somewhat uneven to the reader in that at 18 months he shows higher scores on the voyeurism and stalking scales than at 12 months. However, in my experience, this is not a variable set of results. It would not be uncommon for respondents to vary to a much greater degree over the course of 2 or 3 years in their responding on the QACSO. By the end of treatment, his responses are consistently lower than standardisation scores for sex offenders on all but the voyeurism and exhibitionism scales. His scores on the voyeurism scale remain elevated throughout suggesting that he continues to feel justified in looking at women or at least continues to feel that there is little wrong with looking at women in a sexual manner. His remaining endorsements on the rape, voyeurism and exhibitionism scale generally represented the view that, by the way they dress, women remain responsible for some of the offending behaviour that men might commit. Again, this is not uncommon in offenders, even after protracted periods of treatment. Indeed, it may be a view held significantly by the general public. His continued endorsement of items related to offences against children were specifically on recovery from child sexual abuse. He maintained the view that children would recover from sexual abuse after a few years. On the rape scale, he scored throughout at a level consistent with non-offenders with ID. The only items which he endorsed were those related to victims being somewhat responsible for sexual assault by the way they dressed.

Two other interesting results can be seen in Table 20.2. His total score reduced in an orderly fashion. Despite increases in the final 12 months on one or other of his scales, his total score remained stable. His scores on the social desirability scale remained at an acceptable level. By continuing to endorse a number of attitudes on this scale, assessors can have corresponding confidence in his other responses.

Table 20.3 shows the scores on the QACSO from a man who offended against adult women. At initial assessment, his scores were consistent with the standardisation average for sexual offenders in the areas of rape and attitudes to women, voyeurism,

Table 20.3 Case B. Questionnaire on attitudes consistent with sexual offending

Scale	Baseline	6 months	12 months	18 months	24 months	30 months	36 months
Rape and attitudes to women	7	5	7	4	4	2	2
Voyeurism	5	5	5	2	2	2	2
Exhibitionism	3	5	1	2	1	2	0
Dating abuse	4	4	1	3	0	2	0
Stalking and sexual harassment	9	9	1	4	0	1	2
Homosexual assault	1	1	0	1	0	1	0
Offences against children	3	2	1	3	1	1	1
Total score	32	31	16	19	8	11	7
Social desirability	5	5	5	5	4	5	4

Note: The table shows the repeated measures at initial assessment (baseline) and subsequent 6 monthly assessments after treatment has commenced up to 36 months. Seven scales for offending situations are shown in addition to total score and the social desirability scale.

exhibitionism, dating abuse, stalking and homosexual assault. His scores on the offences against children scale were lower and remained consistently low. This reflects the finding of Lindsay *et al.* (2006b) that, on average, men who offend against adults tend to score lower on the scale of attitudes consistent with offending against children than do child molesters. As treatment progressed, he began to endorse fewer attitudes consistent with offending, especially in the areas of exhibitionism, dating abuse and stalking. It was not until he had been in treatment for 18 months that we began to have an effect on some of his attitudes in relation to rape and sexual assault and voyeurism.

A number of points emerge from this table. Again, progress was not even with increases in attitudes at various points of assessment. However, these increases were not marked. By the end of treatment, although his scores were generally low, he continued to endorse some attitudes in relation to rape and sexual assault, voyeurism and stalking. As with the previous example, these items concerned the way in which women dressed as being mitigation for an incident and suggesting some sexual provocation from the women. His repeated endorsement in relation to the offences against children scale was a persistent mistake he made about the onset of menstruation being consistent with the onset of age of consent. He had high scores throughout on the social desirability scale suggesting confidence in his other responses.

In Table 20.4 we can see the responses from a man who did not show the same degree of change as the previous two examples. His was a violent assault on a woman and, at initial assessment, his scores were significantly elevated in the areas of rape and sexual assault, voyeurism, exhibitionism, dating abuse, stalking and homosexual assault. He scored somewhat lower on the offences against children scale. Although there was some lowering of his scores at 12 and 18 months, there was a significant

Table 20.4 Case C. Questionnaire on attitudes consistent with sexual offending

Scale	Baseline	6 months	12 months	18 months	24 months	30 months	36 months
Rape and attitudes to women	6	7	4	2	6	4	3
Voyeurism	5	5	3	5	5	5	5
Exhibitionism	4	5	4	2	4	2	2
Dating abuse	4	5	2	2	5	1	2
Stalking and sexual harassment	6	6	3	1	6	5	5
Homosexual assault	2	1	2	1	1	1	1
Offences against children	3	3	2	1	6	1	1
Total score	30	32	20	14	33	19	19
Social desirability	5	5	5	4	5	4	5

Note: The table shows the repeated measures at initial assessment (baseline) and subsequent 6 monthly assessments after treatment has commenced up to 36 months. Seven scales for offending situations are shown in addition to total score and the social desirability scale.

increase when he was assessed after 2 years of treatment. During this time, a number of his relationships became disrupted and he began missing his probation sessions and behaving in a more antisocial fashion. He was not charged with breach of probation but was warned about his behaviour. He continued to be confrontational and aggressive in a range of situations and assessment on the QACSO found that he once again endorsed a number of attitudes to the extent that his scores were consistent with sex offenders in the areas of rape, voyeurism, exhibitionism, dating abuse, stalking and offences against children. The elevation of scores on the offences against children scale was surprising. However, it should be remembered that the main risk assessments for future sexual offences include items on general criminality and lifestyle in addition to items on sexual behaviour and sexual preferences. This case underlines the fact that general lifestyle will affect attitudes in a range of areas including attitudes towards sexual offending. The assessor gained the impression that his endorsement of items on the offending against children scale was an indication of his general oppositional stance towards the whole assessment and treatment process rather than any developments in inappropriate sexual preference. He seemed to be dismissive and antagonistic to everyone, including the assessor and the whole test. At this point, his total score was higher than at any other point across the assessments. Although his total score reduced once again at 30 and 36 months, he still endorsed a significant number of items on the rape scale, the voyeurism scale and the stalking and sexual harassment scale. Treatment was not seen as particularly effective and a clear recommendation was made for continued monitoring and continued attendance. His scores on the social desirability scale remained elevated throughout.

The effect of the social desirability scale can be seen in Table 20.5. Both of these assessments were taken prior to the commencement of treatment and it can be seen

Table 20.5 Case D. Questionnaire on attitudes consistent with sexual offending

Scale	Baseline	Baseline 2
Rape and attitudes to women	1	1
Voyeurism	2	2
Exhibitionism	0	0
Dating abuse	0	1
Stalking and sexual harassment	0	1
Homosexual assault	0	1
Offences against children	1	1
Total score	4	7
Social desirability	1	2

that the respondent scored very low across all the scales. This man had been a persistent offender throughout his teenage years with several non-contact offences against males, both adults and children. He had attended residential schools and been in various forms of treatment over the years. His scores on the social desirability scale were below the level one would expect in any group of men and, as a result, I had a great deal of doubt about the reliability of his other responses. He was somewhat more able with a WAIS IQ of 76 and had had a large number of discussions over the years about his sexuality with various therapists and carers. Despite this, he had continued to offend against men and boys and was referred following a series of non-contact offences against both. He was certainly able to furnish me with a range of appropriate responses in relation to the attitudinal questions, but his low score in the social desirability scale suggested that his responses were very much learned rather than a true reflection of his beliefs. Since most men endorse the socially unacceptable nature of questions on the social desirability scale, I suspected that he was trying to present himself in a more acceptable positive light.

These illustrations indicate the way in which repeated psychometric assessment can help facilitators to review an individual's treatment progress. Responses on certain items might indicate that specific aspects of treatment should be repeated or emphasised. Responses across a whole scale might suggest that a module should be repeated for this individual or that their period of treatment should be extended. It may not always be possible for treatment to be extended since the group member's probation might be coming to an end. However, it is still acceptable for such a recommendation to be made and, in my experience, although group members have very little motivation to attend at the beginning and for the first few months of treatment, towards the end of treatment, some may wish to attend voluntarily because they perceive the importance of keeping themselves safe.

Recording Re-offending

Recidivism has been recorded in different ways with different studies. For each staff group it is likely to be a unique method of recording. In some situations, any incident is logged centrally and a permanent record is made available to all legitimate individuals. For example, in maximum security settings, a central information department or security department is likely to record all significant incidents. These can then be recovered by facilitators or clinical teams should they wish to review the success or otherwise of any particular intervention such as sex offender treatment.

Such exact and careful recording is unusual and for most group facilitators, they should attempt to keep their own records of any incidents that occur over the weeks and months of treatment. In our own studies (Lindsay *et al.*, 2004b; Lindsay *et al.*, 2006c) we have a large, area wide network of individuals who invite members of the forensic ID service to all clinical review meetings and case conferences. We record any incident that is mentioned whether or not it is reported to the police or other criminal justice agencies. Incidents are routinely reported by community nursing staff, social workers and so on and it is relatively likely that if any incident came to light, it would be reported to the forensic service. If an individual is incorporated into sex offender treatment, it is highly likely that those involved with that person will report any incident to the facilitators. Indeed, it is our experience that over-reporting is more likely than under-reporting. Therefore, we will hear about new friendships, any observed interactions at clubs or college, alterations in routines, increases or decreases in alcohol and substance abuse and the like.

One of the issues that came to light at an early stage in our service was that the re-offending rates were relatively high. Lindsay *et al.* (2002) reported re-offending rates for sexual offenders at around 20% and for non-sexual (mostly violent) offenders it was between 40 and 50%. Given the significant amount of treatment provided for these individuals, these recidivism rates are disappointingly high. We then looked at the number of incidents committed by individuals 2 years prior to referral (this could only be based on retrospective information and less careful reporting) and the number of incidents at least 2 years and up to 12 years after referral. As has been pointed out in Chapter 4, we found a huge reduction in the number of incidents that were recorded. The clear recommendation arising out of this is that during the initial assessment period, attempts should be made to gather as much information about the number of incidents that have been perpetrated by the individual. A careful record should be kept of these incidents. This can then be compared with the records taken during the treatment phases and at follow-up for years after the person has been referred. In our own service, we have found a highly significant reduction in the number of incidents perpetrated although many of the men may have committed one further offence.

Conclusions

I have tried to suggest a number of fairly easy ways in which treatment can be evaluated as it is being conducted. The PSDR can be filled out quickly during review sessions and incidents can be recorded as they are reported. The peer review system can be incorporated into treatment and is usually enjoyed by participants. It also promotes their sense of ownership of the process in that they are actively involved in evaluating each other. Regular revision can occur through quizzes which are both enjoyable and motivational. The most time consuming assessment is the QACSO. It is also the most technical, requiring a significant degree of sophistication in statistical analysis and corresponding qualifications in psychometric testing. There are a number of other attitudinal assessments available, some of which do not carry the same requirements but they have not been standardised on men with ID. The main message to convey is that assessment is important and ongoing assessment, although it can occasionally seem a diversion from the main business of treatment, is an essential aspect of the treatment process. It allows facilitators to review individual aspects which might be resistant to treatment in addition to overall progress. It reminds facilitators to consider general lifestyle and quality of life in addition to the specific issues related to sexual offending. It also allows facilitators to demonstrate treatment progress to colleagues and officers in the wider service.

References

Abel, G.G., Gore, D.K., Holland, C.L. *et al.* (1989) The measurement of the cognitive distortions of child molesters. *Annals of Sex Research*, **3**, 135–53.

Ager, A. (1990) *The Life Experience Checklist*, British Institute of Learning Disabilities, Kidderminster.

Alder, L. and Lindsay, W.R. (2007) Exploratory factor analysis and convergent validity of the Dundee Provocation Inventory. *Journal of Intellectual and Developmental Disabilities*, **32**, 179–88.

Alexander, R. and Cooray, S. (2003) Diagnosis of personality disorders in learning disability. *British Journal of Psychiatry*, **182** (Suppl. 44), S28–31.

Ammons, R.B. and Ammons, C.H. (1958) *The Quick Test Manual*, Birmingham Publishing Co., Birmingham.

Andrews, D.A. and Bonta, J. (1998) *The Psychology of Criminal Conduct*, 2nd edn, Anderson, Cincinnati, OH.

Barbaree, H.E., Seto, M.C., Langton, C.M. and Peacock, E.J. (2001) Evaluating the predictive accuracy of six risk assessment instruments for adult sex offenders. *Criminal Justice and Behaviour*, **28**, 490–521.

Barratt, E. (1994) Impulsivity and aggression, in *Violence in Mental Disorder* (eds J. Monahan and H.J. Steadman), University of Chicago Press, Chicago.

Bartholomew, K. and Horowitz, L.M. (1991) Attachment styles among adults: a test of a four category model. *Journal of Personality and Social Psychology*, **61**, 226–44.

Bartosh, D.L., Garby, T., Lewis, D. and Gray, S. (2003) Differences in the predictive validity of actuarial risk assessments in relation to sex offender type. *International Journal of Offender Therapy and Comparative Criminology*, **47**, 422–38.

Beail, N. and Warden, S. (1995) Sexual abuse of adults with learning disabilities. *Journal of Intellectual Disability Research*, **39**, 382–87.

Beckett, R. and Fisher, D. (1994) Victim empathy measure, in *Community Based Treatment for Sex Offenders: An Evaluation of Seven Treatment Programmes* (eds R. Beckett, A. Beech, D. Fisher and A.S. Fordham), Home Office, London.

Beech, A.T., Fisher, D. and Beckett, R. (1998) *Step Three: An Evaluation of Prison Sex Offender Treatment Programme*, Home Office, London.

Beech, A.T. and Hamilton-Giachristis, C.E. (2005) Relationship between therapeutic climate and treatment outcome in group based sexual offender treatment. *Sexual Abuse: A Journal of Research and Treatment*, 17, 127–40.

Beech, A., Friendship, C., Erikson, M. and Hanson, R.K. (2002) The relationship between static and dynamic risk factors and reconviction in a sample of UK child abusers. *Sexual Abuse: A Journal of Research and Treatment*, 14, 155–67.

Bender, M., Aitman, J., Biggs, F. and Haug, U. (1983) Initial findings concerning a sexual knowledge questionnaire. *Mental Handicap*, 11, 168–69.

Bickley, J.A. and Beech, A.R. (2002) An investigation of the Ward and Hudson pathways model of the sexual offence process with child abusers. *Journal of Interpersonal Violence*, 17, 371–93.

Blackburn, R., Logan, C., Renwick, S.J.D. and Donnelly, J.P. (2005) Higher order dimensions of personality disorder: hierarchical and relationships with the five factor model, the interpersonal circle and psychopathy. *Journal of Personality Disorders*, 19, 597–623.

Blackburn, R. and Renwick, S.J. (1996) Rating scales for measuring the interpersonal circle in forensic psychiatric patients. *Psychological Assessment*, 8, 76–84.

Blanchard, R., Kella, N.J., Cantor, J.M. *et al.* (2008) IQ, handedness and paedophilia in adult male patients stratified by referral source. *Sexual Abuse: A Journal of Research and Treatment*, 19, 285–309.

Blanchard, R., Watson, M., Choy, A. *et al.* (1999) Paedophiles: mental retardation, mental age and sexual orientation. *Archives of Sexual Behaviour*, 28, 111–27.

Boer, D.P., Tough, S. and Haaven, J. (2004) Assessment of risk manageability of developmentally disabled sex offenders. *Journal of Applied Research in Intellectual Disabilities*, 17, 275–84.

Bonham, G.S., Basehart, S., Schalock, R.L. *et al.* (2004) Consumer based quality of life assessment: The Maryland ask me! project. *Mental Retardation*, 42, 338–55.

Borduin, C.M., Henggeler, S.W., Blaske, D.M. and Stein, R.J. (1990) Multi-systemic treatment of adolescent sexual offenders. *International Journal of Offender Therapy and Comparative Criminology*, 34, 105–13.

Borum, R. (1996) Improving the clinical practice of violent risk assessment. *American Psychologist*, 51, 945–56.

Briggs, F. and Hawkins, R.M.F. (1996) A comparison of the childhood experiences of convicted male child molesters and men who were sexually abused in childhood and claimed to be non-offenders. *Child Abuse and Neglect*, 20, 221–33.

Broxholme, S. and Lindsay, W.R. (2003) Development and preliminary evaluation of a questionnaire on cognitions related to sex offending for use with individuals who have mild intellectual disability. *Journal of Intellectual Disability Research*, 47, 472–82.

Camilleri, J.A. and Quinsey, V.L. (2008) Appraising the risk of sexual and violent recidivism among intellectually disabled offenders. *Psychology, Crime and Law*, in press.

Cann, J., Falshaw, L. and Friendship, C. (2004) Sexual offenders discharged from prison in England and Wales: a 21 year reconviction study. *Legal and Criminological Psychology*, 9, 1–10.

Cantor, J.M., Blanchard, R., Robichaud, L.K. and Christensen, B.K. (2005) Quantitative reanalysis of aggregate data on IQ in sexual offenders. *Psychological Bulletin*, 131, 555–68.

Chevrier, J.M. (1993) *EIHM: Eupreuve individuelle d'habilete mentale*, Tomes 2a et 3, Institut de Recherches Psychologiques, Montreal.

Christiansen, K.O. (1977) A preliminary study of criminality among twins, in *Biological Basis of Criminal Behaviour* (eds S.A. Mednick and K. Christiansen), Gardiner, New York, pp. 177–92.

Cohen, A.K. (1955) *Delinquent Boys: The Culture of the Gang*, Free Press, Glencoe, IL.

Cohen, L.J., Gans, S.W., McGeoch, P.G. *et al.* (2002) Impulsive personality traits in male paedophiles versus healthy controls: Is paedophilia an impulsive-aggressive disorder? *Comprehensive Psychology*, **43**, 127–34.

Cook, J.W., Altman, K., Shaw, J. and Blaylock, M. (1978) Use of contingent lemon juice to eliminate public masturbation by a severely retarded boy. *Behaviour Research and Therapy*, **18**, 131–34.

Corbett, J.A. (1979) *Psychiatric Illness in Mental Handicap*, Gaskell, London.

Courtney, J., Rose, J. and Mason, O. (2006) The offence process of sex offenders with intellectual disabilities: a qualitative study. *Sexual Abuse: A Journal of Research and Treatment*, **18**, 169–91.

Craig, L.A., Stringer, I. and Moss, T. (2006) Treating sexual offenders with learning disabilities in the community. *International Journal of Offender Therapy and Comparative Criminology*, **50**, 111–22.

Crocker, A.J., Cote, G., Toupin, J. and St-Onge, B. (2007) Rate and characteristics of men with an intellectual disability in pre-trial detention. *Journal of Intellectual and Developmental Disability*, **32**, 143–52.

Cummins, R.A. and Lau, A.L.D. (2003a) Community integration or community exposure? A review and discussion in relation to people with an intellectual disability. *Journal of Applied Research in Intellectual Disabilities*, **16**, 145–57.

Cummins, R.A. and Lau, A.L.D. (2003b) The motivation to maintain subjective well-being: a homeostatic model, in *Personality and Motivational Systems in Mental Retardation. A Volume in International Review of Research in Mental Retardation* (ed. H.N. Switzky), Elsevier Academic, San Diego, CA.

Cycle of Abuse (1996) *Report to the Sub-Committee on Crime, Committee on the Judiciary, House of Representatives*, United States General Accounting Office, Washington DC.

Dagnan, D. and Jahoda, A. (2006) Cognitive behavioural intervention for people with intellectual disability and anxiety disorders. *Journal of Applied Research and Intellectual Disabilities*, **19**, 91–98.

Dagnan, D. and Lindsay, W.R. (2008) People with mental health problems, in *Clinical Psychology and People with Intellectual Disabilities*, 2nd edn (eds E. Emerson and C. Hatton), John Wiley & Sons, Ltd, Chichester, in press.

Dagnan, D. and Waring, M. (2004) Linking stigma to psychological distress: testing a social-cognitive model of the experience of people with intellectual disabilities. *Clinical Psychology and Psychotherapy*, **11**, 247–54.

Dahawan, S. and Marshall, W.L. (1996) Sexual abuse histories of sexual offenders. *Sexual Abuse: Journal of Research and Treatment*, **8**, 7–15.

Day, K. (1994) Male mentally handicapped sex offenders. *British Journal of Psychiatry*, **165**, 630–39.

Dolan, M. and Khawaja, A. (2004) The HCR-20 and post discharge outcome in male patients discharged from medium security in the UK. *Aggressive Behaviour*, **30**, 469–83.

Earl, C.J.C. (1961) *Subnormal Personalities: Their Clinical Investigation and Assessment*, Bailliere, Tindall & Cox, London.

Elbogen, E.B. (2002) The process of violence risk assessment: a review of a descriptive research. *Aggression and Violent Behaviour*, **7**, 591–604.

Elliot, D.S., Huizinga, D. and Ageton, S.S. (1985) *Explaining Delinquency and Drug Use*, Sage, Beverley Hills, CA.

Emerson, E. (2003) Prevalence of psychiatric disorders in children and adolescents with and without intellectual disabilities. *Journal of Intellectual Disability Research*, **47**, 51–8.

Emerson, E. (2007) Poverty and people with intellectual disabilities. *Mental Retardation and Developmental Disabilities Research Reviews*, **13**, 107–13.

Emerson, E. and Hatton, C. (1994) *Moving Out: Relocation from Hospital to Community*, Her Majesty Stationery Office, London.

Emerson, E., Robertson, J. and Wood, J. (2005) The mental health needs of children and adolescents with intellectual disabilities in an urban conurbation. *Journal of Intellectual Disability Research*, **49**, 16–24.

Emerson, E. and Turnbull, L. (2005) Self reported smoking and alcohol use by adolescents with and without intellectual disabilities. *Journal of Intellectual Disability*, **9**, 58–69.

Fago, D.P. (2003) Evaluation and treatment of neurodevelopmental deficits in sexually aggressive children and adolescents. *Professional Psychology: Research and Practice*, **34**, 248–57.

Fago, D.P. (2006) Comorbid psychopathology in child, adolescent and adult sexual offenders, in *Comprehensive Mental Health Practice with Sex Offenders and Their Families* (eds C. Hilarski and J. Wodarski), Haworth, Binghamton, NY, pp. 139–218.

Farrington, D.P. (1995) The development of offending and antisocial behaviour from childhood: key findings from the Cambridge study in delinquent development. *Journal of Child Psychology and Psychiatry*, **36**, 929–64.

Farrington, D.P. (2005) Childhood origin of antisocial behaviour. *Clinical psychology and Psychotherapy*, **12**, 177–89.

Fazel, S. and Danesh, J. (2002) Serious mental disorder among 23,000 prisoners: systematic review of 62 surveys. *Lancet*, **16**, 545–50.

Fernald, W.E. (1909) The imbecile with criminal instincts. *Journal of Psycho-Asthenics*, **14**, 16–36.

Fernald, W.E. (1912) The burden of the feeble-minded. *Journal of Psycho-Asthenics*, **17**, 87–111.

Fernald, W.E. (1919) Aftercare study of the patients discharged from Waverley for a period of 25 years. *Ungraded*, **5**, 25–31.

Finkelhor, D. (1984) *Child Sexual Abuse: New Theory and Research*, Free Press, New York.

Finlay, W.M. and Lyons, E. (2001) Methodological issues in interviewing and using self-report questionnaires with people with mental retardation. *Psychological Assessment*, **13**, 319–35.

Furby, L., Weinrott, M.R. and Blackshaw, L. (1989) Sex offender recidivism: a review. *Psychological Bulletin*, **105**, 3–30.

Gallacher, C.A., Wilson, D.B., Hirschfield, P. *et al.* (1999) A quantitative review of the effects of sex offender treatment of sexual re-offending. *Corrections Management Quarterly*, **3**, 19–29.

Galton, F. (1883) *Enquiries into Human Faculty and its Development*, MacMillan, London.

Garlick, Y., Marshall, W.L. and Thornton, D. (1996) Intimacy deficits and attribution of blame among sexual offenders. *Legal and Criminological Psychology*, **1**, 251–58.

Gendreau, P., Grant, B.A., Leipcieger, M. and Collins, S. (1979) Norms and recidivism rates for the MMPI and selected environmental scales on a Canadian delinquent sample. *Canadian Journal of Behavioural Science*, **11**, 21–31.

Gibbons, D.C. and Krohn, M.D. (1986) *Delinquent Behaviour*, 4th edn, Prentice Hall, Englewood Cliffs, NJ.

Glaser, W. and Deane, K. (1999) Normalisation in an abnormal world: A study of prisoners with intellectual disability. *International Journal of Offender Therapy & Comparative Criminology*, **43**, 338–50.

Glueck, E. (1935) Mental retardation found in juvenile delinquency. *Journal of Psycho-Asthenics*, **40**, 267–90.

Goddard, H. (1910) Heredity of feeble-mindedness. *American Breeders Magazine*, **1**, 165–78.

Goddard, H. (1911) The menace of the feeble-minded. *Paediatrics*, **23**, 1–8.

Goddard, H. (1912) *The Kallikak Family: A Study in the Heredity of Feeble-Mindedness*, MacMillan, New York.

Goddard, H. (1921) *The Criminal Imbecile*, Dodd, Mead & Co., New York.

Goodman, R., Simonoff, E. and Stevenson, J. (1995) The impact of child IQ, parent IQ, and sibling IQ on child behavioural deviance scores. *Journal of Child Psychology and Psychiatry*, **36**, 409–25.

Grann, M., Belfrage, H. and Tengstrom, A. (2000) Actuarial assessment of risk for violence: predictive validity of the VRAG and the historical part of the HCR-20. *Criminal Justice and Behaviour*, **27**, 97–114.

Gray, N.S., Fitzgerald, S., Taylor, J. *et al.* (2007) Predicting future reconviction in offenders with intellectual disabilities: the predictive efficacy of VRAG, PCL-SV and the HCR-20. *Psychological Assessment*, **19**, 474–79.

Green, G., Gray, N.S. and Willner, P. (2002) Factors associated with criminal convictions for sexually inappropriate behaviour in men with learning disabilities. *Journal of Forensic Psychiatry*, **13**, 578–607.

Grettan, H.M., McBride, M., Hare, R.D. *et al.* (2001) Psychopathy and recidivism in adolescent sex offenders. *Criminal Justice and Behaviour*, **28**, 427–49.

Griffin, D.W. and Bartholomew, K. (1994) The metaphysics of measurement: the case of adult attachment, in *Attachment Process in Adulthood* (eds K. Bartholomew and D. Perlman), Jessica Kingsley, London, pp. 17–52.

Griffiths, D., Federoff, J.P., Richards, D. *et al.* (2007) Sexual and gender identity disorders, in *Diagnostic Manual – Intellectual Disability* (eds R. Fletcher, E. Loschen, C. Stavrakaki and M. First), NADD, Kingston, NY, pp. 411–57.

Griffiths, D. and Lunsky, Y. (2003) *Sociosexual Knowledge and Attitudes Assessment Tool (SSKAAT-R)*. Stoelting Company, Wood Dale, IL.

Griffiths, D.M., Quinsey, V.L. and Hingsburger, D. (1989) *Changing Inappropriate Sexual Behaviour: A Community Based Approach for Persons with Developmental Disabilities*, Paul Brooks, Baltimore.

Grouio, S., Sakadami, N., Poderi, A. and Alevriadou, A. (1999) Excess of non right handedness among individuals with intellectual disability: experimental evidence and possible explanations. *Journal of Intellectual Disability Research*, **43**, 306–13.

Grubb-Blubaugh, V., Shire, B.J. and Baulser, M.L. (1994) Behaviour management and offenders with mental retardation: the jury system. *Mental Retardation*, **32**, 213–17.

Haaven, J., Little, R. and Petre-Miller, D. (1990) *Treating Intellectually Disabled Sex Offenders: A Model Residential Programme*, Safer Society Press, Orwell, VT.

Hall, G.C.N. (1995a) The preliminary development of theory based community treatment for sexual offenders. *Professional Psychology: Research and Practice*, **26**, 478–83.

Hall, G.C.N. (1995b) Sexual offender recidivism revisited: a meta-analysis of recent treatment studies. *Journal of Consulting in Clinical Psychology*, **63**, 802–9.

Hall, G.C.N. (1996) *Theory Based Assessment, Treatment and Prevention of Sexual Aggression*, Oxford University Press, New York.

Hall, G.C.N. and Hirschman, R. (1991) Towards a theory of sexual aggression: a quadripartite model. *Journal of Consulting in Clinical Psychology*, **59**, 662–69.

Hall, G.C.N. and Hirschman, R. (1992) Sexual aggression against children: a conceptual perspective of etiology. *Criminal Justice and Behaviour*, **19**, 8–23.

Hanson, R.K. (1997) *The Development of a Brief Actuarial Risk Scale for Sexual Offence Recidivism (User report 1997–2004)*, Development of the Solicitor General of Canada, Ottawa.

Hanson, R.K., Broom, I. and Stephenson, M. (2004) Evaluating community sex offender treatment programmes: a 12 year follow-up of 724 offenders. *Canadian Journal of Behavioural Science*, **36**, 87–96.

Hanson, R.K., Gordon, A., Harris, A.J.R. *et al.* (2002) First report of the collaborative outcome data project on the effectiveness of psychological treatment for sex offenders. *Sexual Abuse: A Journal of Research and Treatment*, **14**, 169–94.

Hanson, R.K. and Harris, A.J.R. (2000) Where should we intervene? Dynamic predictors of sexual offence recidivism. *Criminal Justice and Behaviour*, **27**, 6–35.

Hanson, R.K. and Thornton, D. (1999) *Static-99: Improving Actuarial Risk Assessments for Sex Offenders* (User report 1999–2002), Department of the Solicitor General of Canada, Ottawa.

Hanson, R.K. and Thornton, D. (2000) Improving risk assessments for sexual offenders: a comparison of three actuarial scales. *Law and Human Behaviour*, **24**, 119–36.

Hanson, K. and Thornton, D. (2003) *The Static 2002*. Department of the Solicitor General of Canada, Ottawa.

Hare, R.D. (1991) *The Hare Psychopathy Checklist – Revised*, Multi Health Systems, Toronto.

Harris, A.J.R. and Tough, S. (2004) Should actuarial risk assessments be used with sex offenders who are intellectually disabled. *Journal of Applied Research in Intellectual Disabilities*, **17**, 235–42.

Harris, G.T., Rice, M.E. and Quinsey, V.L. (1993) Violent recidivism of mentally disordered offenders: the development of a statistical prediction instrument. *Criminal Justice and Behaviour*, **20**, 315–35.

Harris, G.T., Rice, M.E., Quinsey, V.L. and Chaplin, T.C. (1996) Viewing time as a measure of sexual interest among child molesters and normal heterosexual men. *Behaviour Research and Therapy*, **34**, 389–94.

Harris, G.T., Rice, M.E., Quinsey, V.L. *et al.* (2003) A multi-site comparison of actuarial risk instruments for sex offenders. *Psychological Assessment*, **15**, 413–25.

Hart, S.D., Cox, D.N. and Hare, R.D. (1995) *The Hare PCL:SV*, Multi-health Systems, Toronto.

Hastings, R.P. (2002) Do challenging behaviours affect staff psychological well-being? Issues of causality and mechanism. *American Journal of Mental Retardation*, **107**, 455–67.

Hastings, R., Horne, S. and Mitchell, G. (2004) Burnout in direct care staff in intellectual disability services: a factor analytic study of the Maslach Burnout Inventory. *Journal of Intellectual Disability Research*, **48**, 268–73.

Hayes, S. (1991a) Pilot prison programmes. *Australia and New Zealand Journal of Developmental Disabilities (Journal of Intellectual and Developmental Disabilities)*, **17**, 209–16.

Hayes, S. (1991b) Sex offenders. *Australia and New Zealand Journal of Developmental Disabilities (Journal of Intellectual and Developmental Disabilities)*, **17**, 220–27.

Hayes, S.C. (2002) Early intervention or early incarceration? Using a screening test for intellectual disability in the criminal justice system. *Journal of Applied Research in Intellectual Disability*, **15**, 120–28.

Hemphill, J.F., Hare, R.D. and Wong, S. (1998) Psychopathy and recidivism: a review. *Legal and Criminological Psychology*, **3**, 141–72.

Hingsburger, D., Griffiths, D. and Quinsey, V. (1991) Detecting counterfeit deviance: differentiating sexual deviance from sexual inappropriateness. *Habilitation Mental Health Care Newsletter*, **10**, 51–54.

Hirschi, T. (1969) *Causes of Delinquency*, University of California Press, Berkeley, CA.

Hirschi, T. and Hildelang, M.J. (1977) Intelligence and delinquency: a revisionist view. *American Sociological Review*, **42**, 571–87.

Hogue, T.E., Steptoe, L., Taylor, J.L. *et al.* (2006) A comparison of offenders with intellectual disability across three levels of security. *Criminal Behaviour and Mental Health*, **16**, 13–28.

Holland, A.J. (1991) Challenging and offending behaviour by adults with developmental disorders. *Australia and New Zealand Journal of Developmental Disabilities (Journal of Intellectual and Developmental Disabilities)*, **17**, 119–26.

Holland, A.J. (2004) Criminal behaviour and developmental disability: an epidemiological perspective, in *Offenders with Developmental Disabilities* (eds W.R. Lindsay, J.L. Taylor and P. Sturmey), John Wiley & Sons, Ltd, Chichester, pp. 23–34.

Holland, S. and Persson, P. (2007) *Intellectual Disability in the Victorian Prison System: Characteristics of Prisoners with an Intellectual Disability Released from Prison in 2003 –2006*, Department of Justice, Corrections Victoria.

Hudson, S.M. and Ward, T. (2000) Relapse prevention: assessment and treatment implications, in *Remaking Relapse Prevention with Sex Offenders: A Source Book* (eds D.R. Laws, S.M. Hudson and T. Ward), Sage, Thousand Oaks, CA, pp. 102–22.

Jahoda, A., Dagnan, D., Jarvie, P. and Kerr, W. (2006) Depression, social context and cognitive behaviour therapy for people who have intellectual disabilities. *Journal of Applied Research and Intellectual Disabilities*, **19**, 81–90.

Jahoda, A., Trower, P., Pert, C. and Finn, D. (2001) Contingent reinforcement or defending the self? A review of evolving models of aggression in people with mild learning disabilities. *British Journal of Medical Psychology*, **74**, 305–21.

Johnson, T.C. (1989) Female child perpetrators: children who molest other children. *Child Abuse and Neglect*, **13**, 571–85.

Jolliffe, D. and Farrington, D.P. (2004) Empathy and offending: a systematic review and meta-analysis. *Aggression and Violent Behaviour*, **9**, 441–76.

Kandel, E., Mednick, S.A., Kirkegaard-Sorensen, L. *et al.* (1988) IQ as a protective factor for subjects at high risk for antisocial behaviour. *Journal of Consulting and Clinical Psychology*, **56**, 224–26.

Kaufman, A.S. and Leichtenberger, E.O. (1999) *Essentials of WAIS-III Assessment*, John Wiley & Sons, Ltd, Chichester.

Keeling, J.A. and Rose, J.L. (2005) Relapse prevention with intellectually disabled sex offenders. *Sexual Abuse: A Journal of Research and Treatment*, **17**, 407–23.

Keeling, J.A., Rose, J.L. and Beech, A.R. (2006) A comparison of the application of the self-regulation model of the relapse process for mainstream and special needs offenders. *Sexual Abuse: A Journal of Research and Treatment*, **18**, 373–82.

Keeling, J.A., Rose, J.L. and Beech, A.R. (2007a) A preliminary evaluation of the adaptation of four assessments for offenders with special needs. *Journal of Intellectual and Developmental Disability*, **32**, 62–73.

Keeling, J.A., Rose, J.L. and Beech, A.R. (2007b) Comparing sexual offender treatment efficacy: mainstream sexual offenders and sexual offenders with special needs. *Journal of Intellectual and Developmental Disability*, **32**, 117–24.

Kelly, R.J. (1982) Behavioural reorientation of paedophiliacs: Can it be done? *Clinical Psychology Review*, **2**, 387–408.

Kiely, J. and Pankhurst, H. (1998) Violence faced by staff in a learning disability service. *Disability and Rehabilitation*, **20**, 81–89.

Kirkegaard-Sorensen, L. and Mednick, S.A. (1977) A prospective study of predictors of criminality: a description of registered criminality in the high risk and low risk families, in *Biological Basis of Criminal Behaviour* (eds S.A. Mednick and K.O. Christiansen), Gardiner, New York, pp. 229–44.

Knopp, F.H., Freeman-Longo, R.E. and Stevenson, W. (1992) *Nationwide Survey of Juvenile and Adult Sex Offender Treatment Programmes*, Safer Society Press, Orwell, VT.

Kolton, D.J.C., Boer, A. and Boer, D.P. (2001) A revision of the Abel and Becker Cognition Scale for intellectually disabled sexual offenders. *Sexual Abuse: A Journal of Research and Treatment*, **13**, 217–19.

Kroner, D.G. and Mills, J.F. (2001) The accuracy of five risk appraisal instruments in predicting institutional misconduct and new convictions. *Criminal Justice and Behaviour*, **28**, 471–89.

Lambrick, F. and Glaser, W. (2004) Sex offenders with an intellectual disability. *Sexual Abuse: A Journal of Research and Treatment*, **16**, 381–92.

Langdon, P.E., Maxted, H. and Murphy, G.H. (2007) An exploratory evaluation of the Ward and Hudson Offending Pathways Model with sex offenders who have intellectual disabilities. *Journal of Intellectual and Developmental Disabilities*, **32**, 94–105.

Langdon, P.E. and Talbot, T.J. (2006) Locus of control and sex offenders with an intellectual disability. *International Journal of Offender Therapy and Comparative Criminology*, **50**, 391–401.

Langevin, R. and Curnoe, S. (2002) Assessment and treatment of sex offenders who have a developmental disability, in *Ethical dilemmas: Sexuality and Developmental Disability* (eds D.M. Griffiths, D. Richards, P. Federoff and S.L. Watson), NADD, Kingston, NY, pp. 387–416.

Langevin, R., Lang, R.A. and Curnoe, S. (1998) The prevalence of sex offenders with deviant sexual fantasies. *Journal of Interpersonal Violence*, **13**, 315–27.

Langton, C.M., Barbaree, H.E., Seto, M.C. *et al.* (2007) Actuarial assessment of risk for re-offence amongst adult sex offenders: evaluating the predictive accuracy of the Static-2002 and five other instruments. *Criminal Justice and Behaviour*, **24**, 37–59.

Lezak, M.D., Howieson, D.B. and Loring, B.W. (2004) *Neuropsychological Assessment*, 4th edn, Oxford University Press, Oxford.

Lindsay, W.R. (2004) Sex offenders: conceptualisation of the issues, services, treatment and management, in *Offenders with Developmental Disabilities* (eds W.R. Lindsay, J.L. Taylor and P. Sturmey), John Wiley & Sons, Ltd, Chichester, pp. 163–86.

Lindsay, W.R. (2005) Model underpinning treatment for sex offenders with mild intellectual disability: current theories of sex offending. *Mental Retardation*, **43**, 428–41.

Lindsay, W.R. (2007) Personality disorder, in *Psychiatric and Behavioural Disorders in Developmental Disabilities and Mental Retardation* (eds N. Bouras and G. Holt), Cambridge University Press, Cambridge, pp. 336–59, Chapter 9.

Lindsay, W.R., Allan, R., Parry, C., Macleod, F., Cottrell, J., Overend, H. and Smith, A.H.W. (2004) Anger and aggression in people with intellectual disabilities: Treatment and follow-up of consecutive referrals and a waiting list comparison. *Clinical Psychology and Psychotherapy*, **11**, 255–64.

Lindsay, W.R. and Beail, N. (2004) Risk assessment: actuarial prediction and clinical judgement of offending incidents and behaviour for intellectual disability services. *Journal of Applied Research in Intellectual Disabilities*, **17**, 229–34.

Lindsay, W.R., Bellshaw, E., Culross, G. *et al.* (1992) Increases in knowledge following a course of sex education for people with learning difficulties. *Journal of Intellectual Disability Research*, **36**, 531–39.

Lindsay, W.R., Elliot, S.F. and Astell, A. (2004) Predictors of sexual offence recidivism in offenders with intellectual disabilities. *Journal of Applied Research in Intellectual Disabilities*, **17**, 299–305.

Lindsay, W.R., Gabriel, S., Dana, L. *et al.* (2007a) Personality disorders, in *DM-ID* (eds R. Fletcher, E. Loschen, C. Stavrakakis and M. First), National Association for Dual Diagnosis, Kingston, NY.

Lindsay, W.R., Hastings, R.P., Griffiths, D.M. and Hayes, S.C. (2007b) Trends and challenges in forensic research on offenders with intellectual disability. *Journal of Intellectual and Developmental Disability*, **32**, 55–61.

Lindsay, W.R., Hogue, T., Taylor, J.L. *et al.* (2006a) Two studies on the prevalence and validity of personality disorder in three forensic intellectual disability samples. *Journal of Forensic Psychiatry and Psychology*, **17**, 485–506.

Lindsay, W.R., Hogue, T., Taylor, J.L. *et al.* (2008a) Risk assessment in offenders with intellectual disabilities: a comparison across three levels of security. *International Journal of Offender Therapy and Comparative Criminology*, **52**, 90–111.

Lindsay, W.R., Law, J., Quinn, K. *et al.* (2001) A comparison of physical and sexual abuse histories: sexual and non-sexual offenders with intellectual disability. *Child Abuse and Neglect*, **25**, 989–95.

Lindsay, W.R. and Lees, M. (2003) A comparison of anxiety and depression in sex offenders with intellectual disability and a control group with intellectual disability. *Sexual Abuse: A Journal of Research and Treatment*, **15**, 339–46.

Lindsay, W.R., Marshall, I., Neilson, C.Q. *et al.* (1998a) The treatment of men with a learning disability convicted of exhibitionism. *Research on Developmental Disabilities*, **19**, 295–316.

Lindsay, W.R., Michie, A.M., Whitefield, E. *et al.* (2006b) Response patterns on the Questionnaire on Attitudes Consistent with Sexual Offending in groups of sex offenders with intellectual disability. *Journal of Applied Research in Intellectual Disabilities*, **19**, 47–54.

Lindsay, W.R., Murphy, L., Smith, G. *et al.* (2004a) The Dynamic Risk Assessment and Management System: An assessment of immediate risk of violence for individuals with intellectual disabilities, and offending and challenging behaviour. *Journal of Applied Research in Intellectual Disabilities*, **17**, 267–74.

Lindsay, W.R., Neilson, C.Q., Morrison, F. and Smith, A.H.W. (1998b) The treatment of six men with a learning disability convicted of sex offences with children. *British Journal of Clinical Psychology*, **37**, 83–98.

Lindsay, W.R., Olley, S., Baillie, N. and Smith, A.H.W. (1999) The treatment of adolescent sex offenders with intellectual disability. *Mental Retardation*, **37**, 320–33.

Lindsay, W.R., Olley, S., Jack, C. *et al.* (1998c) The treatment of two stalkers with intellectual disabilities using a cognitive approach. *Journal of Applied Research in Intellectual Disabilities*, **11**, 333–44.

Lindsay, W.R. and Skene, D.D. (2007) The Beck Depression Inventory II and The Beck Anxiety Inventory in people with intellectual disabilities: factor analyses and group data. *Journal of Applied Research in Intellectual Disability*, **20**, 401–8.

Lindsay, W.R. and Smith, A.H.W. (1998) Responses to treatment for sex offenders with intellectual disability: a comparison of men with 1 and 2 year probation sentences. *Journal of Intellectual Disability Research*, **42**, 346–53.

Lindsay, W.R., Smith, A.H.W., Law, J. *et al.* (2004b) Sexual and non-sexual offenders with intellectual and learning disabilities: a comparison of characteristics, referral patterns and outcome. *Journal of Interpersonal Violence*, **19**, 875–90.

Lindsay, W.R., Smith, A.H.W., Law, J. *et al.* (2002) A treatment service for sex offenders and abusers with intellectual disability: characteristics of referrals and evaluation. *Journal of Applied Research in Intellectual Disability*, **15**, 166–74.

Lindsay, W.R., Steele, L., Smith, A.H.W. *et al.* (2006c) A community forensic intellectual disability service: twelve year follow-up of referrals, analysis of referral patterns and assessment of harm reduction. *Legal and Criminological Psychology*, **11**, 113–30.

Lindsay, W.R., Steptoe, L. and Beech, A.T. (2008) The Ward and Hudson pathways model of the sex offense process applied to offenders with intellectual disabilities. *Sexual Abuse: A Journal of Research and Treatment*, in press.

Lindsay, W.R., Steptoe, L., Hogue, T.E. *et al.* (2007c) Internal consistency and factor structure of personality disorders in a forensic intellectual disability sample. *Journal of Intellectual and Developmental Disabilities*, **32**, 134–42.

Lindsay, W.R. and Taylor, J.L. (2008) Assessment and treatment of offenders with intellectual and developmental disabilities, in *Handbook of Forensic Mental Health* (eds K. Soothall, P Rogers and M Dolan), Willan, Cullompton, pp. 328–50, Chapter 13.

Lindsay, W.R., Ward, T. and Morgan, T. (2005) *The Importance and Difficulty of Establishing Relationships in Sex Offenders*. Paper presented at the Good Lives Model Conference, Dundee.

Lindsay, W.R., Ward, T., Morgan, T. and Wilson I. (2007d) Self regulation of sex offending, future pathways and the good lives model: applications and problems. *Journal of Sexual Aggression*, **13**, 37–50.

Lindsay, W.R., Whitefield, E. and Carson, D. (2007) An assessment for attitudes consistent with sexual offending for use with offenders with intellectual disability. *Legal and Criminological Psychology*, **12**, 55–68.

Lindsay, W.R., Whitefield, E., Carson, D. and Steptoe, L. (2004c) *The Questionnaire on Attitudes Consistent with Sexual Offending*. Available from BillLindsay@castlebeck.com to suitably qualified assessors.

Lindsay, W.R., Whitefield, E., Carson, D. and Steptoe, L. (2008b) Factor structure of the 7 scales on the Questionnaire on Attitudes Consistent with Sex Offending. In press.

Litwack, T.R. (2001) Actuarial versus clinical assessments of dangerousness. *Psychology, Public Policy and Law*, 7, 409–43.

Looman, J., Abracen, J. and Niecholaichuk, T.P. (2000) Recidivism among treated sexual offenders and matched controls. *Journal of Interpersonal Violence*, **15**, 279–90.

Luiselli, J.K. (2000) Presentation of paraphilias and paraphilia related disorders in young adults with mental retardation: two case profiles. *Mental Health Aspects of Developmental Disabilities*, **3**, 42–46.

Luiselli, J.K., Helfen, C.S., Pemberton, B.W. and Reisman, J. (1977) The elimination of a child's in class masturbation by over correction and reinforcement. *Journal of Behaviour Therapy and Experimental Psychiatry*, **8**, 201–4.

Lund, J. (1990) Mentally retarded criminal offenders in Denmark. *British Journal of Psychiatry*, **156**, 726–31.

Lunsky, Y., Frijters, J., Griffiths, D.M. *et al.* (2007) Sexual knowledge and attitudes of men with intellectual disabilities who sexually offend. *Journal of Intellectual and Developmental Disability*, **32**, 74–81.

McCord, W. and McCord, J. (1959) *Origins of Crime: A New Evaluation of the Cambridge-Somerville*, Columbia Press, New York.

MacEachron, A.E. (1979) Mentally retarded offenders prevalence and characteristics. *American Journal of Mental Deficiency*, **84**, 165–76.

McGrath, R.J., Cumming, G., Livingston, J.A. and Hoke, S.E. (2003) Outcome of a treatment programme for adult sex offenders. *Journal of Interpersonal Violence*, **18**, 3–17.

McGrath, R.J., Livingston, J.A. and Falk, G. (2007) Community management of sex offenders with intellectual disability: characteristics, services and outcome of a Statewide programme. *Intellectual and Developmental Disabilities*, **45**, 391–98.

MacMillan, D., Hastings, R. and Caldwell, J. (2004) Clinical and actuarial prediction of physical violence in a forensic intellectual disability hospital: a longitudinal study. *Journal of Applied Research in Intellectual Disabilities*, **17**, 255–66.

MacMurphy, H. (1916) The relation of feeblemindedness to other social problems. *Journal of Psycho-Asthenics*, **21**, 58–63.

Marques, J.K. (1999) How to answer the question, "Does sex offender treatment work?". *Journal of Interpersonal Violence*, **14**, 437–51.

Marques, J.K., Weideranders, M., Day, D. *et al.* (2005) Effects of a relapse prevention programme on sexual recidivism: final results from California's Sex Offender Treatment and Evaluation Project (SOTEP). *Sexual Abuse: A Journal of Research and Treatment*, **17**, 79–107.

Marquis, J.N. (1970) Orgasmic reconditioning: changing sexual object choice though controlling masturbation fantasies. *Journal of Behaviour Therapy and Experimental Psychiatry*, **1**, 263–71.

Marshall, W.L. (1969) Cessation therapy: a procedure for reducing deviant sexual arousal. *Journal of Applied Behavioural Analysis*, **2**, 377–89.

Marshall, W.L. (1989a) Invited essay: intimacy, loneliness and sexual offenders. *Behaviour Research and Therapy*, **27**, 491–503.

Marshall, W.L. (1989b) Pornography and sex offenders, in *Pornography: Recent Research, Interpretations and Policy Considerations* (eds D. Zillmann and J. Bryant), Lawrence Erlbaum, Hillsdale, NJ, pp. 185–214.

Marshall, W.L. (2000) Revisiting the use of pornography by sexual offenders: implications for theory and practice. *Journal of Sexual Aggression*, **6**, 67–77.

Marshall, W.L., Anderson, D. and Fernandez, Y. (1999) *Cognitive Behavioural Treatment of Sex Offenders*, John Wiley & Sons, Ltd, Chichester.

Marshall, W.L. and Barbaree, H.E. (1988) The long term evaluation of a behavioural treatment programme for child molesters. *Behaviour Research and Therapy*, **26**, 499–511.

Marshall, W.L. and Barbaree, H.E. (1990) An integrated theory of sexual offending, in *Handbook of Sexual Assault: Issues, Theories and Treatment of the Offender* (eds W.L. Marshall, D.R. Laws and H.E. Barbaree), Plenum, New York, pp. 257–75.

Marshall, W.L., Hudson, S.M., Jones, R.L. and Fernandez, Y.M. (1995) Empathy in sex offenders. *Clinical Psychology Review*, **15**, 99–113.

Marshall, W.L. and Marshall, L.E. (2007) Utility of the random controlled trial for evaluating sex offender treatment: the gold standard or an inappropriate strategy? *Sexual Abuse: A Journal of Research and Treatment*, **19**, 175–91.

Marshall, W.L., Marshall, L.E., Serran, G.A. and Fernandez, Y.M. (2006) *Treating Sexual Offenders*, Routledge, New York.

Maughann, B., Pickles, A., Hagell, A. *et al.* (1996) Reading problems and antisocial behaviour: developmental trends in comorbidity. *Journal of Child Psychology and Psychiatry*, **37**, 405–18.

Michie, A.M., Lindsay, W.R., Martin, V. and Grieve, A. (2006) A test of counterfeit deviance: a comparison of sexual knowledge in groups of sex offenders with intellectual disability and controls. *Sexual Abuse: A Journal of Research and Treatment*, **18**, 271–79.

Miller, R.S. and Lefcourt, H.M. (1982) The assessment of social intimacy. *Journal of Personality Assessment*, **46**, 514–18.

Morey, L.C. (1988) The categorical representation of personality disorder: a cluster analysis of DSM III-R personality features. *Journal of Abnormal Psychology*, **97**, 314–21.

Morrissey, C. (2003) The use of the PCL-R in forensic populations with learning disability. *The British Journal of Forensic Practice*, **5**, 20–24.

Morrissey, C., Hogue, T., Mooney, P. *et al.* (2007a) Predictive validity of the PCL-R in offenders with intellectual disabilities in a high secure setting: institutional aggression. *Journal of Forensic Psychology and Psychiatry*, **18**, 1–15.

Morrissey, C., Hogue, T., Mooney, P. *et al* (2005) Applicability, reliability and validity of the Psychopathy Checklist – Revised in offenders with intellectual disabilities: some initial findings. *International Journal of Forensic Mental Health*, **4**, 207–20.

Morrissey, C., Mooney, P., Hogue, T. *et al.* (2007b) Predictive validity of psychopathy in offenders with intellectual disabilities in a high security hospital: treatment progress. *Journal of Intellectual and Developmental Disabilities*, **32**, 125–33.

Mosher, S. (2009) Staff support, in *Assessment and Treatment of Sex Offenders with Intellectual Disabilities: A Handbook* (eds. L., Craig, W.R. Lindsay and K. Brown), (in press), Chichester, Wiley.

Murphy, G. and Sinclair, N. (2006) Group cognitive behaviour treatment for men with sexually abusive behaviour. Paper presented at 6th Seattle Club Conference on Research and People with Intellectual Disabilities.

Murphy, G., Powell, S., Guzman, A.M. and Hays, S.J. (2007) Cognitive behavioural treatment for men with intellectual disabilities and sexually abusive behaviour: a pilot study. *Journal of Intellectual Disability Research*, **51**, 902–12.

Naik, B.I., Gangadharan, S.K. and Alexander, R.T. (2002) Personality disorders in learning disability – the clinical experience. *British Journal of Developmental Disabilities*, **48**, 95–100.

Nezu, C.M., Nezu, A.M., Rothenberg, J.L. *et al.* (1995) Depression in adults with mild mental retardation: are cognitive variables involved? *Cognitive Therapy & Research*, **19**, 227–39.

Nicholaichuk, T., Gordon, A., Gru, D. and Wong, S. (2000) Outcome of an institutional sexual offender treatment programme: a comparison between treated and matched untreated offenders. *Sexual Abuse: A Journal of Research and Treatment*, **12**, 139–53.

Novaco, R.W. (1975) *Anger Control: The Development and Evaluation of an Experimental Treatment*, Heath, Lexington, MA.

Novaco, R.W. (1994) Anger as a risk factor for violence among the mentally disordered, in *Violence in Mental Disorder: Developments in Risk Assessment* (eds J. Monahan and H.J. Steadman), University of Chicago Press, Chicago.

Novaco, R.W. (2003) *The Novaco Anger Scale and Provocation Inventory Manual (NAS-PI)*, Western Psychological Services, Los Angeles.

Novaco, R.W. and Taylor, J.L. (2004) Assessment of anger and aggression in offenders with developmental disabilities. *Psychological Assessment*, **16**, 42–50.

Novaco, R.W. and Taylor, J.L. (2008) Anger and assaultiveness of male forensic patients with developmental disabilities: links to volatile parents. *Aggressive Behaviour*, **34**, 380–93.

Nowicki, S. (1976) *Adult Nowicki-Strickland Internal-External Locus of Control Scale.* Test manual available from S. Nowiki, Jnr., Department of Psychology, Emory University, Atlanta, GA 30322, USA.

Nussbaum, D., Collins, M., Cutler, J. *et al.* (2002) Crime type and specific personality indices: Cloninger's TCI impulsivity, empathy and attachment subscales in non-violent, violent and sexual offenders. *American Journal of Forensic Psychology*, **20**, 23–56.

O'Conner, W. (1996) A problem solving intervention for sex offenders with intellectual disability. *Journal of Intellectual and Developmental Disability*, **21**, 219–35.

Parry, C. and Lindsay, W.R. (2003) Impulsiveness as a factor in sexual offending by people with mild intellectual disability. *Journal of Intellectual Disability Research*, **47**, 483–87.

Patterson, G.R. (1986) Performance models for antisocial boys. *American Psychologist*, **41**, 432–44.

Patterson, G.R., Reid, J.B. and Dishion, T.J. (1992) *A Social Interactional Approach, Vol. 4, Antisocial Boys*, Castalia, Eugene, OR.

Patterson, G.R. and Yoerger, K. (1997) A developmental model for late onset delinquency, in *Motivation and Delinquency* (ed. D.W. Osgood), University of Nebrasca Press, Lincoln, pp. 119–77.

Payne, R. and Jahoda, A. (2004) The Glasgow Social Self-Efficacy Scale – a new scale for measuring social self-efficacy in people with intellectual disability. *Clinical Psychology and Psychotherapy*, **11**, 265–74.

Perini, A.F. (2004) Staff support and development, in *Offenders with Developmental Disabilities* (eds W.R. Lindsay, J.L. Taylor and P. Sturmey), John Wiley & Sons, Ltd, Chichester, pp. 307–26.

Pithers, W.D., Gray, A., Busconi, A. and Houchens, P. (1998) Five empirically derived subtypes of children with sexual behaviour problems: characteristics potentially related to juvenile delinquency and adult criminality. *Irish Journal of Psychology*, **19**, 49–67.

Pithers, W.D., Kashima, K., Cummings, G.F. *et al.* (1988) Relapse prevention of sexual aggression, in *Human Sexual Aggression: Current Perspectives* (eds R. Prentky and V. Quinsey), New York Academy of Sciences, New York, pp. 244–60.

Pithers, W.D., Marques, J.K., Gibat, C.C. and Marlatt, G.A. (1983) Relapse prevention with sexual aggressors: a self-control model of treatment and maintenance of change, in *The Sexual Aggressor: Current Perspectives on Treatment* (eds J.G. Greer and J.R. Stuart), Van Nostrand Reinhold, New York, pp. 214–39.

Plaud, J.J., Plaud, D.M., Colstoe, P.D. and Orvedal, L. (2000) Behavioural treatment of sexually offending behaviour. *Mental Health Aspects of Developmental Disabilities*, **3**, 54–61.

Polvinale, R.A. and Lutzker, J.R. (1980) Elimination of assaultive and inappropriate sexual behaviour by reinforcement and social restitution. *Mental Retardation*, **18**, 27–30.

Power, M., Champion, L. and Aris, S.J. (1988) The development of a measure of social support: The Significant Others Scale (SOS). *British Journal of Clinical Psychology*, **27**, 349–58.

Proctor, T. and Beail, N. (2007) Empathy and theory of mind in offenders with intellectual disability. *Journal of Intellectual and Developmental Disability*, **32**, 82–93.

Prout, H.T. and Strohmer, D.C. (1991) *Emotional Problem Scales: Professional Manual for the Behaviour Rating Scales and the Self-Report Inventory*, Psychological Assessment Resources.

Quinsey, V.L. (1998) Comments on Marshal's 'Monster, victim or everyman'. *Sexual Abuse: A Journal of Research and Treatment*, **10**, 65–70.

Quinsey, V.L. (2004) Risk assessment and management in community settings, in *Offenders with Developmental Disabilities* (eds W.R. Lindsay, J.L. Taylor and P. Sturmey), John Wiley & Sons, Ltd, pp. 131–42, Chichester.

Quinsey, V.L., Book, A. and Skilling, T.A. (2004) A follow-up of deinstitutionalised men with intellectual disabilities and histories of antisocial behaviour. *Journal of Applied Research in Intellectual Disabilities*, **17**, 243–54.

Quinsey, V.L. and Chaplin, T.C. (1988) Penile responses of child molesters and normals to descriptions of encounters with children involving sex and violence. *Journal of Interpersonal Violence*, **3**, 259–74.

Quinsey, V.L., Harris, G.T., Rice, M.E. and Cormier, C.A. (1998) *Violent Offenders: Appraising and Managing Risk*, American Psychological Association, Washington DC.

Quinsey, V.L., Harris, G.T., Rice, M.E. and Cormier, C.A. (2006) *Violent Offenders, Appraisal and Managing Risk*, 2nd edn, American Psychological Association, Washington DC.

Quinsey, V.L., Khanna, A. and Malcolm, B. (1998) Recidivism among treated and untreated sex offenders. *Journal of Interpersonal Violence*, **13**, 621–44.

Ray, J.A. and English, D.J. (1995) Comparison of female and male children with sexual behaviour problems. *Journal of Youth and Adolescence*, **24**, 439–51.

Reid, A.H. and Ballinger, B.R. (1987) Personality disorder in mental handicap. *Psychological Medicine*, **17**, 983–87.

Reid, A.H., Lindsay, W.R., Law, J. and Sturmey, P. (2004) The relationship of offending behaviour and personality disorder in people with developmental disabilities, in *Offenders with Developmental Disabilities* (eds W.R. Lindsay, J.L. Taylor and P Sturmey), John Wiley & Sons, Ltd, Chichester, pp. 289–304.

Reiss, A.J. and Rhodes, A.I. (1961) The distribution of juvenile delinquency in the social class structure. *American Sociological Review*, **26**, 720–32.

Reiss, S. (2001) *Who Am I: The 16 Basic Desires that Motivate Our Actions and Define Our Personalities. Beyond Pleasure and Pain*, Putnam, New York.

Reiss, S. and Havercamp, S.H. (1997) The sensitivity theory of motivation: Why functional analysis is not enough. *American Journal of Mental Retardation*, **101**, 553–66.

Reiss, S. and Havercamp, S.H. (1998) Towards a comprehensive assessment of functional motivation: factor structure of the Reiss profiles. *Psychological Assessment*, **10**, 97–106.

Rice, M.E., Harris, G.T. and Quinsey, V.L. (2001) Research on the treatment of adult sex offenders, in *Treating Adults and Juvenile Offenders with Special Needs* (eds J.B. Ashford, B.D. Sales and W.H. Reid), American Psychological Association, Washington DC, pp. 291–312.

Romero, J.J. and Williams, L.M. (1983) Group psychotherapy and intensive probation supervision with sex offenders. *Federal Probation*, **47**, 36–42.

Rose, J., Anderson, C., Hawkins, C. and Rose, D. (2007) *A Community Based Sex Offender Treatment Group for Adults with Intellectual Disabilities*. Paper presented at the World Congress of Behavioural and Cognitive Psychotherapy, Barcelona.

Rose, J. and Cleary, A. (2007) Care staff perceptions of challenging behaviour and fear of assault. *Journal of Intellectual and Developmental Disability*, **32**, 153–61.

Rose, J., Jenkins, R., O'Conner, C. *et al.* (2002) A group treatment for men with intellectual disabilities who sexually offend or abuse. *Journal of Applied Research in Intellectual Disabilities*, **15**, 138–50.

Royal College of Psychiatrists (2001) *Diagnostic Criteria in Learning Disability (DC-LD)*, Gaskell, London.

Rutter, M., Maughan, B., Meyer, J. *et al.* (1997) Heterogeneity of antisocial behaviour: causes, continuities and consequences, in *Motivation and Delinquency* (ed. D.W. Osgood), University of Nabraska Press, Lincoln, pp. 45–118.

Rutter, M., Tizard, G. and Whitmore, K. (1970) *Education, Health and Behaviour*, Longman, London.

Salter, A.C. (1988) *Treating Child Sex Offenders and Victims*, Sage, London.

Scheerenberger, R.C. (1983) *A History of Mental Retardation*, Brooks, London.

Schuerman, L. and Kobrin, S. (1986) Community careers in crime, in *Crime and Justice: An Annual Review of Research*, Vol. **8** (eds A.J. Reiss and M. Tonroy), University of Chicago Press, Chicago, IL, pp. 67–100.

Seabloom, W., Seabloom, M.E., Seabloom, E. *et al.* (2003) A 14–24 year longitudinal study of a comprehensive sexual health model treatment programme for adolescent sex offenders: predictors of successful completion and subsequent criminal recidivism. *International Journal of Offender Therapy and Comparative Criminology*, **47**, 468–81.

Sequeira, H. and Hollins, S.A. (2003) Clinical effects of sexual abuse on people with learning disability. *British Journal of Psychiatry*, **182**, 13–19.

Seto, M.C., Cantor, J.M. and Blanchard, R. (2006) Child pornography offences are a valid diagnostic indicator of paedophilia. *Journal of Abnormal Psychology*, **115**, 610–15.

Seto, M.C. and Eke, A.W. (2005) The criminal histories and later offending of child pornography offenders. *Sexual Abuse: A Journal of Research and Treatment*, **17**, 201–10.

Sjostedt, G. and Langstrom, N. (2002) Assessment of risk for criminal recidivism among rapists: a comparison of four different measures. *Psychology, Crime and Law*, **8**, 25–40.

Skirrow, P. and Hatton, C. (2007) Burnout amongst direct care workers in services for adults with intellectual disability: a systematic review of research findings and initial normative data. *Journal of Applied Research in Intellectual Disabilities*, **20**, 131–44.

Smith, M. and Willner, P. (2004) Psychological factors in risk assessment and management of inappropriate sexual behaviour by men with intellectual disabilities. *Journal of Applied Research in Intellectual Disabilities*, **17**, 285–97.

Snyder, J.J. and Patterson, G.R. (1995) Individual differences in social aggression: a test of a reinforcement model of socialisation in the natural environment. *Behaviour Therapy*, **26**, 371–91.

Spielberger, C.D. (1996) *State-Trait Anger Expression Inventory Professional Manual*, Psychological Assessment Resources Inc., Florida.

Steptoe, L., Lindsay, W.R., Forrest, D. and Power, M. (2006) Quality of life and relationships in sex offenders with intellectual disability. *Journal of Intellectual and Developmental Disabilities*, **31**, 13–19.

Steptoe, L., Lindsay, W.R., Murphy, L. and Young, S.J. (2008) Construct validity, reliability and predictive validity of the Dynamic Risk Assessment and Management System (DRAMS) in offenders with intellectual disability. *Legal and Criminological Psychology*, **13**, 309– 21.

Stouthamer-Loeber, M., Loeber, R., Wei, E. *et al.* (2002) Risk and promotive effects in the explanation of persistent serious delinquency in boys. *Journal of Consulting and Clinical Psychology*, **70**, 111–23.

Sturmey, P. (2004) Cognitive therapy with people with intellectual disabilities: a selective review and critique. *Clinical Psychology and Psychotherapy*, **11**, 221–28.

Sturmey, P. (2006) On some recent claims for the efficacy of cognitive therapy for people with intellectual disabilities. *Journal of Applied Research in Intellectual Disabilities*, **19**, 109–18.

Sturmey, P., Taylor, J.L. and Lindsay, W.R. (2004) Research and development, in *Offenders with Developmental Disabilities* (eds W.R. Lindsay, J.L. Taylor and P. Sturmey), John Wiley & Sons, Ltd, Chichester, pp. 327–50.

Sutherland, E.H. (1937) *The Professional Thief*, Chicago University Press, Chicago, IL.

Szivos-Bach, S.E. (1993) Social comparisons, stigma and mainstreaming: the self-esteem of young adults with mild mental handicap. *Mental Handicap Research*, **6**, 217–34.

Switzky, H.N. (2001) Personality and motivational self-system processes in persons with mental retardation: old memories and new perspectives, in *Personality and Motivational Differences in Persons with Mental Retardation* (ed. H.N. Switzky), Lawrence, Erlbaum Associates, Mahwah, NJ.

Switzky, H.N. and Haywood, H.C. (1991) Self-reinforcement schedules in persons with men-
    tal retardation: effects of motivational orientation and instructional demands. *Journal of
    Mental Deficiency Research*, **35**, 221–30.

Switzky, H.N. and Haywood, H.C. (1992) Self-reinforcement schedules in young children:
    effects of motivational orientation and instructional demands. *Learning and Individual
    Differences*, **4**, 59–71.

Talbot, T.J. and Langdon, P.E. (2006) A revised sexual knowledge assessment tool for people
    with intellectual disabilities. *Journal of Intellectual Disability Research*, **50**, 523–31.

Taylor, J.L. (2002) A review of the assessment and treatment of anger and aggression
    in offenders with intellectual disability. *Journal of Intellectual Disability Research*, **46**,
    (Suppl. 1), 57–73.

Taylor, J.L., Lindsay, W.R., Hogue, T., Steptoe, L., Mooney, P., O'Brien, G. and Johnson, S.
    (2008) *Use of the HCR 20 with offenders with intellectual disability*. Paper presented to the
    Annual Conference of the BPS Forensic Division, Edinburgh.

Taylor, J.L., Novaco, R.W., Guinan, C. and Street, N. (2004) Development of an imaginal
    provocation test to evaluate treatment for anger problems in people with intellectual
    disabilities. *Clinical Psychology and Psychotherapy*, **11**, 233–46.

Terman, L. (1911) *The Measurement of Intelligence*, Houghton Mifflin, Boston.

Thornton, D. (2002) Constructing and testing a framework for dynamic risk assessment. *Sexual
    Abuse: A Journal of Research and Treatment*, **14**, 139–53.

Thornton, D., Mann, R., Webster, S. *et al.* (2003) Distinguishing and combining risks for
    sexual and violent recidivism. *Annals of the New York Academy of Sciences*, **989**, 225–35.

Tough, S.E. (2001) *Validation of two standard risk assessments (RRASOR, 1997; Static-99,
    1999) on a sample of adult males who are developmentally disabled with significant cognitive
    deficits*. Unpublished Masters Thesis. University of Toronto, Toronto, Ontario, Canada.

Trent, J.W. (1994) *Inventing the Feeble Mind. A History of Mental Retardation in the United
    States*, University of California Press, Berkeley, CA.

Walker, N. and McCabe, S. (1973) *Crime and Insanity in England*, University Press,
    Edinburgh.

Walters, G.D. (2003) Predicting institutional adjustment and recidivism with the Psychopathy
    Checklist factor scores: a meta-analysis. *Law and Human Behaviour*, **27**, 541–58.

Ward, T., Bickley, J., Webster, S.D. *et al.* (2004) *The Self-Regulation Model of the Offence
    and Relapse Process. A Manual: Volume I: Assessment*, Pacific Psychological Assessment
    Corporation, Victoria.

Ward, T. and Gannon, T.A. (2006) Rehabilitation, etiology and self-regulation: the com-
    prehensive Good Lives Model of treatment for sexual offenders. *Aggression and Violent
    Behaviour*, **11**, 214–23.

Ward, T. and Hudson, S.M. (1998) A model of the relapse process in sexual offenders. *Journal
    of Interpersonal Violence*, **13**, 700–25.

Ward, T. and Hudson, S.M. (2000) A self-regulation model of the relapse prevention process,
    in *Remaking Relapse Prevention with Sex Offenders: A Source Book* (eds D.R. Laws, S.M.
    Hudson and T. Ward), Sage, Thousand Oaks, pp. 79–101.

Ward, T., Hudson, S.M., Johnston, L. and Marshall, W.L. (1997) Cognitive distortions in sex
    offenders: an integrative review. *Clinical Psychology Review*, **17**, 479–507.

Ward, T., Hudson, S.M. and Keenan, T. (1998) A self-regulation model of the sexual offence
    process. *Sexual Abuse: A Journal of Research and Treatment*, **10**, 141–57.

Ward, T., Hudson, S.M. and Marshall, W.L. (1996) Attachment style in sex offenders: a
    preliminary study. *Journal of Sex Research*, **33**, 17–26.

Ward, T. and Marshall, W.L. (2004) Good lives, aetiology and the rehabilitation of sex offenders: a bridging theory. *Journal of Sexual Aggression*, **10**, 153–69.

Ward, T., Polaschek, D. and Beech, A.T. (2005) *Theories of Sexual Offending*, John Wiley & Sons, Ltd, Chichester.

Ward, T. and Stewart, C.A. (2003) The treatment of sex offenders: risk management and good lives. *Professional Psychology, Research and Practice*, **34**, 353–60.

Ward, T., Yates, P.M. and Long, C.A. (2006) *The self-regulation model of the offence and re-offence process: Volume 2, treatment*, Pacific Psychological Assessment Corporation, Victoria BC.

Webster, C.D., Eaves, D., Douglas, K.S. and Wintrup, A. (1995) *The HCR-20: The Assessment of Dangerousness and Risk*, Simon Fraser University and British Colombia Forensic Psychiatric Services Commission, Vancouver, Canada.

Webster, S.D. (2005) Pathways to sexual offence recidivism following treatment: an examination of the Ward and Hudson Self-Regulation Model of Relapse. *Journal of Interpersonal Violence*, **20**, 1175–96.

Wechsler, D. (1999) *Manual for the Wechsler Adult Intelligence Scale*, 3rd edn, Psychological Corporation, Sanantonio, TX.

Wells, A. (1997) *Cognitive Therapy*, John Wiley & Sons, Ltd, Chichester.

West, D.J. and Farrington, D.P. (1973) *Who Becomes Delinquent*, Heinemann, London.

Wierzbicki, M. and Pekarik, G. (1993) A meta-analysis of psychotherapy drop out. *Professional Psychology: Research and Practice*, **24**, 190–95.

Williams, F., Wakeling, H. and Webster S. (2007) A psychometric study of six self report measures for use with sexual offenders with cognitive and social functioning deficits. *Psychology Crime and Law*, **13**, 505–22.

Wish, J.R., McCombs, K.F. and Edmonson, B. (1979) *The Socio-Sexual Knowledge and Attitudes Test*, Stoelting, Wood Dale, IL.

Yates, P.M. and Kingston, D.A. (2006) The self regulation model of sex offending. The relationship between offence pathways and static and dynamic sexual offence risk. *Sexual Abuse: A Journal of Research and Treatment*, **18**, 259–70.

Appendix 1

Vignettes and Scenarios for Problem Solving Exercises

Guidance on how to use these scenarios is given throughout the programme. Chapters 12, 13, 15 and 16 deal with these issues specifically. Many of the scenarios contained in the appendix will be relevant to these chapters. Facilitators should also consider vignettes which are relevant to their own group members.

Recording Sheet

Group Member Name: .... Date: ....

Scenario	Pre-discussion Response	Post-discussion Response

Stalking Scenarios

1. Bert likes a woman named Amy with whom he works. Amy is divorced with two children. Bert is not married and lives alone. They both work and Amy always smiles at Bert. Bert asked Amy to go out for a drink with him but she explained that she did not want to. Bert kept asking Amy to go out with him and begins to follow her around work. Bert is at the cinema on Saturday night and sees Amy outside the cinema by herself. He follows her to the car park where her car is. He

rushes up to her just as she is opening the car door and jumps inside. He is feeling sexy and begins to sexually assault her.

Questions:
Should Bert have asked Amy out?
What should he have done when she refused?
Was it Amy's fault that Bert followed her?
Should Amy have gone to the cinema alone?
What should Bert have done when he saw her at the cinema on Saturday night?
What will Amy do about the assault?
How will she feel after the assault?
How long will it take her to get over this attack?
What will happen to Bert?

Facilitators can adjust the direction of the discussion and the questions according to the needs and requirements of group members.

2. Colin is a 23-year-old man who lives alone in a flat. His neighbour, Wendy, is a 19-year-old student. Colin fancies Wendy but is scared to talk to her face to face. He begins to send her rude letters and makes phone calls to her but he hangs up without saying anything. He watches Wendy from his window. After the letters and phone calls, whenever he sees Wendy she looks very frightened. One evening, he sees her coming back to her flat alone. He leaves his flat and hides on Wendy's landing. When she comes up the stairs she sees him and screams.

Questions:
Should Colin have asked Wendy out?
Was it Wendy's fault that Colin wrote to her and phoned her?
How did Wendy feel after the letters and phone calls?
Would Wendy have gone out with Colin if he had asked?
Should Wendy have been coming home alone?
What should Colin have done when he saw her that night?
What will Wendy do about Colin jumping out and kissing her?
How will she feel after the assault?
How long will it take her to get over the attack?
What will happen to Colin?
What could Colin have done instead of hiding, waiting for Wendy?
What are the other ways Colin could find a girlfriend?

3. Donald is a 27-year-old convicted sex offender. He is walking around town on a Wednesday afternoon when he sees a woman he likes. He begins to follow her around the shops. He stands very close to her several times. He is having sexy thoughts about the woman. The woman starts to notice him and becomes frightened. She is looking around and walking faster as Donald follows her. She goes up to a shop security guard who goes to ask Donald what he is doing.

Questions:
Should Donald have followed the woman about?
What should he have done?
Was it the woman's fault that Donald followed her?
Should the woman be shopping alone?
What should Donald have done when he saw her?
What did the woman do about him?
What is the security man going to do?
What is going to happen to Donald?
How will the woman feel after this?
How long will it take her to get over Donald stalking her?

4. Eric is a 45-year-old man. He sees Kate in a pub. She is waiting for her friend to arrive. Eric talks to her and asks to buy her a drink. She tells him to, 'Get lost.' He is angry and later follows her home to find out where she lives. After that, he stands outside her house a lot and follows her around. He finds her phone number and starts making obscene phone calls to her. She reports this to the police who trace the calls.
   All of the same questions can be asked in relation to each of the scenarios.
5. Fergus is a 47-year-old sex offender. He is walking in the park on a Monday morning when he sees a woman he likes. The woman is walking her dog. She smiles and says 'hello' to him. He begins to follow her round the park. He stands very close to her several times. He is having sexy thoughts about the woman. The woman starts to notice him and becomes frightened. She tells him to go away and leave her alone and goes back to her car. A few days later Fergus is in the same park and sees the same woman. He begins to follow her again. She is very frightened and screams. A man comes running over to help her.
6. Graham is a 24-year-old man. His ex-girlfriend, Gail, dumped him to go out with another man. Graham does not like this and begins to stand outside her house where she lived alone. He keeps on trying to talk to her, but she tells him to go away and leave her alone. He gets angry and makes nuisance phone calls to her. On her birthday, he sends her a big bunch of flowers with a note asking her out. She sees him outside her house and gives him back the flowers and tells him she is getting the police.

Exhibitionism/Flashing

1. Harry is a 20-year-old man who is out with his friends on a Saturday night. He has had six pints of lager and is needing to go to the toilet. He asks the barman where the toilet is. The barman tells Harry that it is up two flights of stairs. Harry has noticed that the ladies toilet is across from the bar and he decides to go there. He goes into a cubicle but leaves the door open. Three women come in and see him having a pee.

2. Ian is a 35-year-old man. He is walking in the park when he feels he needs to go to the toilet. He sees the park attendant locking the gents' toilet. He asks to be let in but the attendant says that he cannot do this as his lift has arrived to take him and he is finished for the day. Ian goes behind a bush to do the toilet. Two boys are playing behind the bushes away from other people and Ian sees them. He stops doing the toilet and begins to get an erection. He shows his erection to the boys.

   This scenario allows facilitators to explore the concept of responsibility. It has a degree of ambiguity in that some of the responsibility can be placed on the park attendant for refusing to open the toilet. Some of the responsibility may be placed on the boys for playing away from the main park areas. Therefore, it is possible to elicit cognitions related to mitigation of the offence and shifting some of the responsibility onto victims or other people in the person's life. Ways of dealing with these ambiguities are explained in Chapters 12 and 13.

3. James is a 30-year-old man. He is at the beach on a sunny day. He has not put his swimming trunks on at home so he asks the ice-cream shop owner if he can change in her shop. She says that she has nowhere private for him to do that and so refuses. He goes back to the beach where he wraps his towel around his waist. He sees a number of females whom he finds attractive and begins to feel sexy. He takes off his trousers and underwear and allows the towel to fall off so that the females can see his penis and backside. All the people around him keep looking at him as he reaches for his trunks.

Sexual Assault against Men

1. Characters: A young man of around 19 years of age. An older man.
   Colin is 18 and he decides to go for a walk in the park. While he is walking in the park, a man comes up behind him and asks him for sex.

Questions:
What should Colin do?
Should Colin have sex with man?
What could happen to Colin if he starts to talk to the man?
What could happen to Colin if he does not have sex with the man?

Colin refuses to have sex with the man and tries to walk away. But the man does not let him walk away. He stands in front of Colin and keeps talking to him. He keeps walking after Colin.

Questions/guides:
What should Colin do now?
Could Colin get away easily?
What might the man do?
How is Colin feeling?
How is the man feeling?

The man forces Colin onto the ground and tries to have sex with him. After forcing Colin to have sex, the man runs off and leaves Colin alone.

Questions/guides:
What should Colin do now?
What could happen to the man?
Why did the man sexually assault Colin?
What could Colin have done?
How could the man be caught?
What could happen to the man?
What could the man be charged with?
How does Colin feel about what happened?
How would you feel if something like that happened to you?
Who was to blame for the incident?

2. Characters: Two men (age can be adjusted according to the age of group members). Bill forced Harry to have sex with him. Harry tried to tell his friends about what happened but nobody believed him. They thought that he was just making it up. Harry's friends think that if he had not wanted to have sex with Bill he could have fought him off.

Questions:
What do you think?
Could Harry have made Bill stop?
If a man doesn't try to fight his way out of being sexually assaulted, does it mean he really wanted to have sex?
Why might a man not be able to fight his way out of a rape?
How does Harry feel about himself?
How does Harry feel about his friends?
How long will it take Harry to get over this?

Harry's friends think that he is just making the story up because he is ashamed that he is gay.

Questions:
What do you think?
Do you think someone would lie about being raped because they were ashamed or embarrassed about being gay?
What will Harry think now?

Age Appropriate Relationships

1. Characters: A babysitter in his twenties. A girl of around 8 or 9 years old (depending on the ages of group member's victims).
Alice's mum and dad are away out for the evening. Their usual babysitter has phoned at the last minute to say she is unable to come. They ask Simon, a

neighbour, if he can babysit and he says 'Yes'. A little while after Alice goes to bed, she wakes up crying after a bad dream. Simon hears her crying and goes into her room. Alice tells him that she has had a bad dream and would like her mum. Simon says she will feel better if he comes into her bed and gives her a cuddle. Alice says 'No' that she wants her mum and does not want Simon to come into her bed. Simon goes into her bed anyway.

Questions:
Was Simon doing anything wrong?
Should he have got into bed with Alice?
What did Alice think Simon was doing?
What could Simon have done instead?
What was Simon thinking about when he got into Alice's bed?
Was Alice too young to have sex?
How did Alice feel when Simon got into bed with her?
Was there anything wrong with what happened?
What will Alice's parents think when they come home?
What will Alice's parents do?
How will Alice feel the next day?

2. Characters: A male and a female teenager both 15 years old.
   Susan and Graham are both 15 years old. They have been going out together for 6 months and are really close. They spend a lot of time together at school and in the evenings when they watch TV and go to the pictures. For the past few weeks, their relationship has been getting more serious and last night Graham asked Susan to sleep with him. Susan had been thinking about this all day and has just told Graham that she would like to sleep with him.

   Questions:
   Are Susan and Graham close to each other?
   Do they want to sleep with each other?
   Are they both consenting to have sex?
   Does Susan feel happy sleeping with Graham?
   Did Graham force Susan to have sex?
   Is it okay for Susan and Graham to have sex?
   Why is it not okay for Susan and Graham to have sex?
   Should Susan ask her family or friends what to do?
   Should Graham ask his family or friends what to do?
   What could happen to Susan?
   What could happen to Graham?
   What should they do if they want to have a sexual relationship?

3. Characters: A woman aged approximately 50 and a man aged approximately 25.
   Ruth and John are good friends. They are going out for walks, to the pictures and going for a burger together. One night after being in a burger restaurant, John

goes back to Ruth's house. John tells Ruth that he loves her and knows that she is older than him but would like to be more than good friends. He would like to have a relationship with Ruth. Ruth agrees and they go to her bedroom and make love together.

Questions:
Is it okay for Ruth and John to have sex together?
Is it okay for a 50-year-old woman to have sex with a 25-year-old man?
What could happen to John?
What could happen to Ruth?
How does John feel?
How does Ruth feel?
Did they both consent to having sex?
Is it against the law?

4. Characters: A male and a female adult around the same age.
   Colin and Alison have been seeing each other for 4 years and they have decided they want to get married in the next year. Before they met, they had both been separated from partners for a long time and believed that they would not start a relationship with anyone again. When they met each other at the beginning, their relationship was based on friendship and they would go out together to the pictures and for walks. They have now started to have a loving sexual relationship.

Questions:
How long have they known each other?
Are they both consenting to have sex with each other?
Is it legal for them to have sex?
Have they just met each other and started to have sex immediately?
How long did they wait to get to know each other properly?
Is there any problem with them having sex?
Is it legal for them to have sex together?

Offending against Children

1. Characters: An adult (age can be adjusted according to the offences and ages of group members). A male or a female child aged 5–10.
   Bob is looking after his young nephew, Connor. Before going to bed, Connor often likes listening to a story. Uncle Bob asks Connor if he wants to sit on his knee while he reads him a story. Connor gets excited when Uncle Bob reads him his favourite story and he bounces up and down on his uncle's knee smiling and laughing at him. Bob enjoys Connor bouncing up and down on his knee and begins to get an erection. Once the story is finished, Uncle Bob asks Connor if he would like to hear another story.

Questions:
Whose fault is it that Uncle Bob gets sexually excited – is it Connor's fault?
Should Connor be sitting on Uncle Bob's knee?
Is Connor thinking about sex when he is on Uncle Bob's knee?
Is Bob thinking about sex?
Why did Bob ask Connor if he wanted to listen to a story?
Is Connor enjoying the story?
Why is Uncle Bob getting an erection?
Does Connor know anything about sex?
What should Uncle Bob do?
What will Bob do next?
What will Connor do next?

2. Characters: A father and daughter.
   James is getting ready for bed when his young daughter, Kate, comes into the bedroom. Kate says she cannot sleep and wants to play a game or have a story. Her dad asks her if she wants to play a pointing game. He asks her to point to her nose, her eyes, and things around the room. Kate gets bored with this game and wants to play another game. Her dad suggests that they play a touching game. He asks her to touch his nose, his stomach and then between his legs. Dad tells Kate that this is a good secret game and that they will play it again some time.
   Facilitators can make up a list of questions and prompts from previous examples.
3. Alex gets on to a bus to go into town for an appointment. The bus is really busy and the only empty seat is next to a young child. He sits down next to the child.

   Questions:
   How does Alex feel?
   How does the child feel?
   What else could he have done?
   What will happen next?
   Who else is on the bus (a neighbour who recognises him, someone who knows that he has offended in the past)?

   Discuss the risks presented in this scenario. Discuss aspects of self-restraint and self-control which might have been employed. Discuss the outcomes. Discuss culpability and responsibility.
4. Characters: A 12-year-old boy or girl and a park attendant.
   Gemma is playing on the climbing frame when Stan comes and tells her that she has to stop playing because he is about to lock up the park. Stan tells Gemma that he has a climbing frame at home and that she can come back to his house for a little while if she would like to. She goes back to Stan's garden to play on the frame and Stan sexually assaults her.

Questions:
Should Gemma have gone back to Stan's house?
What should Gemma have done?
Should Stan have asked her to come back to his house?
Why does Stan have a climbing frame in his garden?
What does Gemma think/feel when Stan says he is locking up the park?
What does Gemma think/feel when she has gone back to Stan's garden?
What does Stan think/feel when he is going back to the garden?
What does Gemma think/feel when Stan begins to sexually assault her?
Who is to blame for the incident?
How would you feel if you were Gemma?
How would it change Gemma's life?
How will Gemma feel over the next few months?
How long will it take for Gemma to get over this?
Who is to blame for the incident?

5. Characters: A child of 5 years old (boy or girl depending on what would be the most appropriate to the offences of group members). An uncle who is babysitting. Mum and dad have gone out for a meal and left Uncle Tom in charge. Tom decides he will watch a video with Alex and tells him to get close while sitting on the sofa. Alex moves close to Tom and feels comfortable beside him. Tom gets sexually excited and abuses Alex.
   The same questions and guides can be used as in previous scenarios.

Public and Private Places

1. Characters: A male and a female adult.
   Walter and Angela are out on a date to the cinema. They go into the cinema and go right up to the back row where they can sit in the darkness. When the film starts, they are holding hands. Walter puts him arm round Angela's shoulder and his other hand on her leg, at first over her skirt and then under her skirt. They both carry on kissing and touching throughout the film. Angela reaches over and places her hand on John's trousers. They keep kissing and touching throughout the film and other people in the cinema begin to watch them.
   Facilitators can develop a number of questions from previous scenarios. In addition, they might ask questions around the following:

   Is it okay for Walter and Angela to kiss and cuddle?
   Is this is a private place at the back of the cinema?
   What might happen next?
   What should they do?
   Where could they go instead?

2. Characters: A male and a female adult.

   Maurice and Rachel are both 23 years old and they have been going out together for the past 3 months. Both their parents think that they are a really nice couple but they do not give Maurice and Rachel any time alone in their houses. One day they get the bus to the local park and they go for a walk. The park is quiet and they both think that they could go to a seat behind the bushes to talk. When they begin to talk, they start touching each other and kissing and cuddling.

   Facilitators can use the same set of questions as in the previous scenario.

3. Characters: A male adult and a female adult.

   Allan and Emily are a married couple. Each week, they go swimming together to their local baths. This week when they go, the changing rooms which are usually mixed are really busy. The only free room is the family changing room which they would have to share. Allan and Emily start to get changed into their swimming costumes and they begin to touch and kiss each other. They kiss each other more and more and start to feel sexy while they are in the changing cubicle.

   Facilitators can use the same questions as in the previous scenarios.

Sexual Assault Including Scenarios/Vignettes in Which Responsibility May Be Misplaced

1. Characters: A male adult and a female adult.

   Anne is waiting at the bar in a pub for her friend to arrive. Her friend is late, and while she is waiting she has a look round the pub. Anne notices a good-looking man at the other side of the pub. She fancies him and she keeps looking over at him. Dave notices that Anne is looking at him. He thinks that Anne must fancy him. He thinks Anne is good looking and he definitely fancies her. Eventually, Anne decides that her friend is not going to arrive so she leaves the pub. Dave decides to follow her and when he gets the chance, he attacks her and sexually assaults her.

   Questions/Prompts:
   Is Anne to blame for being sexually assaulted?
   Is Dave to blame for sexually assaulting her?
   Is Anne's friend to blame because she did not turn up?
   What was Anne doing?
   Who did she see in the pub and what did she do?
   What is Anne thinking?
   What is Dave thinking?
   What does Dave do?
   What is Anne thinking when Dave is following her?
   What is Dave thinking when he is following Anne?
   Who is thinking about sex?
   Who is to blame?

2. Characters: A male adult and a female adult.

   Jane is standing at the bar in a pub waiting for her friend to arrive. Her friend is late and Jane keeps turning round and looking at the door to see if her friend has arrived yet. Paul is standing at the door and notices that Jane keeps looking over and thinks that she is looking at him. He thinks that Jane fancies him. Paul goes over and asks Jane if she wants a drink. Jane says that she is waiting on her friend but because she has not turned up she would like another drink. Paul and Jane talk for a while and then Jane says that her friend is not going to turn up so she is going to go home. Jane leaves to go home and Paul follows her. When he gets the chance, he grabs Jane and drags her into the bushes and sexually assaults her. Facilitators can use similar questions as have been used in the previous scenario. In addition, there are other prompts and questions throughout this appendix which might be appropriate depending on the age, offences and attitudes of specific group members.

3. Characters: A male adult and a female adult (ages may change depending on group members).

   Sadie and Nigel are both 24 years old and are going out on their first date. They are going to go to a restaurant for a meal. Sadie has taken ages to decide on what she should wear. Eventually, she decides to wear a short black skirt and a tight black top. When Nigel comes to get Sadie, he says how nice she looks. Throughout the meal, Nigel keeps on looking at Sadie's chest and after the meal when he is walking her home, he tries to touch her chest. Sadie pushes his hand away and asks him not to touch her. Nigel keeps on trying to touch her and says that it is all right and he won't do anything else. Sadie again pushes his hand away and says that she does not want him touch her. Nigel starts to look at Sadie's legs because she is wearing a short skirt. He begins to feel sexy and starts touching Sadie again. This time he tries to grab her and tries to kiss her.

Questions/Prompts:

Is Sadie to blame for the way Nigel feels because she is wearing a short skirt and a tight top?

Is Sadie leading Nigel on because of what she is wearing?

Is Nigel to blame because he keeps looking at Sadie's chest and her legs?

Is it okay for Nigel to try and touch Sadie?

How does Sadie feel?

How does Nigel feel?

What should Sadie do?

What should Nigel do?

Who is to blame?

Facilitators can add other questions and prompts depending on the characteristics of group members.

4. Characters: A mother, her young son or daughter and a man who helps them in the house and garden.

   Mrs Russell knows Jack well. They live in the same village and Jack has done several odd jobs for her in the house. For example, he put up some shelves in her living room last year and has done some gardening for her. One day Mrs Russell is busy and asks Jack to take her son Tim to play football in the park. While they are at the park, Jack starts to feel sexy. He takes Tim into the woods and sexually assaults him.

   Questions/Prompts:
   Should Mrs Russell have asked Jack to take Tim to the park?
   Should Tim have gone to the park with Jack?
   Should Tim have gone into the woods with Jack?
   Should Jack have taken Tim to the park?
   Who is to blame for the incident happening?

   Facilitators can develop a number of questions regarding the thoughts, feelings and expectations of the mother, the child and the handyman. They can then review the incident specifically enquiring about who has sexual intent. They can then return to the issue of responsibility for the incident.

5. Characters: A married couple.

   Mr Smith is watching his favourite football team playing an important match on television. His wife comes into the room and asks if he would like to go down to the local pub to meet some friends. He says he does not want to go down but she should go. His wife gets dressed to go out to meet their friends. She comes into the room and he says that she is looking nice. She is wearing a short skirt and a tight top. Mr Smith says that he might come down later, in an hour or two after the football match has finished. She goes to the pub and on her way to the bus stop, she notices that a man is following her. Before she gets to the bus stop, the man grabs her and tries to pull her into a garden. He tries to sexually assault her.

   Questions/Prompts:
   Who is to blame for the incident?
   Is Mr Smith to blame because he did not go out with his wife and stayed home to watch television?
   Is he to blame because he said that she was looking nice in a short skirt and tight top?
   Is Mrs Smith to blame because she was walking down to the bus stop in a short skirt and tight top?
   Should she have gone out without her husband?
   Is the man to blame because he assaulted Mrs Smith?

   Facilitators can develop another series of questions and prompts similar to those in the previous scenarios. Again, they can return to the issue of blame after the discussion.

6. Characters: A mother, son and an offender.

   Mrs Brown has a son Andy who is 10 years old (this can be adjusted according to the characteristics of group members). It is 8:30 at night and dark outside. Andy asks his mum for some chocolate and Mrs Brown says there is none in the house. She is busy and says that Andy can go round to the local shop and buy some chocolate. A young man, Jim, sees Andy coming to the shop and goes over to talk to him. While they are talking, Jim becomes sexually excited and says to Andy that he has loads of chocolate back in his flat. Andy goes back to Jim's flat for some chocolate. When they get inside, Jim sexually assaults Andy.

   Facilitators can develop a series of questions and prompts in a similar manner to the previous scenarios.

7. Characters: A male babysitter and a young child.

   Fred is babysitting for his neighbour's child, James, who is 5 years old. When Fred puts James to bed, James asks him for a goodnight kiss. This makes Fred sexually excited and he goes over to kiss James. He becomes more excited when he gives James a kiss and a cuddle and gets into bed with him. Fred rubs his penis against James and tells him that it is a special kind of goodnight kiss and it is much better than a goodnight kiss.

   Facilitators should develop a series of questions and prompts.

8. Characters: Two parents and their daughter. A male sexual abuser.

   Mr and Mrs Brown are out for the day in a local town. They take their daughter, Maggie, to the park. Maggie loves playing in the park and immediately starts playing on the swings. While they are sitting on the bench, Mr and Mrs Brown are getting bored and they decide that they could go to the pub across the road while Maggie is playing on the swings. They tell Maggie that they will just be in the pub and go across for a drink. While they are having a drink, Cameron walks past the park and sees Maggie playing by herself on the swings. He fancies her and goes over to start talking to her. He tells Maggie some jokes and she thinks that Cameron is a nice man. He asks Maggie to come in to the bushes where he sexually assaults her.

   Facilitators can develop a series of questions/prompts.

9. Characters: A male adult and a young child.

   Six-year-old Sophie is out playing on her bike when she gets a flat tyre. She wants to play and knows that her cousin, Joe, is good at fixing bikes. She goes round to Joe's house with her bike and asks him to fix the flat tyre. Joe says that they should go into the shed to get some tools and they both go into Joe's shed with the bike. While Joe is fixing the bike, Sophie is standing very close to him and he becomes sexually excited. He begins to touch Sophie and sexually assaults her.

   Facilitators should develop a number of questions and prompts.

10. Characters: A woman or man depending on the offences of the group members involved. A visiting landlord.

    The landlord has come to visit and has said that he has come to fix the shelves that have been broken in the bedroom. The tenant (name) follows him to the bedroom and shows him where the shelves have been broken and watches while he begins to fix the shelves. The landlord feels the man/woman staring and gets turned on. He pushes her/him to the bed and sexually assaults her/him.

The same questions and guides can be used in this scenario as have been used in previous scenarios by changing the names and situation.

Risky Situations

1. Characters: Sex offender and a relative.
   John has received a 3-year probation order for indecent exposure with a 6-year-old child. His parents have kept this a secret from the rest of the family. John's parents are away for the weekend when his aunt arrives at the house with her two young children. John's aunt wants to take the bus into town and asks John if he will mind watching the children for a couple of hours.

   Questions/Prompts:
   What are the risks in this situation?
   What should John do?
   What will John think/feel?
   What will his aunt think/feel?
   What should John do if his aunt is annoyed with him for not watching the children?

2. Characters: An offender and a child.
   Garry has 9 weeks left on his probation. He sexually assaulted a teenage boy 4 years ago. Garry has got three beautiful dogs and a boy who lives nearby has started hanging around Garry's house asking if he can come in and feed the dogs. The boy has also asked if he can take the dogs for a walk with Garry.
   Facilitator should develop a series of questions/prompts.

3. Characters: An offender and an adult woman.
   George finished his probation a year ago after doing 3 years for sexually assaulting a woman in her twenties. It's George's birthday and he is out on the town with some friends. He meets a woman in a club whom he really likes and she seems to be very keen on George as well. The woman invites George back to her flat and he agrees to go. George thinks that she wants to have sex with him.
   Facilitators should develop a series of questions/prompts regarding the risks in the situation.

4. Characters: A male who is sexually attracted to children, another male who is his friend. His friend's son.
   John has some strong sexual feelings and thoughts for children. He also fantasises about children from time to time. One night, John's friend asks if he wants to come round to the house to watch television. The friends have a 3-year-old son called Peter. John's friend asks him if he would like to help Peter get ready for bed. While he is helping Peter to change into his pyjamas, John's hand touches Peter's back and John begins to get an erection. The next day, John's friend asks if he was free anytime. His friend asks John if he would babysit Peter tomorrow night.
   Facilitators can develop a series of questions/prompts regarding risk.

5. Characters:

   Sam has offended against children in the past. His probation ended a few months ago and he is getting his life back together again. He has just moved house and finds that he has to walk past a school every day to get to the bus stop to get to work. At first Sam walked past the school without stopping. However, now he finds himself stopping at the bus stop next to the school and watching the children go into school at 9 o'clock. He begins to leave work half an hour early so that he can stand at the work bus stop for a longer time to watch the children.

   Questions/Prompts:

   Why is Sam going to work earlier?

   Is Sam doing anything wrong looking at children?

   How is Sam feeling?

   Is anything likely to happen to Sam if he is just standing at the bus stop?

   What happens if the teachers see Sam when they are going into school?

   Will they see Sam day after day?

   What happens if a neighbour looks out the window and sees Sam standing at the bus stop every day for a long time?

   Will anyone phone the police?

   What will the police do?

   Facilitators can develop further questions/prompts depending on the characteristics of group members.

6. Characters: The offender and his friend.

   Peter lives alone in a flat quite close to a burger bar. He cannot see the burger bar from his window but he knows that it gets busy on Saturday. He was once sent to prison for sexually assaulting a young boy. On Saturday afternoons, crowds of young boys gather outside the burger bar to eat their lunch there. One Saturday, one of Peter's old school friends, Tom, comes to visit. Tom has been out of town for about 5 years and knows nothing about Peter's offence. Tom suggests that they go round to the burger bar for a coffee and a doughnut.

   Facilitators should develop questions/prompts regarding risk and courses of action.

7. Characters: A man in his twenties (age should be adjusted to suit the group members).

   Robert is a keen sportsman. He has been a member of a sports club for some time now. He has recently been getting sexy feelings towards young girls. The sports club have decided to give their members a free choice this weekend. They can play a game of golf for nothing or, go to the swimming pool for nothing. Robert is very fond of golf but he knows that there will be lots of young girls in the swimming pool on Saturday and decides that he will be okay. He puts his name down for swimming at the weekend.

   Facilitators should develop questions/prompts regarding risk and options.

8. Characters: An offender (aged change as appropriate to group members). Two young girls (age appropriate to group members).

Steven has just come out of prison for sexually assaulting a young girl. His friends are all going to the pub for a few drinks. He decides to go with them and have a pint of lager. He has a few drinks and then goes off to get fish and chips. When he reaches the chip shop he decides to have chips on their own and gets an extra large portion. He goes out of the chip shop and begins to eat his chips. As he is walking away from the shop, two young girls come up to him and ask for a chip. Nobody else around and it's getting dark. Steven begins to get sexy feelings and the girls keep saying that he has loads of chips and he should give them some.

Facilitators can develop questions/prompts.

Appendix 2

Examples of Quiz Questions

Questions of age of consent:
What does consent mean?
What is the age of consent?
Why do we need an age of consent?
Can a 10-year-old girl decide to have sex?
Would a 4-year-old and a 9-year-old know what sex is?
Do children enjoy having sex with men?
Is it okay for a 12-year-old girl and a 12-year-old boy to have sex in a private place?
Is it okay for two 16-year-olds to have sex together?
How old does a woman have to be to have sex with a man?
How old does a man have to be to have sex with another man?
How old does a man have to be to have sex with a woman?
What would happen to someone if they had sex with someone who was underage?
What would happen to a man if he had sex with someone else who was over age of
  consent? (Emphasise that nothing would happen as long as it was in a private place
  and both were consenting.)
Is it an offence for a 19-year-old woman to touch a 15-year-old boy's private parts?
Is it illegal for an 18-year-old woman to have sex with an 18-year-old man?
Would it be legal for a 22-year-old woman to have sex with a 35-year-old man?
Can a 9-year-old decide to have sex?
It is okay to have sex with a 14-year-old girl who agrees to have sex with you?
Is it legal for two 15-year-olds to have sex with each other?

Questions on dating:
What is a date?
Who is it okay to go on a date with?
Who is it not okay to go on a date with?

The Treatment of Sex Offenders with Developmental Disabilities William Lindsay
© 2009 John Wiley & Sons, Ltd

Where can you go on a date?

What can you do on a first date?

When is it okay to have sex with someone?

Would it be okay to keep kissing and touching a woman after she has asked you to stop?

If a woman is kissing you and then asks you to stop, is she leading you on?

What could you be charged with if you keep kissing and touching a woman even if she has asked you to stop?

What is sexual assault?

What could happen to you if you sexually assault someone?

What does rape mean?

What does consent mean?

How would the woman feel if she was sexually assaulted?

How long would it take a woman to get over being raped?

What would happen to someone if they raped another person?

Questions on stalking:

What is stalking?

Who can be a stalker?

Who could not be a stalker?

Name three things that a stalker might do? (Follow someone, wait on a corner to watch people, masturbate while he is watching people, frighten the person being stalked, feel excited, and so on.)

Give two reasons why someone might want to stalk another person? (He fancies the person, he thinks it is all right to stalk people, he is feeling sexy, he is feeling bad about himself, and so on.)

Is it okay to stalk someone if you have sexy thoughts about them?

Is it okay to stalk someone as long as you do not touch them or speak to them?

Is it okay to follow someone as long as they do not know that you are doing it?

Is there any harm stalking someone?

What is the effect of stalking?

What could you be charged with if you are arrested by the police?

What could happen to a stalker?

Questions on victim awareness:

What is a victim?

Who could be a victim?

What is an offender?

Is it the woman's fault if she goes out in a very short skirt and men follow her?

If a child sits on a man's knee and he starts to feel sexy, is it the child's fault?

If a woman looks at you in a pub, does it mean she fancies you?

If a child undresses in front of you, does it mean they want to have sex?

How would a woman feel if she realised that someone was following her and masturbating?

If someone was sexually assaulted, how long would it take them to get over it?

How long would it take a child to get over being abused?

Questions on public and private places:
What is a public place?
What is a private place?
What is the difference between public and private places?
Is it okay for two men to have sex in a private place?
Name three private places?
Is it an offence to masturbate at an open window in your own house?
Is it okay for two people who are 25 years old to have sex in the park if they both consent?
What would you be charged with if you flashed at a woman on the street from your own front window?
What would you be charged with if you flashed at children in the street from your own front window?
Is it okay to touch someone on their private parts in the cinema?
Is it okay to masturbate in a park as long as no one sees you?

General questions:
What does legal mean?
What does illegal mean?
What is the age of consent for two men to have sex?
What could happen to someone if they have sex with a person who is under age?
Is it legal for a 60-year-old to have sex with a 17-year-old?
Could a 35-year-old woman be raped?
Could a 35-year-old man be raped?
Is it okay to stare at someone?
Is it legal for a 21-year-old man to have sex with an 18-year-old boy?
Could a woman fight a man off if he is trying to rape her?
Could a man force another man to have sex?
Is it against the law to have child porn on the Internet?

Index

Lightning Source UK Ltd.
Milton Keynes UK
UKOW020746190512

192875UK00003B/13/P